Social Death
and Resurrection

Reconsiderations in
Southern African History

Richard Elphick and Jeffrey Butler,
Editors

Social Death and Resurrection

Slavery and Emancipation in South Africa

JOHN EDWIN MASON

University of Virginia Press
Charlottesville and London

50858924

University of Virginia Press
© 2003 by the Rector and Visitors of the University of Virginia
All rights reserved
Printed in the United States of America on acid-free paper
First published 2003

9 8 7 6 5 4 3 2 1

Library of Congress Cataloging-in-Publication Data
Mason, John Edwin.
  Social death and resurrection : slavery and emancipation in South Africa /
John Edwin Mason.
        p.   cm. — (Reconsiderations in southern African history)
Includes bibliographical references and index.
  ISBN 0-8139-2178-3 (cloth : alk. paper) — ISBN 0-8139-2179-1 (pbk. : alk.
paper)
  1. Slavery—South Africa—History.   2. Slaves—Emancipation—South
Africa—History.   I. Title.   II. Series.

  HT1394.S6 M37 2003
  306.3'62'0968—dc21

                                                            2002152295

To my mother, Anna Bernice Hudson Mason,
and in memory of my father, John Edwin Mason Sr.

Contents

Preface

O death, where is thy sting. O grave, where is thy victory?
—1 CORINTHIANS 15:55

When I began this project, I had intended to call the finished product—the book you hold in your hands—*Fit for Freedom*. This was, in fact, the title of the dissertation that served as the book's rough draft. I borrowed the phrase from George Canning, sometime Tory leader of the House of Commons, who used it to explain the purpose of the slavery reform laws that Britain imposed on its slaveholding colonies in the 1820s and 1830s. The laws, he said, were designed to improve the lot of the slave "with a view to fitting him for his freedom" at as early a date as was compatible with the welfare and safety of the colonies.[1] Reform would prepare the way for emancipation by replacing the discipline of the whip with the discipline of virtue, transforming the slaves into sober and industrious free wage laborers. In the dissertation, I argued that the British needn't have bothered. Slaves in the Cape Colony, South Africa, had been demonstrating their fitness for freedom for generations. The moral question of slavery aside, they had proven that they rejected slavery, valued liberty, and were prepared for the responsibilities that emancipation would bring.

My arguments, I believe, were essentially correct, but I have changed the title and much of my analysis to acknowledge the inspiration that I have since drawn from the work of Orlando Patterson and Ran Greenstein and to bring their metaphors of "social death" and "resurrection" to the fore.[2] For Patterson, to be enslaved was to be socially dead, to have no rights that slave-owning society was bound to respect. For both Patterson and Greenstein, resistance to slavery began the process of social rebirth. It mitigated, to greater or lesser degrees, the violence, alienation, and degradation that defined the slaves' condition. When the state abolished slavery and social death was no more, slaves were truly born again.

No slave at the Cape ever used the words *social death* and *resurrection* as I am using them here. The slaves nevertheless devoted much of their energy to resisting the physical violence that their owners and overseers rained down upon them, claiming rights over themselves and their kin, and asserting their human dignity. In doing so, they challenged and compromised social death long before the colonial state granted them their freedom.

I have changed my title and my approach, but not my goals and purposes. I have tried to address two simple questions: What was it like to be a slave? What difference did freedom make? Very early in my research, I realized that while the questions were simple, the answers were not. I could not have completed this project without the help of many friends and colleagues. This is the place to thank them and to absolve them of any responsibility for my errors and omissions.

David Sterling, Laura Struminger, Herb Shapiro, Henry Shapiro, and especially Ann Twinam, present and former members of the history department at the University of Cincinnati, introduced me to the pleasure and pain of researching and writing history.

The late John Blassingame, David Brion Davis, Leonard Thompson, and Robert Harms, all members of the history department at Yale University, directed my dissertation. I owe each of them a very large debt. Members of Yale's Southern African Research Seminar, especially Jeff Butler and Stan Greenberg, welcomed me into the community of southern African studies. Just before I went off to graduate school, Ann Twinam told me that I would learn as much from other students as I did from my professors. She was right. I was lucky enough to have been in graduate school with Karen Sawislak, Patricia Behre, Jennifer Sosin, Carol Sheriff, Jonathan Cedarbaum, Robert Hinton, Jackie Dirks, Katie Snyder, Sean Redding, Diana Wylie, Les Bessant, Kristin Robinson, Robert Shell, then and now the most generous of colleagues, and especially Karin Shapiro and Chris Lowe.

In Cape Town, South Africa, my research would not have been successful without the unstinting assistance of the staffs of the Cape Archives Depot, including Leon Theart, David McLennan, Susan Caetzer, and Annelie van Wyk, and the South African Library, especially Valleri Haddad and Mary Lister. D. J. van Zyl of the department of history at the University of Stellenbosch, and B. A. Le Courdeur of the history department at the University of Cape Town, opened many doors. I am also deeply indebted to the history department at the University of the Western Cape.

The history department at the University of Florida, and Kermit Hall, its former chair, arranged for me to receive a McKnight Junior Faculty

Fellowship, which was funded by the Florida Endowment Fund, under the direction of Israel Tribble. The fellowship made it possible for me to finish my dissertation while finding my feet as a teacher. The project is stronger and my time at the University of Florida was happier because of the support of the friends and colleagues that I met there, especially Hunt Davis, Steve Feierman, Barbara Cooper, Terry Childs, Azim Nanji, Carol Lansing, Steve Grossbart, Susan Kent, Jane Landers, Betty Smocovitis, Murdo MacLoed, Eldon Turner, and Bob Zieger.

The Carter G. Woodson Institute for Afro-American and African Studies at the University of Virginia and its former director the late Armstead Robinson provided me with a place to begin the process of re-thinking and revising. Armstead's kindness and generosity were as overwhelming as his wit and intellect. He is sorely missed. Also at the University of Virginia, the history department and its present and former chairs Melvin Leffler, Peter Onuf, Michael Holt, and Charles McCurdy, made it possible for me to keep the project going, even when its prospects looked bleak. My colleagues and friends in the history department and in many other places in the university offered advice and support whenever I asked. It is my great good fortune to be able to count Joe Miller, Adria Laviolette and Richard Handler, Paul and Mary Gaston, Sophie Rosenfeld, Nelson Lichtenstein, Brian Owensby, Tico Braun, Cindy Aron, Elizabeth Thompson and David Waldner, Reginald Butler, Scot French, Cynthia Hoeller-Fatton, Ed Ayers, Scott DeVeaux, and Dwight Purvis among them.

Bill Anderson can't know how large a favor he did me when he introduced me to Richmond Hill, a place of prayer and retreat in the urban heart of Richmond, Virginia. There, in solitude, I was able to write and to reflect; there in the midst of people who are at once deeply religious and strongly committed to social justice, I was both challenged and comforted. Many, many thanks to its staff and residents, especially the Rev. Ben Campbell and Annie Campbell.

I owe friends and colleagues in South Africa, the United Kingdom, the Netherlands, and Ireland much more than meager words of thanks. Among them are Christopher Saunders, Robert Ross, Sheik Seraj Hendricks, Wilmot James, Jeff Peires, Patrick Harries, Lalou Meltzer, Morgan Kulla, Nigel Worden, Henry Bredekamp, Bill Nasson, Andrew Bank, Colin Bundy, Shula Marks, Leslie Witz, Siraj Rasool, Vivian Bickford-Smith, Tim and Margie Keegan, Francis and Lindy Wilson, Iain Edwards, and Wayne Dooling. In their very different ways, Themba Nolutshungu, Nigel Penn, Charles van Onselen, and William Freund played especially important roles in shaping the book. I will never forget the late Achmat Davids's warmth and hospitality. He welcomed me into his home whenever I was in Cape Town and unfailing shared his unmatched knowledge of Islam in South Africa.

Friends and colleagues in the United States kept me going personally and professionally. I owe much to James Armstrong, Catherine Higgs, George Fredrickson, Jim Campbell, Luise White, Meredith McKittrick, Elizabeth Eldredge, Bob Edgar, Holly Hanson, Jean Allman and David Roediger, Rick Watson, Brian Ward, Jonathan Reynolds, Ron Atkinson, Kerry Ward, Sarah Nelson Roth, Carmel Shrire, Pamela Scully, Laure Dunham, Dan Hallabrin, Geraldine Shaw Bichier, Monica Taylor, Gamin Bartle, and the Hunts and Gores—Alice, Wick, and my godchildren, Ben and Hannah.

John Schroll helped me to breath life into a moribund project. Dennis Marshall made it much more readable.

Rick Elphick and Dick Holway, my long-suffering editors, somehow never lost faith in the book or its author. For that I am deeply grateful.

Cynthia Kros and Alan Mabin have been a part of this project from the beginning. When they met me at Yale, I had only the dimmest notions about South Africa and its history. They took pity on me, thank God, deciding that the more I understood, the less harm I would eventually do. It was Alan who met me at the airport when I arrived in South Africa for the very first time, found me a place to stay for the night, and gave me my first (and still by far the best) tour of Johannesburg. Cynthia understood what I was trying to do in this project before I did and never faltered in her belief it would in the end amount to something. They are much more than colleagues, even though both have been essential parts of my development as a scholar, and much more than friends. They and their children, Will and Linda, have welcomed me into their lives. I feel like family. And there is no better feeling.

Susie Newton-King, who has been with this project almost from the beginning, continues to embarrass me with her generosity and her heart. When I was doing research, she pointed me in directions that I needed to go, making sure that I didn't miss anything that she thought was essential. This was a true blessing; no one understands Cape history better than Susie. When I was writing, she read every word, cautioning, challenging, and cheering me on. When I visit Cape Town, she somehow puts up with my presence for weeks on end. More than that, she has made me a part of her astonishingly eclectic circle of friends, many of whom have become mine as well. This project would have been impossible without her.

No debt is greater than the one I owe to my parents, and nowhere are words more inadequate. With love and gratitude I dedicate this book to my mother, Anna Bernice Hudson Mason, and to the memory of my late father, John Edwin Mason Sr.

Social Death
and Resurrection

Aurora, or the Good Mother's Tale

For we wrestle not against flesh and blood, but against
principalities, against powers, against the rulers of darkness
of this world.

—EPHESIANS 6:12

On Saturday, 26 January 1833, the work day of the assistant protector of slaves began quietly.[1] Several slaves visited his office in Cape Town, the port city and capital of the British Cape Colony, hoping to enlist him and the laws he enforced as allies in conflicts with their owners and others who had wronged them. The first two complaints were commonplace and easily dispensed with. Jeptha,[2] a twenty-eight-year-old field slave whose master's farm lay some fifty miles north of the city, claimed that his master had beaten him, despite his having done nothing to merit it. The protector could offer Jeptha no immediate relief and instead promised to investigate. Rosie, a slave housemaid from Cape Town, asked the protector to help her collect a debt that a Mr. Murrington refused to settle. The amount in question, sixteen rix dollars—an amount that a free servant might earn in a month—was a tidy sum for one such as Rosie. The protector wrote a letter, instructing Murrington, a white man, to appear at a hearing into the matter.

Also visiting the protector on that Saturday was Aurora, wife, mother, and slave. Her simple complaint marked the beginning of a remarkable series of skirmishes—one is tempted to say "epic legal battle"—between Aurora and her family, on one side, and her master, on the other. The record of Aurora's case, like many others found in the archives of the protectors of slaves, shines a bright light on the lives of slaves at the Cape. The information that the protectors and assistant protectors assembled while pursuing the slaves' cases reveals much about their labor and leisure, families and communities, and often stormy relationships with their owners. The records also capture a unusual period in the history of slavery at the Cape. While they do illustrate the factors that made slavery distinct from other forms of forced labor, they also reveal that the slavery reform laws of the 1820s and 1830s, the legal prologue to emancipation, had begun to erode slavery's distinctiveness, increasingly aligning it with forms of racial subjugation and class domination that characterized South African society well into the twentieth century.[3]

For five months during the summer and fall of 1833, Aurora and her husband enlisted the protector and the colonial state that he served in their fight to save their marriage, preserve their family, and lessen the physical violence that they and other slaves endured at the hands of their owner. Aurora, a housemaid, and her husband,[4] Appollos, a coachman who often labored in his master's fields, were both in their early thirties. Malatie, Aurora's daughter, but probably not Appollos's, was twelve. The family's opponent was the man who owned them, Rudolph Cloete, a callow young farmer whose wealthy parents had given Aurora to him as part of his patrimony in 1824, when he was just seventeen and she twenty-two. Cloete's thirty slaves made him one of the larger slaveholders in the Cape Colony and placed him comfortably among the "Cape gentry," a prosperous elite that dominated rural society.[5] The family's legal arsenal consisted of the slavery reform laws; its ambivalent ally was the assistant protector of slaves.

Having walked the twenty miles to Cape Town from the Cloete farm in Koeberg, Aurora appeared at the protector's office on that midsummer's morning to register her complaint. Cloete, she said, had sold Malatie to a certain Mr. Vercuil, and she found it "hard," in the words of the protector's daybook, "to be thus Separated from [her] Child." Not only was Malatie too young to be taken from her, Aurora continued, she was also of "unsound mind" and could not be "without . . . Parental care." She requested "the Interference of the Protector on the Subject." Because the reform laws declared it illegal for a slave owner to sell a young slave child away from its mother, the protector agreed to look into the matter. He arranged for Aurora to be lodged in the town jail pending the outcome of his investigation and summoned Cloete to his office.

Cloete appeared five days later and denied that he had sold Malatie to Vercuil. He said that "he only put her under the Care of Mrs. Vercuil in Order to have her instructed in Some handwork Or Other." It was not his intention, he insisted, to separate mother and daughter permanently, and he had "No Objection, that they should Occasionally Visit each Other." Besides, he said, the Vercuils would soon move into a house on his farm; Aurora would then "have a daily intercourse with Malatie." The girl, Cloete added in passing, had no "defect in her intellects." Aurora, the protector wrote, "Expressed her Satisfaction" with her master's explanation, and the subject, it seemed, was closed.

Less than two weeks later, Aurora reopened the case, again laying a complaint against her master. Cloete, she said, had beaten her. When she returned home after the disposition of her earlier charges, he had taken her "into an Out Room And there upbraided her for having lodged a Complaint." He then administered "Several Severe blows With a Piece of Wood" and struck her "Several times with the fist on the face." Cloete locked her in stocks overnight and kept her in "Solitary Confinement" for more than a week. During that time, Aurora said, he fed her nothing but barley bread and water. After her mistress refused her request to be provided with "Some Other nourishment," she had decided "not . . . to Suffer this treatment any longer." She had loosened some bricks in the wall of the room in which she was being held, and escaped.

Aurora told the protector that she was concerned about the well-being of all thirty of Cloete's slaves, not just herself.[6] She said that her master was "So Severe Upon [us] that it is Impossible to bear it." He had, for instance, recently given a slave named Adonis a severe thrashing, cutting through the slave's skin with his lash. So badly had Adonis been injured, Aurora said, that Cloete believed that he would visit the protector and testify against him. To prevent him from leaving the farm and to allow his wounds time to heal, which would have the effect of destroying evidence of the beating, Cloete confined Adonis in stocks every evening until he recovered. Aurora also told the protector that Cloete had punished his slave Rosina by locking her in stocks despite her advanced pregnancy. She had given birth just "a few moments" after being released. The protector showed little interest in Aurora's complaint concerning herself, but decided that the cases of the other two slaves merited an investigation. He summoned Adonis and Rosina to his office.

On 25 February, Adonis appeared to give a deposition. His version of events differed from Aurora's, but fear and violence were still at the heart of the story. He said that on the preceding New Year's Day, his master had ordered him "to look After Some horses Which had Strayed." He had not been able to find them and ran away "out of fear for a punishment." He was captured six days later. Upon his return to the farm, Cloete locked him in stocks every evening for three weeks, and "when this Punishment was discontinued he Received a beating of 15 lashes with a Cat O'Nine Tails." Rosina testified three days later. She had indeed been pregnant when Cloete punished her, but said that "the last time she was put in the Stocks was about two months before her Delivery & not as Stated by Aurora." The protector felt that Rosina's "Evidence bore Strong marks of being Given Under fear of her Master" and concluded that both slaves had probably endured punishment that violated the statutes that limited the type and severity of the punishments masters could inflict on their slaves. This, he thought, was enough to warrant Cloete's prosecution. The Cape's attorney general, however, declined to take the matter to court, believing that the evidence was too weak to convince a colonial jury of Cloete's guilt. The reprieve did nothing to improve Cloete's behavior.

On 1 March, Appollos, not Aurora, turned to the protector for help. He told the him that Cloete wished him "to leave his Wife Aurora & endeavors by every means to induce him thereto." His master had "already Once Caused him to leave another wife," but he refused to leave Aurora, for whom he had "a great affection." Three days later, Cloete arrived at the protector's office in answer to his summons. Responding to the charges, he said that he had not "in any way endeavor[ed] to force Appollos to leave his wife Aurora." He had merely "asked him to do So, As She is Such a bad Character." He wanted to be rid of her, he acknowledged, but knew that the law would not allow him to sell her away as long as Appollos and she were husband and wife. He had tried to persuade Appollos, a "good slave," to leave Aurora voluntarily. Once Appollos had rejected the proposition, Cloete said, he had "left the Matter at Rest." The protector told Appollos that the law prevented his master from forcibly destroying his marriage and sent him home with that assurance.

Before two months had passed, Appollos was back in the protector's office. Despite Cloete's promises and the protector's reassurance, his master had sent Aurora away from the farm. He could not, he said, "find her Out." He had twice asked Cloete for permission to visit his wife and had both times been turned down. Appollos believed that Cloete had "manifestly done [this] in Order to Compell him to Leave" Aurora, and he "Requested the interference of the Protector on the Subject." The protector once again called Cloete to his office.

Cloete denied that he had sold Aurora: he had merely hired her out to another farmer—a perfectly legal maneuver—"in consequence of her very bad behavior. And her having Expressed A Wish to leave his Service." He admitted that he had not told Appollos where she was. He was certain that if Appollos located his wife he would "Desert And take her with him which he has Already Done Once before." He said that it was "impossible" at the moment to grant Appollos permission to see Aurora "As his Service [was] . . . very Urgently Required On his farm in Consequence of this being Ploughing Season." Cloete promised to allow him to visit his wife "Occasionally" as soon as the heavy work was done.

The protector reported that Appollos "Signified his Satisfaction with his Master's Declaration[, and] the Case was thus arranged."

But because, it seems, Cloete did not follow through and do right by his slaves, the protector had not seen the last of Aurora's family. On 14 May, Aurora told the protector that her master had not "restored" Malatie to her, as he had said he would four months earlier. Before the protector could act, I. G. Meybergh appeared at the office on Cloete's behalf. He insisted that Cloete had indeed arranged for Malatie to be sent to Aurora, "but that Some Unforeseen Circumstances must have interfered." He swore that he would see to it that mother and daughter were reunited, and the protector's day book reports that Meybergh's undertaking appeased Aurora. Five months after it began, the good mother's case was closed, and Aurora and Appollos, Malatie, Adonis, and Rosina disappeared from the official record and from the historian's view.

Few stories from the records of slavery at the Cape can match the richness and complexity of the story of Aurora and the master she had known since his youth. For its narrative drive, it relies on the courage and resourcefulness of Aurora and Appollos and on a husband's love for his wife and a mother's for her daughter. It reveals Cloete's duplicity and brutality, his exasperation with Aurora, and his dependence on and grudging respect for Appollos. It provides a fleeting glimpse of Adonis and Rosina, slaves who chose, for whatever reasons, not to challenge their master as directly as did Aurora and Appollos. Just as importantly, the good mother's tale presents an opportunity to blend storytelling and analysis.

When I began this project, I wanted to know about the work the slaves performed, about the families and friendships they created, about the gods they worshiped, about the ways in which they understood their world and either accepted it or tried to change it. I wanted to know as well what they did with freedom once it was given to them. I was lucky enough to have found myself exploring slavery at the Cape of Good Hope, where colonial officials, such as the protectors of slaves, created and preserved a rich archive within which the voices of slaves and slave owners, free blacks and poor whites have been recorded. From these records I have drawn the many stories that follow.

Telling stories is an essential part of doing history and, to be sure, of being human. People have always told stories and always will. We tell them for all sorts of reasons—to entertain, to instruct, to caution, to arouse, to console. Our stories always have a point, even if it is simply to provoke laughter. Historians, unlike our more subtle cousins the bards, poets, and novelists, feel the need to make our points explicit. We are uncomfortable with the idea that readers or listeners might draw from the evidence we present conclusions other than the ones we intend. We want a thinking audience, but we do not want it to think too much. So we comment on our stories as we tell them. Drawing on the evidence, on ideas about how individuals and societies function, and on our common sense, we tell our readers what it all means; and, just as importantly, what it does not.

This desire to impose order on a turbulent world is just as innate as the compulsion to tell stories. As a historian, I am not particularly comfortable with the thought that the ambiguity that I confront in the archives—the multiplicity of voices, the volatility of facts—will reappear on the printed page like an unwanted guest. But I know that it will. The stories I tell reflect their origins in a society that, like all societies, looked very different to a slave, on the one hand, and a slave owner, on the other. The stories themselves reside in archives that can preserve no more than fragments of the past. Most of what was said and done has been lost forever. Finally, I am painfully aware that what remains must be used with caution. Like all of us, the denizens of the nineteenth-century Cape could be economical with the truth. There is more than a little "fiction in the archives."[7] So rather than try to get our unwanted guest off the couch and out the door, I have learned to live with ambiguity, accepting as inevitable the fact that the stories I tell will have multiple meanings. I console myself with the thought that a well-told tale is richer than any analysis that might try to cling to it.

The stories that I tell will demonstrate that the slaves made history, if not precisely as they would have pleased: their freedom of action was limited by circumstances inherited from the past and by people with whom they shared their present.[8] Aurora's tale reveals some of the ways in which decisions that slaves made and actions that they took forced their masters and the colonial state to respond to them as much as they had to respond to their betters. Some of the choices that slaves made were individual, others were collective; some were self-consciously strategic, others were not. Slaves made all of these decisions in the bustle of ordinary events, not in the quiet of contemplation. If we are to understand the slaves and the ways in which they shaped South African history, we need to grasp as clearly as possible the textures, passions, and routines of everyday life. And for this we need stories.

I have drawn much of my evidence from the reports and other papers of the protectors of slaves, who administered the slavery reform laws, and of the special justices, the colonial magistrates who supervised "apprenticeship" in much the same way as the protectors did the reforms.[9] The most important materials in these two massive collections are the records of hearings, trials, and interrogations that the protectors and justices conducted in the course of investigating slaves' and apprentices' complaints against their masters and masters' prosecutions of their slaves and apprentices. The protectors and justices, or their clerks, recorded the voices of thousands of slaves and apprentices, masters, mistresses, and many other residents of the Cape. They spoke about the events surrounding the complaint under investigation, of course. But the collateral evidence that can be drawn from these reports addresses a wide range of issues, some of it quite far removed from the subject of the complaint. In these records, slaves and apprentices, Khoisan and free blacks, slave owners and poor whites speak about almost every aspect of life in the Cape Colony.

Despite my emphasis on storytelling, I have no intention of shirking my duty to make sense of the tales that I tell. I will offer interpretations based on primary sources that I have read with as much theoretical sophistication and common sense as I can muster. Throughout, I owe a heavy debt to Orlando Patterson and Nell Irvin Painter. From Patterson I borrow a set of intellectual tools that go a long way toward revealing the order and meaning hidden within the messy realities of slavery. One way of understanding Aurora's story and those of the other slaves we will encounter is to draw on Patterson's contention that "social death" has characterized slavery wherever it has existed. Having surveyed scores of slave societies from ancient times to modern, from Asia to the Americas, from Europe to Africa, Patterson argues that slavery is rooted in violence, originating as a substitute for death in war or as a criminal sanction.

To be enslaved was not to be pardoned; slavery was instead "a conditional commutation" of a sentence of death. Slaves, as far as enslaving societies were concerned, owed their lives to their masters. On their own they belonged to no legitimate social order. They had been stripped of all rights and all claims of birth and family and were connected to society only through their masters. Rightless, kinless, and utterly marginalized, they were the most degraded members of slave-owning society. This was social death. Social death, unlike its physical counterpart, is not absolute: it is dynamic, fluid, and contested, above all because slaves refused to accept their condition as permanent. Instead, like Aurora and Appollos, who resisted the lash and asserted their rights of kinship, slaves struggled against social death, "sometimes noisily, more often quietly; sometimes violently, more often surreptitiously; infrequently with arms, always with the weapons of the mind and soul."[10]

Patterson's work on slavery suggests a way of linking the empirical to the theoretical[11]—a way of linking, that is, the unruly facts of slavery to scholarship's insistent desire to codify and generalize. Patterson identifies the characteristics that set slavery apart from all other social institutions. He distinguishes between various classes of unfree people, for instance, differentiating slaves from prisoners, indentured servants, and serfs. He argues that violent domination, natal alienation, and degradation were the "constituent elements" of the social death that defined slavery and distinguished it from other conditions. Violence was at slavery's heart. Acts of violence transformed free people into slaves; through violence, children born into slavery learned what it meant to be a slave; the maintenance of the institution depended on repeated violent acts: "naked force was [slavery's] ultimate and essential sanction."[12] The natal alienation of the slaves derived from their rightlessness and the absence of enforceable claims of kinship. Being rightless, they could not in principle prevent their children from being sold, defend their marriages, or seek the protection of their families. Rightless, powerless, socially marginalized, and thus without honor, slaves were utterly degraded.[13]

Patterson acknowledges that social death describes slavery in the ideal.[14] Actually existing slavery was more complex, "laden with tension and contradiction in the dynamics of each of its constituent elements."[15] Reality was more complex than theory because most slaves refused to believe that they were dead, socially or otherwise. Most were, in Patterson's words, "desperate for life."[16] Although slavery crushed some individual slaves, there is, he contends, "absolutely no evidence from the long and dismal annals of slavery to suggest that any *group* of slaves" internalized their masters' way of seeing things. Like Aurora and Adonis, slaves evaded and resisted violence and fought to maintain ties of kinship and affection. Like them, slaves struggled to assert their human dignity. Patterson writes that because the slave's "kin relations were illegitimate, they were all the more cherished. Because he was considered degraded, he was all the more infused with the yearning for dignity. Because of his formal isolation and liminality, he was acutely sensitive to the realities of community."[17] Slaves wanted nothing more than to become "legitimate members of society, to be socially born again."[18] They longed for social resurrection.

I see social death as more a literary metaphor than a social theory. Metaphors are by nature inexact, both allusive and elusive, and are not to be taken literally. As a metaphor, social death powerfully evokes those aspects of the social order that did the most to shape and define the slaves' outer lives. It has little to say, however, about the slaves' inner lives, despite Patterson's eloquent acknowledgment of slaves' psychological autonomy. My understanding of the psychology of slavery draws inspiration from the writing of Nell Irvin Painter.

Painter has insisted that a "fully loaded cost accounting" of slavery demands an examination of the psychology of slavery. She argues that the violence and sexual abuse that slaves endured, especially during childhood, had damaging psychological consequences. She cites modern studies of those who have suffered repeated beatings and sexual exploitation to show that victims experience "certain fairly predictable effects . . . feelings of degradation and humiliation . . . anger, hatred, and self-hatred." Since "it is doubtful that slaves possessed an immunity that victims today lack," they would have exhibited similar symptoms. This, she writes, constitutes "soul murder."[19]

Painter takes the words *soul murder* literally, arguing that "the beating and raping of enslaved people was neither secret nor metaphorical."[20] While this was as true of the Cape as it was of the American South about which Painter writes, soul murder can equally well be paired with social death as a complementary metaphor. As with social death, soul murder was not absolute, and it was reversible. How closely the slaves' psychological condition in a particular time and place approached soul murder depended on how well slaves and slave owners asserted their contradictory interests, as Painter admits. Southern slaves who were imbedded in networks of kin and fictive kin or who had been touched by religious faith survived slavery "in a human and humane manner."[21] This was sometimes the case at the Cape as well. Things generally turned out badly for the slaves; such was the balance of power in slave societies. But things were rarely as bad as they might have been, because, like Aurora and Appollos, most slaves never ceased to fight for life in the face of soul murder and social death.

During the last decade and a half of the slave era, the period with which this book is most concerned, the colonial state was the slaves' unlikely ally in their skirmishes with their masters and mistresses. Contemporaries were well aware of the incongruity. The slavery reform laws that slaves manipulated, slave owners resented, and protectors enforced were, as the secretary of state for the colonies admitted, "anomalous, and inconsistent." First enacted in the 1820s and designed to prepare the slaves for eventual freedom as sober, disciplined, free wage laborers, they granted rights to those who should, in theory, have had none at all. Colonial officials, at home and at the Cape, needed no one to tell them that this created an irreducible dilemma. In seeking to "enforce justice, and, at the same time to uphold a system which is acknowledged to be essentially unjust," the government, a colonial secretary explained in a dispatch to the governor of the Cape, was attempting "to reconcile things, which are, incompatible." Something had to give, and the secretary believed that it should be the property rights of the slave owner: "so long as Slavery continues, every practical method must be adopted to prevent the abuse of the Owner's powers and to mitigate the hardship of the Slave's condition, so that, if complete justice cannot at once be done, the smallest amount of injustice may be permitted."[22]

It must be said that during the era of reform, and even at the time of emancipation, the British government's ideas about the justice due the slaves stopped far short of overturning the structures of racial oppression and class domination upon which colonial society had been built. As the abolition of slavery neared, another colonial secretary was still speaking of dilemmas, but this time the balance was not in the slaves' favor. Immediately after he asserted that slavery was to be "immediately succeeded by personal freedom, in that full and unlimited sense of the term, in which it is used in reference to the other subjects of the British Crown," he revealed that it was actually to be partial and limited. The slaves newly won rights, he wrote, could not "be unconnected with restrictions against the abuse of them."[23] As Timothy Keegan has noted, British liberalism of the day was "profoundly ambiguous." Its "rhetorical commitment to the legal formalities of equality and freedom was in sharp contrast to its fundamental compatibility with cultural imperialism, class domination, and . . . racial subjugation."[24]

When slaves visited the protectors and demanded that their rights be respected, they declared themselves to be part of the legitimate social order. When they claimed membership in communities of friendship and faith, they denied the marginality thrust upon them. When they resisted the whip, clung to their families, and asserted a sense of honor, they chose social life rather than social death. Slaves became less slave-like to the extent that they succeeded in becoming less violently dominated, less natally alienated, less degraded, and more possessed of civic rights. Well before their final emancipation in 1838, the slaves of the Cape Colony had begun the process of social resurrection.

Metaphors are good to think with, but, like all metaphors, social death, soul murder, and resurrection are not to be taken literally. They do not pretend to the exactness of theory. They suggest that while slavery can be seen as a kind of death, it was not precisely the same thing. And while resistance and emancipation were like being raised from the social grave and psychological hell, they were not this exactly. These metaphors will guide us in our exploration of slavery at the Cape. They will help us to understand what slavery meant to the slaves and allow us to see what was at stake when slaves confronted their masters and when the colonial state intervened. The reform of slavery and the emancipation of the slaves hastened the process of resurrection, but did not end it. The legacy of social death was powerful and deeply embedded in South African life and culture, as subsequent generations have sadly learned.

CHAPTER 1

The State of the Cape

The Cape from its geographical position would become a resting
place for the outcast & [the] dissolute adventurer.

—THE EARL OF CALEDON, GOVERNOR OF THE CAPE COLONY,
1807–11

Lieutenant General Sir Galbraith Lowry Cole was the ninth man to
serve the British Crown as the governor or acting governor of the Cape
Colony after its capture in 1806. Like each of his predecessors, he was
wealthy and well born and disdainful of those who were not.[1] No one at
the Cape could match his riches, and none, as far as he was concerned,
had been gifted with similarly fine breeding. To the governor, it seemed
that the colony and its inhabitants—white and black, master and servant—were well matched. Prospects were dismal everywhere he looked.
In an 1831 letter to the secretary of state, Sir Galbraith reflected despair-
ingly on the difficulties he faced: "The Colony, as you must be aware, is
miserably poor with a semi-barbarous population scattered over an immense tract of bad land."[2]

The view from the governor's house had changed little since the early
years of British occupation of the Cape.[3] Writing to the colonial secretary in 1809, the earl of Caledon, the third governor, feared that his vivid
description of the poverty and backwardness of the rural Cape had "very
probably excit[ed his] Lordship's anxiety for the amelioration of the
Country people." Caledon had suggested, among other things, that the
creation of more magisterial districts was an essential component of any
plan to uplift the settlers and their servants. It could not be expected,
he argued, that the colonists, confined as many were to the arid and
vacant interior, "should make advances in the ways of civilization and
humanity" on their own. The condition of the Khoisan, the indigenous
pastoralists and hunter-gatherers whose lands the settlers had stolen
and who had been reduced to servitude on colonial farms, was even
more deplorable.[4] Any improvement in their material and spiritual condition depended crucially on the "morals and habits" of the settlers.
Hence the governor's proposal to place magistrates among them. These

"enlightened" men would teach the settlers the arts of civilization by example and through practical demonstrations of the majesty and justice of British law.[5]

The governors' remarks reflect the low estimate that British officials, both in London and Cape Town, held of the Cape Colony.[6] Accounts of the Cape published in the late eighteenth and early nineteenth centuries by travelers, settlers, missionaries, and explorers and dispatches and reports sent home by colonial officers stressed the harshness of the climate, the sterility of the soil, and the corrosive effects that these environmental constraints had on the state of civilization in the colony. For a brief period beginning in the second decade of the nineteenth century, official opinion at home and at the Cape had grown more positive. The local administration sensed that it and the "Cape gentry," the prosperous wine and wheat farmers, shared congruent beliefs about the proper subordination of slaves and servants and about security on the colonial frontiers, where the settlers encroached on the lands of independent African societies.[7] Officials at the time also hoped to encourage immigration from Britain. As a result, a competing, almost idyllic, vision of the Cape began to emerge.[8]

By the 1830s, however, the official view had reverted to its earlier position. Much had happened to turn the circle. A scheme to settle several thousand British emigrants on farms on the colony's eastern border had failed miserably.[9] British ideas about relations between masters and their slaves and servants had veered sharply away from those of the Dutch-speaking colonists. Partly as a result, Afrikaners had begun to express a sharp, public antipathy toward British rule.[10] These disappointments had restored a degree of official realism. The Cape was indeed poor, unpromising, and, if measured by the degree of coercion inherent in social relations, barbaric. A German observer, who had been attached to the earlier Dutch colonial administration, wrote in 1812 that the Cape was a "hot, hilly, unfruitful, thinly-inhabited, half-waste country, were scarcely any water was to be had."[11] Most of the British who served at the Cape in the first decades of the nineteenth century would have agreed.

The Social and Economic Geography of the Cape

The Great Escarpment, the "outstanding relief feature" in southern Africa's physical geography, shaped its social landscape as well. A nearly continuous line of hills and mountain ranges, running in a great curve

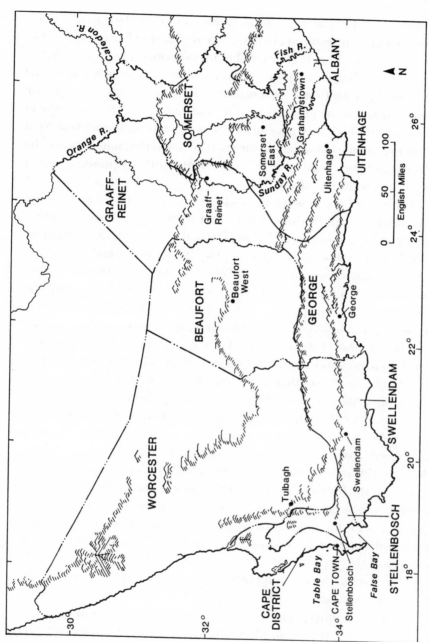

Map of the Cape Colony, c. 1826

from Victoria Falls, in present-day Zambia and Zimbabwe, to the south-western Cape, the escarpment determined patterns of settlement in two important ways. First, it guarded the interior, presenting a formidable, mountainous barrier to human movement when approached from the east, south, or southwest. Second, because it rarely dips below several thousand feet in height anywhere in southern Africa, the escarpment separates the high, dry plateau of the interior from the narrow band of well-watered lowlands along the coast. This discontinuity between the plateau and the coastal lands is "fundamental [to] any consideration of weather in Southern Africa."[12]

Within the Cape Colony, the escarpment produced an arid climate everywhere except in the southern and southwestern coastal plains.[13] Settlement was concentrated in the lowlands; in the interior, it was nec-essarily both sparse and dispersed. The boundless interior plateau— three-quarters of the surface area of the colony—received less than twenty inches of rain per year. The rains that did fall came during the summer, when both temperatures and evaporation rates were highest. As a result, arable agriculture, except in small, irrigated gardens, was im-possible in most of the interior. Only cattle and sheep farming could sustain settler communities, and these farms required vast tracts of land for pasture. In the south and southwestern Cape, however, rain came throughout the year, though most fell during the cool winters. Cape Town, the Cape District, and the district of Stellenbosch were well suited for arable agriculture, as were parts of the districts of Tulbagh (later Worcester) and Swellendam (see map). Settlement, especially within thirty to forty miles of Cape Town, was relatively dense, and this region contained the bulk of the colonial population, slave and free. Physical relief defined a clear-cut pattern. Below the escarpment, there was suf-ficient rain for the farming of crops; settlements and slavery were rela-tively concentrated. It was also there that Cape Town, the only popula-tion center that amounted to more than a village, was to be found. Above the escarpment, the land supported a great many cattle and sheep, but few settlers, servants, and slaves.[14]

The vast amount of land needed for successful stock farming meant that the colony had grown physically large, even as its population re-mained small. In 1806 the colony covered 110,000 square miles—nearly as much territory as the British Isles, including Ireland. It stretched more than four hundred miles to the east and northeast from the capi-tal, Cape Town, and nearly three hundred miles to the north along the Atlantic Ocean coast. According to an 1808 census, only 74,424 people

Table 1.1.   Population of the Cape Colony, 1798–1840

	Whites	Slaves	Free Blacks	Khoikhoi
1798	c. 20,000	25,754	c. 1,700	—
1808	27,956	29,768	(with whites)	16,700
1820	42,975	31,779	1,932	25,975
1830	58,950	33,583	41,958	
1840	70,775	79,480 (Coloured)		

Sources: Calculated or drawn from Richard Elphick and Hermann Giliomee, eds., *The Shaping of South African Society, 1652–1840* (Cape Town, 1989), 524, and Statement of the Population . . . at the Cape of Good Hope in 1808, enclosure to dispatch, governor, Cape Colony, to secretary of state, 16 October 1809, CAD, GH 28/2.

lived within this immense tract of land: 29,768 slaves, 27,956 "Inhabitants," mostly whites, but including perhaps 2,000 free blacks, and 16,700 "Hottentots," or Khoisan (see table 1.1).[15] The figures are probably less exact than they look. Many still independent pastoralists and hunter-gatherers, now known collectively as Khoisan, were regularly overlooked, and Cape Town always contained scores of seamen passing through.

Two demographic facts are especially noteworthy. First, during the early years of British rule, slaves outnumbered all other population groups, accounting for four persons in ten. As this fact suggests, slavery dominated the Cape demographically, and in social, economic, and cultural terms as well. Though the proportion of slaves in the total population fell steadily after the abolition of the slave trade in 1808, the colonial economy continued to rest on a foundation of slavery (see table 1.2). Second, the necessary result of a small population inhabiting a large territory was a sparsely settled colony, except in the far southwest. Nearly one-quarter of the colonial population lived in Cape Town; fully one-half lived in the city, the Cape district which surrounded it, and the neighboring district of Stellenbosch. Yet these southwestern districts accounted for only 5 percent of the colony's land area. Accordingly, population densities varied widely. In the rural southwest, they ranged up to six persons per square mile, and plunged, in the north and east, to below 0.5 persons per square mile.[16]

Slave owners did not constitute a colonial elite. In Cape Town and the colony as a whole, slave owning was widely diffused throughout the settler community. From at least 1750 until 1834, the year of emancipation, roughly one-half of the adult male settlers were slave owners.[17] In 1834,

Table 1.2.   Percentage of Slaves in Total Population

Year	%
1798	54
1808	40
1820	30
1830	24
1834	24

Sources: Calculated or drawn from Elphick and Giliomee, *The Shaping of South African Society,* 524; Statement of the Population . . . at the Cape of Good Hope in 1808, enclosure to dispatch, governor, Cape Colony, to secretary of state, 16 October 1809, CAD, GH 28/2; and D. J. van Zyl, "Die Slaaf in die Ekonomiese Lewe van die Kaapkolonie, 1795–1834" (The Slave in the economic life of the Cape Colony), *South African Historical Journal* 9 (November 1977): 7.

Table 1.3.   Percentage of Total Slaves in the Western Districts: Cape Town and Cape district, Simon's Town, Stellenbosch, Swellendam, and Tulbagh (Worcester)

Year	%
1815	94
1820	84
1829	80
1834	77

Source: D. J. van Zyl, "Die Slaaf," 10.

the 6,334 slave owners in the colony possessed 35,745 slaves, an average of 5.6 slaves per slave owner.[18] If we assume that the proportion of slaveholders in the free settler population held constant during the late eighteenth and early nineteenth centuries, and there is no reason not to, then in 1808 approximately 3,100 settlers would each have held an average of 9.6 slaves. This estimate is consistent with the downward trend in the size of slaveholdings from the late eighteenth century onward. In 1773, for instance, on average slave owners possessed 20.9 slaves.[19] There was, however, considerable regional variation. Slave owning was concentrated in the arable farming districts of the colony, even more so in the early years of the nineteenth century than later (see table 1.3).

The colony's climate and topography determined the geography of production as much as it did the geography of settlement. A British colonial official once spoke of the colonists in terms that reflected the intersection of geography and economics. There were, he said, four "classes" of "Christian," or white, inhabitants: "1. People of the town. 2. Vine-growers. 3. Grain-farmers. 4. Graziers"[20]—that is, three classes below the mountains, one beyond. This scheme is useful not so much because it accurately accounts for the various social classes among the settlers but because it identifies the principal economic activities around which Cape society was built, and places them on the map. Virtually everyone in the colony owed their livelihood either to the port on Table Bay, to wine or wheat, or to livestock. Roughly half of the "Christians" also owed their prosperity to slaves.

Cape Town

Robert Shell describes the Cape as a creole society,[21] and so it was. The colony and its capital owed their existence to their proximity to the shipping routes between Europe and Asia, and the inhabitants reflected that fact. The contrast between the regularity of the city's streets and houses and its exotic citizenry perplexed many visitors. When viewed from a distance, Cape Town seemed almost European. It was a city of right angles, with market squares, bright, rectangular homes, imposing public buildings, and two Protestant churches. Yet the rock wall of Table Mountain, which soared 3,500 feet into the sky directly behind the city, was like nothing seen in Europe. A view of Cape Town streets in the early days of British rule would have looked much like the one a traveler recorded in 1825. It would have identified the city as neither European nor African, but colonial.

> In many of the streets, rows of trees with thick foliage afford an agreeable shade from the heat of the sun and contrast well with the clean white washed houses. The population presents in the streets an extraordinary diversity of race, and variety of costumes, in which respect Cape Town surpasses, perhaps, every other in the world. At the same spot and indeed in the same group may be seen the dwarfish Hottentot clad in woolly sheepskin, the muscular Mozambique slave, black as his neighbor the tall Caffre, the gracefully walking Indian in white robes and turban, the industrious Malay with the conical straw hat, as well as Portuguese, Dutch, French and English colonists, soldiers, sailors and every variety of strangers going to India or coming from it.[22]

Table 1.4.   Population of Cape Town, 1808–1831

	Inhabitants	Free Blacks	Hottentots	Slaves	Total
1808	6,297		435	8,835	15,567
	Christians	Free Blacks	Hottentots	Slaves	Total
1824	8,806	1,843	452	6,763	18,662
	Whites			Slaves	Total
1831*	13,359			5,827	19,186

Sources: Statement of Population . . . at Cape of Good Hope in 1808, enclosure to dispatch, governor of Cape Colony to secretary of state, 16 October 1809, Cape Archives Depot, Cape Town, GH 28/2; Return showing population . . . at Cape of Good Hope in 1824, in Theal, *RCC,* 19:386–87; *Cape of Good Hope Government Blue Book,* CAD, CO 5974.
*In 1831, the population total includes 798 Prize Negroes.

Soldiers, sailors, strangers, and slaves, Hottentots, Caffres, Mozambicans, Indians, Malays, and any number of Europeans—it will do to sort them out.

In 1808, 15,600 people lived in Cape Town.[23] The census of 1808 did not enumerate "Caffres"—that is, indigenous non-Khoisan Africans. There were, in any case, very few in the city. Most Mozambicans would have been counted as slaves; a few might have been "free blacks," a small community not counted separately in the 1808 census. The Indians and Malays were not counted as such and would have been either free blacks or slaves. Nor did the census differentiate between the various European nationalities. It divided the population into "Inhabitants," slaves, and Hottentots, because, for most purposes, those were the lines that mattered (see table 1.4).

For all purposes except this particular census, an "Inhabitant" was a free person of purely European descent or a person Cape society agreed to pretend was of purely European descent. The ancestors of "Inhabitants" or "Inhabitants" themselves had come principally from the Netherlands (the colony owed its life to the Dutch East India Company [VOC]),[24] Germany, France, Portugal, and, lately, Great Britain. "Inhabitant" was a label of both inclusion and exclusion. These so-called Inhabitants were also labeled "white," "European," "colonist," and, very commonly, "Christian"—a term that settlers tended to see as both racially and culturally exclusive, believing that *white* and *Christian* were, or at least ought to be, synonyms.[25] All of these names served to define the civil community and to distinguish those who belonged to it from those who did not. Confusingly enough, locally born whites were sometimes known as "Afrikander" or "Afrikaner"—that is, "African"—an assertion of ownership as much as of belonging. This particular census counted free blacks among the "Inhabitants," an anomaly that had little social significance.[26] Free blacks were descended, in varying combinations, from manumitted slaves, political prisoners transported to the Cape from Asia by the VOC, and white settlers and seamen. Many practiced Islam; virtually all lived in Cape Town.[27] Of the 6,297 "Inhabitants" in the city in 1808, several hundred would have been free blacks.[28]

"Hottentots" were the people whom modern academics refer to as the Khoikhoi and the San, or since they cannot be differentiated accurately within the historical records of the colony, the Khoisan.[29] They were the oldest inhabitants of the Cape and had greeted the Portuguese when European ships first put into Table Bay in the early sixteenth century. They soon began to trade cattle and sheep for iron and copper with the European seamen who interrupted their voyages to the East at Table Bay in order to take on fresh water and victuals. By 1808 the Khoisan of the southwestern Cape had long been dispossessed of their livestock and land. Many had been incorporated into the colonial economy as subordinate laborers; others had been driven beyond the colonial boundaries or killed.[30] In 1808, 435 "Hottentots" lived in Cape Town, among them would have been a number of Bastaard Hottentots, the offspring of white-Khoisan or slave-Khoisan unions.[31] Most "Hottentots" in the colony would have been found in the cattle- and sheep-farming country far to the east.

The census recorded 8,835 slaves in Cape Town, more than the total of "Inhabitants" and "Hottentots" combined. Male slaves outnumbered female, 5,513 to 3,322.[32] Throughout the history of the Cape, the sex ratio among the slaves had been heavily skewed in favor of men in both town and country. The percentage of males in the Cape Town slave population (60 percent) was slightly lower than in the colony as a whole (65 percent).[33] Slave women at the Cape were too few and their lives too harsh for the slave population to have been self-reproducing until after the abolition of the slave trade in 1808.[34] Consequently, Cape slave owners relied on the overseas slave trade to replace slaves who had died and to increase their holdings. Slave ships consistently carried more male captives than female and sold more males to buyers at the Cape.[35]

Virtually all of the imported slaves had left their native lands through Indian Ocean ports and had entered the colony by way of the Cape Town docks.[36] Indian Ocean ports of departure and eventual enslavement in the Cape Colony were all that most newly arrived slaves had in common. They had been stolen from societies spread across the shores of the Indian Ocean, from Indonesia, Ceylon (Sri Lanka), Bengal, Malabar, and India to Madagascar and Mozambique.[37] The origins of the sixty-three thousand slaves imported into the Cape before the British suppressed the trade in 1808 were divided, relatively evenly, between the East African coast, Madagascar, the Indian subcontinent, including Ceylon, and the Indonesian archipelago. The single most important source of slaves during the VOC period was Madagascar. Just behind that island in terms of importance were India and Indonesia. Toward the end of the eighteenth century, Mozambique and other parts of East Africa became the chief areas of supply. The trade was no nation's monopoly. The VOC had imported the greatest number of slaves, but company officials traded privately, the colonists organized expeditions of their own, and English, French, Danish, American, and Portuguese slavers on their way to the New World sold some of their captives at the Cape. Foreign ships became particularly important during the latter decades of the eighteenth century. Overall, an average of from one hundred to two hundred slaves entered the Cape annually from the time the trade was regularized around 1700 to its end in 1808.[38]

The slaves landed at Table Bay and were sold and resold in Cape Town to farmers, merchants, shopkeepers, and tradesmen. Sale ordinarily meant an auction. A Briton noted that the colonists "seem remarkably fond of frequenting those sales which constitute, in the opinion of many, one of their chief amusements. The ladies possess an equal desire of resorting to them, and are not scrupulously delicate in observing those pitiable objects in a state of nudity." The traveler did not hide his anti-slavery sentiments: "It is common to behold aged parents, with their families around them, exposed to public vendition."[39] Slave merchants placed their wares on public display for several days before the auction, and the human merchandise was duly inspected by the colonists, male and female alike. At the auctions themselves, part of the spectacle was the prodding and poking of the slaves by prospective buyers and the leaping and flexing of the slaves themselves, forced by the public to demonstrate their good health.[40] Cape Town *burghers,*[41] having greater access to the slave auctions than their rural countrymen, often acted as middlemen, supplying the needs of farmers in the hinterland as well as buying for themselves.[42]

Captonians traded in much else besides slaves. The city was "a mercantile community whose citizens lived by buying cheap from the farmers . . . and selling dear to the sailors from the passing ships and by exacting a similar profit from trade in the reverse direction."[43] Cape Town was also the seat of the colonial government, supporting a considerable number of officials and their families, and a military garrison. The uses to which the city's slave owners put their slaves reflected the town's commercial and administrative orientation, the slaves working as household servants, laborers, porters, hawkers, and artisans.[44] The slaveholdings were modest. In 1773, 85 percent of the slave owners held nine or fewer slaves; 70 percent owned five or fewer.[45] These figures probably forecast the extent of slaveholding in the early nineteenth century with a fair degree of accuracy. By 1831 the average urban slaveholding had fallen to roughly five slaves.[46]

Most ranks of society were represented among slave owners, from the most powerful—colonial administrators, merchants, attorneys, and wealthy farmers—to the most obscure—shopkeepers, publicans, tradesmen, and artisans. Every ethnic group and nationality among the settlers was represented. While most of slave owners were people of unquestioned (though not necessarily unquestionable) European lineage, a small number were free blacks. In 1816, the year that the colony assembled its first register of slaves and slave owners, approximately one hundred (1.5 percent) of the total number of slave owners were free blacks; none owned more than eight slaves, and all lived in Cape Town or the Cape district.[47] Free black masters and mistresses followed callings similar to those of the lower ranks of white urban slave owners and often employed their slaves in their businesses. There seem to have been no farmers among the free black slave owners.

If the Cape Colony owed its life to its position astride the shipping lanes that connected Europe and the Far East, Cape Town owed its existence to its position midway between the ships in the roadstead of Table Bay and the farms in its vast hinterland. Capetonians bought wheat, wine, vegetables, fruit, and meat from the farms in the interior and sold the produce to the sailors. They bought manufactured goods and exotic commodities from the seamen and sold them into the countryside. Others offered a physician's care, a lawyer's attention, a bed (and often someone to share it), a bottle, or a meal. Cape Town itself produced little. Without the sea before it and the land behind, it was helpless.

Arable Agriculture: Wine, Wheat, and Slaves

British visitors to the Cape often described a colony inhabited by boorish settlers who practiced crude methods of farming and shamelessly abused their servants and slaves. J. W. D. Moodie, a Scotsman who had run a Cape Colony farm for a decade, believed that the travelers wrote too quickly, having seen too little. It had been "the habit of [his] countrymen," he said, "to indulge in an undue contempt of the mode of cultivation practiced by the Dutch colonists, before they have been sufficiently acquainted with the peculiar circumstances of climate and situation by which their customs in this regard are regulated. Imperfect as the agriculture of the [Cape-]Dutch undoubtedly is, we have generally in the course of our experience had reason to see our error, and to entertain more respect for the established usages of the country."[48] There were many "established usages" at the Cape, but one in particular distinguished it from the farms with which European travelers were familiar. That, of course, was slavery. After visiting colonial wine farms, an early-nineteenth-century traveler tallied the "three principal objects for obtaining good wine[:]" "ample buildings," "a store of casks," and "plenty of slaves."[49]

The climate, soils, and demography of the southwestern Cape demanded that arable farming, if it were to be profitable, rely on forced labor. When the VOC seized the Cape Peninsula from the Khoisan in 1652, its plan had been to use the free labor of company employees to supply fresh produce to the refreshment station that it had planted on Table Bay. The scheme failed, largely because the employees proved to be sullen and uncooperative workers. Jan van Riebeeck, the VOC commander at the Cape, then settled free burghers, who remained subjects but not employees of the company, on farms just to the east of Table Mountain. The farms did not prosper, and by 1657 van Riebeeck was making arrangements to import the first large consignments of slaves.[50]

Van Riebeeck had hoped to create a community of small free farmers who would pursue the sort of intensive agricultural production familiar to the Dutch. But the poor soils and winter rains of the southwestern Cape made intensive agriculture on compact farms impossible. The burghers turned first to livestock production, pasturing their animals on the land near their farms, and later to wine and wheat. Both the vineyards and grain fields required large inputs of labor. The vines required almost constant attention during pruning and a sizeable labor force during the harvest. Cape wheat farms produced a relatively low yield per acre, necessitating large farms and many workers. In neither case were the profits great enough to allow the Boers to offer wages and conditions that were attractive to free men and women. The introduction of slavery was an attempt to solve the farm-labor problem.[51] Eventually, the colony's farmers came to rely on slaves to an extent that was rare for non-plantation European colonial settlements. In 1800, for instance, 90 percent of arable farmers owned at least one slave.[52]

Settler farming began to spread out from under the shadow of Table Mountain when the VOC established the village and district of Stellenbosch in 1679. The movement of farmers to the north and east, into the valleys of the southwestern Cape, marked a new phase of colonization. Increasing numbers of inland farmers lived beyond the effective oversight of the VOC, though they were hemmed in by the mountains to their east. They created self-conscious farming and slaveholding communities with economic and political interests distinct from those of the VOC, Cape Town merchants, the Khoisan, and their slaves.[53]

By 1808 the areas of wine and wheat production—the Cape District, Stellenbosch, and the nearer parts of the districts of Tulbagh (Worcester) and Swellendam—extended fifty to a hundred miles beyond Cape Town, at which point inadequate rainfall made cultivation impossible. The total population of this region, including all of Tulbagh and Swellendam, was 32,052. Of these, 10,680 were "Inhabitants," 6,276 "Hottentots," and 15,096 slaves. Of the slaves, 10,219 (68 percent) were male. Most of the slaves, 12,285, were concentrated in the Cape and Stellenbosch districts, the areas of the most productive wine and wheat farms, which made little use of Khoisan labor in either the field or in the home.[54]

Viticulture dated from the late seventeenth century, when the VOC began to import vines from Europe and establish model farms. After a period of experimentation and near failure, the wine farmers developed techniques suited to the cool, wet winters and hot, dry summers of the southwestern Cape. Increasing numbers of farmers entered wine production as the eighteenth century progressed. The initial center of wine making was on the Cape Peninsula, a few miles south of Cape Town. From shortly after midcentury, production in the Cape district stagnated, and Stellenbosch and Drakenstein, thirty to forty miles northeast of Table Bay, became the industry's heartland.[55]

The wine farms prospered. As early as 1798, a British official who served during the first occupation (1795–1803) had characterized the wine makers as "a class of people who, to the blessings of plenty, add the a sort of comfort which is unknown to the rest of the peasantry. They have . . . the best houses and the most valuable estates."[56] The colonial market for wines, supplying internal needs as well as passing ships, had grown steadily throughout the century, especially after about 1780. The number of vines in production doubled in the years just prior to 1806, and profits increased in proportion. Wine farmers invested some of their earnings in land, slaves, and vines, some in conspicuous consumption. It was during this period, and into the 1820s, that the wine farmers built many of the great houses, cellars, barns, and slave quarters that became a particular feature of the colonial landscape.[57]

Wheat, barley, oats, and rye, the "winter cereals," grew best in Swartland and Koeberg, regions that straddled the wine country. They lay among gently rolling hills north of Cape Town, not far from the sea. Swellendam, the third of the major grain districts, was situated just beyond the first range of mountains east of Cape Town. In all three areas, rainfall and growing season temperatures favored the grains.[58] Wheat was by far the major crop, and wheat farmers, like the winemakers, had been able to count on a steadily, if gradually, growing market throughout the eighteenth century. Since grain prices had been at historic highs during the years just prior to the second British conquest of 1806,[59] many of them had reached levels of affluence comparable to the wine farmers. While some farmers produced both wine and wheat, and most ran cattle as well,[60] arable farmers tended to derive the bulk of their income from either vineyards or fields of grain.

Rural Cape slaveholdings were small in comparison with Britain's West Indian colonies. In 1805–6, for instance, only 45 of the 252 slave owners in the Stellenbosch district owned thirty or more slaves, and these holdings accounted for little more than one-fifth of the slaves in the district.[61] Since slaveholdings tended to be small, most slaves, except for the rare rural artisan, worked at a variety of tasks. Male slaves performed every sort of outdoor work, and there was a "regular interchange" of slaves between the wine and the wheat farms, since the peak labor seasons of the two dovetailed.[62] Slave women carried more of the burden of domestic service than did men, and they less commonly worked in the fields and vineyards.[63] Slave children might watch over livestock or the mistresses' younger children; older slaves, as well, often tended livestock.[64]

Without the labor of the fifteen thousand slaves in the southwestern Cape, the colonial economy, based largely on agricultural production, could not have prospered. Slaves produced the wine and wheat that constituted two of the three most important commodities that the colony produced. The concentration of slaves in the Cape's agricultural heartland reflected their central position within the colonial economy. The production of beef and mutton (one-third of the Cape's major commodities) did not depend on slave labor to such an extent. Forced labor, however, remained an essential element of the cattle economy.

Stock Farming: Livestock, Servants, and Slaves

Southern Africa was cattle country and had been for thousands of years. The Khoikhoi and their herds of cattle and sheep had arrived during the early centuries of the Christian era. By the year 1000, Bantu-speaking Africans, too, herded cattle and raised crops throughout eastern and southeastern parts of the subcontinent, including the region that later became the Cape Colony's eastern frontier.[65] The Dutch brought neither cattle nor sheep with them when they invaded and settled the Cape in 1652; they planned to rely on the Khoikhoi to supply their requirements for meat. The trade declined rapidly, however, as the settler demand for cattle and sheep began to outstrip the willingness and ability of the Khoikhoi to match it. In order to build up flocks and herds of their own, the Dutch turned increasingly to coercive means of acquiring the animals they wanted. They raided Khoikhoi herds and flocks and at other times compelled otherwise unwilling Khoikhoi to sell. The ancestors of the settler's herds and flocks were the indigenous cattle and sheep that the Dutch took by force and persuasion from the Khoikhoi.[66]

The Cape suited colonial stock farmers as well as it had Africans, providing an appropriate climate, adequate grazing, and a benign disease environment.[67] The expansion of the cattle economy drove the territorial expansion of the colony during the eighteenth century. As early as the 1680s and 1690s, a shortage of well-watered land and the capital-intensive nature of arable agriculture encouraged young white men in search of a livelihood to turn to stock farming. Cattle and sheep could survive on marginal land where vines and grains could not, and stock farming also required no investment in slaves and little in equipment. Stock farmers could rely on the presence of the port and the gradual growth of the colonial population to create a steadily rising demand for meat. At the same time, the rewards of crop farming diminished rapidly as the soil and climate deteriorated the further north and east that the settlers pressed. These factors promoted the development of one of the most powerful traditions of colonial society. Every man, settlers believed, should work for himself, not others. Most men could achieve this only by farming, and for men of modest means, the farm would have to be a cattle farm on the expanding colonial frontier. Both the number of cattle and sheep farmers and their proportion within the farming community rose dramatically during the eighteenth century. In 1716, for instance, 9 percent of the settler farmers depended on livestock for the bulk of their livelihood; in 1770, the number stood at 66 percent.[68]

In many ways, colonial frontiers were cattle and sheep frontiers. During the eighteenth and early nineteenth centuries, flocks and herds spread out of the southwestern Cape following the routes that the topography dictated—river valleys, coastal plains, and mountain passes.[69] Territorial expansion proceeded quickly (though not without resistance from the Khoisan), propelled by an environment that demanded enormous farms and seasonal migrations. The conquest of the Khoisan, the seizure of their lands, and their incorporation into the pastoral economy as subordinate laborers underpinned colonial expansion. Robert Ross has called these processes the "basic plot of a large part of eighteenth-century Cape history." "As European farmers drove deeper and deeper into the interior of the Cape Colony, they brought about the steady impoverishment of the Khoisan of each successive region. Stock was lifted, grazing and water holes were expropriated, game was exterminated and life in any other status than as labourer for the whites was made impossible."[70]

The Khoisan stubbornly resisted the colonizers, but inevitably fell. Their polities were small, weak, and unstable. They lacked horses and firearms. And European diseases, to which they had little prior exposure, devastated their communities. Such resistance that the Khoisan were able to mount took several forms. They raided settler farms, retreated with their herds beyond the settlers' reach, and, from the earliest days of the colony, went to war. The first Khoikhoi War erupted in 1659, the Khoikhoi fighting the Dutch to a stalemate.[71] Similarly, the last outbreak of concerted Khoisan resistance, the Khoikhoi Rebellion of 1799–1803, ended in a political, not a military, defeat.[72] Nevertheless, the peace terms after the war of 1659 forced the Khoisan to recognize the colony's permanence and opened new tracts of their land to colonial settlement. The terms after the later rebellion marked the end of armed Khoisan resistance within the Cape Colony. The Khoisan had been overwhelmed by the weight of settler expansion and the sometimes reluctant, but always decisive, willingness of the colonial governments to stand behind it.

By 1806 the stock-farming regions—the districts of Uitenhage, Graaff-Reinet, and much of Swellendam and Tulbagh—accounted for three-quarters of the colony's surface area. In 1808, 16,736 people (22 percent of the population of the Cape) lived within the districts of Uitenhage and Graaff-Reinet, the region given over almost exclusively to cattle and sheep: 7,589 "Inhabitants," 6,812 "Hottentots," and 2,335 slaves. Farmers in the Graaff-Reinet district, the center of the stock-farming economy, owned only 1,575 slaves, while employing 4,935 Khoisan.[73]

Khoisan entered the settler economy as forced laborers in one of two related ways. They either sought work with the Boers under the compulsion of starvation brought on by the loss of livestock, land, and game or they were kidnapped and forced into labor as virtual slaves, though they remained legally free. Those who worked for wages were ordinarily paid in kind, not in cash. They received daily rations of food and tobacco and a cow or one or two head of sheep annually. Those who owned cattle or sheep of their own were able to pasture them with their masters' herds and flocks.[74] The Khoisan who lived as virtual slaves were mostly women and children—the victims of formal and informal raiding parties assembled in response to, or in anticipation of, Khoisan attacks. The purpose of these Boer commandos was not only to destroy Khoisan resistance by killing the men, but also to plunder their herds and flocks and to kidnap women and children into servitude. It is uncertain how many of these *krijgsgevangenes* (war captives) or *inboekseling-en* (apprentices, so-called because of the *boek*, or register, in which they were enumerated) entered the cattle economy, though one estimate supposes that there were two thousand in Graaff-Reinet at the turn of the nineteenth century. Colonial law bound the inboekselingen to serve their masters until they were twenty-five years of age, in return for food and clothing.[75] This system of indenture also held Bastaard Hottentots, the children of slave or settler men and Khoisan women, to the service of the farmer on whose farm they were born, again to the age of twenty-five.[76]

The tasks to which farmers put the Khoisan included domestic chores within the farming household and all aspects of cattle keeping and sheep keeping. Both men and women tended the flocks and herds. Domestic work was largely women's work. Khoisan women cooked, cleaned, watched the children of the master and mistress, and kept house.[77] The slaves on the cattle farms worked alongside Khoisan under the same conditions and in the same capacities.[78] Any distinctions that existed in the labor of the two classes of unfree workers were minor. Slave men more often supervised Khoisan labor than the reverse; they seem generally to have held more of their master's trust. Boers who could afford to do so preferred to employ slave women rather than Khoisan as house servants.[79]

All sections of the rural economy had grown steadily, though gradually, during the eighteenth century and into the nineteenth. Growth had come as new farmers entered production and older farmers increased production to meet the demand of a Cape Town market that expanded in an only slightly broken rhythm.[80] The modest wealth of the settler economy was a legacy of conquest, enslavement, and servitude, and its maintenance depended on the ongoing processes of subjugation and exploitation.

Hierarchies at the Cape

Race mattered at the Cape. This assertion will surprise no one who came of age during the second half of the twentieth century. It must be qualified, however. Race did not play precisely the same role in the nineteenth century as it did in the twentieth. Ancestry, skin color, hair texture, and all the other common markers of race did to a significant extent determine where individuals and communities stood in the social hierarchy. But race was by no means the sole determinant of power, rights, and status, and arguably it was not even the most important. Indeed, the term was rarely heard at the Cape, and race was very loosely defined. Gender, wealth, legal status, and reputation mattered just as much.[81] So did the essential question of whether one was or was not an owner of slaves.

The Cape Colony in the first decades of the nineteenth century was very much a "a slave society," and it had been so for a century and a half.[82] Slavery shaped every aspect of Cape society—its laws, customs, and even its language, an evolving creole that would become known as Afrikaans[83]—and it provided the foundation on which the colony had built its economic life. Slavery's centrality also meant, as William Freund has argued, that the first and essential division within the social hierarchy at the Cape was that which separated "the free population at large [from] a subordinate majority of slaves and servants." The boundary ran between the masters, on one side, and servants of all colors and conditions, on the other.[84] Color and ancestry were, according to Freund, of secondary importance. The crucial distinction was between those who worked for themselves or their families and those who worked for others. This opposition has been common in slave societies all over the world. In the slave-owning societies of ancient Greece, for instance, the critical test of the status assigned a given task was not "the nature of the work (within limits, of course) as the condition . . . under which it was carried on. 'The condition of the free man,' said Aristotle, 'is that he does not live for the benefit (or profit) of another.'"[85] Slaveholders in the Cape Colony created and sustained a similar set of values and beliefs, and all colonists, whether they owned slaves or merely dreamed of possessing them, adopted them as their own.

Settlers held that their "proper role" in society was that of a "land- and slave-owning elite, and that manual or even skilled labour in the service of someone else did not befit anyone with the status of free-man."[86] As the colony's chief legal officer put it when explaining to an early British governor the reluctance of Afrikaners to enter paid employment: "When a young peasant marries and sees an opportunity of obtaining land fit for breeding cattle . . . he would act like a fool by leaving that, and hiring himself out to his fellow peasant, in order there, along with the slaves, by a continual labour, to earn . . . only food and clothing."[87] Accordingly, European descent was no guarantee of respectability; the dependent status of white servants relegated them to life among the lowly.

Property-owning colonists and British colonial officials—the respectable element—were of one mind "on such matters as personal dignity, the significance of landowning, and the respect due from the lower classes."[88] They expected deference from white servants as well as black. Governor Caledon expressed some of these prejudices when he explained his order to expel a young Englishwoman from the Cape. He cataloged her crimes and claimed that she shared vices endemic to her class and race. The young woman had left the employ of her master and mistress without seeking permission or giving notice. In common with other servants, Caledon wrote, she had displayed "an hauteur and bad treatment [of her master and mistress] . . . which would probably not have been offered and certainly not have been submitted to in England." The root of the problem lay in the colony's shortage of skilled domestic labor and the bargaining power that the shortage offered the white workers. "European Servants," Caledon complained, "in a Country where they cannot be immediately replaced assume a consequence ill becoming a state of service." He believed that, if he had not punished the young woman, other servants would have "claim[ed] a free agency" that would then have "set at large . . . a discription [*sic*] of people of all others the most troublesome and useless."[89]

There is some evidence that many within the Cape's many-hued working-class community shared a feeling that color did not divide them as much as their subordinate status brought them together. Travelers, for example, described the horse races outside of Cape Town at which "Malays and Negroes mingled with whites, all crowding and elbowing, eager to get a sight of the momentous contest."[90] Reports of friendships between people of various shades and statuses entered the colonial records. Jack, who was a slave, once dropped minor criminal charges against John Quinn, a British immigrant, because he was "a very old acquaintance."[91] Marriages between whites and free blacks were common. The Court of Justice in Cape Town, for instance, once heard a case involving five people of very different backgrounds: Hendrik Theron, an Afrikaner blacksmith; Marie Meyer, a free black woman and Theron's former lover; Mietje Allen, Marie's sister; James Allen, a British immigrant who had married Mietje; and Steyntje, a slave who was a friend of them all. All five were members of Cape Town's multicolored working class.[92] Between 1808 and 1820, 108 marriages took place between whites and free blacks; during the same period, only 102 marriages were contracted in which both parties were free blacks.[93] Because marriage is such a reliable marker of where a "social set" draws it boundaries, these marriages are important evidence of a community of feeling among working-class Capetonians.[94]

The portrait of the Cape as a society divided by class is accurate as far as it goes, but it will not do to ignore the importance of color and ancestry, something that few respectable colonists were also unprepared to do. While a white skin did not guarantee respectability, it was a prerequisite. Though some free blacks acquired wealth in slaves and other property, demonstrated considerable skill in artisanal trades, and became the spiritual leaders the local Islamic community,[95] they were never "respectable." Like white servants and workers, free blacks were denied respectability in terms of social standing and influence.[96]

In common with the other European and European settler societies of the time, race was not well defined at the Cape as noted above.[97] Cape society distinguished between, for instance, whites of various national origins, between Moslems and Christians, between slaves from, say, Malaysia and Mozambique, and between Khoikhoi, San, and Bastaard Hottentots. But while Cape society had yet to elaborate a well-developed racial ideology, "respectable" whites subscribed to a pervasive color prejudice that cut across divisions of class, ethnicity, and religion. As long as there had been European settlement at the Cape, there had been a racial hierarchy. Timothy Keegan argues that "it was unthinkable to the colonists in early South Africa, as it would be to those who exercised power and dominance in the . . . early twentieth century, that the social order might be built on anything other than the foundations of racial . . . exclusiveness and hegemony."[98] In his thorough study of the debate over slavery in the early-nineteenth-century Cape, R. L. Watson concludes that while "overtly racist arguments were peripheral" to the discussion, race did play a part. Virtually all settlers believed that innate biological differences between people of different colors explained variations in culture, power, and status. This conviction was an important part of the ways in which settlers understood and acted in the world. Respectable colonists, both the Afrikaners and the British, "harbored racist assumptions without voicing them publicly." Race, Watson contends, "was certainly a key factor in arranging the colony's social order, and the racial inferiority of non-Europeans was no doubt taken for granted."[99]

Color and ethnic prejudice was evident in colonial practice, if not colonial rhetoric. A former official noted with regret that within Cape society the "difference of colour furnishes . . . but too broad a line of demarcation," leading to discrimination against people who were not white. He believed that whites of every description, including the working class, held themselves superior to nonwhites. "The ceremony practiced by the inhabitants toward each other is sometimes ridiculous, extending even to the lowest class, who in passing pull off to each other their worn-out hats, and bow to the ground. The power exercised over slaves gives to every Christian man (for that is the term) so much distinction, that pomp in rags displays its superiority even in the streets."[100] Despite the rough equality that sometimes existed among members of the working class, race seems often to have trumped class, as can be seen in one of the laws regulating slave behavior: "a constable seeing a slave wilfully jostle or push against a European, even of the lowest class . . . or otherwise insult him, is obliged, in the absence of the master, immediately to apprehend such slave, and have him punished with flogging."[101]

It was not only the slaves who suffered for their nonwhiteness. Whites, a parliamentary commission of inquiry reported, viewed free blacks with "jealously and suspicion."[102] No person identifiable as a free black, Khoisan, or Bastaard Hottentot seems to have held a position in government above the level of manual laborer at any point in the early nineteenth century. It may be, as Robert Ross has argued, that some people of mixed descent came to be accepted as white as late as the end of the eighteenth century.[103] But by the beginning of the nineteenth, whiteness, whether socially constructed or ancestral, marked the men who monopolized civil and ecclesiastical officeholding at the Cape. The leading merchants and professionals of Cape Town were white without exception, and only a tiny handful of landowning farmers in the interior were not white. In Cape Town, a few free blacks owned slaves, and many worked as artisans or kept small shops, but they were subject to disabilities that whites were not. They never held high public office; they found it difficult to purchase land, despite having the legal right to do so; they suffered severe police harassment.[104] While whites were found throughout the Cape social hierarchy, nonwhites were not part of the upper classes.

The slaves, free blacks, Khoisan, and Bastaard Hottentots, who constituted the great majority of subordinate workers in the colony, suffered under oppressive systems of social and labor control by virtue of both their class and their color. Many poor whites, too, were members of the working-class community, but, for them, membership was a function of their class status, a mutable, not inherent, characteristic. By the first years of the nineteenth century, this extensive overlap of color and class had led to the creation of customary color prejudice, despite the presence of significant numbers of whites among the poor. This prejudice was not strictly "racist"; Cape society had not yet closely defined "races" with specific attributes, privileges, and disabilities assigned to each. But there was among the settlers "a clear claim that whites *as whites* (not as free persons) were distinct from all other groups" and that on those other groups "disabilities of various sorts could legitimately be laid."[105] The hierarchies of color and class coexisted easily, at least as far as elites were concerned. While there may have been tension between white chauvinism and the spirit of mutuality that linked working-class whites to nonwhites, there is little evidence that the contradiction caused any social disruption or threatened the general proposition that to be a slave, free black, Khoisan, or Bastaard Hottentot was to exist forever outside the bounds of proper settler society.

The pervasiveness of class and color prejudice at the Cape and the oppression that many nonwhites endured, including, in the case of the Khoisan, kidnapping and forced labor, make it difficult to argue that social death was something that only slaves endured. Yet such was the case. Khoisan and Bastaard Hottentot servants, especially on farms, were indeed violently dominated. Both groups had also fallen, in the estimation of respectable society, to at least as degraded a state as the slaves. Thus Khoisan and Bastaard Hottentot servants shared with the slaves two of the three "constituent elements" that Orlando Patterson has argued define slavery. Violence and humiliation acted with such force in the lives of many individual slaves and servants that, as we shall see, it is reasonable to call what happened to them "soul murder."[106] What set the slaves apart was the third of slavery's constituent elements. Only slaves suffered routine and persistent "natal alienation." Respectable society and its laws denied to slaves all claims on and obligations to kin. Slave parents had as little control over the fate of their children as they did over their own. All could be and were openly and routinely bought and sold. Slaves, unlike others among the oppressed, were decisively cut off from the cultures of their ancestors, another form of natal alienation.[107] This is not to argue that the slaves were more miserable than any group at the Cape. Oppression is not a competitive sport.

The colony that the British seized in 1806 was poor. Its natural endowment was meager, and such wealth as it produced found its way into the hands of the few. For at least two thousand years before the first Europeans arrived, Khoikhoi pastoralists and San hunters and gatherers had been its only inhabitants, leading nomadic or seminomadic lives, scraping a subsistence out of an unforgiving environment. By 1806 a distinctly different society had emerged, a sparsely populated, expansive enclave of settlers, slaves, and servants from Europe, Asia, and Africa. Most of the population clung to the southwestern coast, where rain was regular enough to grow crops familiar to Europeans. In the interior, increasing numbers of settlers and their servants and slaves reproduced, in more senses than one, the pastoral economy of the Khoikhoi. The colony had survived, but few in it had flourished. Like the land, most of the people who lived in the Cape Colony were poor, and four in ten were slaves. Slaves were not the only class of workers who labored for the benefit of others. Most of the Khoisan who remained within the boundaries of the colony had been reduced to the status of servile workers. Whites, too— that is, those whites who had no property and no independent source of income—were to be found in the laboring classes. While a few free blacks owned slaves and other property, settlers rarely allowed even those with wealth to enter the ranks of respectable society. Customary and legal forms of control meant that most free blacks, together with the slaves, Khoisan, and white servants, worked for others under some form of compulsion.

For all of its reliance on forced labor, the Cape produced little of great value. Though most slave owners lived in comfort, the Cape's chief value to the British, as it had been to the VOC, was its position astride the sea-lanes to Asia. Yet holding on to the Cape looked as if it would be an expensive proposition. To find a way to make the colony pay its own way within the empire was the elusive goal of British policy from 1806 until well into the second half of the century. Although the British did not know what commodities might allow the Cape to prosper, they did realize that a servile work force would underwrite whatever prosperity could be won. The problems of commodity production and labor occupied much of the time of colonial officials for many decades to come.

CHAPTER 2

"Breaking the Spell of Subjection"
Slavery in the Age of Reform

> We remain in our usual unsettled and unsatisfactory state. The
> Public mind has been agitated lately.
> —COLONIAL SECRETARY, CAPE COLONY, 1827

Major General Sir David Baird, who in 1806 received the Cape
Colony from the Dutch on behalf of his sovereign, George III, understood that he had been sent to capture his prize for two reasons.[1] First it
sat astride the vital shipping routes between Europe and Asia. Second,
and far less significantly, it might, at some distant epoch, develop into a
significant market for British manufactured goods. No matter what the
Cape's eventual place within the British imperial system was to be, the
mother country insisted that Baird and his successors see to it that the
colony pay its own way.[2] Given the high cost of managing and protecting
the colony, this was unlikely to happen unless the economy grew significantly, and growth, Baird understood, depended on slavery and the
slave trade. Both were "inseparable from the development and utiliza-
tion of the resources of the colony," because the most productive sectors
of the economy depended upon the labor of slaves. Less than a year after he assumed command of the Cape, Baird sanctioned the importation of a cargo of slaves. He wished, he said, "to give every encouragement to the Inhabitants and to contribute by every means in my power
to their welfare."[3] While the new arrivals may have brought joy to the
"Inhabitants," their happiness was surely short-lived, for these slaves
were the last to be landed legally at the Cape.

At virtually the same time that the king's forces were capturing the
Cape, the British Parliament was mustering the votes needed to outlaw
the overseas slave trade. Having seized slave colonies at the tip of Africa
and in the West Indies in the hope of profiting from them, the British
were nevertheless moving to cut off the flow of their most important
source of labor. This was nothing less than "econocide," as far as the
West Indian colonies were concerned.[4] The consequences were not as

severe for the Cape Colony; in fact, the economy grew steadily for almost two decades after the British occupation. But the suppression of the slave trade was only the first in a series of state actions that weakened slavery at the Cape, disquieting the slave owners, inspiring the slaves, and demonstrating that social death was relative, not absolute. Almost unwittingly, the British had initiated a process of social resurrection.

Contradictory impulses shaped British policy. On the one hand, Britain hoped to develop the productive capacities of its colonies, including those that depended on slave labor. On the other, evolving notions about the rights of individuals and the rationality of free markets, including the labor market, were undermining the moral and intellectual foundations upon which slavery rested. By 1806 many in Britain had concluded that slavery must go. But emancipation, most abolitionists felt, should come gradually. To that end, Britain abolished the slave trade and, over the next three decades, enacted laws designed to protect the slaves and to prepare them for life as disciplined, free wage laborers. While there is little evidence that the Cape economy suffered greatly because of these reforms, it is certain that they troubled the masters and emboldened the slaves, profoundly shaking settler society. The masters faced uncertainty about their economic future and about the security of the property that they held in slaves. At the same time, the reforms brought the slaves into the civil community, deeply altering their ideas about themselves, their owners, and the world in which they lived. With the help of the reform laws, they fought and sometimes won battles to diminish the violence, natal alienation, and degradation of social death. Planters in the British West Indies, who endured the same reforms, believed that Parliament was ruining them. Laws designed to improve the condition of the slaves were, they said, "breaking the spell of subjection."[5] Slaves at the Cape would have happily agreed. The slaves' consciousness and the behavior it informed are the subject of the chapters that follow. Here we consider the reforms themselves.

The British Take a Slave Colony, Twice

Imagined riches did not bring the British to the Cape. They knew, even before they conquered the colony for the first time in 1795, that a "very great proportion" of its vast extent was "an unprofitable waste, unfit for any sort of culture."[6] However limited the prospects for farming might have been, the summer harbor in Table Bay and winter harbor in nearby False Bay were invaluable strategic assets, for war and for trade. Fortune had placed the Cape almost precisely midway between Europe and Asia, where the outbound and homeward routes of the spice trade converged. Since the 1590s, it had been the "general rendezvous and place of refreshment" for European merchants and mariners, the stepping stone to the East. The VOC—the Dutch East India Company[7]—established a way station on Table Bay in 1652, and the settlement that became Cape Town grew up around it. The VOC did not interfere with foreign shipping, welcoming the chance to sell supplies to all comers. Among the ships that called were those from Britain.[8]

Throughout the latter half of the eighteenth century, the British had pursued a rich and growing trade with Asia, and especially with India, the jewel in the British monarch's imperial crown. As long as the Dutch controlled the Cape, British ships were welcome. The outbreak of the Napoleonic wars necessarily altered British calculations. A hostile power in possession of the Cape would not only interfere with trade by denying "refreshment" to British shipping, it would also threaten the entire structure of influence and power in the Indian Ocean, if enemy ships began to prey on the gunboats of the Royal Navy. With the advent of war, the fear that the French would seize the Cape prompted the British to act.[9]

Nine British warships dropped anchor in False Bay in June 1795. In early August, the British commander landed his forces, and a month later, the Dutch defenders signed articles of capitulation.[10] Beyond its strategic importance and its glorious land- and seascapes, there was little that the British would have found attractive about the Cape. They had captured their prize during a period of "convulsive disorder." Settlers on the northeastern frontier were in revolt against the VOC and saw no reason to suspend their proceedings in favor of their new rulers; those colonists not in revolt were hostile to the British and engaged in sullen "passive resistance"; and the Khoisan, whom the colonists had reduced nearly to the status of slaves, were soon to rebel.[11] Opinion in London was divided on the wisdom of keeping this unpromising colony any longer than was required to keep it away from the French. As the war subsided, the arguments against the retention of the Cape grew stronger. The British returned the colony to the Dutch (though not to the VOC, which had died, unmourned) in 1803 under the terms of the Treaty of Amiens.[12] During the eight years of the first British occupation, the colonial administration did little to change the status quo and much to preserve it. If they put down the rebellion of the masters, they also suppressed that of the servants. If they eliminated the use of torture as an instrument of criminal justice, they also oversaw the importation of approximately two thousand slaves.[13]

The renewal of warfare in Europe, combined with the weakness and political unreliability of the Dutch Republic, prompted the British to return to the Cape. They appeared in Table Bay on 6 January 1806, in the midst of a particularly hot summer. Sixty-three ships carried sixty-six hundred rank-and-file troops, many hundreds of seamen, and an appropriate number of officers. To oppose them, the Dutch commander could muster no more than two thousand men—regulars, colonists, Khoisan, and Bastaard Hottentots to do the fighting, and slaves to haul the artillery. Only one true battle was fought, and the Dutch lost. On 18 January, the commander of the British forces accepted a second capitulation.[14] The Cape of Good Hope was again a part of the British Empire and would remain so for the next 155 years.

Econocide at the Cape?

In March 1807, Parliament enacted legislation that would lead, eventually, to the abolition of slavery ("An Act for the Abolition of the Slave Trade"),[15] prohibiting British ships from participating in the oceanic trade in slaves and forbidding the importation of slaves into British possessions. Despite the two decades of lobbying that had led to the bill's success, the shift in Britain's position, from that of the slave trade's most active participant to that of its most determined antagonist, was "almost . . . instantaneous" in historical terms.[16] It also seemed to make little sense economically. Britain had been more successful in establishing slave colonies than any other nation, and its industrializing economy, the world's strongest, owed much to the profits of slavery. As Eric Williams argued in 1944, in a conclusion that has not been effectively challenged,[17] "The profits obtained [from the slave trade, slave plantations, and manufacturing that depended on slave-produced commodities] provided one of the main streams of that accumulation of capital in England which financed the Industrial Revolution."[18] David Eltis agrees that the suppression of the slave trade came at the end of more than a century "during which the exploitation of Africans in the New world had become the foundation stone of the British Atlantic economy."[19] Given the centrality of slavery and the slave trade to the British economy, the success of abolitionism after only a generation of antislave-trade politicking stuck many people at the time, and historians of a later day, as a "mysterious triumph."[20]

The earliest historians of abolitionism, writers who were either abolitionists themselves or who closely identified with them, developed a providential explanation of abolitionism. The humanitarians, they declared, were merely the instruments through which the grand design of a higher moral force was made manifest on earth.[21] Williams forever altered the lines of inquiry. His analysis was resolutely materialist, emphasizing the importance of slavery in promoting the emergence of the British industrial economy and its vulnerability when it ceased to play a positive role. By the late eighteenth century, he argued, the slave colonies had become economic liabilities. Slavery was indeed "vicious," providing an opening humanitarian opponents would exploit, but humanitarianism alone, he insisted, would not have ended the slave trade had it remained profitable. The British colonial slave economy had ceased to make economic sense; it was in fact "so unprofitable that for this reason alone its destruction was inevitable." Although slavery's effective demise did not come until 1838, the successful attack on the slave trade was a part of a single process by which it was ended. "The capitalists had first encouraged slavery and then helped to destroy it."[22]

While there is an appealing elegance to Williams's analysis of abolitionism's "mysterious triumph," Seymour Drescher has convincingly challenged much of it. He has demonstrated that the profitability of colonial enterprises that relied on slave labor had not declined significantly at the time of the Abolition Act; nor had the slave colonies become economic deadweight. "Economic interests," he writes, "cannot account for either the timing, the occurrence, or the maintenance of the abolition of the slave trade."[23] David Eltis agrees that "from the viewpoint of economic self-interest, British anti-slavery policy appears wrongheaded enough to qualify for inclusion in Barbara Tuchman's catalog of folly in government."[24]

While Williams misjudged the precise nature of the links between capitalist development and abolition, he was right to suspect that the connections were real and important. David Brion Davis has shown that while abolitionism "served conflicting ideological functions," it did reinforce "the hegemony of capitalist values," especially the beneficence of free wage labor.[25] Robin Blackburn has extended this line of argument by illustrating the ways in which abolitionism appealed to various classes of Britons caught within the psychological and material dislocations of early industrialization. For the middle classes, abolitionism eased anxieties caused by "rampant . . . commercialism and industrialism, the arrogance of the ruling class and . . . even the waywardness of the labouring classes." Radicals in turn "stressed the rights of free labour and the iniquities of a slave-trading merchant and financial oligarchy." For "politically alert members of the ruling order," the abolition of the slave trade was a safe, unthreatening reform.[26] Many hands grasped the dagger of econocide. No factor, save the emancipation of the slaves in 1838, was more responsible for the decline of the British plantation economies than the abolition of the slave trade.[27] At the Cape, no charge of econocide could have been laid. Between 1806 and the mid-1820s, in the face of a tight labor market, the economy perversely boomed.[28]

Word of the parliamentary ban on the slave trade reached the Cape by July 1807. It would take effect on 1 January 1808. The governor, the earl of Caledon, did not welcome the news: abolition in no way served his purposes. Caledon's goal was "to give coherence to the vague and in-choate structure of the Colony, so that it might more adequately be fitted for the place it was finding in the new Empire."[29] Fitting the Cape meant addressing pressing economic concerns. The colony was now a part of a trading empire "vastly larger and more dynamic than that of the VOC,"[30] and, because the Cape "as a strategic calling station" flour-ished in times of war," it had lately experienced a large increase in trade.[31] The boom was accompanied, however, by a chronic trade deficit and a currency that was rapidly diminishing in value.[32] If the colony were to overcome the deficit, steady its currency, and begin to pay its way in the empire, it would have to become more productive. This called for a large pool of cheap, exploitable workers.

In July 1807, Caledon composed a dispatch to the secretary of state and noted, in passing, Parliament's approval of the act abolishing the slave trade. Ostensibly his subject was the "very great expense" involved in supporting the Cape Native Infantry Regiment, but the colony's labor problems were very much on his mind. The Cape Regiment, also known as the Cape Corps, had grown markedly over the preceding several years. It consisted of 800 Khoisan and Bastaard Hottentot rank and file and a white officer corps. The governor wished to cut its numbers by more than half, to 350. The regiment was of little military use, he ex-plained, and the colony would achieve a considerable savings if its strength were reduced. The discharge of more than 400 Khoisan and Bastaard Hottentot soldiers would be doubly beneficial, he argued, since the colonists "would gain the advantage of some useful Labourers, a consideration of much importance, especially since the abolition of the Slave Trade." Caledon enclosed a letter from the *landdrost* of Graaff-Reinet (the district adminstrator and chief law-enforcement officer), stressing the importance of "Hottentot" workers to the local economy.[33] Caledon returned to the labor question in a dispatch written six months later. The end of the slave trade had been "severely felt," he said, and "many of the principal Inhabitants" had spoken to him about a labor shortage. He indicated that the end of the slave trade alone was not responsible for the shortage. Other factors loomed almost as large: many slaves had died during a recent epidemic of measles; the demand for agricultural produce, and, consequently, agricultural labor, had increased due to the presence of the British garrison; and the supply of Khoisan labor had diminished because of recruitment into the Cape Regiment. He now wished to disband the regiment altogether.[34]

The labor shortage—that is, the inability of settlers to find a sufficient number of laborers willing to submit to the low wages and brutal conditions on offer—was a problem that the colonial administrations of the early nineteenth century never completely solved.[35] To a large degree, this was because the British were pursuing contradictory ends. Mary Raynor's remarks about the wine economy apply to the colonial economy as a whole: "Producers were confronted with a paradoxical situation of being encouraged to raise productivity by a colonial government that, at the same time, had acted to cut off the major source of labour."[36] The paradox was inevitable so long as the British were determined to boost agricultural production and, at the same time, to dismantle, slowly, the forced-labor systems at the Cape.

As early as 1810, colonial officials were placing their hopes for economic growth on the wine industry. Writing to the secretary of state, Caledon noted that war had interfered with both production and trade in "the Wine countries in Europe." He suggested that the government consider the Cape as an alternative source and encourage the production and sale of "ordinary Cape Wines and Brandy" by reducing the duty paid on Cape vintages imported into Britain. If the wine farms prospered, he added, the rest of the colony would follow.[37] The home government did not immediately respond. Soon afterward, a new governor, Lieutenant General Sir John Cradock, renewed the lobbying on behalf of the wine industry. Wine, he felt, was the only "article . . . upon which the wealth and commercial character of the colony" could rest.[38] Believing that a better product would find more buyers, he "castigated local farmers and merchants for [the] slipshod methods" that produced poor wines. In order to ensure the quality of vintages, Cradock created the office of the wine taster. Wine farmers responded to Cradock's exhortations, and the acreage under vines began an upward movement that did not end for more than a decade.[39]

Cradock's sense of timing was acute. The home government was at last prepared to do something for the Cape, and in 1813 Britain lowered the duties paid on the wine imported from the colony. The combined effect of reduced tariffs and Cradock's initiatives to promote production "was to usher in a period of unprecedented growth in the wine industry." Between 1809 and 1825, the quantity of wines produced at the Cape increased by 83 percent.[40] Buoyed by the flourishing wine trade, the presence of several thousand officers and men in the garrison, and the exile of Napoleon and his entourage and jailers to Saint Helena (a market that the Cape supplied), the colonial economy entered a period of relative prosperity that lasted until the early 1820s.[41] While the economy grew, the labor supply remained comparatively stagnant. The slave population did grow by natural increase, but too slowly to offset the end of the trade.[42] Slave infants were not, in any case, immediately available as workers. Attempts to smuggle slaves into the colony seem largely to have failed.[43]

Ironically, an outgrowth of the abolition of the overseas slave trade seemed for a time to offer a solution to the labor shortage. Under the terms of the Abolition Act and an order in council that followed (March 1808), slaves imported into British possessions and those captured aboard ships at sea were not to be sent back to their places of origin. Instead, they were forfeited ("condemned," in the sadly appropriate language of the Admiralty courts) to the Crown as "prizes." The courts then freed these "Prize Negroes," or "Liberated Africans," but at the same time "apprenticed" them to settlers for terms as long as fourteen years so that they might "acquire such a degree of practical instruction from the masters to whom they were assigned, as would enable them at a future period to support themselves." The result was the creation of a class of legally free workers whose actual status approached that of the slaves. Between 1808 and 1816, a Royal Navy squadron stationed at the Cape seized ships carrying more than twenty-one hundred captives and brought them to the colony to be indentured. The imports continued until the late 1840s, by which time more than five thousand "Prize Negroes" had been landed at the Cape. Little training followed. Indeed Christopher Saunders has pointed out that colonial masters revealingly referred to the "Prize Negroes" as "Prize Slaves."[44] In the end, the few so-called prizes who entered the colony in any given year made little impact on the overall labor market.

The most significant government attempt to strengthen the colonial workforce in the period following the end of the slave trade involved the Khoisan. In 1809, Governor Caledon issued a proclamation designed, he informed the secretary of state, to foster "the better regulation of Hottentots in service of the Farmers."[45] In fact, the law did less to "regulate" the labor of the Khoisan than to coerce it. The proclamation's preamble claimed that "for the benefit of the Colony at large, it is necessary, that . . . Individuals of the Hottentot nation . . . should be subject to proper regularity in regard to their places of abode and occupations . . . also that they should find an encouragement for preferring entering the service of the Inhabitants to leading an indolent life, by which they are rendered useless both to themselves and the community."[46] To this end, the law required every "Hottentot" to have a "fixed Place of Abode," which in practice meant employment on a settler's farm, and to seek a pass from a colonial magistrate if he or she wished to move. Any Khoisan who did not comply with this last provision was to be treated "as a Vagabond" and as such was liable to being contracted out to a farmer in search of labor. The law also required that farmers enter into written agreements with their Khoisan laborers and empowered magistrates to see to it that both parties fulfilled the provisions of the contracts.[47] The law effectively bound Khoisan to individual settlers for the length of the contract and to the colonial economy permanently. In 1812, Governor Cradock further tightened the constraints that held the Khoisan to settler farms by allowing farmers to "apprentice" the children of his Khoisan workers for ten years.[48]

In 1937, W. M. Macmillan, the leading South African historian of the first half of the twentieth century, argued that initiatives such as Caledon's were attempts to establish greater equality under law while ensuring an ample supply of workers: "The Government had always to reckon with the clamorous colonial demand for labour. . . . All its laws therefore were two-edged. In making well-meant efforts for the legal protection of the Hottentots, they had at the same time . . . been building up a host of provisions to drive them into service, and to keep them there."[49] William Freund has noticed the same conflicting impulses. "British authorities," he writes, "stood for a policy of rigidly subordinating the servants while also protecting them against contractual abuses."[50] This would have been a difficult position to maintain, even in the abstract. In the real world of master-servant relations, the British found that they could not balance the competing claims of the settlers, who wished to reduce their laborers as nearly as possible to the status of slaves, and the Khoisan, who hoped to retain as much of their independence as possible. As far as the status of Khoisan servants was concerned, political and economic interests and cultural sympathy pushed the British and the settlers, for a time, into each others' arms.[51]

The abolition of the slave trade initiated a period during which the British were torn between the desire to abolish seemingly archaic forms of labor discipline and the knowledge that the colonial economy relied on various forms of coercion. This conflict remained within manageable bounds until 1823, when the colonial administration, at the behest of the home government, began to enact a series of laws designed to improve the condition of the slaves and prepare the way for eventual freedom. The result was a weakening of the slave system, not least because of the initiative of the slaves themselves. At almost the same moment, Parliament eased the tariff on foreign wines entering Britain, knocking the bottom out of the market for Cape wines. For slave owners and colonial officials faced with restless slaves and a declining economy, the 1820s and 1830s were years of crisis.

Amelioration

In July 1822, the House of Commons heard a debate on slavery and other matters relating to the Cape Colony. Opening the debate, William Wilberforce, leader of the antislavery forces in Parliament, called for, among other things, the instruction of the slaves in Christianity to counter the effects of Islamic proselytizing and government support for the "amelioration" of slavery.[52] The results were twofold: the appointment of a parliamentary commission to report on the Cape; and a proclamation from the governor, Lord Charles Somerset, designed to civilize, Christianize, and generally uplift the slaves.

Wilberforce spoke at a strategic moment in the history of abolitionism. After a period of dormancy, the antislavery movement experienced a reawakening in the early 1820s. With the death of George III and the ascension of "the spectacularly dissolute and adulterous" George IV, the government could no longer hold off opposition demands for a number of reforms that were related in spirit, if not organizationally—Roman Catholic relief, parliamentary reform, and emancipation.[53] In January 1823, veterans of the anti–slave trade agitation established the Society for Mitigating and Gradually Abolishing the State of Slavery throughout the British Dominions, better known simply as the Anti-Slavery Society.

The society was as much the product of disappointed dreams as hopeful anticipation.

A generation earlier, abolitionists had believed that the suppression of the slave trade "would set in motion a chain of forces, sustained by economic self-interest, that would force planters to improve the treatment of existing slaves" and lead "slowly but irresistibly" to emancipation.[54] The decline of slave populations in many West Indian colonies and reports about the deplorable conditions under which the slaves continued to live convinced abolitionists that only government intervention would better their condition. Initially the call was for amelioration, not immediate emancipation. The abolitionists' modest aims included guaranteeing the slaves access to Christian religious instruction, granting them the right to marry, easing the way to manumission, and ending Sunday labor. Their proposals were designed to prepare the slaves for freedom, in large part through the inculcation of middle-class virtues, while leaving untouched the instruments of discipline needed to protect society from the still barbarous slaves. "The specter of Haiti"— the memory, that is, of the revolution three decades earlier that destroyed the master-class and freed the slaves—haunted the abolitionists. They hoped to avoid "any measures that might undermine law and authority or endanger the long-term productivity of colonial labor."[55] Inevitably, as we shall see, they failed.

In May 1823, Thomas Fowell Buxton, who had succeeded Wilberforce as parliamentary leader of the abolitionists, moved a resolution that argued "that the state of slavery is repugnant to the principles of the British Constitution and of the Christian religion" and ought to be abolished "with as much expedition as may be found consistent with a due regard to the well-being of the parties concerned." Speaking for the government, George Canning proposed a substitute resolution, declaring "the necessity of ameliorating the lot of the slave with a view to fitting him for his freedom at as early a date as was compatible with the welfare and safety of the colonies."[56] The substitute motion carried, and the government was committed to a program of cautious reform. Taking advice from the Society of West India Planters and Merchants, which represented slave-owning interests, the government drew up a model slave code, intending to promulgate it by fiat in the Crown colonies and by persuasion in the legislative colonies. In doing so, the government hoped to offer the abolitionists enough to keep them quiet, while convincing the West Indian planters that reform was politically expedient.[57]

At the Cape, Governor Somerset had already acted. He issued his amelioration proclamation in March 1823, two months before the parliamentary debate on Canning's resolution. Isobel Eirlys Edwards, the most thorough historian of this aspect of Somerset's policy, contended that he did so order to forestall stronger measures from the Colonial Office.[58] In the preamble to the proclamation, the governor expressed the hope that the law would tend to "civilize" the slaves and "ameliorate" their lot, insofar as was "consistent with the security of the state, and with due consideration to the rights and privileges of all." The legislation itself was similarly hedged with qualifications. The slaves were given the right to form legal marriages, if they were baptized Christians and if their masters agreed. These unions, and no others, were protected from disruption by sale. Children under ten were not to be sold away from their mothers, if their mothers were Christians. The testimony of Christian slaves, and no others, was to be accepted in court under oath. Maximum hours of slave labor in the field were set at ten in the winter and twelve in the summer, except for plowing, harvesting, and "extraordinary" occasions. Slave owners were not to punish their slaves beyond "a mild domestic correction," which could amount to twenty-five lashes with a whip. Stating what must have been obvious to all, the final clause stipulated that it was "clearly to be understood, that none of the provisions [of this law would] . . . affect in any degree the property of the proprietors in their slaves, or their just claims to their services."[59] Somerset's proclamation was weaker even than a proposed code that had been drafted by the West Indian planters' committee, which had at least the good grace to suggest a ban on the flogging of female slaves.[60]

Soon after he learned of Somerset's proclamation, Wilberforce wrote to the duchess of Beaufort, Somerset's sister-in-law, to say that he had nothing but praise for the proclamation.[61] This is less surprising than it might first appear. As David Brion Davis has argued, the revolution the abolitionists proposed was a limited one: amelioration and emancipation presupposed continued subordination. The abolitionists' "greatest hope, after all was to transform black slaves into cheerful, obedient and grateful laborers whose wants could be satisfied only by working voluntarily for wages."[62] The Rev. John Philip, superintendent of the London Missionary Society's activities in southern Africa and a man who had seen much more of slavery than either Wilberforce or Buxton, was unimpressed with Somerset's scheme. He doubted that the law would benefit the slaves at all, since it contained nothing that slave owners could not evade.[63] Lord Bathurst, the secretary of state for the colonies, was similarly skeptical. He regretted, he told Somerset, that he had issued a proclamation on so delicate a subject without consulting the Colonial Office. Bathurst was especially annoyed since he was in the midst of preparing a slave ordinance for Trinidad that went well beyond Somerset's in granting rights and protection to the slaves.[64]

Somerset's ineffective proclamation remained in force until 1826. A year earlier, the home government, under pressure from the antislavery lobby, had demanded that the Cape Colony adopt a slave ordinance along the lines of the one the secretary of state had by now forced on Trinidad. The Trinidadian statute offered the slaves more protection than Somerset's and contained enforcement provisions that the earlier law almost entirely lacked. Somerset did his best to delay the impending reforms, and in the end it was left to his successor, Major General Sir Richard Bourke, to publish ordinance 19 in June 1826.[65]

Ordinance 19 extended to all slaves who understood the nature of an oath, not just to Christians, the right to testify in court.[66] Slave children under ten could not be sold away from their mothers, whether or not they were Christians. Although male slaves might still be given twenty-five "stripes," slave women could now be whipped only "to such moderate extent as any Child of Free condition may be." In cases of alleged ill-treatment in which the complaining slave showed signs of a recent beating, the slave owner bore the burden of proving that he or she had not inflicted the wounds. The most significant innovations, however, were the right now given the slaves to purchase their freedom, with or without their masters' consent—the so-called "compulsory manumissions"—and the creation of the office of the guardian of slaves.[67]

The ordinance caused an uproar. Slave owners had three things especially on their minds. First, they feared that a misunderstanding of the law's provisions might incite the slaves to rebellion. In 1825, a mistaken belief that Somerset's proclamation had somehow freed them had allegedly encouraged a group of slaves and Khoisan servants to stage a minor, but bloody, slave revolt in the Worcester district.[68] Second, slave owners found it outrageous that the law gave to "a third person"— that is, the guardian of slaves—"without any right or reason, the odious power of interfering in the arrangement of private affairs." Third, the compulsory manumissions, the slaveholders believed, were an intolerable attenuation of their property rights.[69]

The slave owners were right to be concerned—not about rebellion (there was not even the hint of a slave revolt between 1826 and effective emancipation in 1838), but about the disruptive effects of the guardian's office, compulsory manumissions, and the laws themselves. In the guardian and the assistant guardians scattered throughout the colony, the law had created officials whose job it was to attend trials, hearings, "and all other Proceedings" to which a slave was party, to prosecute masters for violations of the law, and, more generally, "to act [in court] in such manner as may be most conducive to the benefit and advantage of such Slave."[70] To a surprising degree, the guardians acted as the law supposed that they would, benefitting the slaves to the disadvantage of their masters, not least because the slaves insisted on it. Compulsory manumissions did limit slave owners' property rights in their slaves, rights that they believed should be absolute. Owners could not refuse to sell a slave his or her freedom, though they could demand a fair price.[71] Most importantly, the amelioration proclamations and ordinances, even Somerset's, granted rights to those who should have been rightless and a civil and social existence to those who should have been socially dead.

Colonial law now recognized the slaves as members of the political community, not as outsiders, and as autonomous individuals, not simply as extensions of their owners' legal personality. While this did not imply legal or social equality, the law did limit the violence slave owners could direct against their slaves and the degree of natal alienation that they could impose. In doing so, it touched directly on the question of social death. Slaves were now members of the civil community, second-class members, to be sure, but members, nonetheless. The law had compromised social death. This would have been of little more than theoretical interest if not for the actions of the slaves and their guardians. Somerset's proclamation had granted the slaves a modicum of rights, a civil existence, but did not substantially affect the relationship between slaves and slave owners. Ordinance 19 was different. It extended the slaves' rights and, more importantly, provided a mechanism, the guardians's office, through which slaves could assert them. As slave owners feared, the ordinance undermined slavery, in both practical and ideological terms. Although slavery remained in place, it was transformed. The Cape was about to discover that social death, unlike physical death, was not absolute.

The order of the king in council of 2 February 1830 (known also as "the consolidated ordinance") superseded ordinance 19 in 1831. The most important changes reduced the number of lashes that could be applied legally to male slaves to fifteen and prohibited the whipping of female slaves altogether. The order required the slaveholders to keep record books of all punishments inflicted and to submit the books semi-annually to the renamed "protectors of slaves" for inspection.[72] While the title of the officeholders changed from guardian to protector, their duties remained the same.[73] The Consolidated Order sparked a second, stronger round of protests, producing a flood of petitions signed by perhaps one-quarter of the colony's sixty-four hundred slave owners, denouncing the revised law and especially the punishment record books. The protests culminated in a five-day slave owners' riot in the wine country village of Stellenbosch at the time that the books were first to be examined.[74] In the event, the sections of the order mandating the keeping of the record books were never seriously enforced. A further revision of the slave law, effective in 1832, served principally to close loopholes in the Consolidated Order and was the occasion for further protests from the slaveholders outraged by constant tinkering with what they saw as fundamentally unjust laws.[75]

As far as the slave owners were concerned, amelioration came at a particularly inopportune moment. In 1828, ordinance 50 had relieved the Khoisan of the restrictions that the proclamations of Caledon and Cradock had placed on them; it also established their legal equality with whites. The practical effects of the ordinance may be doubted. Life for most Khoisan servants seems to have changed very little. The psychological effects, on the other hand, were significant. The concept of legal equality, even though it may have remained little more than a pleasant idea, disturbed whites as much as it cheered the Khoisan, who clung to it as something of an emancipation proclamation.[76] Even more troubling for the slave-owning class, the colonial economy, especially in wines, was turning sour.

Colonists at the Cape, as C. W. de Kiewiet noted, had never been fully in control of their economic destiny. In the early decades of the nineteenth century, the colony "was fully exposed to the post-war depression by which England and the Continent were stricken. Hard times came in 1820 and stubbornly stayed. The wine trade had passed its peak. . . . A series of crop failures bore witness to the exhaustion of the wheat lands. While government expenditures increased, revenues were depressed by the now chronic weakness of the Rix dollar."[77] De Kiewiet may have misjudged the precise timing of the point at which the Cape's economy took ill, but the decline was unmistakable. The wine industry—the economy's strongest export sector and the employer of the largest number of slaves—led the economy into recession.

The prices that Cape wines earned in the British market fell, beginning in 1823. A year later, five hundred wine farmers and merchants, responding to word that the home government was considering a reduction in the tariff that protected colonial wines, petitioned the government not to take a step that they believed would ruin them. Their plea went unheeded. In 1825, Parliament greatly lowered the duties paid on foreign wine. Under these circumstances, the colony's wines, of dubious quality and produced far from the British market, were at a competitive disadvantage. The industry collapsed, taking the colonial economy with it. For the next several years, wine farmers, merchants, and local officials frequently drew the attention of the home government to the "dismal" state of the Cape economy and to the wine industry in particular.[78]

The reform laws added to the slave owners' anxiety. Though it had never been the abolitionists' aim, much less that of colonial officials, to subvert the subordination of the slaves to their masters, amelioration had that effect. The new laws gave the slaves the opportunity to resist their masters' demands in legally sanctioned and often effective ways. Everything depended, however, on what the slaves did with what the law had given them. As we shall see in later chapters, the slaves proved to be extraordinarily creative in using the laws to protect both customary and legal rights. They manipulated the law and often the protectors who administered them, improving their lives in ways that dismayed their masters and would have surprised the abolitionists. In the slaves' hands, the laws became powerful weapons in their struggles against social death and for social rebirth.

The Slaves and their Protectors

The protectors helped those slaves who helped themselves. It was up to the slave to travel to a protector's office in order to lodge a complaint against his or her owner. Just how slaves learned of the various reform laws is obscure, but informed speculation is possible. The texts of the amelioration ordinances appeared in the colonial newspapers and in the *Government Gazette*. They were no secret to any literate person who had access to one of these papers, which were widely circulated throughout the colony. Many slaveholders learned of the new laws in this way and through local officials, who were supplied with copies of the legislation for dissemination. Some slaves, especially in Cape Town, could read, and they probably learned about the ordinances from the newspapers.[79] Many more would have learned of the reforms indirectly by overhearing their masters speak and argue about them, as the 1825 rebels were said to have done.[80] Slaves who found out what the law offered them would not have hesitated to tell their friends.

There were distinct rhythms to the pattern of the slaves' visits to the protectors. Over the life of the office, the volume of slave complaints rose from roughly two hundred per year in 1826 and 1827 to between four and six hundred by 1833 and 1834.[81] It is likely that two thousand or more slaves, or one in fifteen of the Cape's thirty-five thousand slaves, went at some time or another to a protector's office. Slaves were more likely to visit the protectors during the harvest than at any other time, when, as the principal protector put it in 1833, slaveholders "expect[ed] too much from their Slaves and [were] more prone to Anger and Excitement."[82] Most of the slaves who lodged complaints did so alone. There were, however, occasional instances of collective action. In 1833, for example, two slaves owned by Magtelda Smit complained that they had been punished for no reason other than their refusal to assist in the whipping of another slave.[83] Two years earlier, Isaac and twelve other slaves belonging to Jan Hoets had charged that their master had failed to provide them with wholesome and sufficient food, as the law required.[84]

Alone or as part of a group, many slaves had to travel long distances to reach a protector. Although protectors could be found in ten towns and villages stretching from Cape Town to Stellenbosch to Clan William and Graaff-Reinet, perhaps half of the slaves lived at least a full day's journey on foot from a protector's office.[85] Some slaves were up to the challenge. Martha, a slave owned by Johannes Louw of the Stellenbosch district, walked the thirty-five to forty miles from Stellenbosch to the protector's office in Cape Town while wearing leg irons when she could not obtain satisfaction from the assistant protector in Stellenbosch.[86] T. Venter's slave Jeptha, who lived in the Graaff-Reinet district, walked a hundred miles "over high mountains" to reach an assistant protector.[87]

Once in a protector's office, the slaves found a wary and overworked official who, except in Cape Town and after 1830 in Graaff-Reinet, was a part-time functionary.[88] Circumstances sometimes forced slaves to state their case through the mediation of a translator. It could be a tedious process. Within six months of commencing his job, the principal protector in Cape Town complained that because "the greater part of [the slave population],—particularly from the country,—are unable to speak or comprehend English, and many of them are ignorant of the

Dutch language also, the taking of their own statements . . . necessarily occasions great trouble in interpreting and explaining."[89] Things were, apparently, not entirely different from the eighteenth century, when the slaves widely spoke both "Low-Portuguese" and Malay.[90]

As troublesome as the barriers of distance, language, and the attention-span of the protectors may have been, the protectors' attitudes toward the laws that they enforced and toward the slaves themselves presented even greater difficulties. The principal guardian and, later, principal protector in Cape Town, Major George Jackman Rogers, who had arrived in the Cape Colony as Lord Somerset's aide-de-camp, criticized many aspects of the laws he was meant to enforce.[91] In his 1830 report, for instance, he condemned the new Consolidated Order almost as energetically as the masters. It was with "infinite regret," he wrote, that he felt "bound to declare that the Order in Council does not appear . . . likely to produce any good Effect upon the Moral and social condition of the Slaves." The changes in the slave laws and the debates on abolition in Parliament had kept slaveholders in a state of "constant agitation." This, he claimed, had made them "morose and certainly less kind to their Slaves than formerly." The slaves had come to believe "that their Emancipation must be near, and therefore pay less regard to their Owners, and in short look upon them as their worst Enemies and the impediment to their liberation." As a result, "the tie which formerly existed between the Master and the Slave seems thereby completed [*sic*] severed, the Master does little now for his Slave from real regard, and the Slave nothing for his Master from affection."[92]

Rogers deplored this state of affairs. He wanted to mend, not disturb, the paternal tie between master and slave by conveying to each a sense of their respective rights and duties. He spoke of "the benefits" that had been derived from his policy of reconciling the claims of the slaves with the rights of the masters. It pleased him to note the "many opportunities" that he had been given to bring ill-behaved slaves to "a sense of sorrow and promises of future amendment."[93] Because he held the position of principal protector (or guardian) for all but one of the eight years that the office existed, he was able to stamp his mark on the department. Hence a protector on the eastern frontier wrote of his own desire to "conciliate" any antagonisms that might exist between the master and the slave "rather than to widen any breach caused by the faults of either party."[94]

At other times, however, Rogers's stance toward the slaves could seem positively antagonistic. He once explained delays in processing cases and filing his reports by pinning the blame squarely on the slaves. "It is inconceivable," he grumbled,

> to those who have no means of Observing It, how embarrassing the various Applications for information, Advice and Assistance have become, from a misconception in many Instances of the Powers, with which the Slaves from the Country conceive, or affect to believe, the Protector to be vested, some advancing the most extraordinary requests from actual simplicity, whilst others with the most artful cupidity and affected Ignorance resort to this Office merely to embarrass and waste the time of their Owners.[95]

The slave Floris, for instance, pricked several of Rogers's prejudices. In the course of a hearing into his complaint against his master alleging ill-treatment, it emerged that he had failed to perform the work assigned to him and had been "impudent when upbraided" for it by his master. Rogers threw the complaint out, commenting that Floris "was known at this office as a Stubborn Character."[96] Similarly, Rogers refused to act on Adonis's complaint that his girlfriend's master had beaten him with a broomstick when he visited her without permission. The protector reported that he dismissed the charge because the slave's evidence was weak and "as Adonis was a bad character."[97] As a matter of routine, Rogers and his assistants would not act on the complaints of slaves whose masters could show them to have neglected their work, to have been insolent, or those whom they knew to be troublesome.

It is no wonder that historians have held the protectors, especially Rogers, at arm's length. Isobel Eirlys Edwards, for instance, wrote that the protectors' "sympathy often lay with the masters rather than with the slaves."[98] Mary Raynor has argued that the protectors "showed great solicitude for the feelings of slave proprietors," due, in part, to their "absorption of slaveholders' ideology."[99] While these assessments are accurate as far as they go, they fail to acknowledge the energy and determination with which the protectors sometimes pursued the slaves' interests, as well as the ways in which the slaves were able to manipulate these colonial officers to their own advantage. They also ignore the enmity that slaveholders felt for the protectors, which stemmed precisely from the effectiveness with which the protectors defended the slaves.[100]

Rogers's personal outlook was undeniably paternalist, but his was the paternalism of a British colonial officer, a rather different thing than the paternalism of a colonial slaveholder. As he saw it, the fundamental social relationship was the one that existed between subject and sovereign or the sovereign's representatives, not the relationship between slave and slave owner. The laws he enforced subordinated the master-slave relationship to the relationship between the slave and the colonial state. The admission of slaves into the civil community was not intended to subvert hierarchy of master and slave, yet that was precisely the effect. As Raynor noted, the workings of the protector's office were "fraught with ambiguity."[101]

The sources of this ambiguity lie within the protectors' personal beliefs as much as in nature amelioration. Slavery troubled Rogers, even though he was himself the owner of two slaves—a cook and a seamstress.[102] In the midst of one of his celebrations of the slave owners' concern for their slaves, Rogers interrupted himself to note that slavery was a "Curse which must have Its many attendant Evils wherever it Exists." He added that it "should now be got rid of," though only by "Legal and Justifiable means."[103] The unease that he felt about the legitimacy of slavery may explain the eagerness with which he helped slaves who claimed to be held illegally, wished to purchase their freedom, or struggled to keep their families together. The pressure he received from his overseers in the Colonial Office is also part of the story.

The officials who implemented parliamentary directives regarding the reform of slavery understood very well that it would be fraught with unavoidable ambiguities. Once Britain had made the decision to grant rights to those who, in principle, ought to be rightless, contradictions were inevitable. Officials in the Colonial Office acknowledged that whatever measures local governments enacted to limit an owner's power and "to prepare the slave for freedom" would "infringe on the rights of property." Conversely, any provision that strengthened a master's authority and reinforced "the submission of the slave" would "derogate from the great principle that the labourer is worthy of his hire."[104] But the Colonial Office had no doubt that the evil of slavery far exceeded the wrong of compromised property rights. The officials were themselves supporters of abolition[105] and believed that where rights came into conflict, those of the slave outweighed those of the slaveholder. In his memoir, Henry Taylor, the senior clerk of the Colonial Office during the period of reform, made his allegiance at the time clear:

> We knew what we were about. We had established protectors of slaves in the few colonies in which we had legislative power; they made their half-yearly reports in which every outrage and enormity perpetrated

on the slaves was duly detailed. . . . [W]e wrote despatches in answer . . . distinctly marking each atrocity, and bringing its salient
points into light; we laid the reports and despatches before Parliament as fast as they were received and written; Zachary Macaulay
forthwith transferred them to the pages of his "Monthly Anti-Slavery
Reporter" by which they were circulated far and wide through the
country.[106]

Rogers and his assistants made their every move knowing that their decisions would ultimately be judged by men more kindly disposed to the
slaves than they.

Cape slave owners resented the protectors and the laws that they
enforced and did everything they could to keep their slaves away from
the protectors' offices. Their methods were sometimes violent. Jacobus
Francois Malan, for example, gave his slave Demas fifteen lashes with
a cat-o'-nine-tails because he had lodged a complaint of ill-treatment
with the assistant protector in Stellenbosch. Undaunted, Demas returned to the protector's office and charged his master with having punished him illegally. The protector prosecuted Malan for the second offence, and the court fined him £5 for having beaten his slave without
due cause.[107] Slave owners sought to intimidate slave witnesses as well as
those who lodged complaints. Despite the reforms, masters retained
much of their power over their slaves. They could whip them with impunity, as long as they found a plausible excuse and stayed within the
legal limits; they could assign more onerous work; they could grant or
withhold privileges. The slaveholders proved so adept at suborning the
testimony of slave witnesses that one of the protectors suggested that any
slave who was party to a complaint should be held in the local jail, beyond the reach of the master, until the charge had been adjudicated.[108]
Some protectors adopted this procedure.

Banded together—that is, constituted as courts of law—slave owners
continued to obstruct the slaves' attempts to defend their rights. Until
1828, local boards of landdrost and *heemraden* (local councilor-citizens
appointed by the colonial government) tried cases involving masters
and slaves. The "richest farmers within the districts" dominated these
courts and used them to advance the interests of their class.[109] Since
most of these local notables owned slaves, they tended to be more in-
terested in maintaining the masters' authority than in vindicating the
rights of the slaves.[110] In 1828, the British system of judge and jury replaced the landdrost and heemraden. Convictions continued to prove

elusivé. The problem, said the protector in Graaff-Reinet, was the difficulty of gathering enough evidence of a type that "seemed likely to lead to a conviction[,] at least before a jury." He explained that the juries, "who have chiefly consisted of Slave Holders," held strong prejudices against the slaves: "conviction upon the evidence of slaves is not always to be relied upon notwithstanding the impressive and repeated Cautions conveyed in the charges of the Judge."[111] A few years earlier, similar concerns had led the governor to suggest that jury trials might be inappropriate at the Cape: "The result of some recent trials in cases of maltreatment of Slaves, where the prisoners were acquitted in the teeth of the clearest evidence against them, makes it very questionable if the trial by jury . . . has been a benefit to the Colony."[112]

The wonder is then that there were any convictions at all. E. Hengherr estimated that the masters lost one-third to one-half of the cases that went to trial.[113] The lower figure is probably the more accurate. Convicted slaveholders were subject to fines (in rare instances, the fines reached £10) and to court orders enjoining them to rectify their slaves' grievances. Because most of the slaves' complaints, however, never reached the courtroom,[114] no more than one in six resulted in a conviction. If this is correct, as few as thirty slave owners in the 1820s and a many as seventy in the 1830s would have been convicted each year of mistreating their slaves. That was more than enough to encourage the slaves. As we shall see in subsequent chapters, slaves at the Cape were quite adept at "working the system to their minimum disadvantage."[115]

The Abolition Act, which ended formal slavery while extending the period of effective enslavement, brought the era of amelioration to an close and shut the doors of the protectors' offices. In the four years that followed, the former slaves' relationship to the law and the men who enforced it was considerably more adversarial than it had been during the last years of slavery. Their determination to assert their rights, however, changed very little.

Apprenticeship

The act for the abolition of slavery throughout the British Colonies— "for promoting the Industry of the manumitted Slaves; and for compensating the Persons hitherto entitled to the Services of such Slaves"[116]— passed its third reading in the House of Commons on 7 August 1833; it received the royal assent three weeks later. Parliament acted when it did because the West Indian planters' defiance of amelioration, the brutal suppression of the 1831 Jamaica slave revolt, and evidence of the continued horrors of slavery heard by a parliamentary committee had galvanized public opinion against the institution. Parliament, newly elected under the reformed franchise and eager to legitimate itself, succumbed to public pressure.[117] Under the terms of the act, slavery was to end in the British West Indies on 1 August 1834 and in the Cape Colony on 1 December 1834.[118] Slave owners were to be compensated for the loss of their emancipated property out of a £20 million fund.[119] (The Cape's portion of the compensation money came to £1,247,401.)[120] Although slavery was to be abolished, the slaves were not to be freed.

The Abolition Act initiated a period of "apprenticeship," during which the colonial state would promote "the Industry of the manumitted slaves." All slaves over six years of age were to become "apprentices," bound to serve their former owners faithfully for periods of either six years, in the case of "praedial" apprentices, those engaged in plantation labor, or four years, in the case of "nonpraedial" apprentices—all others.[121] In turn, masters and mistresses were obligated to provide as much "food, clothing, lodging, medicine, medical attendance, and such other Maintenance and Allowance" as the apprentices had received as slaves. The slave owners-turned-employers were either to allow their praedial apprentices to work a few hours a week for themselves or pay them wages for that time. Masters could claim all of a nonpraedial apprentice's time and did not have to compensate them. The act also created "Special Justices," sometimes called "Special Magistrates," who were to oversee the workings of apprenticeship and to punish the misdeeds of both masters and apprentices.[122] The precise nature of the apprentices' duties, the masters' responsibilities, and the special justices' jurisdiction was to be settled by local ordinances.

The Cape ordinance "for giving due effect" to the Abolition Act classified all apprentices as nonpraedial.[123] Their apprenticeships were thus to last for four years and would end on 1 December 1838. Until then, they owed all of their labor to their former masters and would receive no wages. The ordinance required every apprentice "to work and labor in every day in the year,—Sundays and Holidays hitherto usually allowed to the Laboring population excepted,—in the service and for the benefit of his employer." Apprentices were subject to criminal penalties if they "contumaciously" disobeyed the "lawful commands" of their master, worked "indolently, carelessly, or negligently," behaved in an "insolent and insubordinate manner" toward their masters, entered into a "conspiracy" with three or more apprentices against their masters, or ran away.[124] Employers were responsible for the maintenance of their apprentices, and they were not to "whip, beat, imprison, confine in stocks, or otherwise maltreat" them. Since employers could sell the right to the labor services of their apprentices to others, they could, in effect, buy and sell apprentices as they had bought and sold slaves.[125]

The special justices supervised apprenticeship. In theory their relationship to the former slaves was neutral; in practice, it was adversarial. Their role, as they saw it, was to prosecute, not to protect; to act as disciplinarians, not guardians. They could sentence indolent, insolent, or conspiring male apprentices and male runaways to receive as many as thirty-nine lashes. (The legal limit under the last of the slavery amelioration ordinances had been fifteen.) Female apprentices might be confined in jail, but they could not be punished physically. The justices could also fine or imprison employers who contravened provisions of the ordinance.[126]

The regulations that bound the former slaves to their masters and mistresses were so restrictive that Isabel Eirlys Edwards argued that they merely dressed "slavery in the guise of apprenticeship." This was possible because the Abolition Act left the settling of the administrative details of apprenticeship to the colonies, and colonial officials usually shared the slave owners' conviction that the former slaves would not work unless they were forced to do so.[127] In this regard, apprenticeship at the Cape was little different from elsewhere in the empire. Assessing apprenticeship in the West Indies, William Law Mathieson argued that "the Act which abolished slavery did not emancipate the slaves. . . . As a social institution slavery disappeared . . . but it came back as a system of industry, the negroes . . . having to work as slaves . . . [,] being so much the property of their masters that they could be seized and advertised as runaways and were liable to be bought and sold." Apprenticeship, he concluded, was "a system of forced labour."[128]

Parliament had, in fact, anticipated this outcome. The Abolition Act had been framed with the West Indies in mind. The abolitionists believed that West Indian slaves had not been adequately prepared for freedom because local slave owners undermined all amelioration schemes. All sides in Parliament assumed that "the negroes, when freed, would not work of their own will . . . and that the social and economic structure of the sugar colonies would, unless supported, collapse."[129] Accordingly, the abolitionists had gone "out of their way to reassure the planters that emancipation would be accomplished in such a way as to ensure to the West Indian estates a continuing supply of labor."[130]

Apprenticeship was designed to give the former slaves no choice but to continue to work for their masters under conditions that differed little from slavery.

In the Cape Colony, 1 December 1834 "passed quietly and peacefully,"[131] perhaps because the freedpeople knew that little would change. In the months following the Cape's notification of the passage of the Abolition Act, slaves had heard "vague reports of approaching freedom." Many, the protector of slaves in Graaff-Reinet reported, fancied "that their rights were concealed from them, by public authorities, as well as by their Masters" and were anxious to learn the truth. So insistent were the slaves' inquiries in Graaff-Reinet that the protector "felt the necessity of satisfying [their] curiousity to some extent." In the end, a party of distressed slave owners "requested that a slave from each family should be assembled in the Court room and hear the substance of the law read to them." The protector warned the slaves that they were not to be "entirely freed, and that they were bound to show their fitness for freedom."[132] It is likely that similar scenes were enacted throughout the colony.[133]

On the whole, the apprentices remained quiet during the first weeks of apprenticeship. The special justice in Swellendam reported that several masters had complained to him of "turbulent Apprenticed Labourers" shortly after 1 December, but the trouble apparently subsided quickly.[134] In early 1835, Isaac van der Merwe, a farmer in the Worcester district, claimed that his apprentices "were in a state of Mutiny," but this was an isolated incident, and the substance of his charges indicated that the apprentices had done no more than refuse to work. Van der Merwe, an elderly man, was never in physical danger.[135] If most freedpeople anticipated that their lives would improve little under apprenticeship, the next four years confirmed the wisdom of their judgment.

In moving from the oversight of the protectors to that of the special justices, the relationship between the former slaves and the colonial state had undergone a major change. Under the reform ordinances, the state's goal had been to improve the lot of the slaves by intervening in the master-slave relationship. In doing so, it had often acted as the slaves' advocate. During apprenticeship, the state's primary aim was to ensure labor discipline and the continued subordination of the legally-free apprentices to their erstwhile masters. Apprenticeship was part of the process of tailoring new forms of coercion to the needs of the emerging wage-labor economy of a slowly modernizing colony. The laws of apprenticeship emphasized the duties that apprentices owed their masters, rather than any rights that they might enjoy. Henceforth, masters appeared less often as defendants, answering charges brought against them by their slaves, than as plaintiffs, charging their apprentices with a variety of misdemeanors. "From a judicial standpoint," Edwards wrote, "the apprentice was in a sorrier plight than he had been as a slave in recent years."[136]

Evidence drawn from the special justices' reports and record books supports Edwards's conclusion. From the beginning, the justices established a pattern of sternly disciplining apprentices. Masters and mistresses brought their apprentices to the justices for the "domestic correction" that the law no longer allowed them to apply personally, charging them with "crimes" that, as slave owners, they had punished themselves—running away, insolence, drunkenness, destroying property, neglect of duties, disobedience, and idleness. The justices were swift to address the employers' grievances. During the first thirteen months after emancipation, for instance, the justices punished 1,179 apprentices. (The protectors had taken up the cases of about two thousand slaves during the entire eight years in which their offices were open.) Well over half, all of them male, were flogged. The women and 113 of the men were jailed for periods of up to ninety days.[137]

The apprentices, on the other hand, behaved as though their relationship to the law had not changed at all. They took the same sorts of complaints to the justices that they had taken as slaves to the protectors, even though they found relief far less often. The justices sometimes convicted masters and mistresses of mistreating their apprentices, especially if the apprentices could prove that they had been beaten. For example, the special justice in Malmesbury convicted Peter de Wet of whipping his apprentice Brutus and fined him five shillings.[138] The special justice in Worcester convicted Stephanus Botma of flogging Christina, his female apprentice, and sentenced him to pay a £5 fine, £2 of which went to the apprentice. He also heard the case that Christiaan brought against his master, Adriaan Louw. Christiaan testified that Louw had whipped him so severely that he had spit blood. While he was beating his apprentice, Louw had said that "you shall die you dog, because you are not worth the money I gave for you." On the strength of Christiaan's testimony and that of another witness, the justice ordered Louw to pay a forty-shilling fine.[139] Such cases were exceptional. Most often apprentices appeared as defendants, and most often they were convicted of their "crimes."

Some abolitionists expressed misgivings about apprenticeship from the beginning. During the first few months after emancipation, however, official dispatches from the West Indies suggested that the former slaves were quietly going about their duties. By the middle of 1835, reports of continued brutality, often sent by missionaries, had made their way back to Britain. From these and other sources, Thomas Fowell Buxton compiled evidence showing that apprentices were more violently abused as legally free people than they had been as slaves. The campaign against apprenticeship had begun, but it gathered steam slowly. It was not until 1837 that the Colonial Office began to pressure colonial assembles to end apprenticeship before the date stipulated by the Abolition Act. In the West Indies, local ordinances ended praedial apprenticeship on 1 August 1838, two years early.[140] In the Cape Colony, apprenticeship came to an end as scheduled on 1 December 1838.[141] This, and not 1 December 1834, was the day on which the slaves were truly freed.

Old Wine, New Bottles

Many officials at the Cape believed that the ways in which masters and slaves thought about themselves, each other, and the world in which they lived changed radically during the period of amelioration and apprenticeship. In his second semiannual report, the principal protector, Major Rogers, referred to the slaves' increasingly common "acts of insubordination." Although the law had not questioned the subordination of slave to master, the slaves behaved as though it had.[142] Other voices echoed Rogers's sentiments.

Soon after word of the Abolition Act reached the Cape, the acting governor, Lieutenant Colonel T. F. Wade, composed a dispatch in which he described some of the ways in which amelioration and news of impending emancipation had affected masters and slaves. The slaves, he felt, fell into three classes. The first comprised the "almost barbarous beings . . . on the far distant and isolated Farms" of the interior. Despite their ignorance, they had been fully aware of the laws designed to ameliorate their condition, and they had "extensively availed themselves" of their right to seek redress through the protectors' offices. But they knew nothing about and did not anticipate "any measure pretending to do more" than merely reform slavery. The slaves "in the Districts nearest Cape Town," Wade's second class, had more access to the world beyond their masters' farms. They had been "awakened" to the expectation "that they are about to receive some more important but to them as yet undefined benefit." Only the Cape Town slaves, the third class, understood the nature of the changes about to take place. They were, "of course, considerably better educated and more advanced in civilization than in the Districts." Their roles as domestic servants and artisans presented them with the opportunity to hear abolition "hourly discussed." Wade had no doubt that "a desire for freedom [had] of late increased among them."[143] Even the most backward slaves, in Wade's estimation, had "availed" themselves of their newly granted rights. The majority of slaves, those in and near Cape Town, had been "awakened" to the possibility of freedom.

Where Wade sensed optimism among the slaves, he saw only "a dogged gloomy silence" among the slave owners. He did not expect the masters to oppose emancipation openly, but he knew that they viewed the act with "utter detestation." The Abolition Act was only the latest in a series of measures that had alienated them from the British administration and caused them to treat their slaves much differently. Men "who were formerly counted among the best and most considerate Masters in the colony, have ceased to treat their Slaves with their accustomed kindness and liberality, and . . . many, looking upon the Slaves as though *they* were the cause of the approaching crisis . . . transfer to them in ill-treatment no inconsiderable portion of their discontent."[144]

Displaced anger against the government was not the only reason that masters were more often mistreating their slaves. Wade reported that slave owners more and more complained that their slaves now behaved in an "insolent and disrespectful" manner. This, he thought, was "by no means surprising." Anything "short of a servile submissiveness" would constitute "disrespect and insolence," as far as the slave owners were concerned. "[A]nd the Laws enacted "during the last few years have . . . produced in the conduct and demeanour of the Slave, a change that could scarcely fail to be construed into, and indeed, to partake of an insubordinate character."[145] Wade understood the irresolvable contradiction lying at the heart of amelioration: laws that granted rights to the slave weakened the authority of the master.

Those in the Colonial Office who drafted the legislation were also very much aware of the dilemma. James Stephen, counsel to the Colonial Office and later permanent undersecretary, drafted a dispatch in which he discussed the problems that amelioration would inevitably provoke.

No Law can be framed, for regulating the relative rights and duties of the Proprietors and the Slaves which will not, to a considerable extent, be anomalous, and even inconsistent with itself. For the Law-giver is to reconcile things, which are, in themselves, incompat-ible. . . . He is to maintain that domestic authority, without which Slav-ery would be but a name;—while he is gradually to prepare the way for the ultimate removal of those foundations on which that author-ity rests . . . to reconcile these ends with each other . . . is manifestly impracticable.

The result, Stephen acknowledged, might be to provoke insubordina-tion and even revolt among the slaves.[146] This was a risk that Stephen believed that the government must assume. Until slavery could be ended, "every practical method must be adopted to prevent the abuse of the Owner's powers and to mitigate the hardship of the Slave's condi-tion, so that, if complete justice cannot at once be done, the smallest possible amount of injustice may be permitted."[147]

The sense that the relationship between master and slave shifted sig-nificantly in the 1820s and 1830s was common among contemporaries and is shared by modern historians.[148] Yet it is difficult to know how much in the thinking and behavior of masters and slaves was new. In 1833, for instance, the protector of slaves reported that slave owners had claimed "that their Slaves are becoming very insubordinate." He ad-mitted, however, that it did not "amount to very much more of the same sort of Plague[?] always heretofore in practice about Christmas and Harvest time."[149] The extent to which the masters' thinking and behav-ior changed after the reforms is also unclear. J. A. Truter, the chief jus-tice of the colony in the mid-1820s and one of the largest slave owners in the colony, once wrote about the masters' attitudes toward their slaves as they had been before amelioration.[150] He leaves his reader in doubt about the reality of a warm paternalism prior to the reforms. Some slave owners, he acknowledged, were "solicitous" toward their favorite slaves and slave children. On the other hand, most slave owners held "a Colo-nial prejudice" that assumed "that Slaves should be less entitled to claim justice and Christian Charity than free people." He did not share these beliefs, he wrote, because his parents had educated him in "the prin-cipals of our blessed Religion [and] caused the dictates of humanity to be respected in their family." He nevertheless firmly believed that the subordination of the slaves was "absolutely necessary" for the good of society.[151]

The views that Truter and the protector expressed qualify assertions that amelioration had revolutionized the relations between masters and slaves. In fact, continuity as much as change characterized the thinking and behavior of masters and slaves after 1806 and even 1826. Slaves did not awaken on the morning that the guardians' offices opened alive for the first time to the miseries of slavery. And slave owners did not change from kindly patriarchs to sullen despots the moment that a protector first intervened in a dispute between a master and a slave. But the reform laws did, by beginning the process of incorporating slaves into legitimate society and by granting them rights and a civil existence, undermine slavery's ideological foundations. This crack in the edifice of social death would have been of mere philosophical interest if the slaves had not been so determined to put the laws into action. The reforms allowed them to be the instruments of their own partial resurrection.

The dynamics of continuity and change in the behavior of the slaves can be seen in the events of a small 1825 slave revolt. Galant, a male slave of twenty-five, led a revolt of twelve slaves and Khoisan laborers in the Koue Bokkeveld, a sheep-farming region of the Worcester district about one hundred miles northeast of Cape Town.[152] Galant and his comrades killed Galant's master and two other whites before attempting to flee the farms on which they worked. A commando quickly captured the rebels. They were tried and convicted of murder. Galant and two others were hanged.[153] Robert Ross argues that the rebellion itself was not a particularly unusual event. It was part of a "recurring pattern" of small slave and Khoisan uprisings on Cape Colony farms. What made the rebellion "exceptional" was the "ideology behind the murders."[154]

At the trial that followed the rebellion, the prosecutor admitted that "dissatisfaction with the state of slavery" lay behind it. But a longstanding unhappiness alone was not a sufficient explanation; the timing of the uprising was directly related to the efforts to reform slavery. Galant and the others had been motivated by "the idea that [their enslavement had been] prolonged by their masters contrary to the intention of government." Or as the prosecutor later rephrased it, the uprising was the product of "the fire of discontent at the frustrated hope of general freedom" caused by a misunderstanding of what had "been done on the part of Government to ameliorate considerably the state of Slavery." This was a veiled reference to Governor Somerset's proclamation of March 1823.[155]

Galant's testimony supported the prosecutor's contention that he had acted on the basis of a mistaken understanding of Somerset's proclamation. He and the other slaves had heard their masters discussing the provisions of the proclamation. Galant had also heard his master tell another farmer that "he [ought to] keep himself armed in order to shoot the first Commissioner or Englishman who should come to the Country to make the Slaves free, together with the Slaves all in one heap."[156] Although Galant and the others did not understand the details of the slavery reform laws and may not, in any case, have actually believed that they were to be freed, they did sense that their masters felt anxious and vulnerable. They hoped that the government shared their conviction that slavery was unjust, and they may have persuaded themselves that if they won freedom for themselves, the government would support them. When they rebelled, they took advantage of what they saw as a conflict between the powers that controlled their lives, a temporary weakness that they could exploit.[157]

What was new in Galant's revolt was the inspiration he was able to draw from a proclamation that indirectly and partially, but inevitably, delegitimated slavery. What was old was his sense of grievance. The authorities who examined Galant after his capture found marks of severe punishment on his body, the scars of beatings he had received both from his master and in prison, where his master had sometimes sent him to be disciplined. On three different occasions, Galant had complained to colonial authorities either about a beating that his master had given him or about his master's theft of his property. On all three occasions, his efforts had come to nothing.[158] His master's brutality and dishonesty helps to explain Galant's decision to rebel. Somerset's proclamation helps to explain his timing.

The thoughts and actions of all slaves and apprentices owed as much to the unchangeable past as to the fluid present. The balance was not necessarily the same in every aspect of their lives. The broad outlines of work the slaves performed and the conditions under which they performed it changed little during the period of amelioration and apprenticeship. On the other hand, their relations with their masters and mistresses and with each other were altered markedly by changes in the law, ideology, and demography of slavery. Continuity and transformation in the lives of the slaves and apprentices are themes that guide the narratives and analyses that follow.

CHAPTER 3

"A State in Miniature"

The Master's Household

Observe the Dutch children . . . from an early period they acquire
an arbitrary and capricious habit of mind.

—ROBERT PERCIVAL, 1804

Rachiel and Lodewyk's marriage collapsed early in the South African summer of 1832.[1] They had been husband and wife for more than a decade and a half, and Rachiel had borne Lodewyk eight children. Four children were still alive; a son, November, was fifteen. Earlier in the marriage, the family had been whole, with parents and children living under the same roof, but by 1832 the family had not shared a home for many years. Rachiel and the children lived with their master, Willem Jacobus van der Merwe, and Lodewyk lived a half day's ride away with his, Goliath van Heerden. Rachiel, Lodewyk, and their children, of course, were slaves.

Despite the obstacles that distance and their owner's whims presented, Lodewyk visited his wife and children several times a year, and the couple had managed to keep their family intact. The journey was not an easy one, yet as long as the distance was not extreme and his health was good, it was an ordeal Lodewyk gladly accepted. Neither he nor Rachiel seem ever before to have complained openly about their separation. Now, however, the family was threatened. The couple believed that Rachiel's master had sold her to his son, Nicholas van der Merwe, who lived a full day's journey from her husband and her former home. Rachiel's son November would stay behind with Willem Jacobus van der Merwe, separating him from his mother. Because Lodewyk had fallen ill and could no longer travel great distances and because Rachiel was also unable to travel, it seemed to Rachiel that her master had effectively dissolved the marriage. Faced with an impending crisis, Rachiel and Lodewyk turned to the protector of slaves in Graaff-Reinet for help, hoping to keep their family alive.

The protector agreed to look into the couple's complaint and summoned Willem van der Merwe to his office. Though the protector had no authority to unite the couple, since they did not belong to the same master, the law did allow him to prevent the sale of Rachiel away from her son.[2] He would thus have some leverage with which to bargain in Rachiel's behalf. Willem, however, denied that the law applied in the present case. He had not sold Rachiel, he said; he had merely lent her to his daughter-in-law, Nicholas van der Merwe's wife. Rachiel's presence on his son's farm was necessary, he argued, because Nicholas was "nearly blind." He claimed the right to keep November on his own farm, but consented to follow the spirit of the law and allow him to go with his mother. When Rachiel suggested that he sell her to Lodewyk's master, Willem refused; he would not think of selling her. The protector closed the hearing and told Lodewyk and Rachiel that, since they were not owned by the same master, there was nothing more he could do. There the matter rested.

As much as the story of Rachiel and Lodewyk demonstrates their determination to keep their family together,[3] it even more vividly illustrates a slave owner's ability to subordinate his slaves' interests to his own. Slaves and apprentices were inescapably members of their master's household, and their lives were shaped more by the nature of their relationships with members of the patriarchal household than by any other factor.[4] An ideology of paternalism governed the household. The social conventions of the Cape, even after the reforms of the 1820s and 1830s, supported masters in their belief that they should rule their households of wives, children, servants, and slaves as fathers ruled their families, balancing affection with authority. The slaves and apprentices of the Cape resented imposition of the patriarchal authority that so controlled their lives, and they resisted the violence, sexual exploitation, and dependency that so often accompanied it. Many slaves managed to carve out emotional space within which they denied the degradation that accompanied enslavement, asserted a small degree of autonomy, and preserved a measure of self-respect. They struggled, that is, against the forces of soul murder and social death. The household was the site of the larger and smaller struggles, accommodations, victories, and defeats that defined the lives of slaves and slave owners at the Cape.

The Household in Theory

Slavery is implicated in the very origins of the word *family*, which entered English through Latin, *familia* originally referring to a household's slaves. From representing the slaves subordinated to a master, *familia* came to incorporate all persons—wives, children, servants, and slaves—who were subject to the authority of a *paterfamilias,* the patriarch of an extended family of retainers and kin. The idea of family has thus been inescapably associated with power and hierarchy.[5]

The household was the basic social and economic unit of Cape society. In it and through it the slave owners organized production and subordinated their workforce, slave and free. Within the household, the master's wife, children, kin, slaves, and employees pooled income and resources—both voluntarily and under duress—while the master unequally distributed the rewards. By the end of the eighteenth century, the slave owners' ideological commitment to the patriarchal household was clear. Though they did not mount the sort of sophisticated ideological defense of slavery found in the antebellum American South, they did, when circumstances warranted, defend their interests in terms that clearly articulated their understanding of paternalism, the ideology of the patriarchal household.[6]

In 1796, members of the Court of Justice, each of whom is likely to have been a slave owner, responded to the British governor's request to comment on his proposal to abandon the use of torture in the punishment and execution of "blacks," most of whom were slaves. The justices opposed the idea because the proposal would compromise the patriarchal order to which they were committed. Attempts to protect the slaves from violent punishments, the court argued, were misguided. Slaves were naturally barbarous and had to be kept under strict control. The law ought therefore to "leave in the hands of the Master such power as is necessary for him to exercise in the Direction of his Family." The justices then issued a paean to paternalism, unhesitatingly linking the relationship of a father to his family to that of a master to his slave:

> Masters should zealously endeavour to conduct themselves as Fathers rather than Judges in their Families, and act according to the strictest Rules of Virtue and Humanity, not only in punishing but in rewarding. . . . Upon these principles we would flatter ourselves with the hopes that it is not impossible to inspire the Slaves with affection for their Masters, for it is indisputably true that affection is a reciprocal sentiment.[7]

Thirty years later, paternalism guided slave owners in their protests against the slavery reform ordinances of 1826 and 1830.[8] Ordinance 19 infuriated the Burgher Senate (the town council of Cape Town, appointed by the colonial government), in part because it gave "to a third person—the proposed guardian of Slaves—without any right . . . the odious power of interfering in the arrangement of private affairs."[9] If common sense denied outsiders the right to come between a father and his children, neither should the law create an official whose power over the slaves was superior to that of the master. When slave owners in the Cape district learned that the provisions of the order in council of 2 February 1830 would strengthen the slaves' legal protections and further limit their ability to punish them physically, they again framed their denunciation of the law as a defense of patriarchal prerogatives. "Several sections" of the order, they said, were "inconsistent with the welfare" of the colony and "the preservation of good order and discipline in our domestic affairs." Masters could not maintain the "good order and discipline" of their households if outsiders, who understood neither slaves nor slave owners, were determined to interfere.[10]

Similarly, another group of slave owners claimed that the reforms conflicted with their right to govern their households. They spoke of what they called "that inviolable house-right *[huisregt]*, which is held so sacred by [even] the most uncivilized nations."[11] This was an argument about social death, although slave owners did not frame the debate in those terms. Slaves, they believed, could have no independent civil existence. Connected to civil society only through their masters, they ought to have been beyond the notice of the colonial state. When the state recognized the existence of the slaves and granted them rights and protection as individuals, it necessarily threatened "good order and discipline" since slaves could now appeal to an authority to whom even their master was bound to submit.

Not long before emancipation, an eastern Cape slave owner spoke of paternalism in terms that stripped the ideology to the bone. Ultimately, it had little to do with mutual affection and everything to do with violent domination. "I could not rule [my slaves]," he told an assistant protector, "unless . . . I had the power of exacting prompt obedience and repressing insolence with an occasional correction with my hand or whatever I chanced to have in it, *they are children and must be treated as such or [be] spoiled.*"[12] The language of everyday life reflected the slave owners' commitment to paternalism. Dutch-speaking slave owners referred to their slaves as their *volk* ("people"), and at least one English-speaking master called his twenty slaves "my family." Slaves were not simply part of the family, they were children. Slave-owning society referred to a slave man as a *jong* (boy) and a woman as a *meid* (girl).[13] Adult slaves were not literally children, and, being adults, they were dangerous—something slave owners could not but acknowledge. At the time that colonial masters were protesting ordinance 19, slave owners in Stellenbosch wrote to local officials of their need to defend their wives and children "from the dagger of incited slaves. Not alone our Wives and Daughters, but also yours, will in a libidinous manner be prosecuted by our Slaves with rape and defloration."[14]

Paternalism justified both slavery and the oppression of women, who, like children, were weak and dependent, in need of both protection discipline. Patriarchs at the Cape did not dominate their wives and adult female kin in precisely the same way and to the same extent as they did their slaves. Masters routinely beat their slaves, and these beatings were sanctioned in law and custom.[15] There is no evidence, however, that wife-beating—not a "drunken assault . . . or the hysterical attack of a jealous lover . . . [but] chronic battering"[16]—was common or socially sanctioned at the Cape. And while the mistress was junior to the master, she did exert authority over children, servants, and slaves. Slave women, on the other hand, found themselves caught in a triple bind, trapped between ideologies that justified their subordination on grounds of status, gender, and, implicitly, race. The patriarchal household was an instrument designed to control all who lived under the master's authority. It was not always an effective one.

Some writers have argued that ideology was the slave owners' primary means of subordinating their slaves. Slave owners, it is claimed, incorporated slaves into their households as perpetual minors, persuading them to accept their infantilization and subordination and to acknowledge their owners as both father and master. In his early work, Robert Shell called the early Cape patriarchal household "a slightly grotesque mixture of sentimentality and cynicism." But he argued that its exploitative character did not prevent it from becoming the slave owners' most important instrument of domination. The slaves accepted their position as subordinate members of their masters' families, "at least on the surface." Because "[t]he chains of slavery were, in the main, psychological," physical coercion alone cannot explain "how slavery worked at the Cape."[17] Shell's later work brings violence to the fore, while retaining his emphasis on incorporation into the family and infantilization.[18] We can agree that Cape slavery could not have relied solely on violent coercion as a means of discipline without believing that the whips and chains of slavery existed primarily within the minds of the slaves. Paternalism was not hegemonic.

A "hegemonic" ideology implies a form of class rule in which force is masked by consent. Force remains unseen, employed only in moments of crisis. Herbert Gutman, drawing on Rousseau and arguing against Eugene Genovese's interpretation of the antebellum South, defined a hegemonic ideology as one that succeeds in transforming "strength into right, and obedience into duty."[19] Genovese had offered a more flexible definition. Hegemonic rule, he contended, exists when a particular ruling class in a particular historical era is able to contain class antagonisms to "a terrain in which [the legitimacy of its rule] is not dangerously questioned," because of its command of the leading ideas of the time.[20] By either of these definitions, the ideology of the Cape household failed.

The paternalism of Cape slave owners was not in any sense hegemonic. The presence of the *sjambok*[21] was too glaring, the psychological independence of the slaves too apparent, and the anxiety of the masters too obvious. It was not the power of ideas that kept the slaves in their place, but coercion and the demographic, cultural, and geographic realities that dictated "the impossibility of rebellion."[22] The historical record shows that the slaves and apprentices endured, manipulated, and resisted the ideology and the practices that would reduce them to perpetual minors legitimately placed under the care of their masters. They did not accept them, and because they did not, slave owners had to force them to behave.

The violent coercion and physical punishment that slave owners applied to their slaves was sometimes called, in the language of the Cape household, "domestic correction."[23] Anders Sparrman, who spent four years at the Cape during the mid-1770s, reported that locals referred to the beatings they meted out to their slaves as "proper family discipline."[24] Contrary to one historian's contention that domestic corrections were limited to those that a master might apply to his wife and children,[25] they were far more harsh. Throughout the seventeenth and eighteenth centuries and as late as 1823, the laws of the Cape allowed a master or his deputy to lay on up to thirty-nine lashes with a whip, sjambok, leather thong, rattan, cat o'nine tails, "or the like" for any one of a series of "domestic offences," among them wilful disobedience, drunkenness, impudence, escape, neglect of "duties," and theft within the household.[26] The fiscal, or legal officer,[27] who compiled the statutes concerning slavery at the behest of the governor in 1813 felt compelled to apologize for the rigor of the law: "Experience has enough taught us that the generality of slaves always incline to dissolute conduct, and that they take no interest whatsoever in the welfare of their Masters, which frequently obliges the latter, when they cannot confine their slaves within the pale of their duties by reason or verbal correction, to have recourse to corporal punishment."[28] The laws of the Cape reflected social practice, as the fiscal well understood.

The Demography and Architecture of Patriarchy

The precise mix of persons who constituted the households of the nineteenth century is hard to determine. Some of the grand patriarchs of the wine and wheat country counted slaves, Khoisan servants, white employees, sons and daughters, sons- and daughters-in-law, a wife, and sometimes elderly parents and poor relations as members of their household. Hendrik Albertus van Niekerk, for instance, a wealthy wheat grower in the Koeberg district, owned two farms and on them presided over a household consisting of a second wife, a stepdaughter, a son and daughter-in-law, grandchildren, two white workers (a man and a woman), and fifty-six of his own slaves and thirteen of his son's. He apparently employed no Khoisan.[29] Though his son managed many of the farm's affairs, the elder van Niekerk still sometimes whipped the slaves himself, and his authority was final within the household.[30] Justinus Rens, on the other hand, was a poor man who lived alone except for his slave, Camies. He, too, was the lord of his manor. Once, while in a drunken stupor, he beat Camies with a sjambok because he had failed to respond when ordered to "bark like a Dog and Crow like a Cock."[31]

Neither van Niekerk's nor Rens's household was typical of the Cape Colony. The former was much larger than the average, the latter smaller and perhaps more dissolute. Figures for the early 1830s, which generally reflect the composition of slaveholding households between 1820 and emancipation, tell the story. In 1831, only 1,276, or about 1 in 5, slave owners possessed more than 8 slaves.[32] Four years later, in 1834, barely 300 slave owners, or 1 in 22, held 20 or more slaves; 15 slave owners, or fewer than 1 in 420, owned 50 or more—a holding the size of van Niekerk's.[33] The average slaveholding household contained fewer than 6 slaves.[34] These figures are couched in terms that reflect the masters' perspective; from the slaves' point of view, the matter looked much different: fully one-quarter of the slaves belonged to the 300 owners who possessed 20 slaves or more.[35]

The size of the average slaveholding varied regionally. The smallest slaveholdings were in the cattle and sheep country of the eastern and northern Cape, where labor demands were relatively light and Khoisan labor was relatively plentiful. In Somerset, owners possessed, on average, 3.83 slaves, in Graaff-Reinet, 3.99. The largest households were on the labor-intensive wine and wheat farms of the western Cape—on average, nearly 8 slaves per farm. In the Cape district, the average was 7.92, and in the Stellenbosch district, 7.83. In Cape Town, where slaves tended to be employed as indoor and outdoor servants and as artisans, the size of the average slaveholding was slightly below the colonial average (see table 3.1).[36]

Households were likely to include more slave men than slave women. There were, for example, 123 men and boys for every 100 women and girls in Graaff-Reinet. Slave owners possessed 137 males for every 100 females in Stellenbosch, and in the Cape District, 112 males for every 100 females. In Cape Town, male and female slaves nearly balanced each other—105 males for every 100 females.[37] In every district, however, the ratio of men and boys to women and girls was virtually even among slaves under thirty-five years of age.[38]

Within the Cape households, the physical placement of the diverse members was not a matter of chance: the geography of the household reflected the hierarchy within it. Just after the turn of the nineteenth century, Henry Lichtenstein, who spent several years in the colony,

Table 3.1. Average Size of Slaveholding (Selected Districts), 1834

	Owners	Slaves	Average Holding
Cape Town	1,218	5,987	4.90
Cape District	603	4,780	7.92
Stellenbosch	1,097	8,595	7.83
Worcester	471	3,270	6.94
Graaff-Reinet	540	2,157	3.99
Somerset	429	1,641	3.83
Cape Colony	6,334	35,745	5.60

Source: Returns of the total number of slaves in the various districts according to the several classes and values, CAD, SO 20/61.

visited the western Cape farm of "one of the richest colonists in the country." He described the world before him in terms consistent with the slave owners' ideal. The number and size of the farm's buildings, the creature comforts of the interior furnishings in the master's home, and the extent of his herds and flocks were enough to convince Lichtenstein that his host "was a man of no inconsiderable property. Indeed, he maintained a sort of patriarchal household. . . . The family itself, including masters, servants, hottentots, and slaves, consisted of a hundred and five persons, for whose subsistence the patriarch had to provide daily. . . . It . . . may almost be called a State in miniature, in which the wants and means of supplying them are reciprocal, and where all are dependent one upon another."[39] On farms such as this, the architecture and social geography of the household reinforced patriarchal ideology. The master's home occupied a central position. It was often surrounded by barns, storehouses, workshops, cellars, and slave quarters; a low wall encompassed the whole and set the household apart from the gardens, vineyards, and fields.[40] The layout of the farm reflected the ideal patriarchal household, a society unto itself, centered on and dependent on the master. Walls symbolically set the household off from the society beyond.

Although a strict hierarchy was the household's essence, there was little in the way of segregation within it. Separate slave quarters could be found only on the larger farms. Even there, they were often connected to storerooms, barns, or workshops, and always remained within the farm's walls.[41] In the eighteenth century, only one Cape farm had quarters approaching the size of the slave "villages" found on New World plantations;[42] few if any such villages existed in the nineteenth century. One to three slave houses were the rule on the largest farms. Matthys Michielse Basson, a farmer in the wheat-growing district of Swartland, set aside a "Slave Room" for some, perhaps all, of his young male slaves.[43] Adriaan Phillipus Cloete, a substantial wine maker in the Stellenbosch district, kept two slave houses on his farm, one for single men and another for "those that have women."[44] Where the single women lived is not clear, but the arrangements on another Stellenbosch farm may provide the answer. At least three of Daniel du Toit's slaves—two men and a woman—spent their nights in his kitchen.[45] Not only on the poorer farms but also on the wealthiest wine and wheat farms and in Cape Town households, it was common for slaves, often the domestic servants, to sleep in hallways and kitchens.[46]

Middling farmers did their best to create patriarchal social geographies. Lichtenstein's travels took him to the unpretentious farms of the arid Roggeveld. There he found the slave owners and their immediate families living in one- or two-room homes. In the "best houses," the kitchens occupied the second room in the rear of the house. In all of the homes, the kitchen was "equally the [sitting] room for the servants as for the masters." Despite the modest dimensions of the masters' dwellings, about them stood "a number of smaller buildings, simply constructed, which are partly for the slaves and Hottentots, partly for workshops and store-houses." In Swellendam, he encountered farmers who were far from rich, yet they had arranged their farms in ways that allowed Lichtenstein to describe a patriarchal idyll: "The spacious house, the excellent out-buildings, the workshops for the slaves, the stalls for the cattle, a large garden, in the midst of which is a fish-pond . . . the neat lawn before the house, the sleek, fat cattle, all evinced an affluence and spirit of order which make a pleasing impression upon the mind wherever they are to be seen."[47]

Lichtenstein believed that this "patriarchal kind of establishment" was also to be found in the eastern districts, despite the farmers' relative poverty.[48] But George Thompson, a merchant and adventurer who crisscrossed the eastern Cape in the early 1820s, described the home of an ordinary farmer that was hardly patriarchal in its layout. He said that it resembled "a large barn divided into two or three apartments." One of the chambers was the kitchen, which also served as a sitting room and dining room. The master and his immediate family slept in the one or two rooms off the kitchen. Slaves, Khoisan, and guests slept in the kitchen itself. In these kitchens, Thompson often enjoyed, "after a fatiguing day's ride, the most balmy repose; while a swarthy train of slaves and Hottentots were moving round the embers of the fire, wrapped in their sheepskin mantles, and dogs, cats, and fowls were trampling over my body."[49] As Thompson's irony suggests, farm kitchens were rarely pleasant accommodations.

Poverty did not always defeat a master's attempt to establish a patriarchal household geography. Many eastern district slaves lived in straw huts clustered around the master's home. The huts seem typically to have been the homes of married slaves, who may have found it easier than single slaves did to receive the master's permission to live in homes of their own. Telemachus, a slave in the Albany district, for instance, lived in what he called "my straw hut" with his "Bastaard Hottentot" wife and their two children.[50] The relative autonomy of these huts did not always produce marital harmony. The slave Adonis threw his wife out of the hut in which they lived and threatened "to trample her to death if she did not keep away from him."[51] As we shall see in the following chapter, slaves who lived in straw huts no more escaped the pressures of life within the household than those who lived in storerooms and kitchens.

The least fortunate slaves and apprentices were those whose masters were the poorest of the *trekboers*—seminomadic stock farmers. For months on end, they followed their master and his herds from pasture to pasture, resting only briefly at any given spot. The master's immediate family often had only an ox wagon or a tent to sleep in. Occasionally, the master might stay in one place long enough to erect a hut for his wife and children. The slaves and Khoisan servants of these penniless men slept in the open.[52] Sometimes it was just as well for the slaves and servants if their master remained on the road. William Burchell spent a night in a shack that had previously been used to house slaves and Khoisan. He described the dwelling as the worst he had encountered in the colony. Slightly detached from the poverty-stricken farmer's home, it had no windows, was "black as a chimney," and "resembled a *coal-hole*." "The filthiness of the place was so disgusting" that Burchell could not sleep.[53]

The social geography of slavery was most diverse in Cape Town, and it was there that a substantial number of slaves managed to escape the household. The most fortunate lived outside their masters' walls, paying rent out of their earnings as artisans, skilled domestic servants, porters, or hawkers.[54] Most slaves lived within the home of their owner, often sleeping in the kitchen. During the cold and damp Cape winters, masters and mistresses who felt it beneath their dignity to mingle with their slaves may have had reason to regret these arrangements; the only fireplace in many Cape Town homes was in the kitchen.[55] Slaves sometimes inhabited separate quarters in the yards behind their masters' homes. An English officer who had been stationed at the Cape reported that "those slaves who are not highly in [their master's] confidence, or not bred up to household offices, are locked up every night" in a slave house.[56]

The slave-owning household's living arrangements reflected a patriarchal order. On the farms, slaves were asleep in barns, huts, storerooms, or their quarters, while the master and his immediate family slept in the house. Slaves who slept in their master's home did so on kitchen floors; their masters fell asleep in bed. The dichotomies of quarters and house and kitchen and bedchamber held good in Cape Town and the villages as well. Only in the poorest households did masters and slaves share a rough equality of discomfort. The demography and social geography of the household are two parts of a larger story. By themselves they cannot tell us very much about how the members of the household interacted.

The Household in Practice

Many travelers and diarists wrote about their stays in the slave-owning households of the Cape during the late eighteenth and early nineteenth centuries. Few did so without mentioning the graciousness of their hosts and hostesses. John Barrow, no friend of the settlers, admitted that "rude and uncultivated as are their minds, there is one virtue in which they eminently excel—hospitality to strangers. A countryman, a foreigner, a relation, a friend, are all equally welcome to whatsoever the house will afford."[57] This was a rural virtue. Visitors to Cape Town stayed in boardinghouses and inns. In the hinterland, the visitor had little choice but to sleep in a farmer's home or under the stars. A Mr. du Toit, whose home lay on the main road to the interior, told an English visitor that he had received more than 360 "strangers" in a single year. Despite his "very numerous" family and the fact that he was "not over wealthy," he was "like most of the Cape farmers . . . very hospitable."[58] Few of the farmers accepted more than a token payment.[59] But like the fabled hospitality of whites in the American South, settlers extended this courtesy only to those of the same color; slaves and other nonwhites shifted for themselves.[60]

The hospitality of the Boers meant that white travelers freely entered colonial homes, and the writers among them retailed their impressions of life at the Cape to eager audiences in Britain and on the Continent. The households, as the visitors described them, were marked by a chaotic intimacy. An Englishman who stayed overnight on a Franshoek wine farm contrasted what he found there with the "comforts" of rural life in England and southern France. Though the master's house was large and the wine stores and slave lodges extensive, the atmosphere was one of squalor. He described the front room (*voorhuis*) of the big house where "all the members of the family congregate." "Here sits the *Vrouw* [mistress], issuing her commands from an easy chair; here the meals are eaten, the clothes ironed, the psalms sung; here the Dutch-children and those of the slaves, equally dirty, and distinguished only by colour, sprawl

together on the mud floor."[61] Not all Britons were offended by such promiscuous mingling of black and white. Lady Anne Barnard, the wife of
a British colonial official, wrote of her stay at a "very respectable looking
farm house." In the evening, after the wine had been handed around,
"the room filled with slaves—a dozen at least.—here they were particularly clean and neat, Myfrow sat like charity tormented by a Legion of
devils, with a black baby in her arms, one on each knee and three or four
larger ones round her, smiling Benign on the little Mortals who seemd
very sweet creatures and develish only in their Hue—she and her husband having (for a wonder) no children of their own."[62] Yet Lady Anne
was an exception. The slave-owning household shocked more often
than it amused. "The master and mistress, the children without number,
slave boys, slave girls, and Hottentots, are seen running, higgledy pig-
gledy, in all directions: the master holloas, the wife scolds in her shrill
screaming voice, and slaves and children run through all the discordant
notes of confusion, all apparently without meaning, and all for the want
of a little arrangement."[63]

Nearly constant physical proximity, frequent and familiar personal
interactions, and only modestly unequal living conditions in many of the
less prosperous town and country households might have tended to subvert the hierarchy of master and slave. But because the integrity of the
Cape's social structure and the efficient exploitation of the workforce
required the due subordination of the slave to the master, the slave owners developed practices that counteracted the potentially leveling influences of life within the household. A number of "little arrangements" reinforced the hierarchy of paternalism.

Children of the slave-owning class learned from an early age that
their relationship to physical labor and arbitrary violence was very different from that of the slaves. Barrow wrote of the woeful effects "that a
state of slavery invariably produces on the minds and habits of a people,
born and educated in the midst of it. Among the upper ranks it is the
custom for every child to have its slave, whose sole employment is to hu-
mour its caprices, and to drag it about from place to place lest it should
too soon discover for what purposes nature had bestowed on it legs and
arms."[64] Burchell, an Englishman who spent a number of years in the
colony, thought that the children of masters and those of the slaves were
more "playmates" than anything else and that in later years they became
"associates." He denied that the masters were in any sense "cruel and un-
feeling."[65] Most accounts, however, favored a harsher view. Writing in
1829, Cowper Rose echoed Barrow's impressions of thirty years earlier:

"The young Dutch child is early initiated into the knowledge of cruelty, and the little slave who is permitted the honour of sharing its sports, in the duty of submission—for the impatient, angry temper of the one finds vent in blows, beneath which the other is born to crouch; and a lesson learnt in childhood is not easily lost."[66] Rose's concern extended beyond the coarse young master and raised the question of the degraded slave, a topic I address below.

Another Englishman, Robert Percival, probably struck the right balance between cruelty and affection, when he noted that one of the first lessons slave owners' children learned was "to domineer over, and insult the slaves, who are subject to all their whims and caprices. Observe the Dutch children, and those of the slaves playing and mixing together, you will see the former at one moment beating and tyrannizing over the latter, and at the next caressing and encouraging them; so that from an early period they acquire an arbitrary and capricious habit of mind."[67]

In all slave societies, the stability of the system demanded that children learn their proper roles, to command or to obey. Gilberto Freyre wrote of the education and training of the young masters of eighteenth- and nineteenth-century Brazil in terms similar to those that others applied to the Cape. He described "the young Negro playmate of the white lad—a playmate and a whipping boy. His functions were those of an obliging puppet, manipulated at will by the infant son of the family." He quoted a traveler's account of a Brazilian slaveholding household: "As soon as a child begins to crawl . . . a slave of about his own age, and of the same sex, is given to it as a playfellow, or rather a plaything. They grow up together. The slave is sent upon all errands, and receives the blame for all unfortunate accidents; in fact, the white child is thus encouraged to be overbearing, owing to the false fondness of its parents."[68]

Freyre did not ignore the influence that childhood lessons in command had on the character of the daughters of the slave-owning class. "As seen from the veranda of the Big House," he wrote, "[mistresses] still preserved, often, the same evil domination over their housemaids as they had exercised over the little Negro girls who had been their playmates as children."[69] The situation was much the same at the Cape. Barrow and Percival had not exempted girls from their remarks, and an anonymous Briton specifically mentioned female members of the slave-owning family. Slaves surrounded girls from infancy, and "they no sooner begin to move, than they find they are not allowed to assist themselves, but have attendants at their call, over whom they are soon taught, by the powerful examples they see around them, of exercising the imperious tones of command; this, by degrees, is confirmed by habit, and carried with them into active life, when they become mothers in their turn."[70]

Affection between slaves and members of their owners' families was often real. But masters and mistresses had to teach both their children and their slaves that it was never to undermine power relationships within the household. The violence directed more or less often at the slaves and that lurked constantly in the background was the principal means by which masters denied the possibility of equality between themselves and their slaves and coerced the slaves' due subordination. They taught their children to do the same.

Slaves resented the abuse that they suffered at the hands of owners' sons and daughters and deplored the lessons it was designed to teach their own children. For instance, Martha, a slave in the Graaff-Reinet district, took a case to the assistant protector of slaves on behalf of her young son, Adonis. Her child, she said, had been beaten one day while "attending the Sheep together with two of her Mistresses children who are somewhat older." The whipping had left Adonis, who was four, with marks on his back and legs that had been visible for a week; she believed that her mistress's son was responsible. Having no witnesses to corroborate her charges, Martha could do no more than register a protest.[71]

Another slave, Maart, who was fifty-four years of age, charged that he had been beaten by a child. He went to the protector of slaves in Cape Town to complain that his "young master"—that is, his owner's son—had beaten him on the forehead "because he was not expeditious enough in the performance of his work." Maart could not prove his case, and his master's defense underscored the contempt he had taught his son to feel for the slave. The owner, Lieutenant John Steel, convinced the protector that the actual events had been different from those described by Maart. He had ordered Maart to chop some wood; instead, the slave had gotten drunk. Steel's son "seeing the condition He was in, told him that He was a drunken dog, upon which He went away" to complain. "Master Steel" supported his father's version of events. The protector dropped the case, though not before the testimony had established that a white child of the slave-owning class had, with impunity and with the support of his father, called a slave of more than fifty years of age a "drunken dog."[72] No physical violence had occurred, yet the hierarchy within the household had been affirmed.

Many rituals reinforced the lessons that the slave owners and the slaves learned as children about the proper relationship between master and servant. An episode involving the slave Floris and his master Francois Jacobus Roos illustrates several of them.[73] Floris appeared before the assistant protector of slaves in Stellenbosch to charge Roos with having beaten him "in an illegal manner." As he told the story, he had been sick for several days when, one Saturday morning, his master asked him if he were feeling well. He said, "not quite," but that he felt able to "work a little." His master sent Floris to his father-in-law's neighboring farm where he did a light day's labor. He returned home after dark. Floris said that when he arrived back on the farm he went to the kitchen and took a seat near the hearth to rest. Presently, Abraham, another of Roos's slaves, came into the room and told him that his master was calling for him. Floris entered the voorhuis and, he said, "saluted" his master. Roos asked him whether he remembered that it was his job to wash his feet. Floris replied that he did, but that he had only just learned that Abraham had brought the water into the room. "On this," he said, his master beat him with a walking stick "until it broke to pieces." Floris did not resist, but asked his master why he was beating him. Roos did not answer. After Roos had vented his anger, Floris washed his feet and, again, asked him why he had been whipped. His master, he claimed, still did not answer, but called out to Abraham to find another stick. Abraham brought one to him, and Roos gave Floris several more strokes. In closing, Floris told the protector that washing his master's feet was his daily chore, though Abraham had performed the task while he had been ill.

Roos's version of events must be inferred from the answers Floris gave to the unrecorded questions that Roos put to him during cross-examination. Roos hoped to establish that he had not hit Floris more than a very few times. Floris said, however, "I am certain you gave me more than two strokes—the stick would not have broken to pieces with two strokes." Roos also tried to demonstrate that the slave had been insolent. In answer to one of his questions, Floris replied, "I did not . . . say 'You must account to God for having beaten me in this manner.'" Rather, Floris insisted, he had said, "if you were a sensible man you would listen to what I have to say." These words were certainly less impudent than those his master accused him of uttering, but they were by no means subservient. Finally, Roos attempted to show that his slave had not accorded him the expected deference. Floris maintained that he had: "On Sunday morning I was standing in the Kitchen before the fire and did not see you come in, you said Good morning when I immediately turned round and saluted you—You only said Good morning to me once."

Two other witnesses contributed to the narrative. The first, Dr. Daniel

O'Flinn, the district surgeon, testified that he had "inspected" Floris and found "severe livid contusions on the left shoulder and arm, across both shoulder blades, and the left shoulder and arm very much swollen down to the elbow." He believed that ten blows with a walking stick, if "given with force by a strong man," would have caused the wounds. The second witness, Abraham, contradicted much of what Floris had said about the nature of the encounter. Abraham thought that Floris had indeed spoken "in an insolent manner." He said that when Roos asked Floris whether he understood that he was to wash his master's feet, Floris answered "Yes," but asked as well why Abraham could not do the job since he had already brought the water in. Roos told him to repeat what he had said, and Floris, again, asked why Abraham could not do the foot washing for the night. It was then that Roos had beaten him. Abraham added that Floris had not addressed Roos as "Sir, or Master, or use[d] any other form of respect."

Several rituals of subordination are visible in this passage: the foot washing, the salute, the respectful address, the beating. The most striking of the rituals is the washing of the master's feet. Barrow witnessed a similar scene, and his account makes it clear that this was not an exercise restricted to wealthy men, such as Roos. He also suggests that subordination, not sanitation, was the point of the exercise. Barrow described an Afrikaner farm woman of very modest means,

> born in the wilds of Africa, and educated among slaves and Hottentots . . . [who made no] scruple of having her legs and feet washed in warm water by a slave before strangers; an operation that is regularly performed every evening. If the motive of such a custom were that of cleanliness, the practice of it would deserve praise; but to see the tub with the same water passed round through all the branches of the family, according to seniority, is apt to create ideas of a very different nature.[74]

According to Graham Botha, a pioneering South African social historian, this ritual was part of the daily routine in slave-owning households of the eighteenth- and nineteenth-century Cape.[75]

Floris, like Barrow, seems to have understood that the lesson of this daily ritual was humiliation. The act of stooping at the feet of a master or mistress to wash the lowest and dirtiest body parts underscored the degradation of enslavement at the same time that it forced the slave to enact his or her subordination. It was shameful work. Floris had avoided it while he was sick and he tried unsuccessfully to continue to evade it.

Foot washing is, of course, a ritual of humiliation with a long history, familiar to anyone acquainted with John 13:1–20. In that passage, Jesus washes his disciples' feet, a gesture that emphasized his humility. It is a sign as well that though he is their lord (sometimes rendered "Master"), he is at the same time their servant (sometimes rendered "Slave").

There are less onerous rituals of deference contained in the story of Floris and Roos. Slaves were to "salute" their master, greeting before they were greeted. They were to address their owners with terms of respect—as "sir" and "master" (English translations of *seur* and *baas,* both common words in the early-nineteenth-century Cape). Any failure on the slave's part to salute the master and to use the proper forms of address constituted insolence and implied insubordination. Such omissions were warnings that the slaves involved had not fully accepted their roles—cracks in the structure of domination. Floris, despite his protestations of innocence, had apparently not offered his master the deference and obedience that he expected; he resisted the station to which the patriarchal order had assigned him, and he was punished for it. A beating was the ritual of last resort.

The names by which I have referred to the antagonists in the preceding drama—Floris, Abraham, Francois Jacobus Roos—are themselves indicative of the degradation of slavery. They are the names that the record has handed down—a single name for the slaves, two given names and a surname for the master. Colonial records in both the Dutch and British periods commonly referred to slaves by a single name. For slaves who had been imported into to the Cape, the names recorded were usually those given them by their masters, not the names they brought with them. It is not clear who named Cape-born slaves, though certain names, the classical and mocking names, probably originated with the masters. The most common names were the same for imported slaves and those born in the colony—classical and biblical names, teasing epithets, and diminutives of Dutch names, many of them names never borne by whites. Males were also called by the days of the week and the months of the year. For instance, among Jan Hoets's male slaves were January, Maart (March), April, May, Juny, July, Augustus, September, October, November, Zondag (Sunday), Europa, and Africa. Since these men had been born in Mozambique, Malabar, and Timor, we can safely guess that these were not their original names. There are indications that slaves understood that these names were insults. In 1809, for instance, a slave who had been purchased by the London Missionary Society changed his name from Maart, "being so degrading in this country," to Verhoogd, "signifying exhalted [*sic*]."[76] Among the names recorded for Hoets's female slaves were Betje, Spasie, Caatje, Saartje, and Doortje, all diminutives.[77] As we have seen, adult slaves were also referred to as *jong* or *meid;* carefully avoiding confusion, slave owners called slave boys *kleinjong* (little boys) and girls, *kleinmeid* (little girls).[78]

These practices existed from virtually the earliest days of slavery at the Cape and were intrinsic to the incorporation of the slaves into the slave-owning household as permanent minors. The daily use of demeaning or diminutive names was "an important part of the process" by which the masters attempted to infantilize their slaves.[79] Indeed, Orlando Patterson contends that slave owners universally have given their slaves names that advertize and reinforce their subordinate status. He argues that masters have assumed that a name not only denotes the thing to which it refers, but is a symbol for its essence. To strip a slave of his or her original name was to strip that person of his or her identity; a humiliating name was a badge of a degraded status.[80] For a master or mistress to use only a slave's first name was also to deny the significance of slave families by refusing to acknowledge the family name. Mocking names and the absence of family names reflected the degradation and natal alienation of social death.

But just as it cannot be assumed that the slaves accepted social death, it cannot be assumed that they had no surnames; it was simply that surnames did not appear in the records. A similar situation existed in the antebellum American South. As Herbert Gutman has ably shown, American slaves did possess surnames: they chose them for themselves and passed them on through generations. The absence of slave family names in the records, he insists, tells us more about the enslaving society than about the slaves.[81]

Slaves and apprentices at the Cape did possess surnames. Though it was customary to identify a slave or apprentice by a single given name—a custom that for nonwhites continued deep into the nineteenth century—surnames occasionally slipped through. In the protector's reports, we meet a Philida August who married Esau Jacob and took his name, a Piet who was "commonly called Piet Snyder," a Valentyn Snitler, whom we shall encounter again in a later chapter, and a Titus Wilhelmus.[82] There were also the Sissings and the Gileses, families of siblings and their children who were baptized at the same ceremony.[83] By clinging to their family names, slaves symbolically rejected the natal alienation that slave-owning society tried to impose. Slaves did not always reject the contemptuous names their master's gave them. Indeed, slave men's names, such as February, September, and Apollos, became common "coloured" surnames after emancipation. This need not indicate that the slaves had internalized their symbolic infantilization, as we shall discover in chapter 9 within the larger context of emancipation.

The Textures of Household Life

Slave owners never wavered in their efforts to impose their patriarchal worldview on their slaves, and slaves never tired of resisting it. The relationships that evolved in this atmosphere were exceedingly complex, as the following story reveals. One day in October 1832, a slave named Fortuin appeared at the office of the assistant protector of slaves in Stellenbosch to register a complaint against his master, Jacob Eksteen, a middling farmer who owned eleven slaves.[84] Eksteen had beaten him, he said, because of a remark Eksteen's young daughter had overheard him make. The incident began on a Sunday morning, the slaves' customary day of rest, when his master sent another slave to summon Fortuin to the house. Eksteen wanted Fortuin to tend the horses while Phoebus left them to plant some melons in the garden for his mistress. Fortuin said that he did not answer the summons. Soon afterward, his master again called for him, and this time he did appear. Eksteen confronted him about a remark his daughter had passed on to him. She had told her father that Fortuin had "grumbled at having to take care of the horses" because he wanted to mend his clothes instead. Fortuin admitted that he wished to patch his trousers, but insisted that he had not been insolent. He told the protector that, on hearing this, his master had beaten him with a thick stick.

Fortuin said that he left the Eksteen farm the next morning. He went first to Paarl, where he spent the night. The following day he went to the Klapmuts River, where he encountered Piet, a runaway slave. Piet asked him to stay, but he instead went on to Kuils River and the farm of a Mr. Wolff. After he told Wolff about having seen Piet, Wolff assembled a party of armed riders and, with Fortuin leading the way, set off for the place Piet had last been seen. Though Piet had disappeared by the time the party arrived, they spotted a slave named Maart and "a girl" and captured them both. Fortuin said that he then left Wolff and went on to Stellenbosch to see the protector. Under cross-examination, Fortuin denied having called Eksteen's daughter a liar and said that he could not recollect having grumbled. He mentioned that the job of tending the horses had been his "until about two days" before the Sunday in question. His master had removed him from the job, telling him that he had not taken "proper care" of them.

Witnesses added little to the tale. Flora, the cook, said that her mistress had offered to give Fortuin "a piece of tobacco and a piece of soap" if he would relieve Phoebus of the horses for a short while. Her master had indeed beaten Fortuin—two strokes, she said, with a thin stick. She added that by the time Fortuin and Eksteen finished their argument, Phoebus had long since planted the melons. Phoebus confirmed the gist of Flora's testimony and said of Fortuin that he "is not a good slave, he is a great rascal."[85]

Phoebus's typology is as ambiguous as it is pithy. His characterization of Fortuin is open to many interpretations. If Phoebus thought of himself as a good slave, he may have believed that Fortuin was not because he was careless about his work, because he shirked an extra duty, and because his insolence had provoked a mild beating. Phoebus was, after all, given the job of tending the horses after Fortuin had proven unsatisfactory, and he quickly set about the task of planting the melons. Was this the essence of a slave's goodness? Eksteen would certainly have thought so. Or would Phoebus have taken more pride in his ability to avoid friction with his master and the punishment to which it would lead? It is worth noting that had they been asked, Maart and "the girl" would likely have joined Phoebus in calling Fortuin a "great rascal," for reasons that had nothing to do with labor or insolence and everything to do with class and color solidarity.

Fortuin might have told us that he was not "good" because he possessed pride and self-respect. He had been stripped of the job of tending the horses and afterward resisted minding them at all. Did he resent having to relieve another slave of a job that his master thought him incompetent to perform? Fortuin clearly preferred to control his own time, especially his Sundays. It may have been, as another slave owner once put it, that being a bad slave was simply a matter of assuming "a bearing which was quite intolerable."[86] It is not surprising that so many faces of Fortuin appear within the compass of this single narrative. Slaves who were not prepared to play the game according to the rules their masters made or who at some point found it impossible to continue to do so confronted choices that in themselves were "quite intolerable."

Slave owners were as torn by contradictory impulses as their slaves and apprentices. Barend Swartz, a Graaff-Reinet cattle dealer, once ordered his apprentice, Dampie, assisted by several Khoisan, to take three hundred sheep to troops on the frontier. He so trusted Dampie that he gave him a rifle with which to protect the livestock from thieves and "wolves."[87] Dampie disappointed his master. He lost twenty-four sheep on his way to the military encampment and on the return home assaulted Peet, a "Bastaard Hottentot," with the butt of the rifle while in a drunken fury. His master took Dampie before the special justice in Graaff-Reinet, who sentenced him to receive fifteen lashes. But Dampie never felt the lash. Swartz asked that the punishment be "forgiven" since Dampie had always had "a general good character" prior to this incident.[88]

Like Swartz, masters and mistresses were quick to anger and often quick to forgive. A Stellenbosch wine farmer first whipped his slave August for having been "very improper & insolent" and immediately afterward "caused a Glass of Wine to be given him" when he "Begged his Master's pardon."[89] Moses, an apprentice on the farm of Roelof van der Merwe of the Worcester district, narrowly avoided the kind of punishment that August received. During a conversation with several other apprentices, he accused his master of having stolen some cattle. He compounded his crime by repeating the charge to van der Merwe's face. He then dared his master to strike him, knowing perhaps that physical punishment was illegal under apprenticeship. Van der Merwe was so incensed by his apprentice's failure to conform to the norms of deference and subordination that, as he told the special justice, "I was afraid of forgetting myself so I ran away." He reported Moses's words to the justice, who ordered fifteen lashes to be laid on the apprentice's back. Moses was "forgiven," however, "at the earnest request of his Mistress."[90]

It is not clear whether van der Merwe "ran away" because he feared that he would break the law by beating his apprentice, leaving himself open to prosecution, or because he was afraid that he would have badly injured Moses if he had picked up the whip while in a fury. Both readings are consistent with slave owners' behavior. Masters formed friendships, of a sort, with their slaves—friendships that were always compromised by the need to keep the structures of domination intact. Whatever van der Merwe's motives, Moses, like Dampie, escaped punishment and, like August, was forgiven. The absolution the three received was almost certainly sincere, but significantly it came only after the hierarchy of master and slave had been reasserted through violence or the threat of violence. In Moses's case, his mistress, not his master, had intervened on his behalf. Though mistresses were the wards of their husbands, in law and custom, their authority nearly matched that of their husbands in their dealings with other subordinate members of the household.

The Mistress and the Slaves

Patriarchal ideology legitimated the subordination of both slaves and women by viewing them as perpetual children. But it did not reduce married women of the slaveholding class to the level of slaves. They enjoyed privileges of color and status that their slaves could not share, and their wealth derived from the exploitation of their slaves' labor. Patriarchal and colonial ideologies, on the other hand, twice burdened slaves: they were subordinated both by virtue of their status a slaves and as non-whites. Slave women carried the additional burden of gender bias. Between them and their mistresses, there could be no sisterhood of the oppressed.[91] Mistresses and their female slaves and apprentices did, however, share the intimate world of the home in ways that masters and their male and female slaves did not. Slave-owning women rarely worked outside of the household; nor did they often labor in the fields. Much more so than for their husbands and sons, their sphere of daily activity fell within the confines of the farm, town, or village household. Although mistresses were by no means confined to their homes, the rhythms of their lives determined that they would spend most of their time intimately involved with their slaves, coping with the problems inherent in the enslavement of wilful, self-conscious human beings.

Nineteenth-century writers stressed the physical and emotional intimacy of the relations between mistresses and favorites. The women of the household shared the confined spaces of the indoors and were together almost constantly. Lichtenstein visited a prosperous farm in the arable western Cape and found that the women of the household were "constantly busied." It was "no uncommon sight to see all the women of the house, mother, daughters, and female slaves, collected together in the cool apartment of the back of the house, sewing, knitting, or executng several kinds of ornamental works."[92] Samuel Hudson, a Cape settler, diarist, and slave owner, wrote that no secrets could be hidden from "these Slaves who are frequently employed by their Mistresses to worm out every transaction that may occur in the House of their Neighbors. . . . To these favorites they are extremely kind & treat them v. differently from the generality of Slaves."[93] William Bird, the former civil servant and pioneering sociologist, described the relationship in similar terms. The favored housemaids kept "everything in order and were entrusted with all that is valuable,—more like companions than slaves." But, he cautioned, "the mistresses rarely, and the slaves never, forget their relative situations; and, however familiar in private, in the presence of another, due form prevails."[94]

Mistresses turned to violence as freely as did their fathers, husbands, and sons when they could not control their slaves by other means. The weapons of choice were the hand and the whip. A slave woman named Justiero, for instance, charged that her master and mistress regularly mistreated her, "particularly the latter, who is in the habit of beating her with the fists and of placing her by the hands and legs in Stocks." She could not work hard enough to please them, she said, since she was "labouring under a disease." The government surgeon who examined her agreed that she was too ill to work, and the protector took her owners to court.[95] Like Justiero, many slaves were punished by both master and mistress. This pattern was widespread and suggests that masters sometimes felt the need to reinforce their wives' authority with their own. But many women of the slave-owning class were perfectly capable of disciplining slaves by themselves, especially women and children, and they justified their actions in terms similar to those the masters used. Hester van Rooyen, the wife of a small farmer in the Albany district, provides an example. For reasons that were never recorded, she attacked her slave housemaid Candase. As Candase told the story, van Rooyen had hit her with her fists until she fell, had then pounded her head against the ground, and had finally lashed her with a whip. A white visitor, Lena Osthuisen, had tried to pull van Rooyen off her slave, knowing that it was illegal to beat a female slave and that van Rooyen might be fined. But van Rooyen had shouted, "It's my money, my Slave and if I beat her dead it is no ones [sic] business." In court, van Rooyen, whose husband was bedridden and who was herself "within a short time of her confinement," admitted her guilt.[96] Her husband's illness had forced van Rooyen to assume the role of head of household. Her actions and words indicate that she shared with the men of her class and race a set of beliefs about the nature of a slave owner's rights and the colonial state's unwarranted interference in household matters.

There was more to the mistress-slave relationship than violence and resistance. A story told by a slave housemaid named Regina captures some of the contradictory impulses that created tension within slave-owning households.[97] Regina's mistress was Bella de Jong, the wife of Francis de Jong, a farmer in the Albany district. Regina was the family's only slave, having belonged to de Jong since her early teenage years.[98] She was now twenty-three. She told the protector that the trouble began when she and her mistress exchanged harsh words about Regina's children. Both of them, boys, had died as infants. Bella accused Regina of having been a careless mother and said that she was to blame for her babies' deaths. Regina's retort was equally cutting: she said the boys had died because the mistress and her husband did not allow her enough time to care for them and "that if she had another Mistress she could have brought her children up."

The matter smoldered until the next day. In the morning, Regina, her mistress, and the two de Jong daughters were "picking and cleaning corn for the mill." Bella began to scold Regina about her alleged maternal negligence and mocked her by calling Regina, who was pregnant at the time, "big belly." Hearing this, Regina said, the de Jong girls left the house and went out into the yard, apparently sensing the electricity in the air. Regina told her mistress "that she should not say such things before the children as it would make them wicked." Bella responded by ushering Regina into a back room and beating her.

The intimacy of the relationship between Regina and Bella is apparent, as is intimacy's price. Bella had been a part of some of the most private and painful moments of Regina's life, having watched her grow from adolescence into adulthood. She drew on that knowledge when subjecting her slave to scornful teasing. Regina's willingness to rebuke her mistress for the indelicacy of the words she used in front of the children suggests that she had sometimes been able to transcend her role as a slave. Her impertinence was born of the familiarity she and Bella had developed during the decade they had spent together. The two women shared the work of the household and probably living conditions as well. But Bella allowed none of this to subvert the hierarchy of mistress and slave fundamentally. When Regina presumed to speak to her mistress as an equal, her mistress shamed her and later turned to violence—the foundation on which Regina's subordination ultimately rested.

Despite the constant threat of violence, a softer side to mistress-slave relations often came to the fore. For instance, slaves sometimes ran to mistresses for protection when threatened with physical punishment. Dina, an apprentice on Roeloff Petrus Johannes Campher's small farm, sought out old Mrs. Campher, Roeloff's mother, when her son began to beat her for her insolence. The old woman implored her son to stop, "repeatedly saying 'Petrus Petrus,'" but to no avail. Roeloff Petrus was "in a great passion" and exclaimed, "By God I shall now punish her, and she may Complain [to the special justice]."[99] When Grietje, a slave housemaid, tried to punish her own child, the child ran to the mistress for protection.[100]

While slave women and children sometimes formed affectionately intimate relationships with their mistresses, their intimate relationships with their masters often had a bitter edge.

Rape and the Paterfamilias

In the early 1770s, Anders Sparrman visited a farm near Paarl, shared a meal with the white overseer that he met there, and spoke with him of many things. Sex was among the subjects on which they touched. Sparrman's host

> gave me a list (which, by his desire, I took down in my pocket-book, as the result of his own experience) of the constant order of precedence in love, which ought to be observed among the fair sex in Africa. . . . First the *Madagascar* women, who are the blackest and best; next to these the *Malabars,* then the *Bugunese* or *Malays,* after these the Hottentots, and last and worst of all, the white Dutch women.[101]

The overseer had tastes that were unusual, to say the least. The women who most aroused the interest of male travelers, government officials, and diarists were slaves who were "particularly fair in their complexions" and "not destitute of charms to the sensual eye"—descriptions that, apparently, were true especially of slaves in Cape Town.[102] Sparrman's companion did, however, share one attribute with other white men at the Cape. He understood and seems to have exploited the sexual vulnerability of slave women.

The erotic allure of young slave women was explicit in the accounts of the Cape that white men composed. The eroticism of their writing depended as much on taboo—the real or imagined crossing of the social boundaries of class, legal status, and putative race—as on the exotic beauty of the women. The young slave women were "handsome and even beautiful. . . . [They were] as fair as some [women] . . . in Europe. . . . Scarcely any . . . [were not] comely and well-shaped."[103] They were "rather under middle size, with a bust inclined to fulness. They are well proportioned, and usually have teeth white as ivory, and eyes and hair black as jet: they are smart, and fond of dress, in which they excel."[104] Many of the women were "perfectly white," yet, they were also "black" because they were slaves.[105] And because they were slaves, they were available as sexual partners. To put it another way, their relative powerlessness made it difficult for them to remain unavailable.

No one doubted that the fair color of the present generation of slaves was the result of decades of "inter Communion" between "the European and the Slave Woman," the "mixture of Europeans with the Slave Girls," the "connection with Europeans," as writers variously put it.[106] As for the men in question, some accounts leave the impression that they were prosperous outsiders, since a concubine could not be had by a penniless man: "Slave girls are immediately hired of the owner, either by the month or year, or perhaps purchased altogether by some enamoured admirer."[107] Several accounts echo Samuel Hudson, an English slave owner, in suggesting it was Englishmen who were the most active in pursuing slave women: "Many an English Countence you may perceive running through the streets of Cape Town without shoe or stocking—the badge of slavery."[108] One resident of the Cape, a Scot, contended that it was "English labourers," not wellborn men, who lived "in habits of intimacy with the Malay [slave] girls."[109] Rarely did writers attribute the whiteness of the slaves to the lust of their masters.

Nineteenth-century observers tended to assign slave owners the role of pimp, rather than lover. Hudson claimed that it was "too frequently the case that their Masters and Mistresses encourage these connections to improve their breed of Live Stock."[110] An anonymous visitor explained that an "intercourse of this kind becomes a profitable concern to the master of the family, by an addition (if we may be allowed the expression) to his live-stock."[111] A British military officer who served in the Cape during the first occupation wrote of the "Dutch ladies" who "have no reluctance to their slave girls having connection with their guests, in hopes of profiting by it, by their being got with child. I myself know instances where they have been ordered to wait on such a gentleman to [*sic*] his bed room; what followed does not require to be mentioned."[112]

The slave owners were not, according to the chroniclers, the only ones to benefit from these liaisons. The fair, well-dressed young women were "generally in the pay of some resident who furnishes them with their finery which creates no enquiry from their Superiors how they procure these things. It being understood the Slave is handsome and they are the greater part of them Courtezan [i.e., courtesans] and in pay." Besides providing "fashionable dress, to which the slave girl is devoted," the lovers of these women occasionally bought the freedom of the children they fathered, and though it happened less often, a man might also buy the freedom of the woman he kept.[113] A former colonial official argued that the women bore a large measure of the blame for their degradation. A combination of gifts, on the one hand, and the young women's unrestrained sexual ardor, on the other, led them to "court [the] notice" of European men and "not unwillingly yield to solicitation."[114] Commentators on the Cape stereotyped slave women as sensual and abandoned, in much the same way that slave women were described in the Caribbean and the American South. As in the New World, these stereotypes served to legitimate sexual exploitation.[115]

Travelers and diarists at the Cape may have accurately described the appearance of the behavior that they observed, but they did not grasp its meaning. They watched as slave women entered into relationships of concubinage with white men, but they refused to acknowledge the vulnerability and powerlessness and the overt and covert forms of coercion that forced the women into in these liaisons. Even when the relationships were consensual, which they would sometimes have been, they existed within a society in which the range of choices available to slave women was severely restricted.[116] In addition, the activities commentators described were those of male outsiders who were forced to pursue the slave women in public because they were not members of slave-holding households. Most chose not to see the private assaults and seductions of the slave owners.

Otto Mentzel, who lived at the Cape during the 1730s and 1740s, was one of the few male writers who condemned slave owners' exploitation of slave women. The masters were corrupt men who had enslaved the children they had sired, "Their own flesh and blood, begotten of slave women."[117] Mentzel was especially harsh on the slave owners' sons and the society that coddled them. "More often than not," he reported, "[they] commit some folly, and get entangled with a handsome slave-girl belonging to the household. These affairs are not regarded as very serious. The girl is sternly rebuked for her wantonness, and threatened with dire punishments if she dares to disclose who was responsible . . . nay, she is bribed to put the blame on some other man."[118] Lady Anne Barnard, a rare female chronicler of life at the Cape during the slave era, insisted that the sexual abuse of slave women by their masters "often takes place in this country." She wrote of a mistress's rage at her betrayal by her husband and of the shame that she felt because the other woman was a slave. Lady Anne's point was not simply to demonstrate the mistress's lack of sympathy for the slave involved; she also emphasized Cape society's disapproval of masters who involved themselves sexually with their slaves.[119] Samuel Hudson tells a similar tale about a master, a slave woman, and a jealous mistress.[120]

Mentzel, Hudson, and Lady Anne were rare in locating the grimmest forms of sexual exploitation within the patriarchal household. For slave women, the most pressing problem was not concubinage, it was sexual abuse at home. The aggressors were not "European" men, but their masters and their masters' sons. Slave owners rarely flaunted their slave "mistresses." Theirs were private aggressions carried on behind closed doors. Most commentators, by their silence and because of their limited field of view, suggested that slave women ran no risk of direct sexual abuse at their masters' hands. The records of the protectors of slaves, however, speak in a different voice.

Dozens of slave owners found themselves in the protectors' offices facing charges that stemmed from their sexual abuse of their female slaves, both women and girls. Very rarely did a slave's complaint address the problem of abuse directly. The law offered slave women little protection from sexual exploitation. The combination of Roman-Dutch law and the statutes of the Dutch East Indian colonies, which together provided the common law of the Cape, did outlaw "the habit of [masters] indulging in their unruly passions and their making use of compulsory means in forcing a slave to obey any such commands which are contrary to law or morality,"[121] but prosecutions were exceedingly rare. The slavery reform laws, which superseded the common law of slavery in 1823, did not mention sexual assault. Criminal law at the time did little better. The colony prosecuted a slave owner's eighteen-year-old son for the rape of a ten-year-old slave girl in 1831, but the jury refused to accept the testimony of the girl's parents and acquitted the young master.[122]

Rather than confront sexual exploitation directly, slave girls and women fought it indirectly. They attempted to win freedom for themselves or their children through appeals to the extinct common law and to slaveholding society's sense of propriety, by the adroit use of the reform laws, and by the manipulation of the protectors' sensibilities. For instance, Saartje, a Cape Town housemaid, complained to the protector of physical abuse, not sexual exploitation. She said that her master, Charles Mathurin Villet, had beaten her twice "for which she could assign no other Cause than that she would not submit to his addresses" (these were the protector's words). She also accused him of not allowing her to leave his premises on Sundays, a customary privilege. This, she believed, was because Villet was jealous; he had learned "that she would

[soon] take a Husband." Saartje dropped the charges after Villet agreed to allow her to go out on Sundays and visit "that person who wished to take her as a wife."[123] Making clever use of the reform laws and protector's office, Saartje simultaneously deflected Villet's advances and safeguarded her relationship with her intended.

Spas, a slave belonging to Willem Englebrecht of the Somerset district, did complain of sexual abuse, but only to justify her escape from her master's household after she and her husband, Jonas, had been apprehended as runaways. According to the assistant protector of slaves in Graham's Town, she claimed to have "deserted in Consequence of the misconduct of her Young master Cornelis Englebracht who has for some Years forcibly Cohabited with her—that this took place before her connexion with Jonas begun [*sic*] but that Jonas now threatens to kill some one unless this connexion ceases."[124] The choices confronting Spas and Jonas emphasize their powerlessness. If they wished the sexual exploitation to end, they could choose violence, which would certainly have led them deeper into trouble, or escape, a risky venture.

Slave owners and slave owners' sons sometimes seduced slave women with promises of freedom. When these pledges came to nothing, as they generally did, slave women sometimes tried to shame their masters into fulfilling them. Eva, a slave belonging to Barend Liebenburg of the Graaff-Reinet district, went to the protector of slaves and "requested that her master . . . might be ordered to manumit her, agreeably to a promise which he had given her for having carnal connection with her." Though the law did not allow the protector to compel Liebenburg to free Eva, he did call Liebenburg into his office to answer Eva's charge. The protector seems to have believed that the informal pressures he could bring to bear—perhaps assisted by social sanctions—would persuade Liebenburg to free Eva. If this was his strategy, it succeeded. In the protector's office, Liebenburg "denied the promise, but confessed the carnal connection; he declared therefore his readiness to manumit her."[125] In a similar case, Leentje, a Cape Town slave, visited George Jackman Rogers, the principal protector, to report that her master had registered her child as a slave "notwithstanding his being the father of it." There was nothing in the law to prevent a master from enslaving a child born to him of a slave mother, but Rogers took up the case nonetheless. After hearing two witnesses testify that Leentje's master had seduced her with promises of freedom, he decided that the "evidence . . . offered to prove that the master is actually the father of the child is clear, and . . . consistent." He believed that the weight of his office and the threat of public exposure would be enough to "obtain the freedom of Leentje and her child without having recourse to legal measures."[126]

A few years after hearing Leentje's case, Rogers used an explicit threat of public exposure to win the freedom of a slave mother and her child. Magtelda, a fourteen-year-old slave girl, complained that her master had promised to free her if "she allowed connexion with him." The result was a child that she had delivered ten days prior to appearing in the protector's office. Her master, John Saunder, a confectioner, had now taken the child from her, and she did not know where it was. She wanted her child back and demanded her freedom. Magtelda's mother verified her daughter's testimony, and Rogers began an investigation. Saunder at first denied the charges and said that he could prove that Magtelda "had been with other men." But when Rogers declared "his intention of proceeding . . . [Saunder] consented to make her free, and her child never having been registered [as a slave] was free—[Saunder] begged that the Protector would make Magtelda undertake not to give him or his family any further trouble, and engaged that Magtelda's child should be immediately restored to her." Magtelda "was in Consequence immediately manumitted" and the case was closed "to the satisfaction of the mother and daughter."[127]

Men like Liebenburg and Saunder would not have feared public exposure if slave-owning society condoned the direct sexual exploitation of slave women by their masters. There are several indications, besides the master's hesitancy to be exposed publicly, that suggest that respectable society frowned on the sexual abuse of slave women. Mistresses, certainly, did not wish to see their husbands sexually involved with their maids, and they made their disapproval known in forthright terms. Sometimes the master paid a stiff price. Abraham Carel Greyling's wife left him immediately after his slave, Clara, gave birth to a child that she believed was his. Even though Greyling denied that he had fathered the child and blamed his son instead, his wife asked for and received a dissolution of the marriage and a property settlement. A court decided that Greyling's "adulterous intercourse" with Clara and the "continuous quarrels and disputes" had made his wife's home life unbearable.[128] More commonly, however, it was the slave, not the master, who suffered most at the hands of an angry wife. For instance, Samieda, a seventeen-year-old slave housemaid, was "turned out of the House" by her mistress, Mrs. Joseph de Kock, when "having asked [Samieda] who was the father of her Child, she stated Mr. de Kock."[129]

Cape mistresses' dismay over their philandering husbands was not a nineteenth-century phenomenon; nor was their victimization of the slave woman. During the first British occupation, Lady Anne Barnard visited the home of the landdrost of Stellenbosch and witnessed "an affair of jealousy, founded on . . . the partiality of the master to one of his black slaves." Dinner was interrupted one night by an elderly couple, whose problem took up most of the landdrost's evening. The husband's sexual involvement with a slave woman had long caused trouble between him and his wife. He asked the landdrost's permission to sell the slave immediately, and the magistrate agreed, "thinking his hurry a proof that he knew his own weakness and was resolved to put future error out of his power." The couple left, but the wife soon returned to ask the landdrost's permission to whip the slave before she was sold. He refused the old woman's request. The landdrost later told Lady Anne that trouble of the sort that disturbed the couple "often takes place."[130] Lady Anne does not make it clear whether the landdrost was referring only to the sexual abuse of slave women by their masters or the abuse of the slave by both rapacious masters and outraged mistresses. The landdrost probably meant to suggest the latter. A few years later, Samuel Hudson wrote of a farmer, "of some repute," who "frequently had some quarrels with his wife respecting a Slave Maid who unfortunately happened to be more desirable than her Mistress which had caused heart burnings and jealousy and many severe chatisements when ever opertunities [sic] offered by the Absence of the Husband." Eventually the wife murdered the maid.[131]

The sexual exploitation of slave women angered the mistresses not so much because of the harm it did the slaves, but because it was humiliating and because they could do little to stop it. The slave owners' abuse of slave women was both a consequence and a symbol of the patriarchal power that the legal, economic, and ideological structures of the slave-owning society had invested in them. Society did not applaud a master's sexual exploitation of his female slave, but it did everything to make it possible and almost nothing to prevent it. The mistresses' physical abuse of the victim of sexual exploitation was emblematic of their own weakness. Mistresses seldom did as Mrs. Greyling had done and ended their marriage; most were too dependent on their husbands socially and economically to take so risky a course of action. While there can be little doubt that the jealousy and "heart burnings" within the masters' households made life unpleasant for all concerned, mistresses seldom had the capacity to inflict on their husbands pain as intense as that they felt themselves. They lashed out instead at the object of their husbands' affection. They seized on their prerogatives as mistresses, which devolved to them through their husbands, to revenge themselves on the relatively weak and rightless victims of their husbands' aggression.

Neither mistresses nor the law could limit the extent to which masters sexually abused their slaves. Slave women relied much more on their families and their own resources. Magtelda, the fourteen-year-old girl mentioned above, brought her mother, Candaca, with her when she appeared in the protector's office. Candaca, who was a free black, was there to lend her support to her daughter's testimony.[132] In another case, Betje, a seventeen-year-old slave housemaid, at first visited the protector alone. She charged that her "young Master H. Truter had persuaded her to have connexion with [him] promising her to purchase her freedom, to which she had assented, but he had not fulfilled his promise." At the same time, not inconsistently, she claimed that her young mistress, apparently Truter's wife, had struck her and blackened her eye. A "few days afterward," before the protector could investigate the matter, Betje appeared with her mother, Antje, a free woman. The two of them had reached some sort of accommodation with Truter. Betje said that she wanted "to wave her Claim upon Mr. Truter." Her mother, Mr. Truter, and she had "settled the case between themselves."[133] The fact that both Candaca and Antje were free persons may have made it easier for them to oppose their daughters' master. But a parent did not have to be a free person to be found supporting a child in resisting sexual exploitation.

A case involving a slave girl and both of her parents suggests the emotional toll that sexual abuse imposed on slave girls and women and on their families. When Lesaida asked Rogers not to register her child as a slave because her master was its father, her parents, both slaves, accompanied her. Her mother, Sara, and father, February, both testified that Lesaida's master was indeed the child's father. But, they said, it was only "after much difficulty" that they had "obliged [Lesaida] to declare who was the Father of the child."[134] Lesaida's hesitancy to discuss her pregnancy may have been grounded in her fear for her own safety or that of her child. Alternatively, she may have blamed herself for her predicament, as victims of physical and sexual abuse often do, or felt that she had shamed her parents by having violated the mores of her family and community. Any or all of these factors may have produced the "difficulty" Sara and February experienced when they broke the silence with their daughter. The anguish that the incident caused for Lesaida and her parents lurks just below the surface of the protector's report.

Several historians have argued that the experience of slavery was by no means the same for women as it was for men.[135] While all slaves experience social death and soul murder, the nature of these phenomena is different for men and for women. Gerda Lerner has argued that the difference lies precisely in the sexual vulnerability of slave women. While both male and female slaves were subordinated to the power of a master and were thereby denied autonomy and honor, enslavement for women and girls "inevitably also meant having to perform sexual services for their masters or for those whom their masters might designate in their stead. . . . For women, sexual exploitation marked the very definition of enslavement, as it did *not* for men."[136] Nell Irvin Painter contends that soul murder was linked as much to sexual abuse, a particular threat to women, as to the physical violence that affected both men and women.[137] While there were undoubtedly slaves at the Cape for whom the term *soul murder* is appropriate, the slave women and girls who enter the protectors' records seem to have escaped this fate. Aided by their families, their protectors, and the reform laws, they fought back, resisting the men, institutions, and ideologies that would have crushed their souls.

Until emancipation, few slaves ever escaped the household. Relationships within it were sometimes affectionate, often harsh, and occasionally cruelly abusive. Always they were bounded on one side by the masters' efforts to subordinate their slaves and, on the other, by the slaves' attempts to resist that subordination, either overtly or covertly. Relationships typically hovered ambiguously between these poles. As Willie Lee Rose suggested of the American South, it was in the nature of slave-owning households that they "invited love-hate relationships, a certain nervous stability, a discernable atmosphere of tension, and a pervading sense of incongruities locked in interminable suspension."[138] In the Cape Colony, as in the American South, the incorporation of slaves into the household was not an end in itself. Masters subordinated their slaves and apprentices in order to put them to work.

CHAPTER 4

"A Paradise Even When Oppressive"

Skilled Slaves, Domestic Servants, and Urban Laborers

At a nod the cook exchanges his saucepan for a flute, the groom quits his curry-comb and takes his violin, and the gardener throwing aside his spade sits down to the violoncello.

—HENRY LICHTENSTEIN, 1812

Job, a domestic servant and skilled craftsman, and Isaac, a common laborer, once spoke to the protector of slaves in Graaff-Reinet about their lives as slaves.[1] Job identified himself as "the Chief Slave of his Master's indoors" and said that he was a tailor by trade, making clothes for all the slaves on the farm. He added that he was a Christian, could read, and that his master, Gerhardus Lodewyk Coetzee, to whom he had been sold a few years earlier for the remarkably high price of £263, trusted him with the keys to his home and storerooms.[2] He was, all in all, a distinguished man.

Job described the rhythms of work on the Coetzee farm. The day began shortly after dawn for the ten or twelve adult slaves working in the field or in Coetzee's mill and tannery.[3] At eleven o'clock, the slaves ate their first meal, a thick soup of peas, beans, and Indian corn or barley. Occasionally there was meat with the soup. Always there was wine to drink. The slaves received a half pint in the morning and evening, and in summer a third half pint at midday.[4] After eating, the slaves rested, smoking or sleeping for perhaps an hour and a half before returning to work. In the evening, there was more soup, again with a tot of wine. Coetzee's slaves, Job said, did not "reap in the night," but went about other tasks, such as binding sheaves of the harvested grain. Among his other chores, Job fashioned the slaves' clothes. Once a year, he explained, he made each of them a cloth jacket, a "coarse shirt," and a pair of goat-skin trousers. When cooler weather arrived, Job gave them sheepskin jackets and, if there were "skins enough at hand," another pair of pants. Job and his master also saw to it that the slaves got "a skin . . . for shoes, which they [made] themselves." Every day was a working day, but on Sundays the slaves had a little free time during which they tended the vegetables and tobacco they raised on the garden plots that their master had given them. Job said that in the evenings—which he, at least, had to himself—he made clothes for sale, buying coffee and tea with the profits. He had only one complaint: the slaves, he thought, "would be better [off] had they something to eat before going to work in the morning as well as at 11 O'Clock."

Job seems to have found a measure of contentment in his life as a slave. He had earned his master's trust, achieved a notable place within the local hierarchy of the farm, and carved out a small degree of personal autonomy and a somewhat larger amount of self-respect. He was cheating social death. His skills and competence as a worker granted him this relative immunity from the worst aspects of slavery.

Isaac, on the other hand, was angry. His complaint that Coetzee had beaten him for a trifling offense had initiated the investigation that led to Job's deposition. Coetzee, it appeared, had shot a white springbok, "a great Curiousity" because of its color.[5] He had wanted to preserve it and ordered Isaac to skin the animal carefully, making sure not to damage its head and hooves. Isaac, for reasons that have gone unrecorded, botched the job. He cut the head away from the rest of the hide, destroying its value as a trophy. When Coetzee confronted him about his shoddy work, Isaac defended himself "impertinently," according to Job, who was there to witness the incident. At that, "his Master gave him 2 or 3 blows" with a doubled leather strap.

Any number of things might have sparked the incident between Isaac and Coetzee. Those that are visible in the protector's report have to do with Isaac's failure to play the role of a properly subordinated member of his master's household. He labored carelessly, spoke freely, and was punished for it. Those causes that are not immediately visible stem from the quality of Isaac's enslavement. He was a laborer, not a craftsman—a common slave, not a favored one. Slavery for him was a life of drudgery and degradation, as it was not for Job. Long-suppressed anger and frustration may have led him to ruin his master's trophy.

To be a slave was above all to be a worker. Slaves had other identities besides those of laborers, to be sure, and these identities also shaped their sense of themselves. Job, for instance, was proud to be a Christian. But because the slaves experienced labor both extensively and intensively, its emotional and material impact on their lives was profound. As the stories of Job and Isaac indicate, the experience of work was not the same for all slaves. Some slaves derived satisfaction, pride, and a sense of community from their work; most did not. Fortunate slaves in the colony's towns and villages and in the countryside labored at tasks that allowed them to develop technical competence and create physical and psychological zones of personal autonomy. A lucky and industrious few lived almost as free blacks. Slaves such as these, who held soul murder and social death at bay, were silent challenges to ideology of enslavement. The great majority of slaves, however, could not escape the physical and emotional violence of slavery. Even the fortunate ones knew that their luck could change at their master's whim.

Slaves and apprentices were part of a workforce in which the boundaries of color and status were often indistinct. The lives and labors of slave artisans, laborers, cattleherds, domestic servants, and farmworkers blended almost imperceptibly into those of Khoisan, free blacks, Bastaard Hottentots, Prize Negroes, and Bantu-speaking Africans. Slaves sometimes enjoyed privileges and autonomy normally associated with the legally free workers of the colony. Free workers, on the other hand, often struggled under conditions as oppressive as those of the least-favored slaves. In Cape Town, free blacks labored at many of the same occupations as the slaves; they were cooks, domestic servants, laborers, artisans, and porters, who were known at the Cape as coolies.[6] Prize Negroes, rarely if ever possessing skills, worked among slaves as common laborers.[7] Slaves, Prize Negroes, and a scattering of Khoisan worked together in the vineyards, grain fields, and vegetable gardens of the western Cape.[8] In the eastern cattle districts, Khoisan, slaves, and increasing numbers of Bantu-speaking Africans from beyond the colonial frontier herded livestock and raised modest crops of grain on settlers' farms.[9] The intense interaction between slaves and other nonwhite workers, in and out of the workplace, allowed and encouraged them to construct communities and cultures that few whites shared. It was the slaves' natal alienation and status as property—to be bought and sold legally and openly, rather than to be hired and fired or clandestinely enslaved— that prevented the distinction between slave and free from melting entirely away.

Just as color, status, skills, and economic geography worked in sometimes contradictory ways, gender and age differences could both unite and divide. Male and female slaves and apprentices performed many of the same tasks, working as cooks, domestic servants, field workers, and cattleherds. But some jobs were almost invariably held by men, others by women, thus separating the sexes at the workplace. The experiences of work in childhood and old age were specific to slaves of those age groups, yet the fact that all slaves went through the former and many the latter mitigated the tendency that age might have had to fragment the slave community.

The differences of color, status, skill, age, and gender found within workers' communities should not mask the factors that created a common body of experience. The conditions of labor were generally harsh, the discipline rigid, and the rewards exceedingly low. Despite the colonists' chronic complaints of a labor shortage, they could not or would not and certainly did not pay wages and offer conditions that would attract workers who had more than the most limited of options. At the Cape, most people who worked for someone else did so under compulsion.

Young Slaves and Old

Work began to shape the slaves' sense of themselves early in life and ended late. Slave boys and girls began their laboring lives as soon as their masters thought them able, often tending livestock. Elderly slaves worked as long as their masters could extract labor from them, commonly herding livestock, the labor of their youth. Slave owners who testified before the commissioners of inquiry in 1826 agreed that slave children were ready to perform light work by age ten and even "sooner in trifling jobs about the house and farm." They were not fit for heavy labor—what one witness called "profitable work"—until midadolescence. By that point, slave owners believed, boys were physically capable of handling the same jobs as men.[10] The colonial slave registers support the evidence heard before the commissioners. Colonial legislation compelled all slave owners to list their slave property by first name, age or date of birth, "occupation," if applicable, and mother's name, if known. Children below the age of twelve or thirteen were typically enumerated without an occupational listing. Adolescents were most often listed as housemaid, horsekeeper, shepherd, shepherdess, laborer, or similar designation of low skill.[11]

Masters and mistresses disciplined their young workers in much the same way as they did the adults. Violence was essential. As Nell Irvin Painter has shown, masters beat slave children in an effort to inculcate patriarchy's "core values" of submission and obedience and, by destroying the children's souls, to make them "good slaves."[12] Beatings were thus a form of job training. Daniel Johannes Theunissen, for instance, gave the nine-year-old slave Pedro six lashes with a cane for having allowed some pigs to stray into the household garden and destroy the vegetables. Pedro's mother, Sylvia, told the protector that she thought her master and mistress were "rather severe upon herself and Children." To her regret she let her master know how she felt, and he punished her as well.[13] Similarly, Paul Hendrik Stephanus beat twelve-year-old Dina, a girl slave, with a sjambok because some of the goats in her care strayed and were lost. Stephanus explained his actions by claiming that Dina had earned the punishment. She had exposed him "to a great deal of trouble and Expenses not only for her frequently [*sic*] desertion but by her naughtiness."[14]

The children received instruction from older slaves and apprentices as well. Young slaves learned to tend livestock, cultivate the soil, lead the plow, cook, wash, and clean primarily from the slaves who regularly performed those tasks. Sara, a slave cook on a farm near Paarl, taught her daughter the arts of both housekeeping and survival when she warned her "to be careful washing some napkins or she would be again beaten with a horse whip."[15] While it is probable that slave artisans trained their owner's younger slaves in their respective crafts, some learned their trades elsewhere. Lambertus Johannes Colyn, one of the wealthiest wine farmers in the colony, owned eighty-five slaves, including a carpenter, a shoemaker, a tailor, a blacksmith, and a mason. He also owned three young men whom he listed in the slave register as "Apprenticed"—to a carpenter, a shoemaker, and a cooper. Jan Andries Horak, another large slaveholder, owned two boys whom he had apprenticed to a "taylor." Jacobus Petrus Roux of Stellenbosch apprenticed a sixteen-year-old male slave to a carpenter. Neither Horak nor Roux owned slaves who possessed the relevant skills, making it necessary for them to send their slaves away if they were to learn a craft. Colyn, however, did own slave artisans: perhaps he wanted to avoid professional inbreeding.[16]

Slaves and apprentices began to perform skilled labor and the demanding work of the field as their mental and physical capacities matured. They ceased as their powers left them. There was a general agreement among the slave owners who spoke to the commissioners of inquiry that the value of the labor a slave performed began to decline in the slave's forties or fifties. One slave owner claimed that slaves from Mozambique were "past their strength" at forty, but that slaves born in the colony worked well until they were fifty "or thereabouts." Another witness claimed that the slaves could still be worked profitably at age fifty "and sometimes till sixty." A third thought that, "on the average," a slave could work well until age fifty-five.[17]

Old slaves did not retire to lives of ease. They were often literally put out to pasture. Henry Lichtenstein reported that wine and wheat farmers "commonly entrusted" their herds and flocks "to a couple of old slaves or Hottentots."[18] The work was sometimes beyond the capacity of men and women whose strength had been broken by decades of hard labor. Bastiaan, a sixty-three-year-old cattleherd, complained to an assistant protector of slaves that the overseer of his master's farm had beaten him for neglecting the cattle under his care, even though he was too "decrepit" to look after them properly. A physician who examined him found an ulcer on his abdomen and "a rupture." The protector wrote to Bastiaan's master, advising him to "lighten [his] work as much as possible."[19] Another slave owner told his slave April that he would not be given as much food as he wanted because, at age seventy-three, he was "too old to work."[20]

Most slave owners probably took adequate care of their slaves in their old age, but the temptation to squeeze the last possible ounce of profit out of them was strong. Adriana, a fifty-one-year-old slave housemaid, told a protector that "she can no longer do work enough to please her Mistress, that she daily beats or kicks her and tells her that she does not wish to see her face again." The protector sent Adriana to a colonial medical officer, who certified that she was indeed unable to do any but "the slightest work about the house, and that for only a few hours during the day."[21] Pedro, a seventy-year-old slave, was simply abandoned by his master. He was left, a protector reported, "without the means of support he being too old and infirm to procure his food and clothing."[22]

Between the extremes of childhood and old age, slaves and apprentices worked at a variety of tasks, most of them burdensome and unrewarding. This was as true for domestic servants as it was for field laborers. Perhaps because of this, house servants do not seem to have constituted a self-consciously superior caste of slaves. Whatever lines separated them from their comrades were easily and continually crossed.

Domestic Service

Rich or poor, urbanites or country folk, slave owners relied on slaves and apprentices to perform household tasks such as cleaning, washing, cooking, sewing, serving, and making butter and soap. Domestic servants often worked outside the home as well. A valet might work in the fields, and a washmaid might sell pastries on the market square. Most of the time, however, the domestic servants were in the house or near it, within the reach of their masters' and mistresses' eyes, tongues, and hands.

In the 1820s and 1830s, two-thirds of the roughly six thousand slaves in Cape Town worked in domestic service.[23] The proportion in the countryside would have been much lower, but no precise estimate is possible. Many travelers' accounts mention the work of domestic servants. Lichtenstein praised the slave cooks who created the "hotly spiced dishes of the Cape"—food that would have delighted the palate of even the "greatest epicure." One of the meals he so admired was both prepared and served by the slaves of a wealthy farmer in what later became the Worcester district. In this large household, jobs were specialized even among the domestics. While one set of slaves was "eagerly busied in waiting," another stood "about here and there behind the guests, with bunches of ostrich feathers in their hands, which they wave[d] to and fro to keep off the flies."[24]

Earlier in his stay at the Cape, Lichtenstein had encountered a slave orchestra in the home of one of the members of the wealthy van Reenen family. "They played first upon clarinets, french horns, and bassoons. The instruments were good, and there was great reason altogether to be pleased with the performance. . . . They afterwards played upon violins, violoncellos, and flutes, on which they played equally well. It is not uncommon to find the same thing among many families at the Cape." Lichtenstein noted that these slaves were by no means full-time musicians; they were household servants. "At a nod the cook exchanges his saucepan for a flute, the groom quits his curry-comb and takes his violin, and the gardener throwing aside his spade sits down to the violoncello."[25]

Less than a decade later, William Burchell, an English traveler, visited a very different sort of farming household in the cattle country of the eastern Cape. Yet it was one in which a slave servant also filled an important role. He described a family whose home "indicated neither affluence nor comfort," but who nevertheless employed a slave woman and a Khoisan girl to perform domestic chores around the house. Outside, the men—one slave and a few Khoisan—tackled "the more laborious work of the farm."[26]

Both slaves and slave owners thought of many jobs as either a woman's or a man's, at least in the ideal. The range of occupations under which female slaves were listed in the slave registers was much more restricted than for males. A slave woman was almost invariably counted as a house-maid, a nurserymaid, a washmaid, a cook, a seamstress, or, infrequently, a shepherdess. With the exception of the latter, these occupational categories involve domestic service. Men's occupations reflected work in house, garden, and field, and they were employed in a greater range of activities. A man, for instance, might be a coachman, "waggoner," baker, tailor, tanner, houseboy, herdsman, wine "vintager," mason, carpenter, shoemaker, "coolie," gardener, fisherman, blacksmith, cook, common laborer, or overseer.[27]

Slaves and slave owners alike seem to have accepted the loosely defined sexual division of labor. One master, advertising the sale of a "clever African Female Slave, named Carolina," assumed that his readers would understand his meaning when he wrote that she was "a good housemaid, and is well acquainted with female work in general."[28] Similarly, the record of the complaint that the slave Mariana brought against her master indicates that both were aware of Cape Colony conventions about the nature of men's and women's work, though they disputed the precise nature of those distinctions. Mariana claimed that her owner forced her to do the sort of work "exacted from a Male slave and which" she felt that she could "no longer endure." Her master denied that he had violated the customary sex division of labor. "No work," he said, "unsuitable to [her] Sex was required from her." Mariana, he said, did nothing beyond ordinary housework, except "now and then" sell vegetables in the market.[29] Nothing in the record tells us whether or not hawking vegetables was the masculine work that prompted Mariana's complaint; since so many women peddled wares on the streets of Cape Town, something else probably offended her sense of propriety.

The notions of gender roles to which colonial slave owners subscribed defined a woman's place as in and around the home and her work as domestic. Yet Mariana was a slave before she was a woman and could be set to work at whatever tasks needed to be done. Mariana's case illustrates the difficulty that the resulting ambiguity could cause both slave and master. Jacqueline Jones has argued in a discussion of American slavery that slave women lived and worked at the point at which racial and patriarchal ideologies intersected. As women they were assigned to domestic labor and were exploited for their reproductive capacity. As African Americans, they were not protected, as white women were, from the heaviest labor of the house and field. Slave owners took a "crudely opportunistic approach toward the labor of slave women.

[H]ence a slave owner just as 'naturally' put his bondswomen to work chopping cotton as washing, ironing, or cooking."[30]

While Jones's argument is applicable to the Cape in its broad outlines, it was nonetheless true that the job most associated with slave and apprentice women was that of housemaid. It was a role that differentiated their experience of slavery from that of slave men. Travelers and other writers of the period often mentioned the maids, especially the mistresses' favorites. Contemporaries claimed that mistresses, when they could, chose pretty, light-skinned, Cape-born girls and women to be their personal servants, companions, and confidants. These slaves, said William Bird, were the product of generations of sexual mingling between settlers, European visitors, and the slaves. Over the years, a portion of the slave community had "progressed nearly to white," making them, so Bird believed, the "most valuable class of slaves."[31] Bird's notions about human progress are beyond comment, but there is a certain logic to the assertion that mistresses preferred Cape-born slaves as their personal servants. These women would have been more likely than foreign-born slaves to share their mistresses' Cape creole language and culture. All things being equal, they would have fit more comfortably into the role of servant and companion.

As with all slaves and apprentices, domestic servants clashed with their masters and mistresses more often over the work that the servants performed than over any other cause. The intimacy of the household and the almost constant surveillance under which the slaves lived intensified the emotional toll that such clashes exacted. The case of Mina, a slave housemaid in the eastern district of Albany, serves as an example. One day as she tidied up a bedroom, her mistress, Mrs. Willem Meyer, entered and accused her of having neglected some of her other chores. As Mina told it, Mrs. Meyer then struck her with her fist and hit her with the thick end of a sjambok. At the protector's hearing, she attempted to establish that she had endured repeated beatings, but could not. The testimony of witnesses did suggest that she was under great emotional strain. Her mistress's daughter said that she had seen Mina crying on the day in question. She cautioned that this was not necessarily a sign that she had been beaten. Mina, she said, frequently cried when "scolded." Another witness agreed that she was apt to weep when "found fault with." Yet Mina was not simply a victim. A witness called her "a very obstinate girl," suggesting that while she may have been the victim of ongoing psychological, if not physical, violence, she remained capable of asserting herself and resisting her owner's demands.[32] At times apparently trivial incidents ignited violent clashes. Johannes Christiaan Kotze tied his slave cook, Eva, hand and foot before applying fifty lashes with a sjambok, leaving her with "marks and stripes, some of which were [a few days later] in an ulcerated state." Her ostensible crime was her failure to get the day's bread to the table on time and to blame the delay on her mistress.[33] As with Mina, the clash between Kotze and Eva probably had deeper roots than can be seen in the report of her complaint.

Domestic servants do not seem to have formed a self-conscious class.[34] While they did spend much of their time within their owners' households and were more able to form ties of intimacy with their masters and mistresses than were the field slaves, they were also more subject to close, suffocating supervision. Nor did they escape hard work. Their tasks were rarely confined to light duty around the house; they often performed labor as heavy and as deadening as the field laborers. On the farms, they commonly worked in both the fields and the home. Even those in Cape Town could not be sure that fortune would not send them out of the city and onto a farm. The line separating slave and apprentice domestic servants from the rest of the slave community could be very thin indeed.

Slavery and the Urban Economy

When considering the general condition of slaves in the Cape Colony, most contemporaries, including travelers, officials, and the slaves themselves, agreed that slaves in Cape Town were the least unhappy and that those in the countryside were the most disconsolate. John Barrow, who had served as a well-placed civil servant during the first British occupation, described the city slaves at the turn of the nineteenth century as "in general well fed, well clothed, not much exposed to the weather, [and] not put to hard labour." However, "others in the country, whose principal food consists of black sandy bread, and the offals of butcher's meat, who labour from morning to night in the field . . . are subject to bilious fevers, of which they seldom recover."[35] Another British official, writing thirty years later, concurred. A "manifest difference," he thought, "indeed prevails between the treatment, habits, and condition of the Slaves in Cape Town and those in the Country, which is known to create a strong apprehension in the former of being removed by sale to the estates of distant Proprietors."[36] These comments might exaggerate the comfort in which urban slaves lived and worked, if not the rigors of the countryside, but both masters and slaves recognized the contrast between town and country.

Slave masters seized upon that contrast and used it as an instrument of discipline. Two British governmental reports written in 1827 and 1831 noted that disobedient slaves were "frequently" sold into the rural districts "as a punishment."[37] The creation of the office of the protector of slaves in 1826 gave slaves who had been sold or who were threatened with sale away from Cape Town a forum in which to voice their grievances. For instance, another Mina, a Cape Town housemaid, complained that "her Master [had] bought [another] farm about Eight Hours distance from Cape Town and that she did not like to go and live there." The protector told Mina that he "could not entertain such a Complaint" and sent her home. "Complaints of this nature," he lamented, "are frequently made . . . to the great interruption of other business."[38]

It was less the nature of the work than the quality of life that made Cape Town attractive to the slaves. To a much greater extent than in the country, slaves and apprentices in the city participated in the creation of a polyglot working-class community that embraced slaves, free blacks, Khoisan, and poor whites. This community eased the burdens of social death by providing a sense of belonging to a society that was beyond their masters' direct control. In addition, a few skilled slave artisans were able to find a large measure of individual autonomy by living and working outside of their masters' homes. Both the working-class community and the slaves' autonomy depended on the peculiar quality of unfree labor in Cape Town. Many slaves spent their days not in the company of their masters and mistresses, but outdoors among their peers.

Cape Town's beauty and exoticism captured the imagination of nineteenth-century visitors, and the outdoor slaves and apprentices were an important part of the mix. The contrast between the conventional, though spectacular, charms of ocean, bay, and mountain, on the one hand, and the alien sights and odors of its narrow, crowded streets, on the other, jarred travelers' sensibilities. George Champion, an American missionary, described the hubbub in the streets: "Now a cart, now a wagon, now a pleasure vehicle, now a soldier, now a Mosambique, now a Malagash, now a Malay, now a white man. . . . Ere long the night revelry and shouting begin."[39] Chief among those who made the picture so foreign were the African, Asian, and Cape-born black boatmen and porters, slave and free, who greeted the visitors even before they came ashore. Though coolies, boatmen, wagon drivers, and the like comprised only 6 percent of the urban slave population of approximately six thousand in the 1820s, they were everywhere to be seen.[40]

Shore boats went out to meet every large vessel that entered Table Bay. The harbor master boarded to apprise the ship's master of the port regulations, while the medical officer determined whether or not the passengers and crew carried infectious diseases. More interesting to the travelers were the boats manned by people who seemed to be an amalgam of "Hottentot," Malay, and "Hindustanee," and who offered for sale fruit of many kinds, vegetables, meat, "land tortoises," and *kreef,* the local lobster. The boatmen, "a ludicrous mongrel breed," thought one traveler, included slaves sent out to peddle wares for their masters or for themselves, subject to the monthly payment of a fee to their owners.[41] Once on dry land, visitors found coolies waiting to carry their possessions from the waterfront to their rooms or warehouses. Free blacks, slaves, and Prize Negroes monopolized this calling. They were available to all who could pay (and some who would not)[42] to tote loads that frailty or decorum would not allow those from the respectable classes to touch. George Champion found the sturdiness of the coolies "astonishing." "A large chest that in America two men must lif[t], a Malay will carry half a mile without putting it down."[43] When there were no ships' cargoes accumulating on the jetty, no incoming or outgoing passengers to assist, or errands to run, the coolies waited to be summoned for work on the steps of the Stadhuis, opposite Greenmarket Square, near the center of town.[44]

Local ordinances enacted in 1800, 1809, and 1815 were intended to set the hours that the coolies would work and the rates they could charge. The law expected them to be on the job from six in the morning until six in the evening during the summer months and from eight until five in the winter. In both seasons, they were to have an hour's break in the morning and afternoon. In 1827, the regulations entitled them to 1 rix dollar and 4 skillings (R.1 Sk.4) for a full day's work or Sk. 1 for each "errand" in and about town.[45] The fiscal and his deputies had the power to punish summarily all coolies—free blacks as well as slaves—who violated the regulations. Such power seems seldom to have been exercised. A former colonial administrator complained in 1822 that there was "no part of the town regulations . . . worse managed that the regulations of the coolies, except be it that of the boatmen." The tenor of his remarks indicated that the coolies were often able to demand higher wages than the regulations allowed.[46]

Coolies spent most of their time out from under the direct supervision of masters or overseers, but they quite literally paid for the privilege. Speaking before the 1826 parliamentary commission of inquiry, two Cape Town slave owners described the agreements they and other slave owners had made with their slaves who worked as coolies. The first witness, P. M. Brink, said that coolies gave their masters part of their daily earnings in exchange for the freedom to hire themselves out. The other, Gerhardus Henry Meyer, said that he owned two slave coolies and that they each paid him R.18 a month out of their wages. He indicated that coolies generally moved freely about the city, except in the evening when they went "home to their Master's house." Meyer thought few slave owners turned much of a profit from the income they derived from their slaves' wages; rather, it was "a favour to allow a Slave to go out as a Coolie."[47]

In answer to another series of questions, Meyer indicated why he and other slave owners might have been willing to accept a small return on the capital that they had invested in slave property. His "business," Meyer said, had earlier been "more extensive," and he now found himself with more slaves than he could employ. Yet he did not want to sell them since they had served him "faithfully." Rather than disperse his slaves among new owners, potentially breaking apart families and friendships, he hired some of them out as "Common Labourers" to various employers. Two, of course, were the coolies that he had mentioned. Other slave owners, he said, who had come about their slaves by "succession"—that is, through inheritance—were also hesitant to sell the family heirlooms. Meyer felt that circumstances of this sort—the possession of more slaves than could be personally employed, combined with some feeling of duty toward them—characterized the position of most slave owners who hired their slaves out or allowed them to work on their own.[48] A government report of the same era claimed that slaves who had worked "upon their own account" were those whose masters had "rewarded" them for their "superior skill and their good conduct."[49] Other factors influenced the decision to hire slaves out or allow them to work on their own. Because the mid-1820s was a period of stagnant or slowly falling slave prices, the sale of any slave, well-behaved or not, might have been an unattractive proposition.[50] Contradicting Meyer's claim that there was little profit in hiring slaves out, Brink told the commissioners that "poor Persons, Widows, and so forth" and "some wealthy Individuals" relied on hire fees and "Coolie *geld* [money]" for a substantial portion of their income.[51]

While the desire to retain slave property, to reward dutiful slaves, and to secure a steady income were among the motives that prompted individual slave owners to hire out their slaves, the system had evolved in response not to individual desires but to structural needs. Cape Town, like all commercial centers, required a labor force that was able to shift rapidly according to changing demands for labor on the docks, at public works, and in construction, craft production, retail sales, and households. Unless some of the flexibility of a free labor market was added to the slave labor system, the Cape Town economy would suffer. Such was the experience of antebellum American cities. In a study of urban slavery in the United States, Richard Wade notes that the "development of hiring out . . . greatly broadened the opportunity for the use of slaves." It "lessened the rigidity of slavery, allowing a constant reallocation of the labor supply according to demand."[52]

As Andrew Bank has shown, hiring out emerged in Cape Town during the eighteenth century and became a central element in the urban economy as trade, commerce, and population grew in the nineteenth. Despite a series of attempts to reduce the city's reliance on slave labor, an alternative workforce failed to materialize. Individual slave owners who chose to hire out their slaves were responding to the opportunities generated by the steady demand for labor. It is not clear how many Cape Town slaves were hired out, though in the mid-1820s the acting governor of the colony estimated the number at two thousand.[53] This estimate included domestic servants and artisans, as well as coolies.

Coolies joined their masters in viewing hiring-out as a privilege, but their appreciation of the arrangements had little to do with whatever riches they thereby acquired. The income was meager, scarcely enough in most cases to pay the coolie geld that they owed their masters. It was a privilege to work as a coolie because of the conditions of labor, not the wages. Coolies enjoyed an unusual degree of autonomy. They indeed carried heavy loads, too often in the cold rains of Cape Town's blustery winter, but the work was episodic, not continuous, and most importantly it was performed outdoors in the bustle of the city's streets, away from the direct supervision of slave owners and overseers. During the day, coolies came and went much as they pleased. Most returned to their masters' homes each evening, but a few rented rooms well away their masters' premises. Coolies made their own financial agreements with those who hired them, whether for the day or for the task. Although coolies, slave and free, were subject to arbitrary discipline at the hands of the fiscal and the police, this does not seem to have been a major nuisance. Coolies largely escaped violent domination, and, though marginalized by respectable society, they were members in good standing of Cape Town's flourishing working-class community. To a large degree, coolies managed to keep social death away from their doors.

Like the coolies, hawkers helped to propel the urban economy. Housewives and servants did much of their household marketing in the streets, and slaves and apprentices purveyed many of the goods that they bought. Travelers who visited the city during the first half of the nineteenth century described the tents pitched along the road leading out of town and the haphazard displays in Greenmarket Square, at which slaves and free blacks sold fruit, vegetables, baked goods, fish, and sundry items for their masters and for themselves.[54] Several Cape Town slaveholders owned extensive gardens and small stock farms above the city, on the lower slopes of Table Mountain. Slaves tended the plots and picked for market "whatever [was] seasonable." Other slaves gathered eggs and prepared dairy products for sale. The wealthiest of the farmers sent slave men into town twice a day with baskets of goods and derived substantial incomes from the sale. Ox wagons, often driven by slaves, carried produce into town from farms north, east, and south of the city.[55]

Slave women, as well as men, hawked their wares on the streets and in the market squares. Some of the women sold goods not only in Cape Town but in the nearer villages and at country homes. They, and perhaps "an attendant man slave," traded in "an assortment of every article of dress worn by females." At the end of the day, the women returned home to square accounts with their masters and mistresses. According to this report, there had been "instances of chastisement inflicted on the slave, if everything is brought back unsold." The same writer believed that the income the slave peddlers generated, if not sufficient to see that the slave owner's family was "wholly maintained," at least "greatly assisted" in it.[56]

Coolies and hawkers seldom enter the protectors' records. When they do, it is usually in a moment of conflict with their masters and mistresses. The reports reveal, nevertheless, some of the texture of urban slavery. While life as a coolie or hawker was generally preferable to life as a rural slave, even these relatively privileged slaves could not fully escape the discipline and exploitation that were a part of all slaves' lives. Mariana once had a dispute with her master about the proceeds from the sale of the vegetables he had "commissioned" her to take to town. According to her master, she had lost or stolen the profits of one day's sale (R.8), yet he had not punished her for it. Perhaps fearing that her punishment had been merely delayed, not canceled, Mariana had run off immediately after returning home and had stayed away for "several days."[57] Another Mariana, this one a "washmaid," had dared to use "abusive language" when addressing her master and had been "excessively impudent" after he had upbraided her for bringing home R.4 less than he had anticipated from the sale of "some Cakes." Her master, J. van Schoor, a baker, was her employer, but not her owner. He had hired her from Mrs. Ryk le Sueur—one of the widows, perhaps, who lived by retailing the services of their slaves.[58]

Other Cape Town slaves shared the relative autonomy of coolies and hawkers. The men who daily climbed the mountains and hills around the city to cut firewood were another part of that class of outdoor slaves and apprentices who contributed to the creation of the working-class community of Cape Town. By the early decades of the nineteenth century, the land close to Cape Town had been almost completely stripped of timber suitable for use as fuel. Scarcity drove up the price of firewood and made it profitable for slave owners to assign a slave the job of finding and cutting wood. It was not light duty. The slaves trekked up to eight miles beyond the city limits and well up the mountainsides before they reached a suitable stand of wood. Since trees were rare, the fuel the slaves gathered tended to be the roots of shrubs and chopped-up brush. The men tied the wood into bundles, suspended the bundles from both ends of a pole, and carried them back to town over their shoulders. There they took it home or sold it door-to-door and in the streets. As an incentive to carry on with this grueling work, many slave owners split the profits from fuel sales with their slaves or allowed them to sell a portion of the wood for themselves. One traveler mentioned another sort of compensation; he noticed that the woodchoppers had time to socialize with the other slaves, often runaways, whom they met along the way. They could be found smoking, gossiping, and bartering food and trinkets before getting on with their work.[59]

Slave boatmen, coolies, woodchoppers, and hawkers were men and women associated almost exclusively with Cape Town. Slave artisans, as well, largely worked in and about the city. The conditions under which they labored allowed them, like the outdoor slaves, a considerable degree of autonomy and facilitated the contribution they made to the creation of working-class communities.

Fortunate Slaves

Although 'slave and apprentice artisans were concentrated in Cape Town, they could also be found in villages and on the larger farms. The principal protector of slaves once remarked that most farmers "in good circumstances" owned slaves who understood something of the arts of carpentry, blacksmithing, and saddling.[60] While slave artisans many not have been as common in the rural districts as the protector suggested, it is certain that, throughout the colony, slave smiths, carpenters, masons, coopers, tailors, cooks, and seamstresses played an essential role in the Cape economy. They did, nevertheless, make their most important contribution in Cape Town. Andrew Bank has estimated that in the 1820s and 1830s, 25 percent of the Cape Town slaves were artisans.[61] Except for the seamstresses and some of the cooks, the slaves employed in the skilled trades were men.

The owners of slave craftsmen were often in the trade themselves and employed their slaves in their businesses. Jonathan Murry, for example, was a whaler, sailing out of Cape Town. When he decided to quit the business in 1826, he sold his enterprise lock, stock, and slaves. He placed an advertisement in the *Cape of Good Hope Government Gazette*, offering "the whole of his Whaling Gear"—boats, oars, sails, masts, ropes, lances, and harpoons—and ten slaves. The slaves, he said, were "not sold for any faults whatever, but merely on account of the Proprietor wishing to discontinue" his business. Among them were the boatmen Jack, Felix, Azor, Mentor, September ("a complete harpooner and boatman, for which he is well known"), and Africa ("a mason, smith, carpenter, boatman, and also a complete cutter and boiler in a Whale Fishery"). Many slave craftsmen, like September, developed a local reputation for the artistry with which they performed their jobs. Others, Africa is an example, had many skills; Murry was pleased to mention that he would be "a most serviceable Slave to any person."[62]

Cape Town tradesmen in several callings owned slaves who were trained in the craft. When J. J. Smuts, a Cape Town baker, decided to try his luck in another line of work, he placed an ad in the *Government Gazette* offering to lease his bakehouse ("in the best part of the Town, together with the Baking Utensils"). Part of the deal were "three clever Baker Boys"—all slaves.[63] Johannes Rabe, another baker, owned sixteen slaves, five of whom were bakers. James Read, a shipwright, owned two slave caulkers. Adriaan Roux, a tanner in Stellenbosch, held fourteen slaves, six of them tanners.[64] Tradesmen who desired to purchase or hire slaves often found workers in the same way that others sold theirs, by placing want-ads in the local newspapers, seeking, for instance, "Six or Eight Tailor Boys, Slave or Free."[65]

Relations between skilled slaves and their masters and mistresses were no more likely to be harmonious than those between any other slaves and slave owners. Trouble was common and commonly work-related. Castor, a tailor who belonged to a Stellenbosch farmer, was whipped after refusing his mistress's order to immediately finish a pair of trousers for his master. Castor had spent the day working on a jacket and had completed it only in the evening. It was "about Sunset," one of his fellow slaves said, when he quit work, apparently believing that he had put in a good day. His mistress felt otherwise, and his master punished his disobedience with several strokes with a cat-o'-nine-tails.[66] F. H. Truter, a Cape Town baker, also found it necessary to discipline one of his skilled slaves physically. He hit his slave July over the head because, "contrary to orders," he had not used "a particular flour" when baking some loaves.[67] Occasionally it was fellow slaves, rather than masters or mistresses, with whom slave artisans could not get along. Baatjoe's mistress once told of his being put to work alone because "he was of so bad a temper that he could not agree with the other Servants." She added that he was too expert a butcher and too valuable a worker to be considered as a sale item.[68] The assertiveness of these and other skilled slaves suggests that Eugene Genovese's observation about the self-esteem of American slave artisans held true for the Cape. The artisans' skills and the advantages that they derived from them "had the disadvantage [from the slave owners' point of view] of making them considerably less servile than slaves were supposed to be."[69]

Nothing more distinguished slave and apprentice artisans from the others than the amount of money they could earn. These incomes established the economic base from of which they carved out a far greater degree of personal autonomy than most slaves could hope for—and, as we shall see in chapter 8, sometimes paid for the freedom of themselves or their kin. Slave artisans were able to command relatively high wages because of the Cape's shortage of skilled labor and because they were good at their jobs. Two white building contractors told the parliamentary commission of inquiry of 1826 that there was "no difference" between the skills of slaves and those of white men. One of the builders believed that the recent arrival of European craftsmen had made slaves work all the harder. "They do much more work now," he said, "as they are stimulated by competition with the Europeans; they have become both more handy and more industrious."[70]

In his testimony before the commissioners, a member of the Burgher Senate spoke of the wages that the town offered for skilled and unskilled slaves. "Good working" slave laborers drew R.18 a month. Slave masons could earn twice as much—between R.25 and R.40 monthly. Skilled slaves, he said, turned over to their masters about R.1.5 in hire money each working day. Though the sums are obviously awkward to reconcile, the thrust of his testimony indicated that slave artisans turned a profit for both themselves and their masters. Wages in the village of Graaff-Reinet, far to the east of Cape Town, were much the same. A slave laborer earned between R.10 and R.12 a month, a mason, between R.30 and R.40.[71] Slave artisans sometimes supplemented their incomes by teaching others their crafts. A Cape Town slave tailor named Arial (or Ariab) once collected R.30 from Lodewyk Andriessen, a white man, for "having instructed him in the trade of Tailor."[72]

The parliamentary commissioners heard evidence that allowed them to conclude that the owners of the "most skilful" slaves permitted them "to carry on Trades on their own account, and to reside in houses apart from their masters, paying them a monthly sum for the indulgence."[73] John Cannon, a Cape Town builder, told the commissioners that these men were "generally married, and live in houses hired by themselves; sometimes at the house where their Wives reside. When they hire themselves [that is, when they moved from one job to another], the Owner is not consulted."[74] These slaves enjoyed relatively autonomous lives, with the harsh realities of soul murder and social death held at bay, at least temporarily. But it was easy to fail to make ends meet and fall back into a more complete slavery. Adam, a slave carpenter, just managed to avoid returning to his master when he fell about R.66 (nearly £5) behind in the rent that he paid for his lodgings.[75]

Though the slavery reform laws of the 1820s and 1830s had made the personal property of the slaves more secure,[76] little had been done to regulate the relations between slaves who hired themselves out and their owners. The relationships were essentially improvised, and it cannot be surprising that they were often contentious. The case of Adriaan, a Cape Town slave, is an example. Owned by Dirk Sandenburgh, a minor whose property was under the guardianship of his mother, the widow Sandenburgh, Adriaan had hired himself out as a coachman, a skilled domestic servant. He paid his mistress R.20 a month in "hire money" and provided his own food, clothing, and shelter. Adriaan felt, however, that his mistress's demands were "rather exorbitant," since he was frequently "sickly." He asked the protector for help in convincing the widow Sandenburgh to accept a lesser sum. His mistress's elder son answered the protector's summons and argued that Adriaan was a very competent coachman. He had been allowed to hire out at his own request and earned between R.30 and R.40 a month. Sandenburgh added that his mother had recently spent R.85 on medical care for the slave, leading to his complete recovery. He said that, if Adriaan wished, his mother would take him back into her service and furnish him with food and clothing. Adriaan declined the offer, preferring to be a victim of extortion rather than return to conventional slavery.[77]

Money was a constant worry for slave and apprentice artisans, who often found it hard to collect debts. This was the case for a Cape Town mason-slave, Salie. He was part Jan Andries Horak's large slaveholding, which was later controlled by Horak's widow. There were fifty-four Horak slaves, twenty-one of them adult males. Among the men were a shoemaker, a carpenter, a cabinetmaker, and six masons. Salie was the youngest of the masons, and it is possible that one of the older men taught him his trade.[78] He apparently learned well. By 1833 he was acting as a building contractor, entering into agreements with whites not simply to perform masonry work but also to supply the necessary craftsmen. One of his customers once refused to pay his bill because Salie had failed to send "the regular number of Masons" to a construction project. On another occasion, he sought the help of the protector of slaves protector in collecting R.201 (£15) that the socially prominent Pieter Laurens Cloete owed him for "masonry work."[79] The sums of money with which Salie dealt were unusually large, but not unheard of. Piet, a slave shoemaker in the village of Graaff-Reinet, resorted to the law in an attempt to collect the R.107 that a white shoemaker owed him for a consignment of leather.[80] Similarly, Martinius, a slave cooper, once asked the protector for help in collecting R.57 owed to him by a Mr. Jeary.[81]

The skills that fortunate slave and apprentice possessed allowed them to reduce the physical and psychological costs of slavery in a variety of ways. The protector of slaves may have put it too strongly when he said of a slave tailor that he lived "as a free person."[82] But he was right to contrast the lives of slave artisans with those of the majority. With their earnings, many artisans were able to rent rooms or apartments and to establish a life relatively independent of their masters and mistresses. Some escaped slavery altogether by purchasing their freedom. All drew a sense of self-confidence and pride from the expertise with which they plied their trades.

A slave artisan's pride is evident in a protector's report about a slave cooper who felt that his master had slighted him by hiring a white man to do work that had previously been his and by assigning him to tasks that were beneath his dignity. Maart, the protector recorded, said that he was "a Cooper but his Master made him feed the pigs, saying that he was not fit to work at his trade—his Master then employed one Coetzee as a Cooper but has now turned away the said Coetzee and wants him to work at his trade which he is not inclined to do."[83] An apprentice who worked as a blacksmith also demonstrated a self-confidence that his skills had given him. He asked a special justice to release him from his current master and find him one worthy of his talents. "It was the fault of my Master," he said, "that I did not improve in my trade as Blacksmith—Because my Master had not custom enough."[84]

J. H. Hammond, a wealthy American slave owner, would certainly have understood the irritation that slave craftsmen such as these must have caused their masters. "Whenever a slave is made a mechanic," he wrote, "he is more than half freed, and soon becomes, as we too well know, and all history attests, with rare exceptions, the most corrupt and turbulent of his class."[85] Corruption and turbulence might also be called pride and self-confidence, which contradicted the degradation of soul murder and social death. They were traits any slave could possess, given the proper circumstances.[86] Circumstances favored fortunate slaves, the artisans whose self-respect had its source in the skills they possessed and the psychological and physical autonomy that those skills allowed them to create for themselves.

Frederick Douglass, a former slave and a leading American abolitionist, once claimed that life as an urban slave in Baltimore, even "when most oppressive, was a paradise [compared to the] plantation existence" that he had experienced earlier in life.[87] Urban slaves at the Cape would have endorsed his view. Cape Town slaves and apprentices of every station—domestic servants, coolies, hawkers, woodchoppers, and craftsmen—preferred city to country. For most, work in the city was no less strenuous than on the farms, and violent discipline was often a fact of life. But slavery in the city was better because of the autonomy that many slaves enjoyed and the wide range of social contacts that they experienced. Most town slaves exercised a mobility that allowed them and other members of the urban working class to create communities that were relatively independent of their masters.

A notable minority of city slaves labored in occupations that allowed them to achieve an especially high degree of physical and emotional autonomy. Many coolies, woodchoppers, hawkers, and artisans worked outside the immediate supervision of a master or overseer. Within the constraints of satisfying their masters' demands for hire money or sales receipts, they commonly found their own employment and determined the pace at which they labored. The most fortunate of the urban slaves and apprentices secured employment, housing, food, and clothing without their masters' interference. They remained slaves—something the payment of hire money emphasized—but they were no longer their masters' dependents. They experienced much of the independence and responsibility that came with freedom, and they escaped slavery's most debilitating effects. Slavery in the city was slavery, nonetheless. Even the fortunate slaves could not be sure that either chance or their masters would not reduce them to the circumstances of common laborers. The line between fortune and misery was always thin, and urban city slaves sometimes became rural slaves overnight, not out of choice but because their masters demanded it.

CHAPTER 5

"An Unprofitable Waste, Unfit for Culture"

Slavery on the Farms

[When] he has made a garden for himself in one place he is obliged to leave it without reaping the fruit of it.

—PROTECTOR OF SLAVES, DESCRIBING THE FATE OF WELKOM, A SLAVE, 1833

William Wilberforce Bird, formerly a member of the colonial civil service, knew that the state of the Cape in 1822 was not what many in Britain believed it to be. Cabinet ministers, parliamentarians, and well-wishers of all sorts fondly imagined that because the Cape was "Placed in the temperate zone" and "enjoy[ed] a delicious climate[,]" the agricultural pursuits of the recent influx of British immigrants would flourish.[1] This, Bird insisted, was wrong. "Circumstances and restrictions," he wrote, "[will] . . . set at a distance, if not wholly to disappoint, such expectations."[2] While it is not entirely clear which "circumstances and restrictions" Bird had in mind, others did not hesitate to point a finger or two. British writers, especially, had already developed a pair of conflicting interpretations of the Cape's agricultural torpor. The first lamented the moral deficiencies of the Boers, the second the infertile land and merciless climate.

The avatar of the moral declension school of thought was John (later Sir John) Barrow, who served as Governor Macartney's private secretary during the first British occupation and published a lengthy survey of the colony in 1801. A tireless promoter of empire and exploration, he went on to prominence as second secretary to the admiralty and cofounder of the Royal Geographical Society. In his account of the Cape, he attempted to explain the colony's agricultural backwardness. He conceded that a "very great portion" of the colony was "an unprofitable waste, unfit for any sort of culture, or even to be employed as pasture." Yet this was only part of the story. A more important cause of the Cape's malaise was the indolence of the Dutch farmers. Despite the blessings of what he somewhat inconsistently referred to as "the fine climate of the Cape," the Boers engaged "in little or no manual labour." "It is very remarkable," he wrote, that the same people, who are celebrated in Europe for their industry and frugality, should become, in all their colonies, the most indolent and prodigal of all other people." The problem was slavery. No sooner could a colonist afford a slave, Barrow claimed, than he purchased one and ceased to break a sweat on his own behalf.[3] Barrow's analysis, with its appeals to British chauvinism and antislavery sentiments, proved to be highly influential. By 1820, it had become something of a convention to argue that slavery had turned the Afrikaners into a nation of sloths and to speak of colonial farming methods as "rather the rude effort of a savage."[4] This was uncharitable, to say the least, and at least two Britons who had settled for a time at the Cape dissented vigorously.

George Thompson, a Cape Town merchant and sometime explorer, scolded Barrow for his "overcharged picture of the Cape-Dutch boors [Boers]." Barrow, he thought, had understandably seen them through the eyes of a servant of a conquering state and had consequently drawn "an unfair representation of the colonists." They were not as "savage, indolent, and unprincipled" as Barrow had made them out to be. The Boers, Thompson argued, were in fact rather less primitive than the English-speaking, backcountry settlers of North America. They had done well for themselves, despite the disadvantageous position in which geography, the corrupt Dutch regime, and the malevolent influence of slavery had placed them.[5] J. W. D. Moodie, who had tried his hand at farming in the colony and failed, also believed that it had been "too much the habit of [his] countrymen to indulge in an undue contempt of the mode of cultivation practised by the Dutch colonists, before they have been sufficiently acquainted with the peculiar circumstances of climate and situation by which their customs in this regard are regulated." Writers, he felt, ought "to entertain more respect for the established usages of the country."[6]

Moodie and Thompson were more right than wrong. Both men correctly asserted that Cape settlers had adapted well to their environment. In response to the soils and weather, they had adopted distinctly un-European farming methods, often drawing on the knowledge and experience of their African servants and neighbors. In response to their need for large numbers of malleable workers, they had adopted slavery and other forms of forced labor.

The northern European farming techniques familiar to writers such as Barrow were unsuited to the Cape. The colony's agricultural seasons—the reverse, of course, of those in the Northern Hemisphere—were quite different from those in Europe. Winters in the arable farming districts of the western Cape were not so much frigid as wet; summers were both hot and dry. In the cattle country of the north and east, there was little moisture in any season. The climate decreed that productive activities on the wine, wheat, and cattle farms would march to their own distinctive rhythms, the one never coinciding with the others. Within this diversity, however, there were several characteristics that virtually all farms shared.

Most importantly, all sectors of the farming economy relied on some form of forced labor in their operations. On the wine and wheat farms, the workers were predominantly slaves and apprentices. On the cattle farms, Khoisan, Bastaard Hottentots, and Bantu-speaking Africans, who had entered the colonial economy under duress as settlers conquered and commandeered their lands and livestock and fragmented their societies, outnumbered slaves and apprentices. All farmers, as well, were tied to the colonial market. Though many grew much of their own food and fashioned many of their own clothes, they depended on the market to furnish necessities, such as guns and ammunition, and luxuries, such as coffee and sugar. Their desire for these goods and their obligation to pay taxes forced farmers to produce for the market.[7]

Slaves and farm servants also had much in common, living and working under similar conditions, often performing the same tasks and sharing food, lodging, and sexual intimacies. The forms of discipline and supervision that they endured were similar as well. But because they ordinarily had less freedom of movement and lived in regions that were relatively sparsely populated, their range of social contacts was narrower than that of slaves and servants in Cape Town, and the communities that they formed were smaller and less coherent than those in the city. It was much more difficult for slaves on the farms to escape social death's violence and alienation. Not without reason did they prefer town to country.[8] There were, however, fortunate slaves and apprentices on the farms. Especially on the cattle farms, good order and discipline required slave owners to rely on incentives as much as on the whip. Some slaves in the country achieved a considerable degree of autonomy, while others accumulated significant property holdings that in rare instances allowed them to buy freedom for themselves or family members. As in the city, fortunate slaves were able to cheat social death.

Grapes and Grain

Although the wine farms of the southwestern Cape dominated the local economy during the first decades of the nineteenth century, the colony had a well-deserved reputation for producing abominable wines. The brandies, produced in small quantities, were even worse. All, in the words of one English visitor, were "very much inferior to those of Europe."[9] Most Britons agreed. The "multiplicity of bad wines, sent from the Cape," had, said another observer, "sunk the whole" in the British market.[10] During the years that Cape wine entered the home market cheaply, British wine merchants commonly used Cape vintages to dilute better, but more expensive European wine.[11] The only Cape wines generally held in high esteem were those from the estates of Constantia. These vineyards, lying about eight miles south of Cape Town along the peninsula, produced a "sweet, luscious, and excellent wine" for which there was great demand.[12]

Slaves performed most of the labor on the wine farms of the colony; free black, Khoisan, and Bastaard Hottentot workers were comparatively rare. In the Stellenbosch district, for instance, the average wine farmer owned sixteen slaves, twice the number of slaves in the typical Cape slave-owning household.[13] Several farmers spoke of the economics of wine making in 1824 before a visiting parliamentary commission of inquiry. Peter Lawrence Cloete said that he employed twelve to fifteen of his forty to fifty adult slaves in his vineyard, where they tended about 140,000 vines.[14] The other slaves watched his herds and presumably tilled his grain fields.[15] Another winegrower, Hendrik Oostwald Eksteen, calculated that he required one worker for every 10,000 vines, approximately the same number of vines per worker as Cloete.[16] James Christiaan Faure, who owned both a small wine farm and a grain farm, moved his slaves between the farms as needed. He guessed that his 23,000 vines demanded the labor of four adult slaves.[17]

Few wine farmers relied on slave labor exclusively. Faure, for instance, had two "Hottentots" working on his farms. Though they were classed as "free Labourers," their liberty was quite compromised. Faure paid them no wages since they were "young Apprentices, born on the Farm," and he refused to allow them to seek other employment.[18] Eksteen, who owned about thirty slaves, said that he retained "one or two free People," but did not indicate whether they were Khoisan, free black, Prize Negroes, or whites, or whether they were paid.[19] Unlike slaves or Faure's "apprentices," most Khoisan in the western Cape earned cash wages. In 1830, for example, the civil commissioner of Stellenbosch reported that the going rate for Khoisan laborers was 6s. a month with board and clothing, 12s. with food alone.[20] Cloete was a rare winegrower who employed a sizeable number of "Hottentot" servants. He had "about twenty" Khoisan on his farm whom he thought were "indispensable as herdsmen and waggon-drivers." He did not use them as fieldhands or in the vineyard, however, because they could not "be brought to enter willingly in the hard labours of the fields."[21]

The work of cultivating the vines and producing wine and brandy exhausted the energy of a small number of slaves and apprentices throughout the year and of a much larger force during the harvest. During the winter, slaves pruned and planted the vines; in summer, they irrigated the vineyards and cut back the young shoots. Much of this work required heavy digging under the blazing sun or in cold rain. Because the vines grew along the ground "like currant bushes," rather than on trellises, as in Europe, it was almost literally backbreaking labor.[22] During the harvest in late summer and early autumn, wine farmers often supplemented their own workforce with slaves hired from neighboring grain farms. There was, in fact, a "regular interchange" of slaves between the wine farms and the wheat farms, since periods of peak demand for labor on these farms dovetailed.[23] After picking the grapes, slaves extracted the juice and put it into casks to age. Few wine presses existed in the colony, and travelers differed on whether the noxious quality of Cape wines should be attributed to the unwashed feet of the "negro slave men" who crushed the grapes or to the stalks and stems that went into the vat with the grapes.[24] Slaves or Khoisan servants took the wine to market on wagons designed for the purpose, no earlier than the following spring.[25]

Slaves and apprentices performed every chore associated with the making of wine and brandy, from the least demanding to the most delicate. Wine farmers classified most of the slaves on their farms as "labourers," as did wheat and cattle farmers. But especially on the larger wine estates, there was a significant number of highly skilled slave workers. For example, in 1816 Groot Constantia, the farm that produced the finest Cape wines, employed slaves as "waggoners," carpenters, tailors, coopers, masons, and shoemakers, as well as laborers. Some of the skilled slaves, the wagon drivers and coopers, would have been directly or indirectly engaged in wine production. These craftsmen, however, were not the most important slaves on the estate. Three slave "vintagers" seem to have been responsible for ensuring the quality of the wines. Two of these men were in their fifties; one, perhaps still in training, was thirty.[26] Lambertus Johannes Colyn, another prominent wine farmer, also owned a "vintager," as well as craftsmen and common laborers.[27] September, a slave belonging to Joseph de Kock, distilled the brandy made from his master's grapes.[28] While it is likely that the skills that slave vintagers and distillers possessed gave them a sense of accomplishment that partially eroded the degradation that accompanied slavery, the sort of autonomy that Cape Town slave artisans enjoyed was beyond their grasp. The nature of their employment tied them to their masters' farms.

Slave women on the wine farms were less likely than men to be found in the vineyards, but, as was always the practice at the Cape, the farmers did not hesitate to assign women slaves to field work as needed. While this was especially the case at harvest and planting, some women performed heavy, unskilled labor as a matter of routine. Mary Raynor argues that the daily use of slave women in field labor was a nineteenth-century phenomenon, as the demand for labor soared during the wine boom of the 1810s and 1820s.[29] By the 1830s, the presence of women workers in the vineyards was unremarkable. For instance, when the assistant protector of slaves in Stellenbosch heard that Clara, a slave, worked in the vineyards with several male slaves, neither he, his clerk, nor any of the witnesses registered surprise.[30]

Like the winegrowers, Cape grain farmers had developed techniques well suited to the climate, soils, and labor supply of the colony. In a climate such as the Cape's, grain farmers had "to seize the opportunity of ploughing when the ground [had] been softened by recent rains." This was no easy task. Because land was cheap, the soil relatively infertile, manuring expensive, and rainfall light, farmers practiced *ex*tensive agriculture not the *in*tensive farming familiar to Europeans. The broad fields required a plow that was capable of turning large volumes of soil during the short time the ground was soft enough to work. As a result, Cape grain farms were distinguished by the "huge size of their ploughs" and by the teams of twelve to sixteen oxen needed to pull them. The immense plowshare cut a wide furrow, allowing the farmers and their slaves to move quickly through the fields. The wide share had the secondary advantage of suppressing the grass and weeds that choked the grains. Plowing was often a three-person operation—the first worker at the plow, a second driving the oxen with a whip, and a third leading the first pair of oxen with a rein.[31]

Threshing techniques reminded several English visitors of the methods employed by the ancient Israelites.[32] In an elevated location on the farm, slaves first marked out a circular threshing floor, fifteen or twenty paces across. They then built a low, solid wall around the perimeter, leveled the ground, and covered it with a mixture of dung and water to hold down the dust. When the floor dried—it would have become harder than the ground underneath it—they laid sheaves of grain along the inner edge of the wall and turned horses loose in the enclosure. A slave standing the midst of them wielding a whip drove the horses around the circle at a trot. Periodically, other slaves turned the sheaves while the horses rested. After perhaps an hour the slaves would lead the horses out of the enclosure and throw the broken sheaves gently into the air, allowing the wind to separate the wheat from the chaff. The threshing would not yet have been complete. The horses were driven back into the circle, and the process was repeated until the grain had been fully separated from the waste. Inevitably, parts of the threshing floor were broken up and mixed with the grain. This was less of a problem in the eastern districts, where the bits of clay and dung could easily be picked out of the grain. In the western Cape, however, the sandy soil of the floor gave off fine grains of sand that could not be gotten rid of. The result was "exceedingly gritty" bread.[33]

Even though women slaves and apprentices were most commonly associated with domestic service, they routinely labored in the grain fields with men. Though they performed the same work at the same pace as the men, they sometimes suffered in ways that men did not. Child care, for which slave and apprentice women were responsible, presented special problems and was a particular burden for the mothers of infants.[34] They could not take their children with them to the fields, yet young children had to be nursed periodically during the day. One mother, Sara, a slave in the Stellenbosch district, was once working in the fields when Griet, a Khoisan woman, called her "to give her Child the breast." At the house Sara found all the farm's children quarreling and tried to quiet them, all the while attempting to nurse her baby. Her master, who overheard the uproar, accused her of making "a great noise" and ordered her back to the field. Sara refused, saying that her child had not been fed. Her master then grabbed her by the arm and led her to the wagon house, where he locked her in stocks for insolence.[35]

The farm's work, especially reaping and threshing, was labor intensive, and grain farmers put whatever labor they could find to work. Many
farmers employed Khoisan servants as well as slaves. Khoisan laborers
were most common in the eastern Cape, but grain farmers in the west
also employed them as wagon drivers and as field hands at harvest.[36]
Khoisan in Worcester earned between 8s. and £4 10s. a year in 1830, de-
pending on whether or not they supplied their own food. In Uitenhage,
the scale was more compressed—from £1 2s. 1d. to £1 6s. a year.[37] Other
farmers hired white laborers, though in small numbers and without
much success.[38] Sometimes the only nonslave labor on a farm came from
the slave owners themselves or their families. On a farm in the Somerset district, for instance, Jacob Lotter drove his father's plow, one of his
father's slaves leading the oxen.[39]

The grain farmers' greatest demand for labor came at harvest. The
slaves were organized into teams, working under close supervision at the
same task, moving systematically through the fields cutting the grain.
The gangs were largely composed of slaves, sometimes augmented by
Khoisan workers.[40] Especially in the major grain-growing regions of the
Cape and Stellenbosch districts, the grain farmers' personal slaves and
hired Khoisan were often too small a workforce to bring in the crop
quickly enough to avoid losses. As noted above, the farmers found a partial solution in the wine country, regularly hiring slaves from the winegrowers. In 1826, one Stellenbosch grain farmer reported that it had "always been the custom in the Colony" for grain growers "to pay in Corn"
for the use of winemakers' slaves. Payment in kind allowed the grain
growers to avoid depleting their scarce reserves of cash, while the wine
farmers accumulated a store of wheat from which they fed their slaves.[41]

As in the wine country, slaves and apprentices on the grain farms
worked beside people whose color, legal status, customs, and sometimes
language were different from their own. At times they moved from farm
to farm, hired out by their owners. While their worlds extended beyond
the boundaries of the farm on which they lived, they enjoyed less mobility and autonomy than fortunate slaves in Cape Town and on the cattle farms. Hiring out was uncommon; living independently outside of
the master's household was unheard of. Working-class communities
were hard to build. Of all the slaves in the Cape Colony, those on the
wine and wheat farms were least able to fight off the ravages of social
death.

Cattle Country

Few cattle farmers owned as much property or lived in as much comfort as successful wine or wheat farmers. Yet George Thompson argued in 1827 that they were in many ways the most economically secure farmers in the colony. Twenty years earlier, wine makers had clearly been "the most thriving class of agriculturalists; next to them the corn [grain] growers; and the graziers [had] placed lowest on the scale." A variety of factors, Thompson believed, had "combined to modify, if not to reverse this gradation." Most importantly, grain growers and especially wine farmers received a poor return on the capital they had invested in slaves. Stockfarmers, owning relatively few slaves, were not encumbered in this way. What they earned, they kept.[42]

During the late 1810s and early 1820s, winegrowers had indeed borrowed heavily, investing in slaves, vineyards, and land in an effort to cash in on the booming British demand for Cape wines. Wine farmers had put by far the most money in slaves. As noted in chapter 2, when the imperial preference that had underwritten the boom ended in 1825, the bottom fell out of the market for Cape wines. Wine growers found themselves burdened with slave capital on which they could not obtain an adequate return. Thompson did not contend that the wine farmers had become poor or that they lived in squalor, but their wealth was not increasing, while that of the cattle farmers was, he argued, precisely because they did not rely on slaves. There were, as he admitted, other reasons for the cattle country's relative prosperity: stockfarmers bought comparatively few consumer goods, paid little in taxes, and had almost unlimited access to cheap land. But his central point was the cattlemen's greater reliance on Khoisan labor allowed them to avoid debt and utilize their workers more efficiently.[43]

Settlers had depended on the Khoisan for both livestock and labor since the beginning of white settlement at the Cape. The ancestors of the colonial herds were the cattle that the settlers acquired from the Khoisan by trade, raids, and open warfare. Colonial sheep—raised for meat, not wool—were a hybrid of indigenous and Dutch breeds and had also been obtained by fair means and foul.[44] As the Khoisan lost their sheep, their cattle, and their land, they simultaneously lost their independence. Many had little choice but to starve or enter the colonial society as subordinate farm laborers. Because of their centuries-long experience with livestock, the Khoisan were highly skilled at livestock management and quickly learned how to drive draft animals at the plow and the wagon; nor did they have to be taught the arts of milking, butchering, tanning, rendering fat, and crafting leather whips, thongs, and bags. They had long possessed those skills.[45] Because the Khoisan understood the mysteries of the changing seasons and pastures and knew where to find water in the arid land, they became their masters' tutors, teaching them how to survive on the South African veld.[46]

Although Khoisan remained the largest element in the workforce of the cattle farms, there were several thousand slaves in cattle country. Slaves and apprentices were, in fact, often the most trusted servants on the cattle farms. Job, whose story introduced the preceding chapter, lived on a mixed cattle and grain farm and was "the Chief Slave of his Master's indoors."[47] Some slave owners trusted their slaves not only to supervise other slaves and servants but also to trade on their behalf, moving about the countryside with a considerable degree of autonomy, often carrying firearms. Barend Swartz, a cattle dealer, sent his apprentice, Dampie, to Fort Beaufort from Graaff-Reinet (about a hundred miles) with nearly three hundred head of sheep in his care. Accompanying Dampie were three other servants, who were to assist him. His master gave Dampie a rifle "to protect the property entrusted to him."[48]

The degree of mobility and autonomy that Dampie enjoyed was by no means unusual. The nature of stockfarming in southern Africa required cattle and their keepers to travel long distances in search of water and pasture, often spending weeks, even months, away from the master's farm. These arrangements became so commonplace that slaves and apprentices might live unsupervised for weeks on end. Africa, a slave, once told the protector of slaves in Graaff-Reinet a story that illustrates the point.

Africa's master, a farmer named Gerhardus Osthuisen, had decided that he no longer needed Africa's services. He had six "Orlam Bushmen" (that is, semi-enslaved Khoisan) in his employ, a large enough crew to manage his herds and flocks.[49] Osthuisen sent Africa, with his wife and children but otherwise alone, to Graaff-Reinet, a six-day's journey by foot, to be sold by a Mr. Ardendoff, a butcher and trader. On Osthuisen's behalf, Ardendoff asked R.1,000 (£75) for Africa, but could find no buyers. He took Africa with him when he crossed the colonial boundary at the Orange River on a trading mission, leaving Africa's family behind. Africa soon parted company with Ardendoff, however, because of a quarrel he had with one of the butcher's servants. Before he left, he exchanged some of his clothes for four oxen and, with Ardendoff's blessing, set out to return to the Cape colony. On his way back, Africa met several Boers driving herds before them. None of them attempted to apprehend him as a runaway; rather, they offered him food. Nearing the colony, he bartered the oxen for a horse and returned to Graaff-Reinet. Africa stayed at Ardendoff's home until the butcher returned from beyond the border and then asked him what he and his family ought to do. Ardendoff told him to return to his master's farm, but provided no food for the journey. The family arrived at Osthuisen's farm desperately hungry. They had subsisted on the road by begging food from the white farmers who passed by on their way to pastures beyond the border. Africa mentioned that his family had nothing to eat because he "had no gun to shoot game." Having found no one at the farm, Africa and his family returned to Graaff-Reinet to ask the protector of slaves for help.[50]

Africa's story underscores the autonomy and mobility that he and other cattle country slaves might routinely possess. His master trusted him to take himself and his family to Graaff-Reinet for sale, and Ardendoff, who was to sell him, did not fear that he would run away when he left his service to return to Graaff-Reinet. Africa twice bartered property of his own for that of others and was apparently accustomed to the procedure. He was familiar with both guns and horses and regretted that he did not have a rifle with him on his return journey to Osthiusen's farm. Africa's routine mobility, his experience with horses, trading, and guns, and the trust that his master and his erstwhile employer placed in him made his experience of slavery quite different from that of most other Cape Colony slaves.[51] There was a significant number of slaves in the cattle country who lived as Africa did, however. As was the case with the fortunate slaves of Cape Town, the circumstances of their lives were little different from those of the free servants on settler farms. Their relative autonomy, their family bonds and community ties, and their modest property holdings meant that they experienced slavery differently from their less-favored brethren. Most crucially, they were better prepared to ward off the ravages of social death.

A Few More Fortunate Slaves

In Cape Town, as we have seen, fortunate slaves hired themselves out, paid for their own lodgings, and created relatively autonomous lives. On the farms, hiring out was almost unheard of. But many slaves and apprentices did raise garden crops on plots supplied by their masters, and the most privileged were able to pasture livestock of their own on their masters' lands. Slaves bartered, sold, loaned, and traded the produce of their gardens and the increase of their flocks and herds. With the proceeds they fed and clothed themselves and their families and bought goods that their masters would not supply, up to and including their freedom.[52] These privileges allowed the most fortunate slaves to live, in effect, as labor tenants. Their owners, that is, gave them land on which to raise crops or pasture livestock, in exchange for the labor that they performed. Much of the time the lives of these fortunate slaves were indistinguishable from those of the free servants with whom they lived and worked.

The slaves were, of course, a distinct class, and they suffered disabilities specific to themselves: the law defined them more as property than as people; they were subject to harsh legal coercions; they and members of their families were subject to sale; and their rights were limited, even after the reforms. The realities of social death never entirely disappeared. But the law had always recognized that "conscientious masters" commonly allowed their slaves to accumulate property and that the slaves were "at liberty to dispose of [their property] as they please."[53] The reform laws of the 1820s further protected the slaves' property rights.[54] Thus they allowed masters and slaves to work out a compromise. Slave owners permitted fortunate slaves to live almost as though they were free servants, not out of the kindness of their hearts, but in order to control their troublesome property more effectively.

Arrangements of this sort have been common in modern slave societies because both masters and slaves had something to gain.[55] In his survey of the historiography of American slavery, Peter J. Parish insists that rewards and incentives, similar to those just described, played an essential role in maintaining discipline. He argues that because the lash and the difficulty of escape severely narrowed the slaves' options, they were "receptive to the idea of making the best of their lot" by accepting the privileges and indulgences their masters and mistresses offered. Both the slaves and the slave owners benefitted: "It made for a quieter life. The relentless use of unbridled repressive force would have been a heavy drain on the owners as well as an appalling ordeal for the slaves." Parish cautions that it was "only the presence or the threat of coercion which permitted the resort to persuasion": "Coercion could be relaxed if, and only as long as, gentler measures worked."[56]

In many ways, circumstances were much the same at the Cape. On a foundation of coercive violence, colonial slave owners built a superstructure of rewards and incentives.[57] Though this outcome was the same in both the Cape and the American South, the struggles between the slaves and slave owners that produced it were not. At the Cape, particularly in the rural districts, the slaves' lives were not closed by the near impossibility of successful escape, but, as we shall see in the next chapter, opened by the relative ease with which they could run away. The privileges that slave owners offered can be seen as bribes that slaves extracted in order to keep them on the farms.

Although the privileges that fortunate slaves enjoyed were commonplace, one protector of slaves in the eastern Cape thought that most slave owners were in principle "opposed to the acquisition of property by slaves," fearing that it would weaken rather than strengthen their hold over them, "render[ing] the slave[s] independent."[58] This attitude parallels the apprehensions slave owners expressed over the fortunate slaves of Cape Town. Slave owners adopted the system of incentives reluctantly, and slaves accepted them grudgingly. Rewards and incentives were not freedom, but the sense of autonomy that the acquisition of small amounts of property created was more attractive to most than running away into the arid expanses of the east.

A significant number of slaves and apprentices benefitted from the privileges that their owners offered. The principal protector of slaves once noted that "The Slaves in the Country have their little gardens out of which they raise much [*sic*] vegetables . . . which They sell."[59] "Industrious Slaves," he elsewhere remarked, earned as much as £5 to £15 a year "by cultivating Potatoes, Pumpkins, Melons, Beans, Peas, Indian corn, etc." and carrying them to market in their master's wagons.[60] He regretted that some of the slaves spent their earnings "Drinking and Gambling."[61] In the "far [eastern] Districts almost all well behaved and Provident Slaves breed goats and Sheep, and . . . not a few of Them possess Horses and other Cattle to a larger amount which Their Owners allow to run and Graze on their Extensive Cattle Farms."[62] Though the protector did not indicate what proportion of slaves were "well behaved and Provident," the records indicate that it was substantial.

Garden plots were not an unalloyed blessing. In fact, it is precisely because such privileges sometimes caused tensions between masters and slaves that we know something about how the system worked. Aggrieved slaves and apprentices took their complaints to protectors and special justices, and there they entered the colonial records. In one case, Isaac van der Merwe, a farmer in the Worcester district, allowed his apprentices to raise crops for themselves, and they, in turn, marketed their produce and spent or saved their earnings, just as labor tenants might have done. Van der Merwe had apparently given a plot to each of the twenty-five apprentices on his farm, and he allowed them to use his wagons to take their produce to the village of Worcester for sale. One of his apprentices claimed that his garden allowed him to earn R.40 (£3) a year, with which he bought clothes. Another said that the proceeds from his plot brought him R.20 (£1 10s.) and that he purchased thread and soap for himself, as well as clothing. But while this arrangement seems to have suited van der Merwe—his apprentices largely fed and clothed themselves—it did not entirely please the apprentices. And it appalled his sons.[63]

One of the van der Merwe apprentices told the special justice that during the previous fourteen years he had received very little clothing from his master—just two pairs of pants, three shirts, and a jacket. His irritation stemmed from his knowledge that van der Merwe had both the customary obligation and the legal duty to cloth him properly. While the apprentices may have enjoyed the opportunity to market produce on their own behalf, this man at least resented the resulting abrogation of one of his master's obligations. On the other hand, van der Merwe's sons claimed that the privileges that their father had allowed his servants had given them airs. The relative autonomy and freedom from coercive discipline that the apprentices enjoyed had loosened the restraints on their behavior. They were often "very insolent," the sons claimed, and when they returned to the farm in their master's wagons, they came back drunk.[64]

Welcome though gardens usually were, slaves could not always be sure that the energy they expended on their crops would be rewarded. The protector of slaves for the eastern district recorded the grievance of Welkom, the slave of a Graaff-Reinet master. He complained, wrote the protector, that "his Master is in the habit of hiring him out with his wife and children, for one month to one person and two months to another, in Consequence of which[, when] he has made a garden for himself in one place he is obliged to leave it without reaping the fruit of it."[65]

At other times, disputes over the ownership of market produce led to trouble between masters and slaves. In the Stellenbosch district, Isaak, Pieter Cillier's wagon driver, charged his master with beating him "for having put some Chilies upon a wagon proceeding to Cape Town." Isaak claimed that his master had accused him of stealing the peppers; he insisted that he had grown them himself. Cillier admitted to having whipped Isaak, but explained that his neighbors had told him that his slaves were stealing fruit and vegetables from their gardens and taking them to Cape Town in his wagons for sale. In response, Cilliers had ordered his slaves not to carry personal property in his wagons. On the day that he beat Isaak, he had dispatched him to Cape Town with a wagonload of wine. He heard the wagon stop just after Isaak drove off and went to investigate. He found Isaak loading a bag of "chilies, onions, and other articles" onto the wagon. Cilliers did not know who owned the chilies and did not particularly care. He punished Isaak, he said, for disobeying his order not to use the wagon on his own account.[66]

Slaves' garden plots were so common a feature at the Cape that it is likely that conflict was the exception rather than the rule. Present's case provides an example. He lived on his master's farm in the Graaff-Reinet district with his wife, a Khoisan woman, and their children. His master provided the family with "all food and other necessaries" as well as "land to cultivate." Present had managed to turn vegetables into livestock by bartering the produce of his garden for sheep and cattle. In the eight years during which his current master had owned him, he had accumulated two cows, two calves, forty sheep, twenty goats, and a horse.[67] Present was by no means the only slave to have a livestock holding of this size.

On the stock farms of the eastern Cape, slaves and apprentices commonly owned cattle and horses, and sometimes several dozen smaller animals such as sheep and goats.[68] Jeptha, a slave on a Graaff-Reinet stock farm, acquired, over the course of a decade, fifty-one goats, thirty-one sheep, ten head of cattle, and four horses.[69] November, a slave belonging to the estate of the recently deceased Cobus van Heerden of Graaff-Reinet, owned even more stock, but his story emphasizes how difficult it was for slaves to accumulate property, even when they did so under their masters' sanction.

In 1833, November owned 254 sheep and goats and 9 head of cattle.[70] He told the protector of slaves in Graaff-Reinet that he had earned, bought, or bred all of his animals. His livestock grazed on his master's land, intermingled with his master's flock and herds. All the servants on the farm, slave and free, owned some stock, and they all apparently ran their animals with those of their master. To distinguish the stock that belonged to each of them, van Heerden and his servants clipped their animals' ears in distinctive patterns. Periodically, all involved gathered to count the holdings of each individual. At the time that November spoke to the protector, he, another slave, and his master's son had made the most recent count of November's property, and they had agreed on the numbers. Trouble began for November after he successfully prosecuted his late master for having punished him "unjustly." Van Heerden was fined and apparently decided to recover his losses by stealing from his slave.[71] In the wake of his conviction, he sold or slaughtered one of November's cows and 50 of his sheep and goats, and he had "paid away in wages to the Hottentots Dragoon and Cout and the Mantatee September 12 Goats[,]" without compensating November for any of them.[72] An additional 35 of November's sheep and fifteen goats were missing. Van Heerden, November said, had gone so far as to alter the marks on some of the animals to match his own. Now van Heerden's widow refused to allow November to reclaim his livestock. The protector intervened on November's behalf. After a lengthy hearing, the widow van Heerden agreed to return all November's cattle to him "together with a Cow in lieu of that which was killed and 300 Sheep and goats." As November's case demonstrates, the slaves' hold on their property was tenuous. Slave owners who granted their slaves the privilege of owning herds and flocks did so half-heartedly.

The practice of allowing slaves to raise livestock was similar to the arrangements farmers made with African servants. Almost from the beginning of colonial agriculture, payment in kind had been a more important part of free laborers' incomes than cash wages. As early as 1695, the conquest of Khoisan lands and the subjugation of Khoisan societies had advanced far enough that some Khoisan had been forced to enter the colonial economy as farm laborers. Their masters might give them a small number of calves or lambs annually, plus tobacco, alcohol, and food, instead of paying wages. By the early nineteenth century, the practice of paying Khoisan servants in kind rather than cash was well established, especially in the eastern districts.[73] While some received monetary payment, a government report noted that in Uitenhage "the usual annual wages frequently consist of an ox, or a cow and calf, which are allowed to graze with the cattle of the farmer." The report added that "in this manner the Hottentots have in some instances been able to accumulate and to preserve the earnings of their labour."[74]

When Bantu-speakers entered the colonial economy, farmers reproduced the labor relations they had established with the Khoisan. Like other servants, they often lived on white farms as labor tenants. Eastern Cape farmers had begun to employ Xhosa workers in the late 1770s. The incorporation of Xhosa and other Bantu-speaking Africans, such as Tswana and the "Mantatees," into the settler economy as subordinate laborers accelerated as colonial military forces seized Africans'

land and legislation provided for the employment of these "native for-
eigners" as contractual workers. The ordinary payment for a year's labor
was one cow or its equivalent in smaller stock. The colonists offered
these terms because the shortage of labor was acute, cash scarce, and
Bantu-speaking African societies largely intact, making it difficult to attract workers.[75] Slaves and apprentices were well aware of the terms under which their comrades labored. Slaves who understood the ways
in which labor tenancy agreements worked did not hesitate to share
their knowledge with their friends. For example, Damon, a slave on a
farm in the Somerset district, once earned his master's wrath by telling "a Bechuana [Tswana] residing on the place that he might if he
chose do like other Bechuanas, earn Cattle, Sheep and Goats and select
a place for himself to live upon . . . that he might commence Farming
for himself."[76]

Slaves ordinarily received their livestock in the same way and at the
same time as the free workers on the farm. On one farm, the master's
sons rounded up the "Young cattle" once a year and the slaves and Khoisan laborers "claiming the Calves come forward and say which is theirs."
The sons marked the calves of each laborer by clipping its ears in a
unique pattern. These particular calves had come from the farm's herd,
but, on at least one earlier occasion, a slave and a Khoisan worker "returned from Kaffirland [Xhosa territory] with a troop of cattle," some of
which they distributed to their master's servants.[77] It is not clear whether
this episode was a legitimate trading expedition or a cattle raid. Both
were common events in the eastern Cape.[78] There were more exceptional ways in which livestock passed from master to servant: Isaac Pretorious, for example, once gave his slave Jephta six sheep in compensation for having broken his jaw.[79]

Slaves and apprentices who possessed livestock behaved no differently than the whites, Khoisan, and Xhosa around them; they bartered,
bought, and sold the animals and also lent them out. With the profits,
they purchased not merely commodities but sometimes freedom itself.
Adam, an apprentice employed by a Uitenhage district grain farmer, acquired cattle with the produce he grew in his garden. With the cattle he
purchased his freedom. Adam's master had given him land on which
he planted both a vegetable garden and a small vineyard. He marketed
his crop, and over the years he bought several oxen, two of which were
trained for the yoke and quite valuable. But his proudest possession was
his liberty. After selling some of the oxen, he bought his way out of apprenticeship several months before the apprenticeships of the former

slaves were due to expire.[80] Adam had not merely challenged social death or limited its impact; he had defeated it.

Cupido, a slave in the Somerset district, similarly wanted to buy his freedom. He told an assistant protector that he feared the consequences of his mistress's death. Her children had never treated him well, and he did not wish to be inherited by any of them. He owned nineteen head of cattle, he said, and had a claim of R.20 against one of his deceased mistress's sons. This, he hoped, would be enough to satisfy his mistress's heirs. When the protector approached family members with Cupido's offer, they agreed to consider the matter.[81] Sometimes, property-owning slaves paid for the freedom of family members, rather than themselves. Samson, a slave in the Somerset district, gave Anna Erasmus one cow and twenty-three sheep and goats; in return, Erasmus released Samson's wife, a Khoisan woman, from her labor contract.[82]

Slaves and apprentices tried in many ways to build up their holdings, but the deals that they made did not always go smoothly. After arguing with Jantje Keyser, a Khoisan, over the precise terms of a barter agreement, Isaac, a slave, took the case to an assistant protector for adjudication. Isaac claimed that Keyser had undertaken to give him a horse and other animals in return for two oxen and a cow. Keyser did not dispute the nature of the transaction, but he claimed that he had already delivered the horse and asked Isaac for more time to come up with the ten sheep that he still owed.[83]

Slaves and apprentices also dealt in cash, or tried to. Maria, a slave in the Albany district and one of the rare female slaves who owned livestock, went to an assistant protector of slaves in order to recover a debt. Piet Retief, soon to become one of the leaders of the Afrikaner exodus from the Cape Colony known as the Great Trek, owed her R.249 for the 141 sheep and thirty goats he had purchased from her. Maria told the protector that after eighteen months of "repeated applications for payment," Retief had yet to respond to her requests. Her master, Joseph van Dyk, supported her claim. He said that the animals "were bona fide her property" and produced a receipt Retief had signed acknowledging the debt.[84] It is not clear whether or not Retief ever paid Maria the money he owed her.

Like the other cattle-keeping peoples of southern Africa, both black and white, slaves entered into loan arrangements involving cattle. These agreements had long existed in southern Africa. Centuries before the arrival of the whites, more prosperous Khoikhoi had "often lent out their cattle to poor clients who herded them in return for a percentage of their yield."[85] Similarly, among Bantu-speaking Africans "loan beasts would be used by the borrower until they were reclaimed. . . . The owner would divide up the increase, and perhaps the original stock, giving some to the borrower outright."[86] In both cases, the granting of loan-cattle was an exercise in patronage. Wealthier persons hoped to build a loyal following and, as J. B. Peires suggests, by controlling cattle, to control men.[87] Settlers also lent livestock to poorer clients and kin; the borrower gained half the yearly increase, and the lender perhaps won a client.[88]

The slaves' loan-cattle agreements paralleled those of other southern African pastoralists. For example, Manas, a Graaff-Reinet slave, gave Roset, a slave woman who belonged to another master, two cows and two heifers (young cows—usually ones that have not calved) to keep for him in exchange for half the increase. The arrangement worked well for between ten and sixteen years (witnesses' accounts vary). Manas's cows were prolific and eventually numbered twenty. Things soured when Roset's master, Johannes Oberholzer, took four of Manas's "breed" from her and trained them as wagon oxen. Two of the four died, and Oberholzer sold the others, keeping the profits for himself. Later he sold a bull and a cow belonging to Manas. When Oberholzer died, Roset tried to reclaim Manas's livestock and her own from the estate, but was not able to since all of Manas's oxen now had Oberholzer's mark on them. Neither Manas nor Roset were able to recover their stolen property.[89]

Cases like those of Manas and others seen above emphasize the fragility of the slaves' grip on their livestock. Slave owners continually looked for ways to take with one hand what they had given with the other. At times, they simply stole from their slaves, and only occasionally did they bother to contrive an excuse. For instance, James, a slave, charged his master with having stolen six of his goats; the slave owner had given the goats "to a Mantatee," James said, on the "false pretence of [James] having taken some money from that person."[90] The slaves' grip on their property was weak because their privileges masked, but did not eliminate, their subordination to their masters and mistresses. They remained subject to violent domination, and their power to resist their masters' and mistresses' extortion was relatively weak. Slaves and apprentices nevertheless generally believed that it was preferable to accept the enticements they were offered and to make the best out of the difficult circumstances of enslavement. They acquired property and, with that property, were able to buy and barter better food and clothing than they or their families otherwise would have known. Sometimes, though rarely, they managed to free themselves or their kin.

As in the city, masters and mistresses in the countryside put their slaves and apprentices to work as the needs of the household and the demands of the workplace dictated. Slave owners were not especially concerned with distinctions between house slaves and field slaves or between male slaves and female slaves. They could not afford to be. Few farmers possessed enough slaves to allow a strict division of labor by either gender or skill. Many slave owners were similarly unconcerned by differences of status and ethnicity among their subordinate workforce. Slaves and apprentices worked beside and under the same conditions as Khoisan, Bastaard Hottentots, and Bantu-speaking Africans. Masters treated all of their laborers in much the same way, to the point of allowing some slaves and apprentices to live as quasi tenants.

Despite the advantages that fortunate slaves enjoyed, they might be reminded of their status at any moment. Fortuyn is an example. One day on a farm in the Somerset district, two mares, one belonging to Fortuyn, the other to his master, Gerhardus Swart, got into the household garden and began to destroy the crops. Fortuyn and his master chased the horses out of the garden. Swart caught his own mare and began to beat it. He ordered Fortuyn to snare his horse and to bring it to him so that he could punish it as well. Fortuyn, whose mare was "heavy in foals and [would] be injured if beaten," refused. When Fortuyn let his horse escape over a fence, Swart instead beat his slave. Fortuyn knew his rights. He went immediately to the office of the assistant protector of slaves in Somerset and charged his master with having beaten him without cause and with unlawful severity. Swart was convicted and fined.[91] If violent domination was never far below the surface of slavery, neither was resistance to it.

CHAPTER 6

"Words Will Not Suffice"

Violence and Resistance

It must be looked on as an extraordinary event to find a Slave who would not rejoice at any mischief that might befall his master.

—COURT OF JUSTICE, CAPE COLONY, 1796

The similarities between slavery and capitalism troubled Karl Marx. Both systems required ruling classes to devise mechanisms that would ensure that laborers, slave or free, were "labourious beyond their wants." That is, they had to forced somehow to work harder than was required to satisfy their needs in order to support their owners and employers as well. There were important distinctions between slaves and free workers, of course, and one of the critical differences was the nature of the coercive force that compelled workers to support both themselves and their masters and bosses. The free worker chose between hard labor and starvation, the slave between hard labor and the lash.[1] Coercion was indirect in the first case, direct in the second.

Marx was out to score a polemical point by demonstrating that free wage laborers were in an important sense unfree. It did not serve his purpose to acknowledge that the rewards and incentives that we explored in previous chapters sometimes spurred on the labors of both slaves and free workers or to acknowledge that they toiled long and hard out of an internalized sense of duty. Marx was nevertheless more right than wrong about slavery. Slavery was a relationship of domination. As individuals, slaves were violently dominated by their masters, and as a class, by slaveholding society. Violent coercion was the bedrock on which the system rested.[2] Only when this foundation had been firmly established could slave owners turn to less coercive means of controlling their slaves. Violence was sometimes masked, but it never disappeared.

These are by no means peculiarly Marxist insights: they are central to Orlando Patterson's argument that slavery is social death,[3] as well as to most other analyses of the institution.[4] Nowhere was slavery's violence a secret; nowhere was it disguised. In the Cape colony, it was a matter of both public record and public and private spectacle. Colonial officials, the protectors of slaves, and slave owners themselves acknowledged the centrality of violence in the maintenance of the master-slave relationship. Travelers and residents such as Anders Sparrman witnessed and wrote about it as well. Sparrman, who spent several years in the colony during the late eighteenth century and who was generally sympathetic to the Dutch settlers, reported that "many a time, especially in the mornings and evenings, have I seen in various places unhappy slaves, who with the most dismal cries and lamentations, were suffering the immoderately severe punishments inflicted on them by their masters."[5] In 1813, the Cape's chief legal officer defended the slave owners' right to beat their slaves in a memorandum he wrote for the governor. When persuasion failed, the fiscal contended, slave owners had no choice but to resort to the whip. "Experience [had taught the colonists] that the generality of slaves always incline to dissolute conduct, and that they take no interest whatsoever in the welfare of their Masters, which frequently obliges the latter, when they cannot confine their slaves within the pale of their duties by reason or verbal correction, to have recourse to corporal punishment." The fiscal attempted to show that the law prohibited capricious or wanton punishment, yet the limits of the permissible violence were broad. In colonial law, the definition of punishable "domestic offences" included "neglect of work," insolence, escape, theft within the master's household, and drunkenness. "Domestic correction" could amount to thirty-nine lashes with a whip or the sjambok.[6] A legally permissible beating might put a healthy adult male to bed for several days.

In 1826, the first of the effective reform laws limited the number of stokes that a master might apply to a male slave to twenty-five. The same ordinance allowed female slaves to be whipped over the shoulders only "to such moderate extent as any Child of Free condition may be."[7] The ordinance angered the slave owners,[8] and even the newly created principal guardian of slaves doubted that the new reforms were useful. Stern discipline was needed to control "ill-behaved slaves, of which it must be supposed there are . . . not a few." Such slaves were "the greatest possible torment to their owners." This, the guardian thought, was particularly true of the "female slaves, for whom there is now no punishment but slight correction, which on some of those masculine Mosambique [sic] women, in many instances stouter and more hardy than European men, amounts to no punishment, and only increases their ill-behavior."[9]

By 1831, the reform laws had reduced the maximum number of strokes that could be laid on the backs of male slaves to fifteen and had prohibited entirely the corporal punishment of female slaves. Women could, however, be placed in stocks and on restricted diets.[10] The new law, like the first, outraged the slave owners. Among the many petitions they sent to the governor protesting the restrictions was one from several dozen slave owners of Graaff-Reinet. They lamented the new limits on physical punishment and complained that "it were greatly to be wished that the slaves and Hottentots were actually such as they are considered by the Government,—this would be fortunate for the Proprietors and render it possible to rule them without beating, but there are few who can be ruled by words. . . . [I]f words will not suffice[,] the rod must be applied[,] more especially in the case of an uncivilized people."[11] As one of the protectors acknowledged two years later, "Slavery must always be a system of Coercion."[12]

Not every slave felt the lash, and not every slave owner wielded one, but most owners whipped and most slaves bled, at least occasionally. Violence hung in the air. It could not have been otherwise. Violence was, as Patterson argues, a "constituent element" of slavery, a crucial aspect of social death. Acts of violence transformed free people into slaves. Once enslaved, men, women, and children endured violent punishments. But just as importantly, violence and the threat of violence were forms of social control, continually reminding slaves of their relative powerlessness.[13] The whippings and beatings were physical acts with psychological consequences. It is likely that all slaves some of the time and some slaves all of the time succumbed to what Nell Irvin Painter has called "soul murder."[14] We have seen evidence of slaves who had internalized feelings of degradation and self-hatred in previous chapters, and we shall see more in the pages that follow. But we have also learned that this is only part of the story.

Most slaves and apprentices did not submit passively to the beatings that their owners inflicted any more than they meekly accepted other aspects of social death. In large and small ways, they resisted the violence directed against them and the labor it compelled them to perform. Not every slave engaged in active resistance, just as some were never whipped. But most did find ways to resist the degradation of physical punishment and to assert an important degree of psychological autonomy. As was so often the case during slavery's last decade, slaves sought the aid of the protectors and the laws that they enforced in their struggle for personal and collective resurrection.

Discipline and Disciplinarians

Coercion was the means, labor was the end. In every sector of the Cape economy, in town and countryside, in the home and the fields, masters, mistresses, and overseers beat their slaves and apprentices more often for "neglect of work" than any other offence.[15] The slaves were seldom willing workers, to say the least. Nigel Worden argues that owners ordinarily punished their slaves themselves and that the whip was the instrument of choice. "Whipping . . . inflicted considerable pain . . . providing a striking [demonstration] to the victim and other slaves . . . of the visible authority and supremacy of the master."[16]

The routine violence of the households sometimes horrified even the protectors and special justices. The special justice in Graaff-Reinet, for instance, heard the case that Christiaan Raby brought against Solomon, his apprentice. Raby claimed that one Sunday after traveling to Graaff-Reinet by wagon to attend church he knee-haltered his horses and left them in Solomon's care. The apprentice, however, failed to keep an eye on the animals. They strayed and three were lost. At the justice's hearing, Solomon admitted that he had allowed the horses to wander, but "at the same time [he] show[ed] his back with old marks of a very severe punishment which he says was inflicted by his Master." Shaken by what he had seen, the justice called a halt to the proceedings.[17] Similarly, another special justice dropped the charges a master had pressed against a woman apprentice when, "on examining her body, it was found to be disfigured by a great number of old scars & bruises. In answer to [a] question, as to how she came by them, she stated that her late Master & Mistress,—the Parents of her present Owners—, had been exceedingly cruel to her and had given her those marks prior to the year 1835;—which statement her present owner Ath. Nel, corroborated." "My feelings," the justice wrote, "were . . . shocked."[18] Brutality on such a grand scale was by no means universal; some masters and mistresses rarely beat their slaves. When Damon, a fifty-seven-year-old slave, charged his master with having hit him with the handle of a spade, he said that he had never before been beaten.[19] But, as Damon had now learned, all slaves and apprentices—domestics and field workers, men and women—risked violent punishment when they failed to fulfill their master's or mistress's demands.

While most slave owners supervised and disciplined their slaves personally, some depended on overseers. Often the overseer was the *klein baas* (translated as Young Master in contemporary accounts), either a son or a son-in-law of the *groot baas* (big boss) or *ou baas* (Old Master). Less frequently, slave owners hired white men or free blacks as *knechts* ("overseer," "overlooker," or "manager"). Still less common, but not unknown, were slave overseers. In the eighteenth century, these men were called *mandoors*,[20] a word that does not appear in the protectors' reports or other English accounts of slavery in the nineteenth century.

Since the material welfare of the slave owner's son or son-in-law depended on the economic health of the farm and since he stood to inherit some or all of the estate, the interests of the klein baas largely coincided with those of the ou baas. Here again, nothing was more likely to lead to a beating than a conflict over labor. Jan Laubscher, Albertus Jacobus Laubscher's overseer, laid forty lashes on the shoulders, back, belly, and loins of Carel, his father's slave, because the slave had left two sheep behind when bringing the flock home one evening.[21] Similarly, Johannes Petrus van Zyl whipped Adam, a slave, for "neglect of duty," at the insistence of his mother, the widow van Zyl. Van Zyl applied the lashes with a cat-o'-nine-tails that he had soaked in salt water. After the beating, he ordered Carel's back and shoulders to be washed in the "Pickle" solution. The assistant protector of slaves who heard the case commented that this "Mode" of punishment was "calculated to produce greater Suffering than the mode of domestic Punishment [normally] employed in this Colony." The apothecary who examined the slave thought that the saline solution, while indeed increasing the pain when applied to raw wounds, might have prevented the wounds from becoming infected. Van Zyl claimed as well that he had been concerned to forestall the "inflamation" of Carel's injuries. The protector felt the punishment exceeded the crime and convinced a court to fine van Zyl and his mother £20.[22]

In the town and in the countryside, the sons of slave owners began their lessons in slave management early in life. Several visitors to the Cape noticed that one of the first lessons that the children of slave owners learned was "to domineer over" the slaves, "beating and tyrannizing" them.[23] They had to learn the habit of command, as well as the art of inflicting physical abuse without flinching. Willem de Klerk, who was sixteen, seems to have applied himself to his lessons. He punished his father's slave Aaron, who was thirty, because, as a witness put it, "they had a difference about the milking of some Cows." After beating Aaron, Willem threw him to the ground, tied a leather strap around his neck, and nearly strangled him. This sort of punishment was legally inappropriate, and the magistrate who tried the case fined Willem and his father £1.[24]

Another youth, the son of an English-speaking slave owner, beat Maart, a fifty-four-year-old slave, "because he was not expeditious enough in the performance of his work."[25] In 1830, the son of M. van der Spuy, a Koeberg grain farmer, twice found himself answering charges of having mistreated slaves. On the first occasion, he gave January, a thirty-six-year-old, "about Six Stripes" with a whip, but said that he "was sorry for having done so." The protector reported that he "warned this young lad not to take it upon himself to strike any of the Slaves & He . . . earnestly promised to attend to [the protector's] suggestions" not to do so in the future. Young van der Spuy broke his promise, as, it seemed, he must if he were to be the baas someday. He appeared before the protector soon afterward, admitting that he had, as charged, slapped another slave in the face four or five times.[26]

Less frequently, hired hands managed and punished the slaves and apprentices. Worden shows that these knechts were found on only a minority of the Cape farms during the eighteenth century,[27] and there is no indication that things had changed by the nineteenth. The overseers were sometimes Bastaard Hottentots or free blacks, but were most often former soldiers or seaman or locally born white men. Usually, knechts were found only on the largest farms; always they earned little respect.

After traveling throughout the colony during the first years of the nineteenth century, Henry Lichtenstein concluded that "among white people . . . there are none who lead such wretched lives" as the knechts. Many were "worn out invalids" with few skills, who could find no other work. They earned little, saw virtually no one other than their "black subjects," and, Lichtenstein claimed, were known throughout the Cape as "the drunkards."[28] Though Lichtenstein may have exaggerated the knechts' degradation, there is no doubt that they occupied a very low position in the social hierarchy of the Cape.[29] The low status of the knechts stemmed from several causes. They were landless, slaveless men in a society in which land and slaves were the principal source of wealth and respectability. They also tended to be "the sort of men who had climbed their way up from the lowest levels of north European society."[30] Holding a degraded office and spending their working lives among the dishonored, they had not climbed far.

Overseers had to strike a balance between their bosses' demands and the slaves' recalcitrance, generating the maximum possible profit for the former by extracting as much labor as possible from the latter. Unlike the slave owners' sons and sons-in-law, the hired knechts were easily replaced,[31] and, of course, they never stood to inherit part or all of the farm. This placed them in an awkward position. They had to drive the slaves hard enough to satisfy their employer, while avoiding the open rebellion or hidden resistance that would disrupt the farm's routine. Their attempts to tread this fine line sometimes entered the colonial record.

Dirk Cloete, a wine farmer in Stellenbosch, once ordered his knecht, Jacobus Estenhuysen, to lay twelve lashes on his slave cattleherd, Antoin, for having allowed some horses to stray. Estenhuysen instead gave Antoin only ten lashes, "which he thought were enough," telling him that, if his master asked, he should say that he had received twenty-five.[32] Estenhuysen's actions illustrate Eugene Genovese's observations about the overseers in the American South. While owing their jobs to their employers, they "knew that they would not keep their jobs without some degree of support [from the slaves], and, accordingly, they tried to curry favor."[33]

The slave owners of the Cape understood the complex nature of the relationships between themselves, their overseer, and their slaves. They watched their knechts as closely as the knechts watched them. Johannes Albertus Laubscher, for instance, supported his overseer, Jan de Kock, in his wrangle with Clara, his slave, but he did not act without weighing the matter carefully. Clara said that one Monday morning de Kock struck her several times with his fist while dragging her away from her work in the vineyard. He then took her to an outbuilding and locked her in leg stocks for the day. Clara said that her crime had been to leave the farm without permission early Sunday morning to attend services at a missionary's meetinghouse.[34] After being let out of the stocks, she went to the assistant protector's office in Stellenbosch and charged de Kock with mistreating her. De Kock, preparing to defend himself, asked two male slaves who had been working with Clara in the vineyard whether they had witnessed the altercation. Both men told him that they had seen him give Clara a mild slap and lead her away, but nothing more. Meanwhile, Laubscher, who had been away from his farm that Sunday and Monday, apparently began his own investigation when he learned that Clara had pressed charges, interrogating the two slaves with the help of the local veld cornet (prominent citizens who helped the landrosts in policing) and two white neighbors. Laubscher wanted to know precisely what had happened between Clara and de Kock. The slaves repeated the story they had told de Kock; they had seen him slap her once and take her away. One of the neighbors accused the slaves of lying and threatened to harm them if they persisted in their claim that de Kock had struck Clara at all. After hearing the slaves' account, Laubscher chose to defend his knecht at the protector's hearing. In the protector's office, however, the two slave witnesses felt secure enough to recant their earlier version of the events and corroborate Clara's story. Despite the new evidence, Laubscher continued to stand by his overseer.[35]

Slave owners rarely failed to defend their overseers in disputes with their slaves and apprentices. A competent knecht—such as de Kock, whom Laubscher trusted to maintain discipline in his absence—was vitally important to the efficient functioning of the farm. To favor the slaves over the knecht would have been to subvert the knecht's authority and his ability to extract labor from the slaves. On the other hand, an incompetent overseer—one who was continually in open conflict with the slaves—would not have long maintained his employer's confidence. Such a knecht would not have been an effective manager of his slave workforce and would have been an economic liability. A conscientious master might trust his overseer enough to leave the farm in his care, but not enough to accept his word against a slave's unconditionally.

Slaves, free blacks, and Bastaard Hottentots sometimes acted as their owner's or employer's overseers. Anders Sparrman encountered a slave "who had the absolute management" of a farm and ran it "skillfully."[36] In 1816, a slave overseer supervised the 105 slaves on the Constantia estate, Hendrik Cloete's well-known vineyard south of Cape Town.[37] In the same year, Baatjoe, a slave, was an overseer on Jan Hoets's wine and wheat farm on the Cape Peninsula; Hoets manumitted Baatjoe in 1827, probably as a reward for loyal service.[38] In 1831, Baatjoe, now a free black and still one of Hoets's overseers, appeared at a protector's hearing as a witness, defending his master against charges made by thirteen of his slaves that he refused to supply them with sufficient food.[39] In Stellenbosch, Christiaan Coenraad Basson's "Bastaard Hottentot" overseer, Philemon Roos, "cohabited" with one of his slaves and had a daughter by her. Roos's position was difficult; he sometimes had to stand by while his master and mistress physically punished his wife and child for various offenses. He lost his job when he complained of Basson's brutality after watching him beat his daughter for having allowed some calves to stray.[40]

Violent domination was the foundation on which slavery was built. Yet at the same time that it ensured the subordination of the slave to the master, it laid the groundwork for resistance. More than "any other aspect of their bondage," Robert Ross argues, "the Cape slaves seem to have resented and reacted against the degradation and the physical pain of being whipped."[41] Evidence drawn from the protectors' reports lends some support to Ross's claim; slaves and apprentices often responded to the lash and the forced labor process with resistance.

Everyday Resistance

An example will illustrate some of the dynamics of slave and apprentice resistance. D. I. G. Putter, a Graaff-Reinet farmer, took Jacob, one of his apprentices, to the special justice for punishment. According to Putter, Jacob had committed two serious offenses: he "overdrove" a pair of oxen when returning them to the kraal, causing one to be "so much injured as to endanger [its] life." And when Putter hired Jacob out to several of his neighbors, he "converted [the hire money] to his own use" rather than bringing it home to his master. Putter's witnesses supported his charges. One had seen Jacob driving the oxen "in a furious manner"; another said that though he had paid Jacob 1½s. a day "to break stones[,] he would do no work." Jacob made no defense. He admitted that he had received hire money from three men, including "a Person of colour called Geduld," and that he given none of it to his master. The special justice sentenced him to receive fifteen lashes.[42]

It is not hard to list the things that Jacob had done to anger his master. He had abused his master's animals, stolen his master's unearned profits, and refused an employer's orders to work. It is more difficult to uncover what he thought he was doing; that is, to determine how he would have explained his actions to himself and to others. Jacob may have been a lazy, vicious, and dishonest man; he may have been responding to momentary provocations; or he may have been self-consciously challenging the nature of his apprenticeship. Since he was no more than human, the range of Jacob's thoughts and emotions surely covered all of this territory at various times and in various circumstances. Historians of slavery have noted that the line between the desire to avoid hard work and deliberate protest or resistance is often indistinct.[43] Since the historical record is too skimpy to allow a multidimensional portrait of Jacob to be drawn, it will be more useful to view him within the context of the community of slaves and apprentices.

Some slave owners and travelers understood slave behavior in terms of racial or ethnic characteristics. The idea had long been abroad that some slaves were more deceitful and thievish by nature than others. What had earlier been an elaborate hierarchy of prejudices about the inherent characteristics of slaves from various ethnic backgrounds had, by the 1820s, settled into a three-tiered system.[44] Most whites believed that Cape-born slaves were the best and the brightest, that Mozambican and Malagasy slaves were dull, but well suited to heavy, repetitive labor, and that Malays and other Asian slaves were clever, treacherous, and dishonest.[45] But this crudely racist argument was never universally held. Writing in 1813, the fiscal suggested that unacceptable slave behavior might be generated by something other than genetic predisposition. In doing so, he set the stage for viewing Jacob's actions as resistance.

Slaves, the fiscal once argued, harbored a "secret hostility towards their masters."[46] He later added, "Experience has . . . taught us that the generality of slaves always incline to dissolute conduct." Slaves were not, however, innately dissolute. The inherently antagonistic relationship between masters and slaves had shaped their characters. Slaves took "no interest whatsoever in the welfare of their masters" and "would readily oppose their Masters and shake off the Yoke of Slavery . . . in case they were not kept in order by fear."[47] The Cape's Court of Justice, the colony's highest court, had argued along similar lines during the first British occupation. "A State of Slavery," the justices told the governor, "is always accompanied with a certain Enmity against Masters, in so much that it must be looked on as an extraordinary event to find a Slave who would not rejoice at any mischief that might befall his master. . . . It rarely happens that when a Slave sees a plot formed against the life or property of his Master, he endeavours to prevent the execution of it."[48] The fiscal and the court shared an assumption that is held as well by most modern students of societies stratified by hierarchical relationships and differentials of power and wealth. There will always be "a basic antagonism of goals between dominant and subordinate," engendering a constant testing, by each side, of the limits of its freedom to pursue its interests.[49] The rich and the poor, the powerful and the weak, will often be at each other's throats.

The tactics the slaves employed to blunt their masters' efforts to dominate them and expropriate the fruits of their labor were those that James Scott calls the "weapons of the weak." Like most subordinated classes throughout most of history, slaves and apprentices confronted people and institutions that were too powerful for them to oppose openly by adopting "the ordinary weapons of relatively powerless groups: foot dragging, dissimulation, desertion, false compliance, pilfering, feigned ignorance, slander, arson, sabotage, and so on." In a reference to the socialist German playwright Bertolt Brecht, Scott calls these "Brechtian . . . forms of class struggle."[50] Historians of seventeenth-, eighteenth-, and nineteenth-century slavery at the Cape (notably, Nigel Worden, Mary Raynor, and Robert Ross) have found ample evidence that the slaves employed these everyday forms of class struggle. Each has described what Raynor refers to as a "tradition of resistance."[51]

Not all historians of slavery have been prepared to call the various weapons of the weak "resistance." Writing of American slavery, George Fredrickson and Christopher Lasch, for example, have asked historians to make the "conceptual distinction between resistance and noncooperation." They admit that it is "easy to show that Negro slaves did not always cooperate with the system of slavery." It is more difficult, they insist, "to prove that noncooperation amounted to political resistance." Malingering, they suggest, "may have reflected no more than a disinclination to work." Fredrickson and Lasch refuse to accept the argument that everyday forms of class warfare constitute resistance. For them, "Resistance is a political concept"; it must be "organized collective action which aims at affecting the distribution of power . . . [or] more broadly . . . any activity, either of individuals or of groups, which is designed to create a consciousness of collective interest." Brechtian struggles—unorganized and individualistic—do not qualify.[52] While Fredrickson and Lasch are probably correct to insist that resistance must have political implications, they have drawn the boundaries of the political too narrowly. The weapons of the weak are indeed weapons of political struggle.

Scott has answered arguments that closely parallel those of Fredrickson and Lasch. These positions, he contends, "fundamentally misconstru[e] the very basis of the economic and political struggle conducted daily by subordinate classes—not only slaves, but peasants and workers as well—in repressive settings." It is a "simple fact that most subordinate classes throughout most of history have rarely been afforded the luxury of open, organized, political activity. Or, better stated, such activity was dangerous, if not suicidal." To look for formal political resistance "is to look largely in vain." Most forms of subordinate resistance "stop well short of outright collective defiance." The everyday resistance of peasants and slaves has well-suited their historical circumstances. Brechtian forms of resistance "require little or no coordination or planning . . . make use of implicit understandings and informal networks . . . often represent a form of individual self-help; [and] typically avoid any direct, symbolic confrontation with authority." Such resistance is relatively low-risk. Yet cumulatively, it can force the superordinate, whether as an individual or as a class, to grant concessions to the subordinate, again as individuals and as a class. Scott admits that it is difficult to discern resistance "when it comes to acts like theft." "Slaves in the antebellum United States South who secretly butchered their master's hog may have been asserting their right to a decent subsistence, but they were just as surely indulging in their fondness for roast pork." The pleasure the slaves derived from feasting on their master's hog did not, however, vitiate the theft as an act of resistance. "It is precisely the fusion of self-interest and resistance that is the vital force *animating* . . . resistance."[53]

Writing of Cape slavery, Ross and Worden work from assumptions similar to Scott's, but they differ from him in one crucial respect: they do not see slave resistance as arising from a community of values, understandings, and norms; rather, they see slave resistance as "individual [and] un-coordinated." There was little, they argue, in the way of "collective resistance."[54] Yet Ross and Worden ignore many of their own findings when they fail to notice that much of the resistance that they describe presupposes a community of beliefs and values that validate individual acts of resistance. Scott has cautioned against discussing resistance as merely a set of behaviors; this would be to reduce resistance to the level at which one might "explain how the water buffalo resists its driver to establish a tolerable pace of work." Unlike the buffalo, humans are "gifted with intentions and values and purposefulness that conditions their acts." "The meaning that the slaves gave their acts . . . constitutes the indispensable background to their behavior."[55] It is possible to uncover this background to resistance at the Cape.

While it is true that most slaves and apprentices individually resisted their owner's claims over their bodies, minds, and labor, instances of collective resistance were common. Runaway slaves, for instance, often received help from their comrades in making good their escape or found semipermanent refuge with *droster* gangs (the word *droster* is taken from the Dutch *drossen,* to run away or desert), as we shall see below. Occasionally, too, slaves brought collective complaints to the protectors of slaves. In 1831, Isaac and twelve other slaves belonging to Jan Hoets charged their master with failing to provide wholesome and sufficient food.[56] In 1833, Lendor, Arend, Isaac, and John, all slaves belonging to Matthys Michielse Basson, told the protector that their master gave them too little to eat and that he locked them up in the "Slave Room" at night. Not only was their complaint collective, but so was the offense that led their master to confine them in their room. As Basson put it, they were all "in the habit of running out at night to visit farms of his neighbors."[57]

Of greater significance than runaway gangs and group visits to the protectors' offices was the ethos of resistance and solidarity that slaves shared even when they were not engaged in collective acts of resistance, as even the principal protector of slaves dimly perceived. Soon after the creation of his office, he reported on the difficulty he encountered in establishing the facts of the cases that the slaves brought to him. Many slave witnesses, particularly those from Mozambique, were "without religion" and under "no moral obligation to declare the truth"—or so the protector believed. Among these slaves,

> the desire of assisting a comrade or friend is, I am afraid, a powerful inducement to . . . advance as true, statements which further inquiries often prove to be false, and their cunning in concealing, under assumed ignorance, that which they do not wish to be known, and in evading questions which would expose their inconsistency, renders their depositions at all times doubtful.[58]

The protector did not pause to ask himself whether it was possible that the slaves believed that the moral obligations that they owed to each other were more urgent than their duty to speak the truth to a representative of the laws that enslaved them.

Patterns of collective thought and action can best be seen in the slaves' resistance to violent punishment. For instance, November and two men named Present were among the many slaves who shared a hatred of physical punishment, whether directed against themselves or others. In 1833, November brought a complaint to the assistant protector of slaves in the Somerset district. He said that J. D. Cilliers, who managed his owner's farm, had whipped him with a cat-o'-nine-tails though he had done nothing to deserve it. November told the protector that the incident began when Cilliers had ordered him to call all the "servants" into the house. November thought that this was because Cilliers wanted to beat another slave, Apollos, whom he had threatened. November wanted no part of it, and he and two other servants, both named Present, hid in the farm's goat kraal in order to avoid either assisting in the whipping or witnessing it. Cilliers eventually found the slaves and beat them for disobeying his orders. The protector dismissed both November's complaint and the similar charges that the other men had pressed against Cilliers. He told them that they ought to have followed orders.[59] By their actions, November and his colleagues had twice demonstrated shared beliefs about violent punishment. Together they had refused to assist in or witness the beating of another slave, and together they had left the farm to complain about the punishment they themselves had received. They had operated within what might be called the moral economy of the lash.

In appropriating the phrase *moral economy* to my own purposes,[60] I mean to suggest that the slaves and apprentices of the Cape Colony had developed a moral code by which to judge the physical punishment to which they were subject. In this "moral economy," slaves acknowledged that some beatings were inevitable, if not legitimate. But their code set rules governing the distribution of the violence—determining, that is, the circumstances under which a master or mistress might justifiably punish a slave. The moral economy of the lash drives the action in the story of Mey, a slave who did not resist a first beating that he received; while regrettable, it did not fall outside of the moral economy. But he did protest a second whipping, which he deemed out of order.

One spring day in 1832, Mey and several other slaves on a wheat farm in the Cape district had returned to work from their midday meal a half-hour late.[61] Seeing this, their owner, Hendrick Albertus van Niekerk, ordered his son to lay between fifteen and twenty-five lashes on the backs of each of them. None of the slaves resisted. A few days later, Van Niekerk ordered Mey to carry some bags of chaff from one part of the farm to another. He worked slowly because the wounds from the beating he had received had not yet healed. Van Niekerk told Mey to move more quickly, but the slave was unable to comply. Angered by what he believed was his slave's disobedience, van Niekerk gave him another ten lashes with a cat-o'-nine-tails. Mey believed that this whipping, unlike the first, was undeserved, and, as he told the protector, he had "therefore . . . come to Complain." Here was the moral economy of the lash in action.

Mey's words might seem to be slender reeds on which to hang so heavy an argument, but there are other supports. Mey's fellow slaves offered testimony that addresses the problem. In the protector's office, they spoke of the first whipping, the one that came after they had tarried in returning to work, the one that all eight slaves had undergone, the one that they had not resisted. The first slave witness, Carolus, gave evidence that confirmed Mey's account as far as the initial beating was concerned. He said that their master's son had whipped him, Mey, and the seven other slaves, "by directions of his Old Master . . . for not Attending at the regular hour to their Work." Carolus told the protector that he "should never have thought of Coming to Complain" because he thought "himself to have deserved the punishment which he received," having knowingly stayed away from work longer than he should have. This punishment, because it was just, was tolerable. George, the slave whom the others testified had suffered the most from the blows, likewise said that he believed that he had no grounds for complaint. He added, however, that he did think that "he had Received rather a Severe punishment for the fault committed." The beating, though harsh enough to have caused him to comment, had not violated the norms of the moral economy of the lash. The protector assimilated the testimony of four of the other slaves into a general statement. They had not complained about the punishment because they imagined that they had "deserved" it. They acknowledged that they had "neglected to go to their Work at the Proper time and therefore," they explained, they "did not Suppose they could have been Considered to have any Grounds of Complain." This last point is highly ambiguous.

The protector would have his readers understand that the slaves admitted that they had been wrong in not going about their work as they should and that the punishment they received had been deserved. But it is equally possible that they failed to complain because they "did not Suppose they could have been considered," by someone other than themselves, "to have any Grounds of Complain." The slaves almost certainly understood that their own notions of just and proper punishment did not accord with those of the protector, the official who had the power to bring their master to book. Slaves sometimes went to the protectors hoping for justice, but not expecting it. When the punishments that they received did violate both the law and the moral economy, they did not hesitate to turn to the law. Mey's second beating is an example. It violated both Mey's sense of the moral economy and the letter of the law. Van Niekerk was punished for assaulting his slave without due cause. As we shall see below, when the transgressions against the moral economy of the lash fell short of what slaves believed the law would notice, they often found other ways of policing the boundaries. The moral economy was subject to negotiation.

The van Niekerk slaves were hardly alone in possessing a sense of just and unjust punishment, and Mey was only one of many slaves who complained to the protectors when their masters violated these norms. Cases in which slaves complained of "unjust" or "undeserved" punishment appear frequently in the protectors' reports. The English words are those of the protectors or their clerks, translating and paraphrasing the slaves' testimony. The insistence that the punishment in the particular circumstances had been improper, however, derived from the slaves themselves. A few representative examples will illustrate the point. One slave, Africa, who was said by a witness to have provoked his master with "insolent conduct," protested that he had been "most unjustly punished."[62] The record of the charges filed by another slave, Blom, could not have been more explicit: he told the protector that his master had punched him in the face and whipped him with a sjambok. But, the protector reported, "he did not come to complain of the severity of the beating . . . but because it was undeserved."[63]

In a case similar to the one brought by November and the two Presents, two slaves in their late teens, Hector and Abraham, claimed that they had been "undeservedly punished." Their master's overseer denied that this was the case and said that he had beaten them with a walking cane "for having refused, when desired so to do, to hold a Slave who was to be punished."[64] Like Hector and Abraham, slaves commonly refused to assist in or witness the beating of their comrades. The principal protector was aware of the slaves' obstinacy. In 1830, he wrote that far too often slaves who had been ordered "to Witness, the Punishment of their fellow Slave, have purposely got out of the way, and some even have peremptorily refused to be present."[65] The moral economy of the lash seems, as far as many slaves were concerned, to have denied that slaves were obligated to assist in or witness the whipping of a comrade. According to Peter Kolchin, slaves in the American South also developed a set of norms that determined the legitimacy or illegitimacy of beatings. He argues that "central to the whole process of resisting punishment was the slaves' belief that the intended discipline was unjust and undeserved. . . . For most [slaves] it was the injustice of the punishment rather than the physical pain it produced that provoked fury and resistance."[66]

The slaves and apprentices often focused their resistance not at enforcing a moral economy but directly at the forced-labor process, resisting exploitation at the point of production. While resistance often expressed itself as a sudden flaring of temper directed at an immediate catalyst, it was rooted in the routine oppressions of slavery. The underlying sources of resistance are important. They are the personal and

160 Social Death and Resurrection

community values that motivated the specific acts of resistance. Slaves did not resist every injustice or every command. Calculating the probable consequences of their actions, they generally picked the moments carefully. Most resistance was clandestine; their thoughts were expressed with caution. But at times of extreme emotional tension, anger, or exhaustion, slaves behaved in manner they otherwise would have checked and uttered words they more often repressed.

The weariness of a lifetime and a resigned acceptance of the consequences of her actions are evident in the fifty-five-year-old Amilia's account of her run-in with her mistress. Amilia lived on a farm in the district of Graaff-Reinet, where she struggled under the dual burdens of domestic service and farm labor. She had taken the household laundry down to the banks of a creek one day and had begun washing when her mistress scolded her for using dirty water and ordered her to move upstream. Amilia told an assistant protector that she had said that "her body was too full of pain to go further, and that her mistress had better go home, as she had already destroyed all the Strength of [her] body, and that she was now no more able to do anything." Her mistress assaulted her forthwith.[67] This was open resistance, a direct challenge to her mistress's authority. Amilia's complaints were private thoughts ordinarily uttered off-stage; her outright refusal of her mistress's command was the sort of thing that she would rarely have attempted at all. Similarly, Valentyn Snitler, a slave whom we meet again in the next chapter, spoke words in a moment of anger and physical weakness that he would otherwise have left unsaid. During a heated argument with his master, he "commenced to cursing and swearing, and holding his finger in his Master's face said 'We have been created by one God and I am as good as you.'"[68] Snitler had *openly* denied the legitimacy of his master's authority—the very antithesis of Brechtian resistance. Drawing on religious teachings, he denied the assumption that he was by color, class, and status inferior to his master.[69]

Amilia's and Snitler's words and deeds were unusual; most slaves and apprentices who chose to resist did so covertly. Slave owners understood the nature of the game. They knew that most of their slaves, at least some of the time, would intentionally evade work or perform it poorly, abuse farm animals, or simply run away. And they understood that the slaves would lie about what they had done. While the slave owners may have been committed ideologically to the notion that their slaves were congenitally lazy and unprincipled, they knew that often the slaves purposefully resisted the extortion of their labor.

The tangible rewards of everyday resistance were usually limited: slaves might win a few hours rest from their labors; or they might have the satisfaction of a measure of revenge against their masters. Something like this was the case for Solomon and Tom, two of Peter de Wet's apprentices. De Wet took them to the special justice's office in Malmesbury for punishment, saying that they were "extremely idle" and that when "he turn[ed] his back they neglect the work." A day earlier, he had first found them asleep in the fields, then sitting absent-mindedly by a fire. He asked the justice to punish both of them.[70] It cannot be known whether Solomon and Tom shared beliefs about the injustice of laboring for the benefit of another, whether they had given in to fatigue, or whether both possibilities were true. The records of other cases are more revealing, however.

Salomon [sic], a slave in the Stellenbosch district, claimed that his master beat him daily and forced him to work even though he was "sickly." According to his master, Hermanus le Roux, and another witness, Salomon took revenge on his master's crop: "Mr. le Roux coming into the garden, found Salomon with a spade, instead of loosening some onions as he had been desired, wilfully cutting off the tops and destroying all he could."[71] Throughout the colony, masters and mistresses believed that slaves and apprentices worked with deliberate slowness and sometimes spoiled their work by design. Christiaan Kotze held this opinion about his apprentice William. The apprentice complained to the special justice in Malmesbury that his master had beaten him for "going crooked" with the plow. Kotze, defending himself, said that he had "marked off the ground with bamboos" and ordered William to lead the plow "knowing that he could do it properly, which he took pains in teaching him." William, however, "would not do it right." Kotze changed horses, but his apprentice "persisted in spoiling the work." Kotze admitted that he had been "so provoked" that he had given William "a few slaps." Afterward, William "did well for a short time but again went wrong."[72] Other slave owners, too, had no doubt that their slaves and apprentices worked poorly out of malice, not incompetence. Petres de Waal once testified that his apprentice Celia was "in the habit of disobeying him every day—if he tells her to take the horses in one direction She is sure to go in the other." He added that feigned stupidity was not her only offence. She was "a thief & a drunkard & is well known to the Resident Magistrate as such."[73]

Charges of heavy drinking were also involved in the case that Rachel, a slave housemaid, brought against her master and mistress. The issue turned, however, on whether she was truly ill, as she claimed, or was merely pretending. Rachel told the protector of slaves that her owners had denied her medical care because they "thought [her] illness feigned" even though she had been laid up for some time. Her master replied that he had brought in "a Medical Gentleman" who had told him to consult a midwife. The midwife prescribed "some Medicine" and told Rachel to stop drinking wine. Consuming too much alcohol was something her master said that "she was apt to do." In an effort to resolve the case, the protector advised her master to send her to the government hospital in Cape Town, where she would be "better taken care of, and be out of the reach of liquor."[74] Rachel's drinking had perhaps blinded her master and mistress to her illness. But because slaves had long angered their masters by faking illnesses, they undoubtedly also suspected that she was not truly ill.

A feigned illness—or an illness said by the owner to be feigned—could be as contagious as a real one. Anders Sparrman, who had been trained in medicine, told of helping "two female Malabar slaves . . . find their legs again, who, out of mere idleness, had kept to their beds for several days under pretense of illness."[75] Albert Meyberg wanted the special justice in Malmesbury to punish Adam, his apprentice, because he claimed to be sick whenever "work is to be done." Meyberg had asked "a Medical Man" to examine Adam, and the doctor had pronounced him healthy and able to work. But Adam persisted in his refusal to work, and Meyberg found that "his other apprentices [were] now following the same plan & he has sometimes five or six out of . . . work," each claiming to be ill.[76] A shared ethic about the injustice of forced labor, rather than a virus, was the likely cause of this local epidemic.

There were many other forms of everyday resistance. It was a commonplace at the Cape that slaves and apprentices were given to abusing their masters' livestock. The attorney general once complained of the notorious "brutal violence of [apprentices] towards animals under their charge."[77] Jacob, mentioned above, drove a pair of his master's oxen "in a furious manner," severely injuring one of them.[78] Christiaan Kotze lost one of his horses and saved the other only "with difficulty" after one of his apprentices, Carl, mixed sand with their feed. Carl had apparently withheld the horses' feed until they were hungry enough to eat "sand mixed with a little wheat & he did so to kill them." At a special justice's hearing, Carl acknowledged giving the horses "dirty wheat" and said that he "wished them dead because his master scolded him for not feeding them."[79]

Such everyday resistance did not necessarily result in an immediate improvement in a slave's circumstances. Slaves and apprentices who, for example, abused farm animals did not confront their masters openly; they took no action that would result in immediate benefits for themselves. Such resistance was often, at best, a form of revenge and a sign that they did not accept their enslavement as legitimate.

Resistance to the forced-labor process was not the sole preserve of laborers and domestic servants. Skilled slaves and apprentices also resisted. Like the unskilled, they commonly employed the weapons of the weak. Mrs. M. E. Bain, for instance, once charged Christiaan, her shoemaker apprentice, with "contumaciously" refusing to work. A witness, John Saur, said that Christiaan was frequently careless and inattentive to his work. He often arrived at the workshop late and became "obstinate" when spoken to about it. He had given Mrs. Bain "much trouble . . . particularly since the absence of Mr. Bain who [was] employed on the frontier with the troops."[80] Betsey, a "Hottentot" woman, testified that Christiaan had behaved impertinently and had refused to make a pair of shoes on the morning of the hearing. Christiaan did not defend himself, probably realizing that any defense he might make would be futile. Acting on behalf of the colonial state and in support of the absent patriarch, the special justice sentenced Christiaan to receive ten lashes and noted that he had previously admonished him for his "bad conduct and coming late to work."[81]

Skilled slaves also frustrated their masters by deliberately producing substandard results, despite their competence in their crafts. Pierre Roche, of Simon's Town, described his slave Dappat as "a most incorrigible bad Character who at various times . . . had been punished by Sentence of different Magistrates for his misbehavior, adding that [Dappat] was a most able Mason but very obstinate and disobedient in the performance of his Work."[82] Though skilled slaves and apprentices often derived pride, personal autonomy, and an improved standard of living from their skills, many were exploited as directly as unskilled laborers. Some refused to employ the skills they had developed and others practiced them poorly in an effort to deny their masters the full benefit of their labor.

The slaves' widespread avoidance of work, their willingness to abuse farm animals and to perform less than their best work, and their susceptibility to imaginary diseases testify to the existence of shared notions regarding the injustice of forced labor. Slaves and apprentices taught each other the arts of resistance—as slave owners such as Albert

Meyberg (seen above complaining of an epidemic of bogus infirmities) suspected. Sometimes the culture of resistance was passed from mother to child, as is shown by the following two cases from the Graaff-Reinet district.

In the first, W. S. Basson charged Sabina, his apprentice housemaid, with theft. He claimed that shortly after he had left his home one day, Sabina sent her son, December, into the garden to steal some fruit and that she had later given the fruit to a "Hottentot" woman. A witness, Alima, who was Sabina's daughter and too young "to understand the nature of an oath," confirmed Basson's statement and added some detail. She said that on the day in question, her mother sent her into the Basson house to see whether or not her master and mistress were at home. When she told her mother that they were out, Sabina sent December into the garden. He soon returned, bearing apples and grapes wrapped in an handkerchief. At the special justice's hearing, Sabina admitted her guilt and was sentenced to seven days in jail on half-rations.[83] Sabina had instructed her son in the ethics and techniques of theft. At the very least, December had learned that it was acceptable to steal from one's oppressor and that, if one were not to be caught, one must pick one's moment. If Basson was correct in asserting that Sabina had given the fruit to a "Hottentot" woman, December may have also learned that the liberated booty ought to be shared with other subordinate members of the household. Sadly, Sabina had failed to teach her daughter the importance of keeping her mouth shut.

Another female apprentice taught her son both to steal and to evade work. Hester Hasselbach, a "laundress" in the village of Graaff-Reinet, claimed that Catherine, her apprentice, refused to work, used abusive language when addressing her, and induced her son, Jacob, to steal and to neglect his work. Like Sabina, she did not teach her child to keep secrets. Jacob, called before the special justice, said that his mother told him "when he was sent out by his Mistress he might stay and play and on another occasion she told him to take every opportunity he could to steal . . . and he acknowleg[ed] that he had at different times stolen two shillings and six pence [*sic*] from his Mistress."[84]

Although the slaves and apprentices at the Cape shared habits of mind that legitimated Brechtian forms of resistance, the consequences of employing those methods were not always foreseen by those using them nor applauded by those on the sidelines. Workers who malingered on the job, for instance, sometimes caused trouble for those who did not. Africa, a slave on a Stellenbosch grain farm, got no support from his comrades when he complained about the whipping his master's overseer had given him. Moses, a slave witness, testified that it had been Africa's task "to make the sheaves" while the other slaves reaped. But Africa "would not work equally with the other slaves, although one of the best workmen." Because he "had purposely worked negligently," Moses said, Africa had received fifteen lashes.[85] Moses's testimony carried with it an implicit criticism of Africa's recalcitrance and no defense of his actions, probably because it meant more work for himself and the other slaves in the field that day. Witnesses in similar cases made explicit the criticism that Moses only implied.

Silvester, an apprentice in the Worcester district, often left his master's property without permission in order to visit his wife, an apprentice on a nearby farm. He spent his nights with her and frequently did not return until late the next morning. Other apprentices complained that when Silvester was not on hand to do his job, they had to do it for him.[86] In another case, Lea, a cook, was responsible for preparing the meals for both her master's family and her fellow apprentices. She was habitually slow in getting the apprentices' meals to the table. Consequently, a witness said, "the Men are dissatisfied & . . . cannot get on with their work."[87] The slave ethic sanctioned resistance and the slave community supported it, but not beyond the point when resistance would cause other slaves or apprentices to suffer.[88]

Slaves and apprentices used the weapons of the weak to deny their masters' claims and to advance their own interests within the confines of slavery. Everyday resistance mitigated slavery materially and psychologically, but it could not end it. Escape was the single form of everyday resistance that could bring an end to slavery, if only one person at a time. In choosing to escape, slaves and apprentices reproduced a pattern of resistance that subordinate classes have often employed. "Throughout the centuries," Barrington Moore has pointed out, "one of the common man's most frequent and effective responses to oppression [has been] flight."[89] Cape Colony slaves and apprentices, women as well as men, were well acquainted with this response.

Escape

It has been difficult to estimate how many slaves ran away or how often they tried, though historians agree that both numbers were "high."[90]

Contemporaries would have concurred. Slave owners complained about runaway slaves, and colonial officials drafted laws to suppress the practice. In the mid-1820s, a government report observed that from 1658 onward "mention is made [in colonial records] of the frequent Desertion of Slaves."[91] The principal protector of slaves noted the same phenomenon, reporting in 1834 that desertions were chronically "very numerous."[92] There the matter has rested. Historians have described in great detail the dynamics of escape, but their descriptions have been qualitative, rather than quantitative, because only once, on the eve of emancipation, did anyone count the number of runaway slaves in the Cape Colony.[93]

In 1835, the colonial government completed a census of the slaves, as a part of its plan to compensate the former slave owners for the property losses they suffered with the emancipation of the slaves.[94] The assistant commissioners of slave compensation listed slaves who were runaways, as of 1 December 1834 (the date of formal, but not effective, emancipation), separately from those still in their masters' custody.[95] The commissioners found a total of 35,745 slaves in the colony, deserters included. Of the total, 427 (1.2 percent) were runaways. The number of runaways, however, varied regionally. The rate of desertion in Cape Town was lower than elsewhere in the colony. In two representative Cape Town subdistricts, only nine (0.6 percent) and four (0.3 percent) of the slaves were deserters. In the arable farming country of the western Cape, the number of runaways was somewhat higher than the colonial average. In a grain-farming subdistrict of the Cape district, fifty-three (1.7 percent) of the slaves had escaped their masters. In a Stellenbosch wine-farming subdistrict, fifty-seven (1.3 percent) of the slaves had run away. Comparably high rates of desertion were found in the sparsely populated cattle districts of the eastern and north-central Cape: fifty-four (1.7 percent) of the slaves had run away from Worcester district masters. In Graaff-Reinet, the corresponding figure was thirty-five (1.6 percent). By far the highest proportion of deserters in any slave community in the colony was in the far eastern Somerset district, where fifty-four (3.2 percent) of slaves had escaped.[96] As might have been anticipated, slaves deserted most often in the rural southwestern districts, where the work was heaviest and in the east, where the probability of successful escape was the greatest.[97] Slaves ran off the least often in Cape Town, a place of residence for which they commonly expressed a decided preference.[98]

While the absolute number of runaways may not seem particularly high, numbers can deceive. The census presents a still life. A more accurate picture would show slaves in motion—some in the act of running away, some eluding capture for days, months, or years on end, and others returning to their masters, either voluntarily or under duress. The number of slaves living in the colony who at some time or another had been deserters would have far exceeded 427; there were no doubt thousands, many of whom would have been repeat offenders. The number of slave owners who had suffered the sometime loss of their slaves' labor would have been correspondingly large, and so would the runaways' impact on Cape society.

Slaves were in the habit of running off at precisely those moments when their masters could spare them the least. As the principal guardian of slaves reported in 1827, "In the harvest and sowing times, when the services of the Slaves are most required, frequent desertions take place."[99] It was then, he later wrote, that "the masters being very anxious about the salvation of their Crops are often induced to expect too much from their slaves."[100] The small size of the average slaveholding exacerbated the masters' problems. The 1835 census showed that the average slaveholding was 5.6 slaves. If all of an average master's slaves were healthy adults of prime working age—an unlikely event—a single escape would have reduced the slave workforce by nearly 20 percent. Wine farmers, who were the largest slaveholders in the colony, on average owned sixteen slaves,[101] eight to ten of whom might have been able-bodied workers. For them, as for most slave owners, the loss of a single slave laborer was a serious economic burden. Robert Ross contends that the bleeding from the slow hemorrhage of escape was so severe that it was an important factor in slave owners' calculations about where and how to use slave labor.[102]

The figures from the 1835 census took no notice of a runaway's age and gender. Other sources make it clear, however, that escape was the enterprise of young men. Slave owners sometimes advertised for the capture of their runaways in colonial newspapers. The notices indicate that runaways tended to be young, rather than old, and male, rather than female. For instance, nineteen notices of escaped or captured runaway slaves were placed in the *Cape Town Gazette and African Advertiser* (often known as the *Government Gazette*) during 1826. Only three were for females. In 1832, when fifty-one such advertisements appeared in the *Gazette,* the proportions of male and female deserters were similar: nine of the ads requested the apprehension of female slave deserters; the over-whelming majority, forty-two, or 82.4 percent concerned males. In 1826, slave owners listed the ages of only three escaped slaves, all of them male; their ages were twenty-two, twenty-three, and thirty. In 1832, when twenty ages were noted, all but two of them for males, the average age was 25.8. Eldest were fifty-year-old men (the ages were no doubt ap-proximate); the youngest was a girl, aged thirteen.[103]

The newspaper advertisements are suggestive, not conclusive, but they reinforce the impression left by the protectors' reports that most runaways were young men. Other aspects of slave life also support this conclusion. The work of rural slave women, though not confined to their masters' homes, did not take them away from the farms as often as did the labor of slave men. As we saw in chapters 4 and 5, men were more frequently hired out to neighboring farmers; they followed the masters' herds and flocks on the seasonal migrations between summer and winter pastures, much more often than women; and they alone worked as traveling artisans. Male slaves were more familiar with the lay of the land than female slaves and were, consequently, better placed to locate the food, water, shelter, and hideaways necessary for a successful escape. They were also less likely to work under close supervision in and around their masters' home. Just as importantly, slave families tended to be matrifocal, and slave women assumed the primary responsibility for child care, as we shall see in chapter 8. Because they so valued their children and because escape with children in tow was doubly difficult, slave mothers rarely chose to run away. In the United States, as well, slave women ran away far less often than slave men, and the responsibilities of child care were an important reason why this was so.[104] Nevertheless, some slave women at the Cape were not to be stopped, and they some-times took their children with them when they escaped. Sarah, for in-stance, a slave who ran off in 1834, took her three-year-old daughter with her.[105] For slaves of any gender, escape was difficult. A successful escape required strength and physical stamina, as much as courage, luck, and opportunity. Older slaves, on the whole, were at a physical disadvantage and were disinclined to run away.

Slaves and apprentices ran away for a variety of reasons. The most common reason may have been, as Ross suggests, "punishment or the fear of it."[106] For instance, Eva, one of the few deserters who was not only a woman but, at forty-six, much older than the average runaway, ex-plained her escape in particularly revealing terms. After her master had recaptured her, she said that "she merely wanted to conceal herself for a few days as her Mistress was beating her too Much." Because Eva was the mother of three children, two of whom were thirteen and ten, it is perhaps significant that she had planned a temporary, not permanent, escape.[107]

The punishments that led slaves to desert were often tied to the forced-labor process. This was true for Arend, a slave on Adriaan de Kock's Koeberg wheat farm. He appeared at the protector's office to press charges against his master. De Kock, he told the protector, had beaten him with a walking stick, without cause, while he was working in the fields. This beating had not satisfied his master, Arend said, and he had gone into to his house to fetch a cat-o'-nine-tails. Arend, understanding very well what was about to happen to him, ran off. He returned to the farm a few days later and again was beaten. De Kock's testimony filled in some of the silences in Arend's story. Labor discipline had been the point of the exercise. De Kock said that he had struck his slave for being "very negligent . . . whilst cutting the harvest." The protector refused to prosecute de Kock. As far as he could determine, Arend's punishment had been lawful and just. His master had beaten him first because of his malingering and later for running away. It is not clear whether Arend believed that the initial beating had violated the moral economy of the lash; it is certain, however, that his desire to avoid a second beating was the principle factor that drove him to desert.[108]

The social and physical geography of the Cape Colony provided the slaves and apprentices with several avenues of escape. The slaves, whose ancestors had come from widely scattered societies in the Indian Ocean basin, southeast Africa, and Europe, varied greatly in appearance. Their hair might be straight, wavy, or tightly curled, their skin dark, medium, or fair, their features sharp or broad. One could not have said what a typical slave looked like. One master described his escaped slave Salomon as having "a stout figure, white complexion, light blue eyes, [and] light brown curly hair."[109] While I have no evidence that slaves ever passed themselves off as white, they did masquerade as a members of other social groups. In 1834, for example, F. J. Bestbier offered a reward of R.20 for the apprehension of two of his slaves. One, Felix, was a tailor who, Bestbier believed, passed himself off as a free black; Hendrick, the other deserter, pretended to be a Bastaard Hottentot, or so his master claimed.[110] A slave owner on the eastern frontier felt that his escaped slave Damant, who had "the appearance of a Bastard," would play on his looks in an attempt to enter the Cape Regiment, a unit of Khoisan and Bastaard Hottentot troops that was commanded by white officers.[111] A little more than a year later, another eastern Cape master notified the special justice in Graaff-Reinet that his apprentice July was "now serving in the Army at Fort Beaufort." July's "yellow complexion" allowed him to pass as a Khoisan or Bastaard Hottentot and enlist.[112]

Rather than enlist, slaves and apprentices more frequently used their indeterminate appearance to hire themselves out to employers while claiming to be free blacks or Bastaard Hottentots. Spadille, a runaway apprentice, supported himself for nearly a year by hiring himself out "to different people in the Country on his own account."[113] William Stephanus Smith, a farmer in the Graaff-Reinet district, took his recently recaptured housemaid, Aploon, to a special justice for punishment. She had deserted several weeks earlier and had survived by hiring herself out to an employer in Graaff-Reinet village.[114] In the southwestern grain district of Malmesbury, Piet, an apprentice, eluded his master for three months and, during those months, hired himself out "as a free person."[115] Hendrick, another western Cape runaway, passed as a Bastaard Hottentot and supported himself by "cutting Oats [for wages] at Eerste River."[116] These and many other slaves and apprentices survived by taking advantage of both their looks, which for many did not distinguish them from free blacks, Khoikhoi, or Bastaard Hottentots, and the Cape's chronic labor shortage, which prompted many employers to avoid asking prospective workers potentially embarrassing questions.

There were other ways to survive as a deserter. Annette, an apprentice on a farm in the Graaff-Reinet district, was one of many runaways who "secreted herself in the mountains" and "lived on the wild berries and roots." She managed to stay alive for three weeks before her master captured her.[117] Jacob, a Cape district slave whom the protector described as "a very bad subject," supported himself while he was a deserter by hiring himself out to several different employers in Cape Town and by engaging in petty theft. He eventually pleaded guilty to charges of burglary and was sentenced to jail for the theft of a chest, clothes, a bridle, and a saddle.[118] It was common for runaway slaves and apprentices to engage in petty crime to support themselves. Maladieu, another deserter caught in Cape Town, admitted that he and two other runaways had been guilty of a series of housebreakings and thefts.[119] As Maladieu's case suggests, escape was not always an individual act. The droster or runaway gangs were legendary.

Eighteenth- and nineteenth-century accounts of life at the Cape often complained that Table Mountain was "much infested with runaway slaves, who lurk[ed] in the caverns and recesses of the mountain, and sometimes attack[ed] travelers who [were] not sufficiently protected by numbers."[120] Most of the Table Mountain runaways were slaves, though some were Khoisan and others were whites escaping Dutch or British military and naval service. At least one, Joshua Penny, was a young American who had been pressed into the Royal Navy.[121] Though the runaways derived some of their sustenance from crime, they also relied on help from their friends. The runaways developed a regular trade with the slaves who daily climbed the slopes of the mountain searching for firewood. They cut wood and bartered it for "a little Bread, Tobacco & Fish," brought to them by the city slaves. The deserters avoided recapture "as they [had] so many hiding places and are so well acquainted with . . . the mountain" and because their fellow slaves rarely turned them in.[122]

Droster gangs were common in the mountains of the southwestern and northwestern Cape. The gangs commonly included Khoikhoi and Bastaard Hottentots who, like the slaves, were fleeing oppressive conditions on colonial farms.[123] Gang members sometimes eluded capture for years on end, periodically dropping out of the mountains to raid settler farms, counting on the cover of darkness and the isolation of the Boers to protect them. In 1827, for example, a court in Stellenbosch convicted seven slaves belonging to five different masters and "the Hottentot Hendrick their accomplice" on charges of desertion, vagrancy, and "repeated cattle thefts." The gang had survived in the mountains outside the village for at least several months.[124] Earlier in the same year, the court had convicted Michiel, one of the most notorious runaways in the colony, of desertion. A slave belonging to A. B. van Reenen, Michiel had been charged with "deserting, about three years since . . . vagabondizing and committing various acts of robbery in the district of Stellenbosch." The prosecutor contended that he had "secreted himself amongst the Kleindrakenstein mountains, where he became the leader of a gang of run-away Slaves, who committed numerous acts of burglary and cattle thefts." So irksome did Michiel and his band become that the government offered a £20 reward for the leader's capture. Several commando parties went out in search of him, "but without success, although some of his gang were taken," before a final commando brought him in. The sentence that the court imposed was severe. Michiel, the court said, would be "exposed at the usual place of execution with a rope around his neck, and confined for life in irons on the public works."[125]

The only location in the colony that can be said to have sustained a lasting community of runaway slaves was Hangklip (Hanging rock), on the mountainous southeastern shore of False Bay. As early as 1725 and for the next hundred years, escaped slaves lived in the rock shelters above the coast and survived by fishing, raiding the flocks and herds of neighboring farmers, robbing travelers, and bartering with Cape Town slaves, who were a day's journey away by foot. Though Hangklip was quite close to Cape Town, the droster's hideout was relatively secure. Commandos arriving on horseback could be seen miles away, and the rugged terrain meant that the horses would eventually have to be left behind. The rocky shoreline prevented any approach by sea. From time to time, commandos captured one or even several of the deserters, but the community survived. While the site seems to have been continually occupied from the early eighteenth century until emancipation, it did not reproduce itself biologically. It gained and lost members as slaves escaped to join the gang and others were apprehended.[126]

In the eighteenth century, it seems that the Hangklip deserters were solely slaves.[127] By the nineteenth century, that had changed. In 1826 the assistant guardian of slaves in Stellenbosch reported on the trial of six slaves, five men and one woman, who "were part of a large group of runaways who infested the Hangklip Mts., and subsisted by what they could steal." Captured with the six slaves was "their accomplice, the Hottentot Jan." The charges the drosters faced included desertion, vagrancy, cattle theft, and repeated burglaries. Despite reports such as this one, it is difficult to determine how many slaves may have lived at Hangklip at any given time. Ross, who has identified fifty slaves who were connected to the community at some point during the eighteenth century, contends that no more than ten occupied the site at any given time.[128] Whatever the size of the Hangklip group, droster gangs tended to be small. Though they allowed some slaves to escape their masters for extended periods of time, they rarely touched the lives of most Cape Colony slaves.

Permanent escape was more of a possibility in the far eastern and northeastern districts, where slaves sometimes fled the colony altogether, hoping to find sanctuary among the independent and semi-independent African societies on and beyond the colonial frontier. From almost the earliest days of the colony, slaves periodically escaped to Khoisan communities beyond the reach of colonial authorities. Though many were incorporated into these societies, slaves could not always be sure of a warm welcome. Either under duress or because they hoped to win favor with the colony, the Khoisan sometimes returned slave deserters. As the colony expanded during the course of the eighteenth century and as colonists conquered and destroyed Khoisan communities, slaves began to seek a haven with still independent chiefdoms and bands well to the north of the colony. Slaves were at times also welcomed by the "numerous small groups of herders, hunters, and raiders" along the Orange River, "who were only too happy to acquire all the manpower they could." Slaves could become full members of these new communities, such as the Griqua, which derived their members and culture from both indigenous societies and settler societies.[129] Slaves knew as well that Xhosa chiefdoms east of the colonial border would sometimes welcome and protect them and eventually incorporate them. A late-eighteenth-century traveler remarked that the Xhosa admired and made use of the "warlike" character of the runaway slaves.[130]

Because frontier societies tended to embrace and protect escaped slaves, few of the runaways who found shelter there enter the colonial record. One who does, Philip Byers, a slave belonging to Mathias Jacobus Pretorius of the Graaff-Reinet district, ran away several times, often staying away for months at a time. He once ran off to the Griqua settlement of Philipolis and lived there for some time until Pretorius tracked him down and took him home.[131]

Inviting though it might have been, the frontier was not always a land of liberty. The story of another slave droster, Frederick Opperman, illustrates the point. He escaped to the border community led by Jan Bloem II, the son of a white father and Khoisan mother. He stayed with Bloem for seven years, serving him as a blacksmith. Though Opperman was grateful for the protection Bloem offered, he became convinced "that it was too dearly bought by his dependence." All of his earnings went to Bloem. At the first opportunity, he sought refuge with Adam Kok, a Griqua leader who granted him considerable freedom. While with the Griquas, Opperman built up considerable property holdings by working as a smith and developing a large clientele among the "white, black, and yellow" farmers, herders, hunters, and outlaws of the frontier.[132] As Opperman learned, escape was an imperfect solution to an intractable problem. Escape, like all other forms of everyday resistance, had limited and sometimes cruelly compromised results. Slaves might escape slavery, but at the same time sacrifice their family ties and find neither true freedom nor material comfort. The act of escape, which slaves and apprentices repeated hundreds of times every year during the nineteenth century, nevertheless reflected and reinforced a habit of mind that denied the legitimacy of their masters' control of their minds, bodies, and labor. Dramatic though it might have been, it was but one of many ways in which slaves refused to accept social death.

Violence is inherent in slavery. The act of enslaving the original generation of slaves involves the violence of warfare or kidnaping, and violence is central to the task of reducing the children of subsequent generations to a servile condition. Violence is not only a necessary part of reproducing slave systems from generation to generation, it is crucial to the survival of master-slave relationships from moment to moment. Violence and the threat of violence demonstrated, in symbol and in the flesh, the power of the master or mistress and the subordination of the slave.

As this chapter has shown, most slaves and apprentices resented slavery, and most resisted the violence that their masters and mistress directed at them at least some of the time. While they rarely rose in rebellion, they often engaged in small acts of physical or ideological defiance. The slaves knew that they were weak and recognized that open resistance would bring them few results and much suffering. Consequently, they resorted to the weapons of the weak—weapons that required little planning or organization and were difficult for their masters to detect or prevent. Everyday resistance freed few people from slavery, but it forced slave owners to recognize, in ways that they otherwise would not have, that their slaves were not the childlike beings that they pretended they were. And it forced many to reach a compromise with their slaves, not by eliminating the violence inherent in slavery, but by holding it in reserve.

Everyday resistance tended to be the work of individuals, yet most slaves and apprentices shared habits of mind that sanctioned resistance. They collectively resisted the lash, succumbed to counterfeit epidemics of disease, and aided and abetted escapes. Incidents of everyday resistance are evidence of both a spirit of mutuality and of an ethic that delegitimated their subordination to the their masters and encouraged resistance. The slaves did not believe themselves to be socially dead, and by their resistance they showed that they were not.

Evidence of the slaves' and apprentices' resistance to social death is found not only in their everyday acts of defiance, but also in their religious beliefs and family life. The slaves acted least like slaves and most like fully human, autonomous human beings when they assumed the roles of mother or father, daughter or son, or child of God. The creation of slave and apprentice families and religious communities were not always self-conscious acts of resistance. But, as we shall see later, faith and family profoundly challenged social death. When combined with everyday resistance to the lash and to labor exploitation, they allowed the slaves to make themselves, if not free, then much less than fully enslaved.

CHAPTER 7

"A Faith for Ourselves"
God and the Slaves at the Cape

The interest of the Master is the same as that of Government,
whose principal object is the real happiness of each subject in his
relative situation in life.

—SIR JOHN TRUTER, CHIEF JUSTICE OF THE CAPE, 1812

An unjust king asked a Sufi what kind of worship is best. He
replied, "For thee the best is to sleep one half of the day so as not
to injure the people for a while."

—SAYING ATTRIBUTED TO SA'DI

T he records tell us little about Valentyn Snitler, but we do know that
he was impetuous and devout, a volatile combination in one both young
and enslaved. One day in the spring of 1832, during a heated argument
with his master, Jacobus Stephanus Vermaak, Snitler blurted out an eloquent and audacious statement of faith, for which his master beat him.
A few days after the quarrel, having accompanied his master to town on
an errand, he stole away to register a complaint with the protector of
slaves in Uitenhage.

Vermaak, Snitler told the protector, had whipped him unjustly. His
master, he said, had given him ten stripes with a cat-o'-nine-tails, despite
his plea that he was too sick to work. When the protector learned that
Vermaak was also in Uitenhage, he invited him to tell his side of the
story. Vermaak said that insolence, not indisposition, provoked the beating. On the day in question, he had been unhappy with Snitler's work.
When he spoke to him about it, Snitler had answered "in a very impertinent manner that he was not well." Vermaak said that he had then ordered him to take some medicine, and he had refused. Vermaak told
him that his choices were to accept the medication or go back to work.
At that, Vermaak continued, Snitler had "commenced to cursing and
swearing, and[,] holding his finger in [my] face said 'We have been created by one God and I am as good as you.'" This had been too much for
Vermaak, who had reached for his whip.

Snitler, the protector reported, at first denied Vermaak's version of events, but, when pressed, admitted that it was true. Others, he said, had encouraged him to press charges that he now acknowledged were false. On hearing this confession, Vermaak forgave his slave, bringing the case to a close.[1]

This story shares its basic plot with hundreds of others in the archives of the Cape Colony's protectors of slaves. An exasperated slave spoke too directly to his master, who interpreted outrage as insolence and punished his slave accordingly. The slave complained about the beating to a protector of slaves, who conducted an investigation. The slave's insubordination having been established, the slave dutifully acknowledged that he had been in the wrong and deserved his punishment. This story, like the others, is about violence and degradation, soul murder and social death. It is also about the ambiguities of resistance. Snitler, like most slaves, found it impossible fully to accept the ideologies and social practices of the slave system; and he found it equally difficult completely to reject them. The notion that slaves were innately inferior to their owners and owed them unquestioning obedience was, like the whip, part of the fabric of daily life. So, too, were the slaves' anger and resentment. The result was often the sort of double consciousness that Snitler displayed. He recognized the injustice of slavery and his own inherent equality with his master; at the same time, circumstances forced him to concede that he owed his master some degree of deference and obedience. Two warring souls in one dark body.[2]

If the story's plot is mundane, its details are not. Snitler's stunning declaration of faith and assertion of equality direct our attention to the way religion shaped a particular slave's ideas about the world and his place in it. Snitler was one of the thousands of slaves who had been exposed to one or both of the dominant religions of the Cape, Christianity and Islam. We cannot know whether the God that he invoked in his confrontation with Vermaak was the God of the Gospels or of the Quran; nor can we know whether he was a formal convert to one of these faiths or simply a man who had somehow learned something about one or each of them. We do know that he had absorbed two of the central teachings upon which the faiths are built. He believed that there was but one God and that this creator God had made him, in some essential sense, Vermaak's equal. These lessons supplied the ideas and the language that he used during his confrontation with his master. As Snitler saw it, God had not created inferior and superior orders of humankind, and Vermaak had no business acting as if God had. In refusing to submit to his master's unreasonable command and in asserting his dignity as his master's equal, he rejected social death and demonstrated that his soul was very much alive. Theology trumped ideology, if only for the moment.

By the 1820s and 1830s, a large minority of the slave and apprentice population had joined Muslim and Christian communities within which slaves and nonslaves were able collectively to mount sustained and sometimes effective challenges to the degradation and alienation of soul murder and social death. Few slaves professed Islam when they arrived at the Cape, and none were Christians. There was, in fact, no widely shared faith among the thousands of captives that the slave ships carried to southern Africa.[3] Yet by the fourth decade of the nineteenth century, several thousand slaves and Prize Negroes, mostly in and around Cape Town, had formally converted to Islam, and many more floated around the edges of the Muslim community. Although only a handful of slaves had been baptized as Christians, more than two thousand attended missionary schools or regularly heard the gospel preached in churches, chapels, and mission stations. As different as Islam and Christianity might be theologically, each provided a spiritual, psychological, and physical sanctuary for those who walked through their doors.

To both converts and the curious, Christian and Islamic theology offered coherent bodies of thought that could be turned against the ideologies of slavery.[4] The religious critique of slavery allowed slaves to redefine themselves as children of a merciful and compassionate God, equal to all other people in God's sight—a stark contrast to the ways in which colonial society defined them. Christian and Islamic theology also set standards against which converts judged their owners and the society that held them in chains. Especially within the Muslim community, slaves put theology into practice. Schools, mosques, and other places where the faithful gathered were physical spaces within which converts became full members of a community—the Islamic community—rather than marginal members of colonial society. Muslim converts, and to a lesser extent slaves who attended Christian schools or who elsewhere heard the gospel proclaimed, experienced belonging instead of alienation, respect instead of degradation, love instead of domination. Religion's gifts to the slaves and Prize Negroes were tools, both spiritual and practical, with which they could begin the arduous task of psychological and social resurrection.

A Lesson from the Cape Town Goal

In 1835, Barnabus Shaw, a Methodist missionary who had arrived at the Cape from Britain nearly two decades earlier, was "called upon to visit three Mohammedans, under sentence of death." Although they were Muslims, they were so receptive to Shaw's preaching that he was moved to ask them why they had chosen Islam instead of Christianity. The oldest, who had been born a slave, said that his master had taught him nothing about religion. Speaking now for group, he said that they converted to Islam because "Wy waren verlaten om een geloof voor zelfs te zooken" (We were left to seek a faith for ourselves).[5] This delightfully ambiguous answer is open to several interpretations, all of which may be true. Shaw believed that it indicated the extent to which colonial churches and missionary societies had neglected the slaves, a sentiment that was uncharitable, but not entirely inaccurate.[6] As J. S. Marais wrote many years ago, until the end of the eighteenth century "nothing that is worthy of mention was done by the church or a missionary society toward the christianization of the slaves."[7] Churches and missionary societies were more active during the first four decades of the nineteenth century, but by the time of emancipation, the gospel had reached only a minority of the slaves. As a result, many of the slaves who got religion got it through their own efforts, and, Shaw believed, got it wrong.

Alternatively, the converts may have been alluding to the slave owners' refusal to spend very much time worrying about the state of their slaves' immortal souls. From the beginning of the slave era until its end, few slave owners sought to convert their slaves to Christianity, and most were undisturbed by the idea that their slaves might embrace Islam. J. T. Bigge, writing on slavery at the Cape in an 1831 report to the British Parliament, offered two explanations for this anomalous state of affairs. First, slave owners mistakenly feared that slaves who converted to Christianity acquired a claim to freedom. Second, and perhaps more importantly, they viewed "with apprehension any measure which might have a tendency to abridge the relative distance between Master and Slave."[8] Slave owners saw no good coming out of conversion to Christianity, which had the potential to undermine the hierarchy of master and slave, and were indifferent to Islam, which could neither free the slaves nor narrow the social divide that separated them from their owners.

The remarks of the condemned convert might also have been a reference to what Bigge called the slaves' "manifest preference" for Islam.[9]

Most observers acknowledged the phenomenon and believed that this had more to do with sociology than theology. William Elliot, a Christian missionary who proselytized among Cape Town Muslims in the 1820s, wrote of the "perfectly natural" pleasure that Muslim slaves derived from "being of a religion different from and opposed to that of their owners." "If the Cape proprietors of slaves were Mohammedan," he wrote, "the majority of the slaves would immediately become Xtian."[10] Ironically, if not surprisingly, many slaves seem to have been just as determined as their owners to preserve the "relative distance" that separated them.

Despite the ambiguity of Shaw's account, it teaches one unarguable lesson about the converts he met: they sought God. Faith, Karen Armstrong has reminded us, is a fundamental part of human existence. People began "to worship gods as soon as they became recognizably human." Faith has allowed men and women to express "the wonder and mystery that seem always to have been an essential component of the human experience of the beautiful yet terrifying world."[11] Few worlds were more terrifying than the one in which the slaves and apprentices of the Cape found themselves, and, for many, religion was an important part of their lives. Historians of slavery worldwide have long recognized that spiritual hunger always accompanied enslavement. Commenting on slavery in the American South, Paul Radin wrote that slavery "was bound to leave the victims with a sense of degradation and sin." As a consequence, slaves adopted, recreated, and invented religions in which they found "cleansing and its concomitant rebirth."[12] In his discussion of conversion to Islam among the slaves of nineteenth-century Bahia, in Brazil, Joao Jose Reis emphasizes the slaves' search for community and "spiritual security."[13]

We know little about the faiths that slaves took with them to the Cape from South Asia, Madagascar, and East Africa, except that all but one were lost. These religions, divorced from their social and cultural roots, lacked the institutions, organized clergy, and sacred scriptures that would have allowed them to survive in a strange and hostile land. Islam alone endured to compete with Christianity for the slaves' allegiance. As we shall see, its Sufi *tariqa* (brotherhoods), mosques, and schools, its *shaykhs* (spiritual heads of Sufi brotherhoods) and imams (spiritual heads of mosques), and sacred text, the Quran, gave it a human and institutional infrastructure that only Christianity could match. These infrastructures allowed both religious communities—Islamic and Christian—to incorporate a diversity of new converts while maintaining the integrity of their doctrines and the coherence of their social identities.

Religious transformation, especially widespread conversion to one of the world religions such as Christianity or Islam, has been a touchstone of the modern world.[14] Historically, the spread of these faiths has often been associated with empire. Such was the case at the Cape, though with a twist. Christianity and Islam both reached the southwestern corner of Africa aboard the ships of the empire-building VOC, or Dutch East India Company. Christianity arrived with the company's sailors and settlers; Islam accompanied their prisoners, servants, and slaves.

The Company, the Church, and the Slaves

From the settlement's beginnings in 1652, the VOC supported the Dutch Reformed Church (DRC) financially and administratively, paying clergy salaries and prohibiting the public observance of other religions, including other Christian denominations, until the latter part of the eighteenth century. This was hardly a sign of deep religiosity. For at least the first century of settlement, DRC ministers were more concerned with the outward display of religious conformity than with the nature of their parishioners' spirituality.[15] There was a similar lack of enthusiasm for missionary work. The DRC virtually ignored the slaves and Khoisan, leaving them to the tender mercies of the VOC.

Early in the colony's life, VOC officials hoped that the slaves and Khoisan would adopt Dutch as their language and Christianity as their faith. This had less to do with religious enthusiasm, which was as lacking among the officials as the settlers, than with desire to establish and maintain Dutch cultural and political hegemony. In the 1650s and 1660s, several Khoisan received religious instruction, and one was baptized, but none were comfortable with their new lives. Most returned to their communities of birth; one, initially the most promising, ended her days on Robben Island, an isolated, miserable, drunken wretch.[16] Following these failures, the VOC all but ignored the Khoisan. The slaves were a different story. In 1658, Jan van Riebeeck, the VOC's first commander at the Cape, opened a school for young slaves in which they were taught the Dutch language and the rudiments of reformed Christianity. Gifts of brandy and tobacco encouraged them in their studies.[17] The company continued to operate schools for its own slaves until it surrendered the colony to the British in 1795. Instruction, often by slave and free black teachers, was perfunctory. The schooling, such as it was, did lead to baptism. Between 1665 and 1795, the DRC baptized more than two thousand slaves, an average of more than fifteen a year. The vast majority shared two characteristics: they were children, and their owner was the VOC itself. There is no evidence that either the VOC or the slaves attached religious significance to these baptisms. The company conferred no special rights upon the baptized, and no visible community of Christian slaves emerged during this period.[18]

Unlike the VOC, most private slave owners had no intention of sharing Christianity with their servants and slaves. For them, Christianity was as much a social identity as a faith. Whites called themselves Christians—meaning they were in a category separate and distinct from the slave, Khoisan, and Bantu-speaking African "heathens" among whom they lived. *Christian,* Timothy Keegan argues, was a racial term as much as it was a cultural one, referring to the "community of European origin."[19] As far as settlers and most DRC clergymen were concerned, Christianity, far from being a universal faith and identity, was their exclusive birthright.[20] It confirmed their sense of inherent superiority at the same time that it marked the boundaries of their community. The term *heathen* stigmatized slaves and Khoisan as inherently inferior and permanently excluded from proper society. Since the status was hereditary, it carried its own unstated racial assumptions. Settlers doubted that baptism could make slaves or Khoisan truly Christian in the religious sense of the word, and they insisted that it could not do so in its social or political connotation. Seventeenth- and eighteen-century settler Christianity served the colonists' interests, reinforcing their dominance and their slaves' and servants' subordination.

As we shall see, by the end of the eighteenth century, settler society was slowly turning away from the language of religion and toward the use of the language of race to define and justify hierarchies of power and status. This allowed some slave owners, especially in the more prosperous southwestern Cape, to support the conversion of slaves and Khoisan to Christianity without fear that this would undermine existing patterns of domination. These slave owners, however, remained a minority.

Throughout the slave era, settlers worked hard to maintain their Christian identity, whether in Cape Town and its well-populated hinterland or in the isolation of the frontier. Family devotions were a regular part of settler life. Slaves and Khoisan servants were often present as the head of the household read from the Bible and led prayers and psalms.[21] In this daily exercise of patriarchal authority, settlers forced slaves to worship their Christian God, even as they excluded them from their religious community and denied them access to the grace of salvation.

Henry Lichtenstein's account of household devotions on a cattle and sheep farm in the Roggeveld illustrates how the rituals surrounding these services reinforced the slaves' and servants' subordination. Lichtenstein wrote that every day began "with a psalm being sung, and a chapter from the Bible being read." The entire household, including all the slaves and Khoisan servants, was required to attend. In the evening

> the whole collective body of people belonging to the house were again assembled. In the first place came a female Hottentot, with a large tub of water, in which the feet of every individual in the [white] family, from the father to the smallest infant, were washed. A table was next set out, at which all the christians seated themselves; the slaves and Hottentots squatting, as in the morning, round the room. The father then read some extracts from his old sermons, which was followed by the whole company singing a psalm. The ceremony was concluded by the evening blessing.[22]

Foot washing (a ritual of humiliation) and squatting against the walls of the room (literal marginalization) meshed seamlessly with this celebration of settler Christianity.

Other settler religious practices confirmed belonging for whites and exclusion for nonwhites. On the frontier, settler families traveled for days to attend quarterly communion services at which they reaffirmed their ties to the "Christian" community.[23] Slaves and servants went along to attend their masters and mistresses, but could not take part in the services. Settlers also saw to it that their white children were baptized; slave and servant children, no matter who the father might be, were not. Baptism had as much social as religious significance; it was an indispensable prerequisite for admission to burgher status. As Keegan writes, it opened the door to "differential access to the legal system and to the protections and patronage of government."[24] It can hardly be surprising that the proportion of privately owned slaves among the slaves who were baptized during the VOC period started small and fell steadily.[25] The pattern was slow to change. Even though from the 1790s onward increasing numbers of slaves had access to Christian preaching and instruction, baptisms were few. More than two thousand slaves were attending services and receiving some Christian schooling by 1824, but only eighty-six were baptized between 1810 and 1824.[26] One reason for the paucity of baptisms was, as Bigge pointed out, the settlers's resistance to "any measure which might have a tendency to abridge the relative distance between Master and Slave."[27] But there was another consideration. Slave owners feared that baptism would lessen their property rights in their slaves and might even free them. While this had never actually been the case, there was some substance to these concerns.

In 1618, a synod held in the Dutch town of Dort had laid down the canons of the DRC. Slavery was among the questions that the synod addressed. After much discussion, it declared that slaves who had been baptized ought to be freed and, in any event, could not be sold out of the household into which they had been born. According to Richard Elphick and Robert Shell, the canons of Dort "periodically pricked the consciences of clergy concerned with Cape practice." In 1708, for instance, the Reverend E. F. Le Boucq complained that "baptised slaves, and their baptised children . . . are frequently alienated [that is, sold] here and used as slaves, which is contrary to Christian liberty."[28]

Such complaints had little impact on the behavior of either the private slave owners or the VOC. Private slave owners baptized very few slaves, and the VOC, which baptized many, freed almost none. Determined to bring Dutch practice into line with Dutch theology, the VOC decreed in 1770 that all Christian slave owners were bound to educate their slaves in the Christian religion, that all slaves who wished to be baptized should be, that no baptized slave could be sold, and that all baptized slaves should be allowed to purchase their freedom if they could. The decree, which stopped far short of freeing any of the slaves, was widely misinterpreted, many slave owners believing that it required them to manumit slaves who had been baptized. They were wrong, but could legitimately worry that the decree would have lessened their property rights in their slaves, had it ever been enforced, which seems never to have been the case. Nevertheless, the decree resulted in the almost complete cessation of slave baptisms.[29] And, in a fitting irony, it contributed to the spread of Islam among the slaves.

Islam in Exile

In early 1808, two years into the second British occupation of the Cape Colony, Governor Caledon dispatched a letter to the colonial secretary in London deploring Islam's success in attracting slave converts and reporting steps he had taken to stop it. He felt that newly imported slaves, who were mostly from Mozambique, were the most susceptible. They arrived at the Cape "in total ignorance," he wrote, "and being permitted to remain in that state . . . for the most part embrace the Mahomedan faith." He was "Anxious to undermine" Islam and "to afford these unfortunate people the consolation of a purer religion." Since ignorance was the root of the problem, knowledge was surely the cure. He had therefore "empowered" the ministers of the DRC and Lutheran churches in Cape Town to appoint instructors "for the duty of promulgating the Gospel to the slaves belonging to the members of their respective congregations."[30]

Caledon was by no means the only colonial official to be concerned about the spread of Islam among the slaves. By 1808, the Muslim community had entered a period of rapid growth, especially in Cape Town and the surrounding countryside. What had been something of an underground faith, tolerated so long as it remained below the horizon, had become remarkably visible during the 1790s. Public worship commenced early in the decade; the first Islamic school opened in 1793 and the first mosque sometime between 1795 and 1804.[31] The schools and mosques provided energetic shaykhs and imams with the institutional infrastructure they needed to be able to attract large numbers of converts from the relatively mobile slave population in and near Cape Town. But the rise of Islam at the Cape came only after a century of slow preparation.

Most Cape Muslims regard Shaykh Yusuf al-Taj al-Khalwati al-Maqasari (more commonly, Shaykh Yusuf of Macassar) as the founder of their community. Scholar, statesman, and Sufi mystic, he was exiled to the Cape in 1694 because of his role in leading opposition to Dutch expansion in the Indonesian archipelago. He and his large retinue immediately became the most visible Muslim community south of the Limpopo. The shaykh and his party were not, in fact, the first Muslims to enter South Africa; he owes his place in the popular imagination to his fierce resistance to the Dutch, his religious writing (much of which is still extent),[32] his piety, and his reputation as a healer and miracle worker.[33] The symbolism is also appropriate. Yusuf's story embodies the community's history of exile and dispossession.

The men and women who planted Islam in South Africa were laborers, exiles, *bandieten* (convicts), and slaves that the VOC transported to the Cape during the seventeenth and eighteenth centuries. The first sizable group of Muslims to arrive at the Cape may have been Mardyckers, from Amboyna in the southern Moluccas, who landed in 1658. Little is known about them. Although the company seems to have registered the Mardyckers as slaves, it explicitly granted them limited religious

freedom.[34] At the Cape as elsewhere in the VOC's possessions, the statutes of Batavia allowed the private, never public, practice of Islam, while
prohibiting proselytizing.[35] Official attitudes toward Islam were thus in
place virtually from the beginning and did not change until the end of
the eighteenth century. Islam was tolerated—never encouraged, never
seriously repressed.[36]

The Mardyckers' influence on the religious history of the Cape seems
to have been minimal. For Muhammed 'Adil Bradlow, the arrival in 1667
of three exiled Sufi shaykhs, the Orang Cayen (men of power), marks
the true beginning of Cape Muslim history. Conventionally, this history
falls into "two more or less discrete periods." During the first, the late
seventeenth century through the late eighteenth, small Muslim communities coalesced around Sufi shaykhs, such as the Orang Cayen and
Yusuf. The second, more public, period began with the opening of the
first Islamic school and mosque at the end of the eighteenth century.[37]

The Orang Cayen were among more than one thousand exiles that
the VOC transported to the Cape in its ongoing efforts to crush anti-
colonial resistance in the Indonesian archipelago. The company immediately sent two of the Orang Cayen, both of whom were Sufi shaykhs, to
the company's forest in Constantia hills in an attempt to isolate them
from slaves and free blacks in Cape Town. Shaykh Yusuf arrived three
decades later accompanied by an entourage of nearly fifty, including
wives, children, servants, slaves, and several imams. The VOC sent them
to Zandvleit, a farm even further removed from Cape Town than Constantia. Again the goal was to isolate them from potential converts. Bradlow contends that the effort failed.[38] Out of the sight but never completely out of mind, the shaykhs quietly attracted followers from among
slaves and free blacks, instructed them in the tenets and practices of
Sufism, and initiated them into their respective Sufi tariqa,[39] thereby
laying the foundations of Islam at the Cape. Bradlow argues that before
these men died they ensured the survival of their tariqa, and of Cape Islam, by investing others with the authority to initiate new members. In
this way, "several *tariqas* came to be established at the Cape, each with
[its] own network of shaykhs and *murids* [initiated members of the ta-
riqa]."[40] Hence, during the seventeenth and most of the eighteenth centuries, there were several distinct Muslim communities at the Cape—
small, secretive, isolated, and organized around the practices of Sufi
mysticism.

Bradlow's account initially received a cool response. One writer called
it "interesting and imaginative" but "no more than hypothetical."[41] The

problem, as Bradlow himself admitted, is one of sources.[42] The earliest Cape Muslims produced no written documents that survive.[43] In building his argument, Bradlow relied largely on the oral traditions of the Cape Muslim community and on the presence in the immediate vicinity of Cape Town of several venerable *kramats*—the tombs of shaykhs and imams who have come to be regarded as saints. The oral traditions he collected trace the local origins of particular tariqa to one or another of the exiled shaykhs. Kramats on and near the Cape peninsula have been associated with particular shaykhs and imams for, in some cases, nearly three hundred years, and have long been places of pilgrimage for local Muslims, who visit them to venerate the saints and to be healed or blessed.[44] In addition, Bradlow was able to draw on Suleman Essop Dangor's 1982 biography of Shaykh Yusuf, which discusses his membership in the Khalwatiyyah tariqa and provides translations of some of his devotional writings.[45] Bradlow had seemingly hung his argument on the slender threads of memory and circumstance. But these threads are not as weak as they might appear, and his argument has recently been echoed by other scholars.

In an unpublished manuscript written not long before his death, Achmat Davids, a prolific and pioneering historian of Islam at the Cape, accepted the contention that the Constantia exiles established the Qadariyyah tariqa at the Cape. He goes on to argue that Qadariyyah doctrines decisively shaped the beliefs and practices of the Cape Muslim community.[46] Elsewhere he links two of the most distinctive Cape Muslim ceremonies, the *ratiep*, a rite involving prayers, chants, and displays of bodily endurance, and the *rampie-sny*, a celebration of the Prophet's birthday, to Sufi practices. He suggests that the ritual observed and described by the Swedish traveler Carl Peter Thunberg in 1772 was a rampie-sny, a rare piece of evidence linking the days of the early shaykhs to the more thoroughly documented period that began at the end of the century.[47]

Yusuf da Costa also accepts the role of the Constantia shaykhs in the planting of the Qadariyyah in the colony. He believes as well that there "can be little doubt" that Shaykh Yusuf "continued to practice [in exile at Zandvleit] . . . the religious rites and ceremonies associated with his order," the Khalwatiyyah, including the initiation of members. He argues that Yusuf's tariqa influenced Muslim burial rituals, as reported by a traveler in 1797 and as practiced in the western Cape up to the present day. By the end of the nineteenth century, he writes, several tariqa had become "part of the Islamic fabric at the Cape."[48]

An emerging consensus suggests that Sufi tariqa have been present at the Cape from virtually the beginning of colonial settlement and that they have strongly influenced the development of local practices and beliefs. It is probably best to claim no more than this; too little can be known with certainty and too much must be supposed. Muhamed Auwais Rafudeen, for instance, has recently concluded that accounts of Shaykh Yusuf's exile, which often claim that Zandvleit became a refuge for runaway slaves and spiritual home for a multitude of converts, are ridden with unsubstantiated claims.[49] Despite these limitations, Sufism's presence and importance has been firmly established.

The second era of Cape Muslim history began as early as the 1770s, when, as Bradlow writes, "one begins to witness a shift in emphasis towards more overt, unified forms of organization."[50] This part of Bradlow's argument conforms to the earlier conclusions of Davids and Robert Shell.[51] Substantial growth in the size and cohesiveness of the Cape Muslim community began in the late eighteenth century and continued into the nineteenth. The Dutch colonial government's growing toleration of Islamic worship was one of the critical factors that contributed to this process. The Dutch certainly did not welcome public Islam, but neither did they suppress it. By the 1770s, Muslims regularly held services in private Cape Town homes, and officials did not try to stop them. Indeed, we know of these practices in part because the European traveler Thunberg described such ceremonies in his widely circulated narrative.[52] By the 1790s, Muslims were holding open-air Friday services in a quarry just beyond the Cape Town limits, unmolested by the authorities.[53] Finally, authorities did not interfere when local Muslims opened a school in 1793 and the first South African mosque sometime between 1795 and 1804.[54]

Factors internal to the Muslim community were just as important as external ones in initiating and sustaining the community's growth. The newly opened schools and mosques laid the institutional foundation for sustained growth and consolidation. Both Davids and Bradlow also see the release from prison in 1793 of Tuan Guru, a political exile from the Ternate Islands and an extraordinarily learned Muslim scholar, as a key event in the reconfiguration of the community.[55] Tuan Guru was instrumental in the creation of both the first school and the first mosque at the Cape. Beyond that, he seems to have been the figure who reconciled the earlier tariqa-centered Islam of the seventeenth and eighteenth centuries with the mosque-centered religious practice of the nineteenth and twentieth.

This reconciliation was possible, Bradlow contends, because Tuan Guru was thoroughly grounded in Islamic scholarship and, at the same time, well versed in Sufi traditions.[56] Davids noted that Tuan Guru's manuscript "Ma'rifah al-Islam wa al-Iman" (Manifestations of Islam and faith), composed while he was imprisoned on Robben Island, combined a discourse in Islamic law with an acknowledgment of his intellectual indebtedness to Muhammed Yusuf ibn al-Sunusi, a leading Sufi philosopher.[57] Davids argued that the "Ma'rifah" was the founding text of the Cape Muslim community, creating a theological framework within which slaves and free blacks, many of whom were small slave owners, could "function together [in a religious body] without threatening their respective stations in life."[58] Tuan Guru, a slave owner himself,[59] offered slaves the possibility of upward mobility within the Muslim community and "a fair degree of protection from . . . harsh treatment" by their Muslim owners, while avoiding any condemnation of slavery itself.[60]

Increasing official toleration,[61] a coherent theology, and a growing institutional infrastructure laid the basis for rapid growth in the number of Muslims in the Cape Colony between 1800 and the years following the de facto emancipation of the slaves in 1838. By the end of 1824, there were two large mosques and five smaller ones in Cape Town.[62] In the same year, the community supported three or four schools, the largest enrolling 491 children and adults; by 1832, there were twelve.[63] Shell's research makes it clear that the growth of the Muslim population more than kept pace with the development of the community's infrastructure. From fewer than one thousand in 1800, the colony's Muslim community grew to more than seven thousand in 1842, with sixty-five hundred in Cape Town alone (Islam at the Cape was and has remained largely an urban religion). Most of this growth was through conversion, not natural increase or immigration.[64] None of this pleased the British administrators of the early-nineteenth-century Cape. They could see no good and much harm coming from Islamic conversion and felt compelled to stem the tide.

Faithful Slaves

When Governor Caledon told the colonial secretary that he had made arrangements for the DRC and Lutheran church in Cape Town to spread the gospel among the slaves, he said little about the reasons for his hostility to Islam. It would have been superfluous; the Colonial Office undoubtedly shared his conviction that Christianity was, as he put it, the "purer" religion. Other officials at the Cape agreed on the superiority of Christianity, but they analyzed the situation in decidedly secular terms. Much like the VOC and in contrast with the settlers, the British administration believed that Christianity could act as "an agent of tranquility and social order."[65] Chief Justice Sir John Truter, for instance, felt that since Christianity had a "good influence on the character of the free," it could not "fail to have the same effect on slaves . . . rendering them even in their humiliating situation useful members of society." Writing in 1812 to Caledon's successor, Sir John Cradock, he explained that the "true interest of the master is . . . to have *Christian* slaves, that is those who cordially embrace the Christian religion, and who therefore become faithful slaves. . . . [T]he interest of the Master is the same as that of Government, whose principal object is the real happiness of each subject in his relative situation in life."[66] A decade later, H. T. Colebrooke, one of the commissioners sent to the Cape by the Colonial Office to assess Lord Somerset's administration, offered his own analysis of the religious lives of the slaves. Unlike Truter he was less impressed with the blessings of Christianity than with the curse of Islam. He argued that the large number of Muslim converts among the slaves "must be deemed a political evil." "The difference in colour [between slaves and slave owners]," he continued, "furnishes already but too broad a line of distinction. Add the difference of religion [and] . . . . A hostile feeling, nursed by religious animosity, may excite the slave against the master."[67]

The colonial government's plans to promote Christianity and combat Islam involved moving in three directions at once. It supported the work of Christian missionaries among the slaves; it repealed the VOC decree of 1770 requiring Christian slave owners to educate their slaves in Christianity and prohibiting the sale of baptized slaves; and it opened schools for the poor, including slaves, in which the fundamentals of Christianity formed the principal subject.

Governor Cradock in 1812 asked his legal officers to draft legislation that would repeal the 1770 decree. He argued that all of the government's "endeavours to extend Christianity . . . can have but a very limited effect while some Part of the ancient Dutch Regulations subsist, which affect the complete Property of the Master in his Slave if he became a Christian." As long as the law remained in effect, the doors of the churches would remain closed to the slaves. Cradock wanted slaves to receive "the Benefit of Christianity," but this would happen only if conversion left "the exact Property of the Master in the Individual . . .

unimpaired."[68] Justice Truter agreed that the benefits of bringing Christianity to the slaves needed "no demonstration" and that the "principal obstacle" to be overcome was the VOC decree. The law was ill-suited to conditions at the Cape, and neither he nor his recently deceased predecessor, he wrote, "could deduce from the true principals of our religion why a slave here cannot be a *slave* and at the same time a *Christian*."[69] The colony's chief legal officer also supported repeal, believing that once it came into effect "it will probably soon be seen that many [slaves] will be baptized and confirmed in the Christian faith."[70] Accordingly, on 9 October 1812 Cradock issued a proclamation declaring the decree null and void.[71]

Cradock understood that the slaves could not convert themselves and believed that schools had to be part of the process. In 1809 he had appointed a commission to look into the state of education at the Cape. The commissioners lamented the miserable condition of colonial schools and reported that most poor children, black and white, received no formal education at all. They recommended that the government establish free schools for the poor, including slaves.[72] A few years later, the circuit court reported that in the eastern districts slaves received no instruction and that opportunities were slight even for white children.[73] In 1813, in an effort to remedy the situation, Cradock created "a common and extensive fund" for the support of free schools for the poor (the fund relied on voluntary contributions). A commission—the Bible and School Commission—was appointed to administer the fund. As the commission's name suggests, the fund's goal was to promote the "religious and moral improvement" of children from "the lower stations of society." Free schools, to which slave children were admitted, duly appeared in Cape Town, though there were none in the country districts.[74] The schools do not seem to have produced the results Cradock desired. Few slaves attended and even fewer were baptized.

In 1823, another governor, Lord Charles Somerset, resumed the effort to bring light to the slaves. His proclamation of March 1823, designed to Christianize, civilize, and improve the lot of the slaves,[75] required slave owners in Cape Town and the villages in which free schools had been established to send slave children between the ages of three and ten to school at least three days a week. Rural slave owners generally evaded this provision as they did most of the others in the proclamation.[76] Later that year, a government report found that fifteen hundred slave children and adults, or roughly one slave in twenty, were attending school, mostly commission schools in Cape Town. When the report looked at baptisms, it discovered that in the decade and a half since Caledon first raised the issue, fewer than ninety slaves (approximately 1 in 350) had been baptized.[77] Neither changes in the law nor the opening of schools had succeeded in bringing Christianity to more than a handful of slaves. The colonial government had done its best and failed. At the same time, however, evangelical Protestant missionaries were trying their hand.

Georg Schmidt, a missionary sent to the Cape by the United Brethren, or Moravians, arrived in 1737 and quickly established two patterns that shaped missionary activity in southern Africa for the next century and a half. He directed his attention toward the Khoisan and earned the distrust of both the established church and the colonial administration. By 1743 he had been deported for baptizing five Khoisan, an act that flew in the face of both ecclesiastical protocol and local mores.[78] Missionaries who appeared subsequently, notably those of the London Missionary Society (LMS), who began to arrive in 1799, tended to follow the Moravian example of avoiding the settled parts of the colony, where most of the slaves lived, and proselytizing within Khoisan or Bantu-speaking African communities. The exception to the rule was the Cape's own South African Missionary Society (SAMS), which focused its efforts primarily on the slaves and servants of Cape Town and its densely settled hinterland.[79]

SAMS was an outgrowth of both a religious revival among the settlers in the late 1780s and the return of missionary societies in the 1790s, after the hiatus brought on by Schmidt's deportation. Its leading figure was M. C. Vos, the pastor of the DRC congregation in Tulbagh. According to R. L. Watson, Vos was "conspicuous as the only member of the Dutch Reformed clergy recorded as speaking against slavery."[80] However much he might have "wished that name of slavery was never known among us," Vos was himself a slave owner;[81] he said that the neglect of the slaves' immortal souls concerned him more than the actual conditions under which the slaves lived.[82] In this he was not alone. As lamentable as the material circumstances of the slaves' lives might have been, most missionaries believed that true slavery was slavery to sin and that "true freedom was only to be gained through the knowledge of God and the self that conversion gave."[83] Radicals who were prepared to challenge social norms, such as J. T. van der Kemp, James Read Sr., and John Philip, were few and far between. Even they were more likely to press the cause of the Khoisan than that of the slaves, believing that the British antislavery movement had already set the institution of slavery on the course to eventual extinction. The Khoisan, on the other hand, had been neglected.[84]

The refusal by SAMS to look beyond the slaves' spiritual needs allowed it to attract support from portions of the settler population. Within five years of its founding in 1799, its membership had reached four hundred. Most of the members were burghers of the southwestern Cape, some of whom were prosperous slave owners. Money was never a problem, but the society required more than financial resources if it were to reach the slaves.[85] It also needed the slave owners' cooperation because, as Elizabeth Elbourne and Robert Ross point out, missionaries who hoped to work among the slaves were utterly dependent on the slave owners' goodwill. Missionaries had to seek the slave owners' permission to enter their households; slaves needed permission to leave them. Accordingly, missionaries appealed to the slave owners' interests, arguing that Christian slaves were more trustworthy servants. Slave owners remained skeptical.[86] It is doubtful whether the South African Missionary Society ever succeeded in persuading more than a minority of slave owners to allow their slaves to receive religious instruction.

Nevertheless, SAMS soldiered on, carrying out its work in private until 1819, when it began to hold public services in Cape Town, Stellenbosch, and Paarl.[87] By the 1820s, SAMS was cooperating with the LMS-affiliated Cape Town Auxiliary Missionary Society (CTAMS), which supported additional missions to the slaves in Port Elizabeth, Uitenhage, and Grahamstown and issued periodic reports on the progress the missionaries had made. In 1825 the CTAMS admitted that on the whole its successes were few, though it preferred to view them as the "first fruits of a more abundant harvest." Indeed, there were some success stories. Vos was still active in Tulbagh, and the missionary in Paarl, the Reverend Mr. Evans, was attracting so many new adherents that he now needed a larger building.[88] Two years later, Evans reported that he held morning and evening services on Sundays, devoted Monday evenings to religious instruction, Friday evening to public worship, and Saturday evenings to prayer services. Although he did not indicate how many attended these functions, he did note that ninety-eight children and adults attended the school he ran on weekday mornings between 8:00 and 10:00, while forty-three attended evening classes.[89] In 1829, the new man in Paarl, the Reverend Mr. Kitchingman, was holding three services on Sundays and preaching on Friday evenings to "both slaves and many of their owners."[90] In Stellenbosch, the Reverend P. D. Luckhoff took his wife with him when he "visited the slaves in their hovels, and persuaded them to . . . cleanse their evil-smelling abodes, and to attend the services and evening schools which he had inaugurated."[91] At the same time, the Reverend William Elliot was attracting eighty to a hundred slave children and adults to his evening classes in Cape Town and fifty to eighty to worship services on Sunday afternoons.[92]

The historian J. S. Marais estimated that, overall, twenty-two hundred slaves throughout the colony were regularly attending Christian services by the middle of the 1820s. As many as fifteen hundred attended schools in towns and villages throughout the area from Cape Town to Graaff-Reinet. The instruction was designed primarily "to fit them for church membership"; in Stellenbosch, for instance, slaves learned to read and memorized hymns, passages from the Bible, and portions of the Heidelberg catechism.[93] None of the missionaries seems to have preached against slavery. Instead, their message to the slaves "was generally one of the necessity of obedience, of resignation to one's fate, and of the hope for glory in the world to come."[94]

By the 1820s, a significant minority of slaves, especially in the more densely settled parts of the colony, were being exposed to Christianity. Few were baptized, but far more heard the Word. The old settler prejudice against the Christianization of slaves and servants was beginning to break down. But this was happening slowly, as contemporary reports confirm. William Bird, the former colonial official and pioneering sociologist, maintained in 1822 that many slave owners clung to their "stubborn objections" to "the encouragement of Christianity." Some still believed that baptized slaves had to be freed, though the sentiment, he acknowledged, was not universal.[95] The Wesleyan missionary Barnabus Shaw wrote that while "some of the slave proprietors of Cape Town encourage the diffusion of religious knowledge among their slaves," others continued to be opposed.[96] Chief Justice Truter, whom Shaw knew well, was said to be the very model of the enlightened slave owner;[97] another master, a Stellenbosch farmer and owner of a slave named Lena, was not. In 1826, Lena visited the protector of slaves to complain that "her master would not allow her to attend church, although she had been brought up in the Christian religion, and that he will not cause her to be christened." The protector, guided by the reform laws that promoted the Christianization of the slaves, ordered Lena's owner "to comply with her request, that she should be allowed to go to church, and to be christened."[98] A few years later, Marie, a slave housemaid in Albany, went to the protector with a similar complaint. She said that her owner,

Mrs. John Rafferty, prevented her from attending church services, despite "longstanding requests." Once again the law favored the slave: the assistant protector in Albany directed Mrs. Rafferty to grant Marie's wish.[99]

Neither Lena's nor Marie's difficulties would have surprised the missionaries, especially those of the LMS, who, one of them wrote, were "hated with a perfect hatred," in large part because of their mission to the slaves and Khoisan. Jane Philip, the wife of John Philip, the most visible of the LMS missionaries, linked this hostility to the Dutch settlers' dislike of all things British and to the slave owners' "violent opposition to the British government in consequence of what they call interference between them and their slaves"—that is, amelioration.

Yet change was in the air. Elbourne and Ross are right to contend that in the nineteenth century settlers were more likely to support the conversion of their slaves and servants than had been the case earlier.[100] Significant numbers of slaves were attending schools and churches with the consent of their owners, especially in the southwestern Cape. In 1825, CTAMS reported that farmers in Paarl "allow their slaves to leave their employment in the morning of a weekday, to attend divine service, and do so themselves in the afternoon."[101] Shaw spoke of the "unspeakable delight" he felt when leading services near Cape Town in the 1820s and 1830s at which "masters and mistresses united with the darkest of Africa's sons in singing the praises of God." Among those present, on at least one occasion, was Justice Truter.[102] Writing in the third decade of the nineteenth century, H. T. Colebrooke, a commissioner of inquiry, argued that opposition to the conversion of slaves was "wearing away." "Masters, it is affirmed, begin to find that their slaves serve not the worse for instruction received in religious duties. Missionaries, who devote themselves especially to the religious instruction of slaves, (and there is one in each of the principal towns,) have increasing congregations."[103] This "wearing away" was especially noticeable in Cape Town and its hinterland.[104]

In 1952, Abraham Leslie Behr concluded, optimistically, that in the early nineteenth century a "new spirit was being evolved, in complete contrast to the type of prejudice that had prevailed at the end of the eighteenth century and that had opposed the baptism of slaves."[105] Behr may have been right about the effects of this new spirit, even if he was wrong about its nature. Openness to conversion did not imply openness to equality. The ethnocentrism and cultural chauvinism that had characterized settler thinking about the slaves, servants, and indigenous people among whom they lived were giving way to explicitly racist ide-ologies.[106] As the nineteenth century progressed, settlers were more in-clined to see race rather than religious affiliation as the crucial marker of social identity, drawing the line between white and nonwhite rather than between Christian and heathen. Indeed, the conversion of small numbers of slaves and Khoisan was enough to cause something of a crisis within the DRC. By 1829, its local synod felt it necessary to affirm that "the Lord's Supper should be jointly celebrated by all members . . . without distinction of colour or descent."[107] Just prior to final emanci-pation, James Backhouse, a missionary who traveled throughout the colony, discovered that the "prejudices of those who had been accus-tomed to hold their fellow men of a darker skin in bondage, were yet too strong, in many places, to admit them to join with themselves in public worship."[108]

It is hard to know what the slaves made of the missionaries' efforts to woo them. Few Christian slaves or slaves who were attracted to Chris-tianity enter the colonial records as individuals. In order to understand the slaves' response to the missionaries, it might be worth considering the fact that the relatively large number of slaves attending government and missionary schools resulted in surprisingly few baptisms. It is un-likely that this is due entirely to slave-owner resistance. When mission-aries, government officials, and other observers spoke of settler resist-ance, it had to do with their refusal to allow slaves to *attend* church and school, not to preventing those who were already being taught and preached to from being baptized. Indeed, missionary laments about the paucity of baptisms were often coupled to celebrations of their success in attracting students and congregants. When speaking about the Wes-leyans' work in Cape Town during the 1820s, Shaw, for instance, said that although the schools had "prospered delightfully," the missionaries could not yet "perceive that *immediate fruit* [that is, conversions] which we so earnestly desired."[109] In the same way, the 1825 CTAMS report noted, on the one hand, that 150 slaves attended services in Paarl and, on the other, its regret that so few slaves had been brought formally into the church.[110] The most comprehensive figures available, noted above, indicate that while twenty-two hundred slaves regularly attended church and fifteen hundred were enrolled in schools in the mid-1820s, the number baptized in the previous decade and a half "did not exceed 86."[111] Given the disparity between the number of students and number of converts, it is plausible to suggest that at least some of the slaves were using the missionary and government schools for their own purposes.

The experience of Imam Muding, one of the leading figures in the Cape Town Muslim community in the first decades of the nineteenth century, illustrates the point. Though not a slave himself, he was the son of a slave and representative of slaves and free blacks who sent their children to the government and missionary schools or who attended those schools themselves without the expectation that they or their progeny would adopt Christianity. Muding said that his four children went to both "European schools," where they learned to read and write Dutch, and an Islamic school, where they studied Arabic and the Quran. According to Muding, many other free Muslims sent their children to European schools.[112] But it was not just free Muslims who sent their children to government and missionary schools. Slave parents, Muslim and non-Muslim alike, did so as well. In 1821 Shaw reported that slaves, "free persons of colour," and "several children of Mohammedans" attended the Wesleyan "heathen school" (or school for heathens—the term was the Wesleyans') in Cape Town. Though the school was "well attended," few converts had been won.[113] By 1839, one year after final emancipation, about 230 children were attending CTAMS' Dorp Street school. The society itself estimated that up to half "of these [were] children of Mohammedan parents." They, along with the equally numerous children who were neither Muslim nor Christian, learned Dutch and listened to the missionaries' religious appeals, but only a handful joined the church.[114] In fact, the 1820s and 1830s were a period during which converts flocked to Islam, not Christianity—a fact that missionaries such as William Elliot, who worked among Cape Town Muslims on behalf of the SAMS, ruefully admitted.[115] It would appear that as far as most slaves and free blacks were concerned, schools were a place to acquire skills, such as literacy, which would allow them to deal more effectively with colonial society, rather than places to find God.

Elbourne and Ross argue that the missionaries' message to the slaves was one of obedience and resignation.[116] If so, it is not surprising that few slaves sought to be baptized. Exhortations of resignation to one's fate could not address a slave's most pressing spiritual and emotional needs. Admonitions to obey masters and mistresses could not resurrect a soul that slavery had murdered. The few who did find comfort in Christianity may have done so because they interpreted Scripture for themselves. Shaw, for instance, met an unbaptized slave woman who asked him to pray with her after hearing another slave read a passage from the Gospel of Matthew that had "particularly delighted" her: "Come unto me all ye that labour and are heavy laden, and I will give you rest." One suspects that she longed to rest in *this* world, not the next.[117] The slaves' disinterest in the Christianity of the state and the missionaries can be seen as a rejection of slavery and the slave owners' world of social death.[118] But the Christian's failure to convert the slaves does not explain the Muslim's success.

Conversion and the Search for Community

Robert Shell has done more than any other scholar to establish the Islamic community's rapid growth during the first decades of the nineteenth century. From fewer than one thousand in 1800, the number of Muslims at the Cape grew to more than seven thousand in 1842, most of whom lived in Cape Town. Virtually all this growth was through conversion, not natural increase or immigration; most of the converts were slaves or Prize Negroes.[119] Having established the remarkable extent to which Islam attracted converts, Shell turned his attention to explaining why it was able to do so. He explicitly rejects the possibility that spiritual concerns and what he calls "cognitive factors" had anything to do with conversion in this period. The grounds for conversion were "quite mundane and practical." Converts went to Islam in an effort to overcome their "economic marginality" and "racial exclusion." They went to achieve a higher social status or to find a community with which to identify and by which to be embraced, to prepare to marry a Muslim spouse or to be eligible for the solemn rites given the Muslim dead—"a cradle-to-the-grave range of social services." They went because the Muslims welcomed all, regardless of color, status, or ancestry, in great contrast to the racial exclusivity of most local Christians.[120]

Shell has undoubtedly identified some of the more important grounds for conversion at the Cape, all of which were related to slavery. Slaves, as Orlando Patterson has shown, were outsiders, the socially dead. Prize Negroes, who had only recently been stolen from their homes and thrust into a brutally alien environment, shared their fate. Precisely because they were socially dead, they were "desperate for life."[121] Converts to Islam who were slaves and Prize Negroes sought and found membership in a community distinct from that of their masters. In doing so, they established a degree of cultural autonomy and diminished their social marginality. Arguing along these lines, Achmat Davids demonstrated that a considerable degree of upward mobility was possible within the Muslim community, even for slaves. Several Cape Town imams were freedmen, and Achmat van Bengal was still a slave at the time he was appointed assistant imam of the Dorp Street mosque.[122] It was not only within the Muslim community that a convert's status could improve; some whites held Muslims in higher regard than other blacks, in part because they abstained from alcohol.[123] Likewise, Muslim ceremonies to mark pivotal stages of life—birth, marriage, death—would certainly have been attractive to those whose progress through life was otherwise unnoticed.[124] All of these are important considerations and were surely part of what led men and women to convert. Yet none of this advances us beyond the missionary William Elliot's 1829 discussion of conversion to Islam at the Cape. For him, conversion was an attempt to deny slavery its due.

Elliot's professional bias may have obliged him to discount the spiritual aspects of conversion to Islam.[125] Nevertheless, he knew the Muslim community well, and was, in fact, "rather a favorite" with them. His account of Islamic conversion is quite elegant, as far as it goes. He conceded that the "pomp and circumstance" of Muslim ceremonies attracted some converts. But the principal reason for conversion was "totally unconnected with religion."

Anticipating Patterson's concept of social death, Elliot wrote that slaves were "not recognized as . . . member[s] of society," no matter how kindly they might be treated by their owners. They remained "base fragment[s], detached from the family of man." Conversion to Christianity brought little relief. A Christian slave "may indeed be admitted into a Christian church, and may partake of the privileges of Christian communion. . . . But excepting when he is within the walls of the church, he is scarcely more a member of society than when he was an untaught heathen. There is a wide difference in colonial estimation between a Christian slave and a Christian man." In stark contrast, a slave who converted to Islam became "a real, not nominal member of an extensive society. . . . [I]t is not in the mosque alone that he feels himself a social being; in every house inhabited by a Musselman he finds a home and a brother."[126] One can hardly ask for a better description of social death and (at least partial) resurrection. But as an explanation of conversion it is incomplete. Elliot and his twentieth-century counterparts dismiss compelling evidence that spiritual concerns brought converts to Islam and that the rebirth of the socially dead at the Cape had something to do with God.

Conversion and the Search for Meaning

Nearly a decade ago, Richard Elphick lamented the marginalization of religion within South African historiography and called on historians and other scholars to study "the thought and actions of religious people—their doctrines, rituals, spiritual experiences, individual and corporate mentalities . . . with the utmost seriousness and . . . empathy."[127] It is a challenge that historians of Islam at the Cape have not entirely met. While they have produced convincing discussions of the "mundane and practical" grounds for conversion, the phenomenon has been analyzed as if God had nothing to do with it. These analyses are not so much wrong as they are partial.

Emefie Ikenga-Metuh has insisted that any account of conversion must be multicausal, not monocausal.[128] Robert Hefner adds that conversion is a matter of "faith and affiliation": it implies "the at least nominal acceptance of religious actions or beliefs deemed more fitting, useful, or true" and "the acceptance of a new locus of self-identification, a new, though not necessarily exclusive, reference point for one's identity."[129] Historians of Islam at the Cape have had a tendency, as Richard Eaton put it in another context, to "see any religion as a dependent variable of some nonreligious agency, in particular an assumed desire for social improvement or prestige."[130] Conversion was not like applying for membership in a country club and cannot be understood as an exercise in pure pragmatism. Muslim converts in South Africa longed "to find meaning and value in life, despite the suffering that flesh is heir to."[131]

Shell ties his dismissal of spiritual motives for conversion to an attack on Robin Horton's influential thesis on religious conversion in Africa.[132] A quarter-century ago, Horton drew on examples of conversion to monotheistic religions in small-scale African societies to argue that conversion from polytheism to monotheism was likely to occur when previously isolated societies were brought into contact with a much wider world through, for instance, incorporation into a colonial empire. Prior to the establishment of wider contacts, the social life of people in a small-scale society was largely confined within the geographic and cultural boundaries of their "microcosm." In their religious practices, they paid considerable attention to lesser spirits, who sustained the microcosm, and very little to a supreme being, who was more closely associated with the wider world, the "macrocosm." When the boundaries of the microcosm began to collapse and the macrocosm began to impinge strongly on everyday life, people experienced a religious crisis. The practices and beliefs associated with the lesser spirits could not explain or help people to control events that accompanied incorporation into the macrocosm. They began to pay less attention to the spirits and more to a supreme being, a god who transcended local boundaries and affiliations. As Horton put it, people "groped toward a more elaborate definition of the supreme being and a more developed cult of this being" in an attempt to cope with the larger world of which they were now a part. This process, in his estimation, opened the door to both Christianity and Islam.[133]

Horton has come in for his share of criticism. Research has shown that the crises that accompany incorporation into a macrocosm are not always catalysts for conversion and that religions oriented toward the microcosm sometimes "dig in, reorganize, and survive." Robert Hefner argues that Horton, nevertheless, "properly draws our attention to how incorporation into a larger social order acts as a catalyst for conversion [to monotheism] and the reformulation of indigenous religion."[134] Elizabeth Elbourne, who has studied conversion to Christianity among the Khoisan in the early nineteenth century, accepts the premise that societies and individuals "in a state of profound crisis . . . are more prone to seek new [spiritual] explanations and meaning systems" than are stable people and communities.[135]

Shell will have none of this. He claims not only that monotheism was "not clearly understood" by Muslim converts at the Cape, but that conversion was "accelerated by magical practices and syncretistic mysticism . . . unrelated to monotheism."[136] In fact, the contrary was the case. Shaykhs within their tariqa and the emerging Quranic schools ensured that the converts understood the fundamental teaching of Islam, a radical monotheism: "Your God is one God. There is no God but Him. He is the Compassionate, the Merciful."[137] And it is precisely "magic" and "mysticism" that provide us with some of the best evidence of the intensity with which converts worshiped God. Their devotion also shines a light on the spiritual concerns that drew them to Islam.

It would be hard to find a cohort of enslaved and oppressed converts better educated in the tenets of their religion than the Muslim converts of the Cape. Sufi orders flourished. The first Islamic school opened in 1793; three decades later, Cape Town was home to several of the schools, the largest enrolling nearly five hundred students. What lessons did the imams teach? "To look up to God for all good, and to fear Him," said one. This imam taught his pupils "to read and write Arabic"; "to observ[e] the facts prescribed by the Koran, [to attend] the service of the mosques, and [to make] their wives and children conform to these rites."[138]

Davids was able to expand on these remarks. The "Ma'rifah" of Tuan Guru was at the heart of the school curriculum. His grounding in Ash'arite theology led Tuan Guru to stress the "rational unity of God," and his exposure to al-Sunusi's Sufism allowed him to borrow a Sufi liturgy that "proved the most popular and convenient part of the manuscript for rote learning." The liturgy became known as the *twintagh siefaats,* the twenty attributes of God. Student notebooks dating from the first decade of the nineteenth century and containing transcriptions of this liturgy still exist in private collections in Cape Town.[139] Muslim converts at the Cape were thus well drilled in the fundamentals of Islamic monotheism.

The "magic" and "mysticism," too, were thoroughly Islamic. "Malay magic,"[140] especially the power to heal, drew converts to the Cape Muslim community—as the hope of being healed has drawn so many people to religion in so many different times and places.[141] Many "Malay Doctors" appear in the street directories of early-nineteenth-century Cape Town, and a belief in the power of learned Muslims to cure (and to curse) was shared by many in the colony, Muslim and non-Muslim, black and white.[142] Tuan Guru's "Ma'rifah" contains a number of prescriptions for spiritual remedies. Were these doctors and prescriptions somehow un-Islamic? Hardly. The prescriptions were normally composed of two elements, the earthly and the spiritual. Imams and shaykhs recited passages from the Quran while administering physical (often herbal) remedies.[143] What was called "Malay magic" at the Cape was simply "Islamic medicine" elsewhere in Africa.[144]

About three hundred *hadiths* (traditions relating the deeds of the Prophet Muhammed) deal with medicine and related topics. Sufi shaykhs are especially associated with healing. Sufis believe that shaykhs are inspired by the Prophet and expect them to safeguard the body as well as the soul. Ismail Abdulla notes that in West Africa and the Magreb, where Sufi orders flourish, the shaykh has become an important part of "the medical experience of . . . Islamic peoples."[145] The same is true elsewhere in the Muslim world; converts' hunger to be healed is part of what draws them to the Muslim community. Far from being unrelated to monotheistic spirituality, this "pragmatic" desire to be cured cannot be separated from the converts' faith in God, whence comes the power to heal.

The Muslim practice at the Cape about which Shell is the most skeptical is the ratiep. He acknowledges that this rite brought converts into the fold, but he maintains that it was both syncretic and unrelated to monotheism. Drawing on the authority of I. D. du Plessis, he says it was "originally a Hindu dance from Bali."[146] While agreeing that the ratiep was one of the "strategies" that shaykhs and imams employed in order to attract converts, Davids similarly implied that it was less than orthodox;[147] elements of Islamic spirituality were present in the ratiep, but, he argued, it also drew on "animistic ritual practices."[148] It seems more likely, however, that the ratiep, at least initially, was an utterly orthodox expression of Sufi devotion.

Although the ratiep was central to Islamic practice at the Cape for two centuries, no reference to it appears in Cape Muslim sources from the eighteenth and early nineteenth centuries. We see it through the eyes of whites who learned about particular performances only when something went wrong or when, as writers, they happened to observe them. Hundreds of ceremonies must have passed privately and without incident. Some did not, making various forms of the ratiep one of the best documented expressions of nineteenth-century Islamic spirituality in the Cape Colony.

The ratiep has had a checkered career. Whites have largely viewed the it as a peculiar ceremony of colorful but outlandish folk. In 1854, some called, unsuccessfully, on the government to suppress it, complaining that the noise disturbed the peace of the city.[149] Even within the Muslim establishment, the ratiep fell into increasing disfavor as the nineteenth century progressed,[150] perhaps because, as some suggested, it had become mere entertainment devoid of religious significance.[151] But there is no reason to believe that the men whose 1813 performance led to the death of one and the imprisonment of another were not every bit as sincere as they were unlucky.

The first written account of a ratiep is found within the records the 1813 trial of Griep, a free black from Mozambique, on charges of having caused the death of another free black, Abdul Zagie, during a ceremony at the home of the free black Hammat of Macassar. Griep admitted that he had been at fault. One evening at about midnight, he said, he and several other men had "performed the . . . *Callifat.*"[152] While rotating the tip of a sword on the stomach of a supine Zagie, he had intoned "some mystic prayers." Unfortunately, the sword caused "the entrails of said Abdul Zagie [to spill out of] his Belly, whereupon [Griep] sewed up the Wound, continually repeating his prayers." Griep's fervent prayers were to no avail: Zagie died within the hour. The court condemned Griep to labor in irons on the public works for three years.[153] As we shall see, nothing about Zagie's death suggests that this was anything other than a rite gone wrong.

Other accounts of the ratiep come from the pens of white observers. Although the ceremonies varied, the similarities make the connections clear. George Champion, a Christian missionary, wrote of "a confused noise of singing, beating of drums" and of men dancing with chains and "performing a variety of eccentric movements."[154] Alfred Cole, who attended a ratiep in the middle of the century, was less horrified than amused, as he freely admitted. The "comic parts" of the ceremony struck him "so forcibly . . . that the grandeur of the occasion was quite lost." His description, however, remains valuable for its detail.

> It was evening, and I was conducted into a large room. Candles were stuck in silver sconces, fastened to the walls in profusion. Round the room were several old Malays, squatting on mats, dressed in gala costume. In the centre of the room a quantity of perfume was burning. Three or four younger Malays kept marching round the room, and they and the old gentlemen kept up a sort of grunting, whining chorus . . . [and I] was afterwards informed that they were chanting sentences from the Koran. Suddenly the young gentlemen began to throw themselves about in gladiatorial attitudes, singing faster than ever. Thereupon the old gentlemen shouted louder. Then the young men stripped off their shirts. [They] danced, and jumped, and shouted, till they left little pools of sudorific exhalations on the floor. Then a boy came shouting awfully. . . . [A]t the same moment two of the young men seized the boy, and plunged a sharp instrument like a meat-skewer through his tongue—at least so it appeared. . . . [T]he boy looked quite happy and contented with his tongue on a skewer. . . . [Then] one of the young men took a dagger and plunged it into the fleshy part of his side . . . then walked round and showed himself. There were a few drops of blood apparently flowing from the wound. . . . Another man thrust a skewer through his cheek, and came and showed himself also. Then some red-hot chains were brought in, and thrown over an iron beam, when another of the Malays seized them with his bare hands, and kept drawing them fast over the beams. All the while . . . the Malays kept up their hideous shrieking of the

Koran sentences. . . . The noise, the sight, the weapons, and the red-hot chains, together, formed a scene bordering on the diabolical; except that there was such evident jugglery in the whole affair.[155]

Cole's was not the only such account. In 1861, an anonymous contributor to the *Cape Monthly Magazine* reported on a ratiep involving more than fifty men. Once again the observer refused to take the ceremony seriously. An "old priest," he wrote, "scattered a few grains of incense on a brazier . . . [and] began to recite a few verses of the Koran in a sort of high-pitched tremulous chant." After prayers, invocations, and hymns accompanied by the beating of tambourines, one of the participants, "while in a slow dancing step," plunged daggers into his stomach without apparent injury. The atmosphere grew frenzied. At one point, twenty men were "circling slowly round and round, throwing themselves in the most extravagant attitudes, plunging . . . their long keen daggers through the heart and lungs." At the end of the ceremony, the old priest obsequiously approached the writer, promising even greater feats. With that, he wrote, the "awful, mystical ceremony dwindl[ed] into a mere sleight-of-hand."[156]

Was the ratiep mere jugglery—a slight of hand? Perhaps by midcentury it sometimes was. But let us then go back to the early part of the century, back to a time when an educated Muslim visitor to the Cape praised the "many pious good" Muslims he met and said nothing about unworthy or un-Islamic ceremonies and beliefs.[157] If we, unlike Champion and Cole, take the ratiep seriously, it will tell us quite a bit about the spiritual concerns that brought converts to Islam. Through the ratiep, adepts negated aspects of slavery's social death and at the same time expressed their deep devotion to God. Before we can understand how this was so, we will need to know a little more about Sufism.

Sufism, "the guardian of the path of inwardness," is the form in which Islamic spirituality has most often "revealed itself in history."[158] Its roots lie in the Prophet Muhammed's "powerful mystic experiences briefly described . . . in the Qur'an."[159] Like mystical movements in Christianity, Judaism, and Buddhism, "the Sufi path is a . . . discipline of mind and body whose goal is to directly experience ultimate reality."[160] Sufis believe that only in this way can men and women attain a true knowledge of God, knowledge beyond rational thought and human perception. The Sufi ideal is a "state of annihilation"—"the systematic destruction of the ego [leading] to a sense of absorption in a larger, ineffable reality."[161] This state allows Sufis to know "the One who is God in His absolute Reality beyond all manifestations and determinations, the One to whom the Quran refers as Allah."[162]

Sufis, like the mystics of other religions, insist that "the mystical journey can only be undertaken under the guidance of an expert . . . [who can] guide the novice past perilous places."[163] Hence, the shaykh, the spiritual master, is an "indispensable element" within Sufism, gathering disciples around him for instruction and initiation.[164] Sufis have adopted a number of disciplines to help the initiate attain a state of transcendence. Among the most common have been fasting, silence, celibacy, and the *dhikr,* the rhythmic chanting of prayers and liturgies. Some tariqa also use music, song, and dance in an effort to trigger ecstatic states.

The ceremonies of one of the oldest tariqa, the Rifa'iyyah, often involve practices very similar to the ratiep—dancing, the chanting of the dhikr, and, at moments of ecstasy, falling "upon objects such as serpents or knives."[165] These rituals have been associated with the Rifa'iyyah wherever it has been found.[166] In the Indonesian archipelago, one of the most distinctive Rifa'iyyah rituals is known as the *rapa'i;* in Malaysia it is called the *dubbus,* from the Arabic word for an iron awl. During the rapa'i, members of the tariqa pierce their bodies with swords, knives, and awls. The point of rite is to demonstrate the power of God, which allows "the adept to come out of the ceremony without his body showing any evidence of having been harmed."[167]

There are, of course, clear parallels between Rifa'iyyah rituals and the ratiep. They have been part of Islamic practice on the Indonesian islands from the time Islam first arrived, in the fourteenth and fifteenth centuries. They were, that is, part of the religious world in which the exiled shaykhs of the seventeenth- and eighteenth-century Cape came to maturity. Yusuf da Costa writes that it is "highly probable" that the ratiep has its roots in the practices of Sufi tariqa, though he ties it to the Alawiyyah, not the Rifa'iyyah.[168] Whatever its provenance, in the early nineteenth century the ratiep was an important expression of Muslims' faith and a genuine attempt to touch the face of God.

Like all religious rituals, the ratiep expressed meanings that were multiple and elusive. Most importantly, it satisfied the Sufi imperative to lead believers toward an experiential, rather than rational, knowledge of God. It would have been especially attractive to nonliterate or semi-literate converts such as slaves, Prize Negroes, and free blacks who struggled to find meaning in the words of the Quran. The ratiep also demonstrated the power of God to protect the believer from physical peril. This freedom from corporal reality doubtlessly appealed to slave converts. Their owners expressed their domination of their slaves in large part through the slaves' bodies. It was the body that the owner bought and sold, the body that the owner put to work, the body that the owner raped and flogged. The ratiep provided slaves with a sphere within which their owner's claim to and power over their bodies could be challenged.[169] The believers' triumph over fire and steel made this quite plain. So, too, did the cures of the "Malay doctors."

Through the ratiep and the healing power of Islamic medicine, slave and Prize Negro converts repossessed their bodies and demonstrated their mastery over them. This was possible only through faith in their single and unitary God. The ratiep also embodied an alternative world-view that starkly contradicted the ideologies and practices of slavery, colonialism, and white supremacy. As Sufis soared above the mundane and pragmatic world of daggers, red-hot chains, and slave owners' whips, they validated Islam's claims of embodying a superior "cosmology and . . . moral order in a world of duplicity."[170] The ratiep reinforced the lesson that the imams taught slave and Prize Negro converts: though their bodies were enslaved, their souls were free.[171]

Writing about slavery in the United States, Nathan Huggins argued that while many slaves never engaged in overt acts of resistance, they nevertheless "died whole persons . . . able in their souls to meet their God without shame."[172] Two factors above all others allowed slaves to claim their full humanity—their families and their faith. We shall discover in chapter 8 that slave families played a similar role at the Cape. In the present chapter, we have seen that religion, especially Islam, provided enslaved and oppressed converts with a way of understanding the secular world, of judging it, and of living with a measure of dignity within it. The ratiep in particular led converts toward a deeper and more powerful truth than the truth of slavery. God entered their lives to reconstruct souls that slavery and white supremacy had made every effort to destroy. The message of slavery was soul murder and social death; God's message was life. To the heart of the believer, the violence and frenzy of the ratiep brought the quiet of inner peace.

CHAPTER 8

"Habits of Intimacy"
Slave Families

> Jacob said to Laban, "Send me away, that I may go unto mine own place, and to my country. Give me my wives and my children, for whom I have served thee, and let me go."
>
> —GENESIS, 30:25–26

September was a fortunate slave.[1] He was a property owner and a family man, facts that set him apart from most slaves in the Cape Colony. In June 1835 he was legally an apprentice and lived in a straw hut on his master's farm in the Uitenhage district with his wife and seven children, who, like him, were apprentices. September's master, Petrus Gerhardus Human, a man of modest means whose only apprentices were September and his family, had given him permission to run a small herd of cattle on the farm's pastures. Several of the animals were valuable milk cows. Although few apprentices could have matched September's material and emotional resources, he was not satisfied with the circumstances of his life, and he took his grievances to the special justice in Uitenhage.

Some of September's problems were of long standing. Human, for instance, did not give his apprentices enough food to satisfy them. The family's basic diet, September said, was "two basins full of [bean] Soup" each day. In the morning they also received "a slice of Bread and a piece of Meat, half the size of my hand." At dinner meat was added to the soup. "This food," September argued, "is not sufficient for us." Human was equally stingy with the clothing he provided his apprentices. September told the justice that the clothes he wore were all that he owned. When he washed them he was "obliged to stay naked behind the Bush" until they dried.

There was little September could do to clothe himself or ease his family's hunger despite the cattle that he owned. Although the statutes establishing apprenticeship guaranteed his right to own and dispose of property,[2] his master had ignored the law's provisions. About three months before September took his troubles to the special justice, Human had sold five of September's milk cows, all of them "with Calf," without his permission. He promised his apprentice that he would compensate him in either cash or kind, but, September said, he had "waited patiently" and "received nothing." September might never have sought the justice's help, however, if his master had not first beaten him and later driven him, his wife, and four of their seven children off the farm.

As September told it, his master had sent him to "water the gardens" a few days before he made his complaint. Before doing so, he "went and fed [his] children first." His master met him on his way to the garden and asked him why he had taken so long to begin his work. September replied that he had been seeing to his children. His response and his delay angered Human, who beat him over the wrists, arms, and head with a stick. The beating sent September to bed for two days; on the third day his master forced him out of his hut and back to work. September brought an initial complaint to the justice soon afterward. When he returned home, Human ordered him off the farm and told him "to go the same road back again." He insisted that September take his wife and four of his children with him. Human would not, however, let the three eldest children—all girls—leave. The three girls worked in both house and field and their labor was apparently too valuable to be lost. September returned to the special justice, hoping that the law would reunite his family. The justice was uncertain whether or not the statutes allowed him to intervene in the case.[3] He asked the advice of his superiors in Cape Town, and in the meantime committed September and his family to the Uitenhage jail "for food and protection." The outcome of the case is unknown.

In slavery and apprenticeship, men and women such as September and his wife created families. And, like September's, those families were fragile. Prior to 1823, the laws of the Cape Colony offered slave marriages and slave families no protection. Slaves were property first and people second. As the colony's chief legal officer put it in 1813, they could not possess "those rights and privileges which distinguish the state of the free in civil society." They could not legally marry, and they had no rights over their children. The law recognized that slave men and women might be attracted to each other, and it allowed them to "cohabit" without the benefit of state or clergy. But cohabitation carried no rights. Nor did slaves have any enforceable rights or claims over their children.

Children born to slave mothers were by definition slaves, the property of their mother's owner.[4] Denied all claims of matrimony and kinship, they were, in Orlando Patterson's words, natally alienated.[5] Denied the rights and privileges of membership in civil society, they were also socially dead.

Slaves struggled against natal alienation and social death, and the reform laws of the 1820s and 1830s helped. Believing that slavery ought, someday, to be abolished, yet certain that the slaves were not fit for freedom, Parliament and the Colonial Office promulgated reforms that they hoped would civilize and Christianize the barbarous and heathen slaves.[6] Stable slave families were to be both the instruments and results of this process. Ordinance 19 of 1826 granted Christian slaves the right to marry. At the same time, it prohibited the separate sale of husbands and wives belonging to the same owner and the sale of children under the age of ten from their mothers.[7] The order in council of 1830 strengthened these protections. Husbands and wives, whether formally married or having "reputed" marriages, were not to be separated by sale, and children were not to be sold away from either parent.[8] The reform laws did not, however, protect families whose members belonged to different owners, nor did they protect families from disruption by being hired out. The slaves clung to these laws in their efforts to protect the families they had created, but no law could fully shelter them from the overwhelming power of their owners. Slave families and apprentice families were as porous as they were fragile.[9] In neither law nor custom could they properly defend their boundaries. Such families were a subordinate part of the slave-owning household, and were necessarily open to the master's interference. Petrus Human, for example, stole from September's family and attempted to break it apart. Yet the significance of the story of September's family lies in its life, not its demise.

September, his wife, and his children were representative of the thousands of Cape Colony slaves and apprentices who created and sustained families despite the pervasive and malign influence of their masters and mistresses. The widespread creation of these families seems to have been a nineteenth-century phenomenon. In the eighteenth century slave, families were rare.[10] In the last decades of the slave era, the demography of the slave population changed; no longer was extensive family formation precluded. Most importantly, the number of young men and young women within the slave community was increasingly equal.[11] It is impossible to know precisely what proportion of slaves and apprentices were members of families. No census of slave families was ever attempted, and government slave registers mention only the mother, never the father, of slave children. Other sources, including the records of the protectors and special justices, settler memoirs, and travelers' accounts, clearly indicate that the slave families were commonplace. We know, for instance, that by no later than 1830, considerably more than 50 percent of the slave population was Cape-born; at the very least, a majority of slaves were members of, or had been members of, a family of mother and child.[12]

Slave families assumed a variety of forms. Most slave families were single-parent families, and most single-parent families were matrifocal. By *matrifocal* I mean that these families were headed by women and that the women assumed the primary burdens of ensuring the families' survival. It will not do to suggest that they were matriarchal; the power of the master, the patriarchal head of the slave-owning household, overwhelmed any slave mother's authority.[13] Married couples and families composed of two parents and their children also appear frequently in the records. Some families, such as September's, fit the notional Western norm of two parents and their children, sharing a residence. But often, husbands and wives belonged to different masters and lived within the separate slave-owning households. In these cases, the mother almost invariably cared for the couple's children, the property of her master. Slaves sometimes married free people; the children of these marriages were free if their mothers were free, slaves if they were enslaved. Throughout the colony, slaves married both Khoikhoi and free blacks. More often in Cape Town than in the countryside, lower-class white men married slave women. Any of these core families might be extended vertically through generations or horizontally to incorporate kin by blood and marriage.

The diversity of slave family structures was the product of many factors. The laws of the Cape promoted matrifocality. The small size of the average slaveholding forced many slaves to seek marriage partners outside of their master's household. The unbalanced sex ratio in the slave population meant that some slaves would have to embrace non-slave partners or none at all. Slave owners also played a part. Driven by a variety of motives, they routinely granted their slaves permission to marry. Some masters and mistresses were indulgent; others hoped that children would result, a natural increase in their property holdings; all must have understood that slaves who had a family to protect were likely to be less rebellious than slaves who had nothing to lose.

The slaves themselves, of course, played a more important role in the creation of slave families than either their owners or the law. Slaves devised complex family and marital structures in response to the demographic, legal, and personal constraints under which they lived. Masters rarely forced slaves into marriage; it was a choice that the slaves made for themselves, if not under circumstances of their own choosing. They married partners with whom they had an affinity. If they found no likely prospect within their master's household, they looked elsewhere, forming what American slaves called "'broad marriages"; that is, they left their masters' farms and households to marry "abroad."[14] If no eligible slaves were available or if they calculated that it would best serve their emotional needs or material interests, they married free persons.

Lawrence Stone cautions that the functions the family has fulfilled and the definitions that have been applied to it have been "many and varied." A family provided a sexual outlet, emotional support, and economic assistance for its members. The degree to which any one of these elements was present varied over time, space, culture, and class. The word *family* itself, Stone notes, has been used to mean anything "from the conjugal pair to the 'family of man.'"[15] Because slave family structures were so diverse and because they most often were customary, not legal arrangements, any definition must be appropriately elastic. In this chapter, *marriage* refers to a loving, if not necessarily stable, sexual and emotional partnership between a man and a woman;[16] no marriage ritual was necessarily involved. *Family* refers to a loving partnership among persons who were, or considered themselves to be, bound by the rights and duties accruing to kin.

Although the slaves created these families, they would not have been able to do so without the acquiescence of their owners, suggesting that slave owners believed that the families served their interests. Indeed, some historians have thus viewed the slave family as a form of social control. Willie Lee Rose, writing of American slavery, speaks of the slave family as "a most significant bulwark of slavery as a working system." The loyalty that slaves felt toward their families made them reluctant to endanger them by challenging their master's authority. While Rose acknowledges that slavery was "at bottom based on force," she argues that most "intelligent planters attempted to see that slaves would have something to lose" should they choose to rebel.[17] Other historians have seen slave families principally as a form of cultural resistance and a "refuge from the rigors of slavery." Slaves were able to achieve a marked degree of cultural autonomy within their families, a social space within which they could counteract the psychological degradation inherent in slavery.[18] Both views contain a large element of truth. The slave family was a contradictory institution. Slave owners must have known that slaves who were members of families would be less likely than other slaves to rebel, escape, or otherwise defy their authority. At the same time, families gave slaves and apprentices the physical and emotional space that they needed to think and act in ways that checked the processes of soul murder and social death. Nevertheless, the slave family remained a family of slaves. While the families the slaves made were sometimes "havens in a heartless world,"[19] they were also arenas within which the slaves turned the stresses of slavery back upon each other, and institutions that the slave owners used as instruments of social control.

The Demographics of the Slave Family

In 1834, approximately 35,750 slaves lived in the Cape Colony, an increase of roughly 6,000 in the three decades since the abolition of the slave trade.[20] Of these, one-quarter lived in households of twenty or more slaves, the threshold at which the slaves might expect to be able to form families from within their owner's household.[21] The growth of the slave population had come in part because the sex ratio among the slaves had evened considerably since the beginning of the century and because there were simply more slave women of child-bearing age (see table 8.1). The more evenly balanced sex ratio meant that it was increasingly likely that slave men and women would find marriage partners in the slave community. While the ratio was becoming more even for the colony as a whole, it still varied regionally. In Cape Town and the Cape district, for instance, the numbers of males and females were nearly even; in the Stellenbosch district, they were wildly askew. The sex ratio in the Worcester and Graaff-Reinet districts approximated the colonial average.[22] In all districts and towns except the Stellenbosch district, the sex ratio was virtually even among slaves aged thirty-five and younger—slaves who accounted for 64 percent of the slave population.[23] Slaves and apprentices who could not find slave or apprentice partners (or did not wish to find them) sometimes formed families with free blacks and Khoisan, whose combined numbers exceeded those of the slaves. In both of these groups, the sexual imbalance was less marked than among slaves.[24] The more balanced gender ratio among the slave population in the nineteenth century and the availability of nonslave partners

Table 8.1.   Percentage of Males and Females in the Slave Population

Year	Males (%)	Females (%)
1806	65	35
1820	60	40
1829	57	43
1834	54	46

Source: Reprinted from D. J. van Zyl, "Die Slaaf in die Ekonomiese Lewe van die Westelike Distrikte van die Kaapkolonie" (The slave in the economic life of the western districts of the Cape Colony), *South African Historical Journal* 9 (November 1977): 8.

Table 8.2.   Percentage of Children in the Slave Population

Year	%
1815	21*
1824	35*
1833	39†

Sources: D. J. van Zyl, "Die Slaaf in die Ekonomiese Lewe," 8–9, and report, protector of slaves, Western Division, 20 January 1834, Public Record Office, London, CO 53/57.
*Under 16 years old
†Under 18 years old

promoted family formation and allowed the slave population to become self-reproducing for the first time.[25] For the same reasons, children comprised a growing proportion of the slave population (see table 8.2).

Husbands and Wives

Slaves and apprentices married each other out of what were at once the simplest and the most complex of motives—love, companionship, and sex. Slaves and apprentices may well have sometimes married free persons for reasons that were more calculating than affectionate—the children of free mothers were freeborn, and free partners sometimes bought the freedom of their enslaved spouse[26]—but when they married within the slave or apprentice community, they sought lovers and friends. Slave marriages were "warm," rather than "cold," "companionate," rather than "instrumental."[27]

The ceremonies slaves and apprentices performed on the occasion of their marriages are hard to recover. Few travelers or government officials commented on the subject. William Burchell, normally an acute observer of the early-nineteenth-century Cape, believed that the near absence of formal marriages among the slaves signaled the scarcity of marital relationships.[28] One contemporary account reported that local imams—the "Mohammedan priests" of English-speaking writers—regularly performed marriage ceremonies for Muslim slaves.[29] Beyond Islam, travelers and officials saw nothing but sexual anarchy. An Anglican priest, writing in the 1820s, lamented the slaves' "unrestrained" sexuality, and a former colonial officer insisted that their "conduct . . . is not restrained by either moral or religious ties, and both sexes follow the natural impulse of their passions with African ardour."[30]

Comments such as these reveal more about the observers than the observed. In 1837, for instance, the colony's attorney general discussed an apprentice's marriage in terms that reveal the prejudices of his race and class. The special justice of Swellendam asked for his advice regarding the case of a woman apprentice who, "having one child by one man, turns him off, and takes another as a husband." Her master later sold "her service" to another farmer who lived about ten hours away, "and her intercourse between her and her [second] husband is thus interrupted." The woman heard that her second husband had fallen ill, and she was "anxious to visit him." She asked her master for permission to leave the farm to see him and was refused. The special justice asked the attorney general whether the woman's master could legally deny her permission to visit her husband. The attorney general replied that he considered "the woman under consideration simply as a whore, and not the wife of any person." Her master was perfectly justified in refusing to allow her to visit "the man with whom she cohabits."[31] The attorney general's analysis was as crude as his language. While the lives of slaves and apprentices were not guided by the moral imperatives of early Victorian England, they were not as anarchic as the writings of nineteenth-century British gentlemen would suggest.

The emotional ties that bound together the apprentices Rosette and Orestes were especially strong. They were a married couple belonging to Martinius Snyders, a wealthy farmer in the Worcester district.[32] They repeatedly escaped together and jointly brought complaints against Snyders to the special justice, risking and accepting severe punishment for doing so. In March 1835, Rosette successfully prosecuted Snyders on charges of having beaten her. Orestes accompanied Rosette when she made this complaint and seems to have been lodged with her in the Worcester jail, pending the outcome of the case. After paying the fine to which the justice had sentenced him, Snyders himself complained about Orestes's "long absence . . . without cause." The special justice cautioned Orestes that if "his Wife . . . should again have cause of complaint against her Master, he was not to accompany her." If he did, the justice told Orestes, he "would most assuredly Punish him."

Orestes did not take the justice's advice. In August 1835 Rosette brought another charge of ill-treatment against her master, and Orestes came with her once again. This time Rosette did not sustain her charge. Two of Snyders's other apprentices testified that he had merely "shoved" Rosette out of the house after she had become uncontrollably insolent. The justice dismissed the case. Snyders, who was present at the hearing, then charged Orestes with desertion. The justice sentenced Orestes to receive twenty-four lashes, "having been warned . . . not to leave his Master[']s place." The justice "admonished" the couple, and they "promised to conduct themselves better for the time to come." They had merely told the justice what he wanted to hear. One day later, on the journey back to Snyders's farm, Rosette and Orestes ran away. Rosette was captured quickly, but it took a week for Snyders and his son-in-law to track down Orestes. When they did, they brought him to the special justice for punishment. The justice ordered that thirty-nine strokes be laid on Orestes's back. He declined to punish Rosette. He sent them home with Snyders's son-in-law "with a promise on their part to return home and conduct themselves better—instead of which, they ran away . . . and went to Cape Town."

This time, Rosette and Orestes eluded all attempts to retake them until mid-February 1836. When they appeared before the special justice, they admitted their guilt and said that "they had left their Master because they did not chose to remain any longer with him, that they would sooner undergo any Punishment . . . and that they would not stop if sent back [to Snyders's farm]." The justice did not disappoint the couple; he sentenced Orestes to receive thirty lashes and each of them to a month's hard labor. At the end of their confinement, the justice brought the couple before him and again "desired them to return to their Master." Both refused. Orestes replied that the justice "might send him, but he would not stop." Rosette said much the same thing "in an Insolent manner." The couples' refusal to return to Snyders's farm and their willingness to undergo such harsh punishment perplexed the justice. Rosette would only say that her master persisted in violently mistreating her and that she would never return to him.

She was as good as her word. She escaped again, made her way to

Cape Town, and somehow managed to bring her case to the attention of the governor, who ordered the colonial secretary to investigate the matter. After hearing the special justice's account of the affair, the secretary supported the course of action that had been followed. "The Magistrate [special justice]," the secretary advised, "should just go on as he has done in regard to these two indomitable apprentices—punishing them to the utmost for every succeeding offence. This will be expensive and very troublesome to him and the Employer, but the lives of these apprentices will thereby be rendered so thoroughly (and so deservedly) miserable, that none will be tempted to follow their example."[33] "Indomitable" indeed. This heroic couple baffled the special justice and infuriated the colonial secretary. Their stubborn determination to resist the violence their master directed at Rosette, their stoic acceptance of the consequences of that resistance, and their commitment to each other were not traits that the colonial state wished to encourage in the lower classes.

The complaints that Rosette and Orestes brought to the special justice did not touch directly on the integrity of their marriage. The trouble grew out of Snyders's violent abuse of Rosette, not an attempt to separate her from Orestes, but their resolve to stay together is readily apparent. The same is true of other slave and apprentice couples. July and Greya, for instance, both Cape Town slaves, visited the protector to complain that they could no longer endure their mistress's abuse. They demanded that she sell them, but not individually; they insisted on being sold as a couple.[34]

Many masters and mistresses were unable to resist the temptation to interfere in their slaves' marital relations. When they did, the slaves did not often accept the meddling without a fight. A case that involved the wife of slave owner Willem Johannes Jooste and his female slave Kaatje furnishes an example. Mrs. Jooste[35] beat Kaatje with a horsewhip because she did not wish her to "cohabit" with David, another slave. Jooste had ordered Sara, one of Kaatje's daughters, who was apparently not David's child, and Phillippina, another slave, to hold Kaatje down while she beat her. At the protector's hearing, neither Kaatje nor Mrs. Jooste explained why the slave's relationship with David so angered her mistress. But the protector did establish that Mrs. Jooste had indeed punished Kaatje illegally, and he persuaded her to allow Kaatje to "cohabit" with David. Upon hearing this, Kaatje withdrew her complaint, as Mrs. Jooste had no doubt hoped that she would.[36]

The marriage of another slave, Jacob, was similarly threatened by an owner's interference. Like Kaatje, he sought a protector's help. Jacob told the assistant protector of slaves in Worcester that his master, Frans Johannes Marais, had "banished" his wife, who was also a slave, from his farm and told her never to return. (Why Marais chose to rid himself of his own slave is not known.) The protector sensed the depth of Jacob's loss and addressed a letter to Marais in which he "exhorted him to appease [Jacob's] feelings, in having his wife returned home." When Jacob arrived back at his master's farm, he discovered that his master had left for Cape Town. He gave the letter instead to his mistress, who read it and immediately sent a messenger on horseback to intercept her husband and ask him to return. Marais turned back and, on reading the protector's letter, asked Jacob how he dared to leave the farm without his permission. Jacob told his master that he had visited the protector to learn whether or not it was legal to "separate man and wife." Marais then gave Jacob eighteen lashes, perhaps because he had been insolent, perhaps simply for initiating an independent course of action that had threatened the hierarchy of master and slave. After the beating, Jacob went back to the protector and pressed charges of ill-treatment against his master. The protector opened legal proceedings, but the case was settled before the issue could come to trial. Marais agreed to allow Jacob's wife "to return home," and Jacob dropped the charges in exchange.[37]

Slaves and apprentices who, like Kaatje and Jacob, shared a home with their spouses understood how fortunate they were. Most slaves and apprentices were not able to defy the demographic realities of the Cape and find partners within their masters' households. For them, one of the few options was to seek a partner from beyond the household, forming a "'broad marriage." No slave marriage could exist without the owner's acquiescence, and this was all the more true of the 'broad marriages. Such marriages could not have been formed nor could they have survived without the considerable degree of personal mobility owners granted their slaves. Urban and rural slave owners routinely granted their slaves permission to visit spouses and children who resided elsewhere—perhaps daily in Cape Town, once or twice a week in the densely settled wine and wheat country, less often in the cattle districts. For instance, Hendrik Sturk, a Cape Town shopkeeper, punished his slave Africa not because he had gone to visit his wife but because he had "overstayed his leave."[38] Spatie, a housemaid on a Stellenbosch wine farm, and her husband, Arend, had long sustained a 'broad marriage with her master's approval. "But now of late," she told an assistant protector, he "has prohibited . . . Arend to visit her." Though the reform laws did not protect 'broad marriages, the protector deferred to Cape custom and dispatched a letter to Spatie's master "in which he [was] desired to allow Arend to visit [Spatie] as before."[39] In a similar case, Erasmus Venter, of Graaff-Reinet, stopped his slave Adam from traveling to his wife's residence, but only because he was under the mistaken impression "that she was then the wife of another."[40]

'Broad marriages often ran into problems that could not be easily sorted out. In 1833, a Mr. Phillips, of Cape Town, reported that he was "compelled" to turn to the police because the slave Adonis, his slave woman's husband, "continually entered his house at night and stayed all night" without his permission. He had told Adonis that he would not refuse such an "indulgence" if he secured "a pass" from his master, but he had not done so. Adonis had added to his crimes by prodding his wife to behave insolently toward her master and by verbally abusing Phillips himself.[41] It was not only masters who were sometimes annoyed by the inconveniences surrounding 'broad marriages, as we see in a tale involving an apprentice, a master, and a second apprentice. Wouter de Wet had taken Silvester, his apprentice, to the special magistrate in Worcester for punishment. Among Silvester's misdeeds were his nocturnal wanderings. De Wet said that he had warned Silvester three or four times over the preceding year "not to sleep out at night without my leave." He had told his apprentice that he "could visit his wife twice a week, Wednesdays and Saturdays," if only he first asked permission. But twice-weekly visits were not enough for Silvester, who continued to spend his nights with his wife "contrary to . . . orders." This caused trouble because he often failed to return early enough in the morning "to feed the horses." Abraham, another de Wet apprentice, supported his master's complaint. Silvester, he said, commonly returned home after daybreak, too late to tend the horses. As a result the task fell to "some one else." He, Abraham added, was that "some one else."[42]

By no means were 'broad marriages an uncompromised solution to the problem of creating and maintaining slave and apprentice families. Family members seldom saw as much of each other as they would have liked; and other slaves might be burdened with additional duties. The presence of a 'broad marriage within the household placed slave owners in an awkward position. On the one hand, they understood that households tended to be small and that their slaves would typically find spouses elsewhere. They knew that to deny their slaves permission to marry outside the household would be to exacerbate their slaves' discontent and to run the risk that their slaves would strike back. On the other hand, the very mobility that made the marriages possible had the potential to disrupt the household. Slaves who received their owner's permission to visit a spouse outside the household sometimes stayed away longer than their owner would have liked. This was not only an act of defiance, but because households were small, it was a threat to productivity. Most slaves probably did not greatly abuse the privilege; if they had, 'broad marriages would have disappeared. Slaves understood the various difficulties that a 'broad marriage entailed, and they tried to unite their marriages when they could.

Although success was elusive, slaves and apprentices regularly appealed to the protectors and special justices for help in bringing their families together. Castor, a Cape district slave, told the protector that he wanted to be "sold in [Cape] Town where his Wife and Children reside." At the protector's hearing, his master, the wealthy Sebastian van Reenen, agreed to sell him, provided a purchaser could be found. He may have been willing to part with Castor because he had been troublesome, making a number of unauthorized trips to see his family. At the protector's hearing, van Reenen grumbled that "Castor had now again left his place without any Cause."[43] Slave owners often showed the sort of casual indifference to slave families embedded in van Reenen's off-handed remark that Castor had left his farm "without cause." Sina, a slave on another Cape district farm, ran into a similarly unsympathetic slave owner when she asked a protector's "assistance to get her sold where her husband resides." Her husband's master, "having been acquainted with the case," simply "declined the purchase."[44]

Some slave and apprentice marriages—both 'broad marriages and coresidential—were troubled. Although evidence of marital discord appears less frequently than that of harmony, there is enough to suggest that unhappy marriages were not uncommon. The slaves' powerlessness relative to their owners, and their inability to protect themselves, their spouses, and their families from the interference of their masters and mistresses, exacerbated the tensions that exist within all families. Slave families had few institutional supports on which to lean when the pressures of enslavement drove them apart. The protection that the law offered slave marriages was imperfect. Religion similarly touched most slaves lightly.[45] If travelers and officials were wrong to claim that the slaves had no moral compass, they were correct in suggesting that few structures existed that could compel the slaves to adhere to the moral codes to which they subscribed. The result at times was conflict.

The proximate cause of trouble within slave and apprentice marriages was often a husband's alleged infidelity. Sara, for instance, told the assistant protector in Somerset that her husband, Jacob, had taken another wife and that she "wish[ed] him to be prevented from having any intercourse with that woman." The law gave the protector no authority to intervene directly, but he wrote to Sara's master, Cornelis Meyer, asking him to use "his influence and authority to settle the matter between Man and Wife." Meyer responded that he knew nothing of Jacob's "improper conduct" and added that Sara quarreled "continually" with her husband. He agreed to "investigate" the situation and attempt to "reconcile" the couple.[46] While Meyer may have been insensitive to Sara's plight, other masters did demand that their male slaves remain faithful to their wives. Dina and her husband, Spadille, both belonged to the same master, Hendrik Passenfuss. When Spadille left Dina for a "Hottentot" woman, Passenfuss ordered him instead "to keep Dina as [his] Wife."[47]

Some male slaves and apprentices seem to have believed that they had the right to form and dissolve marriages freely. For instance, February, the slave of Johannes Andries Ostenhuisen, complained that his master had beaten him in part because he had struck Doortje, "a bushwoman,"[48] who had formerly been his "wife." He told the protector that "he kept her for two months until he thought another young woman was old enough, when he took her for a wife and left Doortje, in Consequence of which there are continual quarrels on the place between Doortje and him."[49] The case of two apprentices, Absolm and Regina, similarly suggests that the informality of slave marriages encouraged some men to take them lightly.

Absolm initiated the case when he charged his master with having illegally sent his wife, Sarah, and his child by her to another farm. He said that his master did this despite his knowledge that Sarah was his wife. Regina, an apprentice who at the hearing claimed Absolm as her husband, appeared at the special justice's office in defense of her master. She said that Absolm had been her husband for five years and that she had borne him two children. One had died; the other was still an infant. She slept in the same room as Absolm, though not in the same bed, and both she and her master had always considered him to be her husband. Sarah, she said, had lived on the farm for two years: she slept in the same room as Regina and Absolm and she, too, had borne a child for Absolm. Regina insisted that Absolm had never told her that he considered Sarah to be his wife. The special justice who heard the case decided that he could not prevent Absolm's master from sending Sarah away.[50] Absolm seems simply to have assumed that he was within his rights to change partners at his whim.

The slaves' triumph was not that they married and created strong, stable, double-headed families, but that their marriages and families existed at all. Despite disruption by sale, loan, and hiring out, despite weak legal protection and the near absence of religious sanction, and despite the ubiquity of 'broad marriages, many of the relationships between slave and apprentice husbands and wives were loving, supportive, emotionally fulfilling, and long-lived.

Matrifocal Families

Slaves and apprentices preferred double-headed families, but this was not the most common family form. Most were matrifocal. Law, custom, and demographics determined that most slave and apprentice families would be headed by an single adult and that the family head was usually a woman. While assertions about the structure of slave and apprentice families must be made in the absence of quantitative evidence, the preponderance of qualitative evidence strongly suggests that most families were matrifocal. They may not have been so throughout the life of the family—the disruptions of death, sale, and other factors prevented any single form of slave family from achieving stability—but in most families, most of the time, husbands and fathers were absent. Even when husbands were intermittently present, as in 'broad marriages, mothers had the greatest measure of influence and responsibility within the family, and they received more affection and loyalty in return.

Matrifocal families were a product of both the structural constraints of slavery and the customs and laws of slaveholding society. While the law did not determine the behavior of either the slaves or the slave owners, it did underwrite matrifocal families to a far greater extent than double-headed ones. Until the formal abolition of slavery in 1834, children followed the condition of the mother. Any child born to a slave woman was a slave and became the property of her owner, no matter what was the legal status or social standing of the father. Until the era of amelioration, slave marriages received no legal protection, and neither mothers nor fathers possessed parental rights.[51] The slavery reform laws of the 1820s and 1830s gave slave marriages a measure of legal standing, but this protection was at first restricted to Christian marriages and, throughout the reform period, applied only to marriages in which both partners were the property of a single owner. While slave children were not to be sold away from their mothers, slave fathers had enforceable claims over their progeny only after 1831.[52]

The law reinforced the tendency within settler culture to view child care and child rearing as naturally the mother's responsibility. Many slave owners, if not the slaves, understood the slave family as encompassing only a mother and her children and acted on that understanding. The records of the protectors of slaves and special justices also support the claim that slave and apprentice families were predominantly matrifocal. In most cases involving parents and children, only the mother is visible. Some of these cases concerned slaves' attempts to prevent the sale of their children, a process that, because of the provisions of the slave laws, would commonly have involved mothers, not fathers. But many other cases present circumstances in which either parent could have acted on behalf of the child. Here again mothers appear far more often than fathers.

The matrifocal family was not simply the product of oppression. The slaves adapted the institution to their own purposes, making it a means of coping with the stresses of slavery. Two slave families headed by women serve as examples. Marie was a housemaid in the Somerset district whose impoverished master had turned her and her two children out of his house because he could no longer afford to feed, clothe, and shelter them. He ordered Marie to find work to support herself and her family. She found employment in the village of Somerset and managed to keep her children from going hungry. Marie's diligence ensured the survival of herself and her children, but because she received no wages, only food and shelter in exchange for her labors, she and the children wore clothes that were "old and nearly worn out."[53]

Rosetta, another slave housemaid and mother, found herself in similar straits. She had once filed charges of mistreatment against her master, Johannes Hubertus Theunissen, and had seen the protector reject them. In retaliation for what he called an "unfounded complaint," Rosetta's master ordered her out of his house. Rosetta took her youngest daughter, Clara, with her when she left. In the fourteen months since that time, Rosetta had hired herself out as a maid in Cape Town and, she said, had "faithfully paid her Wages"—that is, her hire money[54]—to her master. She managed at the same time to care for her daughter. Now, however, Theunissen "was about taking Clara from Cape Town into the Country" because she was now old enough to be "useful." Rosetta turned to the protector for help. Although the law did not protect Rosetta in these circumstances, the protector arranged a settlement. Theunissen agreed to allow Clara to visit her mother "whenever Mrs. Theunissen came to Town (which is very often)." If Rosetta "behaved herself better for the future," he would permit her "to come to his place now and then to visit her Children." Rosetta accepted these terms, both because she "wished to remain in Town and her Owner [lived] only two hours from it" and because she had little choice. Theunissen had every legal right to take Clara away.[55] His power to disrupt the family by laying claim to Clara's labor overwhelmed Rosetta's ability to resist the process.

Like all mothers, slaves and apprentices worried about their children's safety. When, for instance, Willem Johannes Basson sent his apprentice Sabina to the farm of another Boer for four months, she was apprehensive about leaving her seven-year-old daughter behind. When she returned, she discovered that her child, Almina, was "very much marked as if from a cruel beating." Almina told her mother that Basson had whipped her with a sjambok and that her mistress had beaten her as well. Sabina pressed charges of mistreatment against her master. At the office of the special justice in Graaff-Reinet, the surgeon who examined Almina testified that he had found "severe marks" on her back and loins. The justice fined Basson £3 and instructed him not to separate mother and child again.[56] It is possible that Basson would have beaten Almina whether or not her mother had been present, but it is certain that Sabina could offer her daughter no protection when she was away.

Sabina's case suggests the depth of affection and concern that existed between slave mothers and children. A more fully documented, and at the same time more ambiguous, incident is even more persuasive. Lea, a slave, and her three daughters lived with their master, William Thomas Brown, a Graaff-Reinet surveyor, and his wife.[57] One morning on the stoep in front of the house, one of the girls, also named Lea, committed some minor offence, and her mistress beat her for it. Young Lea ran crying to her mother for protection, wrapping her arms around her waist. The elder Lea pushed her child away and told her that she could "not speak concerning you." Previous run-ins with Mrs. Brown had taught her that it would have been a dangerous impertinence to attempt to stop her mistress from beating her child.[58] When the elder Lea pushed young Lea away, the girl slipped off the stoep and fell one or two feet to the ground, screaming all the louder. Brown and his wife now directed their anger at the mother and locked her in leg stocks. Lea was convinced that she had done nothing to earn her owner's wrath. She believed that she had not been disrespectful to her master and mistress while Mrs. Brown was beating her daughter; she had not shielded young Lea from the blows.

Brown saw it differently, and Lea spent two successive days in the stocks.[59] Lea's daughters came to chat with her several times while she was in the stocks, and their presence comforted her. On one occasion, she laughed and sang with her daughter Philidia, angering Brown, who believed that she was taking her punishment too lightly. When Lea complained that she was uncomfortable, Philidia brought her a pillow to sit on. Soon after Brown released her from the stocks, the mother made a complaint of mistreatment against her master, and the protector of slaves took the case to court (the charge was a technical one: that Brown had employed illegally designed stocks, which caused great discomfort). On the day of the trial, mother and daughter, the two Leas, kissed before entering the courtroom to testify. In court, Brown did not deny having placed Lea the mother in the stocks; his defense rested on the claim that she had been insolent to him and his wife and that she sometimes beat her children. The elder Lea admitted that she occasionally hit the girls, but only, she said, when they deserved it. The court found Brown guilty of employing an "illegal mode" of punishment and fined him £10.

Lea and her daughters displayed a wide range of emotions in their interactions with each other, some of them directly determined by their status as subordinate members of Brown's household. On the morning of the original incident, the elder Lea's fear of her mistress was stronger than her concern for young Lea's distress. At other times, the family's slave status seems secondary. There was playfulness in the mother's singing and laughing with Philidia. Philidia, in turn, demonstrated worry and sympathy for her mother when she was in pain. Lea, by her own admission, could be a stern mother, physically disciplining her children if she felt that they had earned it. Yet on the morning of her trial, she expressed her love for young Lea in a thoroughly conventional manner, kissing her and wishing her a "good morrow."

Slave and apprentice children returned the love their mothers gave them, as Philidia and young Lea had done, and it is not surprising that occasionally the child, rather than the mother, sought the protector's help in keeping the family whole. Lena, a sixteen-year-old slave in the Worcester district, preserved her family by indirect means. She once charged her mistress with having hit her several times across the face, back, and neck. A slave witness supported Lena's claim. Her mistress denied having struck her and produced "a Certificate from her Medical Attendant" in which Lena was described as showing no signs of a beating.

With the proceedings deadlocked, Lena proposed to withdraw her complaint, "provided She be allowed to live with her Mother at Tulbagh." Her mistress accepted the compromise.[60] Lena had done as so many slaves had done before her. She had used the protector and the laws he enforced as means of persuading her mistress to do something she would not otherwise have done. The threat of a trial was real enough to convince Lena's mistress to accept her slave's offer of a settlement.

Slave families were often both matrifocal and extended. Extended families, by their depth and resiliency, compensated for the instability of the nuclear family and were especially important as providers of child care in the absence of one or both parents. Sara, a twenty-four-year-old slave housemaid who felt that her extended family was threatened, visited the protector in an attempt to preserve it. She told the protector that her mistress, the widow Pretter, a Cape Town shopkeeper, "was going to sell her into the Country." She did not wish to go because "[her] mother and Child reside in Cape Town." The widow Pretter denied the charge. Sara, she said, had exasperated her; she "was continually running away" and had a "thievish disposition." Determined to be rid of Sara, she said she would sell grandmother, mother, and child "in a lot." The widow's plans were perfectly legal, and the protector dropped the case.[61]

The double-headed families, 'broad marriages, and matrifocal nuclear and extended families seen thus far were families composed exclusively of slaves or apprentices. These families probably accounted for most of the slaves and apprentices in the colony, although a substantial minority were members of families in which some kin were slaves and others free. As we have seen, historians of the Cape have recognized that one of the ways slave men coped with the colony's persistently unbalanced sex ratio was to take Khoisan and Bastaard Hottentot women as wives.[62] Historians have not, however, analyzed these marriages in detail. Nor have they acknowledged the extent to which slave women took Khoisan, free black, and Bastaard Hottentot men as husbands. These marriages were, however, quite significant. As F. M. L. Thompson has noted, "who marries whom, without courting alienation or rejection from a social set, is an acid test of the horizon and boundaries of what each particular social set regards as tolerable and acceptable, and a sure indication of where it draws the line of membership."[63] Marriages between slaves or apprentices and free people were the principal institution within which boundaries of culture and ethnicity were dissolved within working-class communities at the Cape, making them the incubators of "coloured" South Africa.

Families—Slave and Free

Like slave families, mixed slave/free families exhibited a variety of structures. But because the free partner in slave/free marriages was at greater liberty than a slave to choose the place of his or her employment and residence, slave/free families seem to have been more often both double-headed and coresidential than were slave families. Most of the other constraints under which slave families suffered applied to families of slaves and free people: the law hardly noticed them, and they were subordinate units within the slaveholding household. Though the number of slave/free families was smaller than the number of slave-to-slave (or apprentice) families, their significance should not be dismissed. Through them, slaves, free blacks, Khoisan, and Bastaard Hottentots came to form diffuse working-class communities, distinguished from communities of whites.

Demography determined that some slave men would not be able to find slave women to marry. Many of these men therefore married Khoisan and Bastaard Hottentot women. They rarely married free black women, probably because poor white and free black men considered free black women to be desirable partners and could offer the women more security and material comfort than could a slave man.[64] Slave men married Khoisan and Bastaard Hottentot women, less desirable partners in the eyes of free blacks and whites, because they were available— but also for love, companionship, and sex. A protector's case involving Maart, a slave, provides evidence of the depth of feeling that could exist between slave husbands and Khoisan or Bastaard Hottentot wives.

Maart told the protector that his master, Johannes Hubertus Theunissen (whom we have already encountered in this chapter, driving Rosetta and her daughter off his farm) had accused his "Hottentot" wife of "idleness," though an illness had confined her to bed. Maart's wife had been offended and had left Theunissen's farm. Maart said that he found "it hard to be separated" and that he had "followed" his wife; he had, that is, in going after her, run away. He also complained that "his Master was constantly reviling him" because he was a former convict. He asked to be sold to someone else. The protector did what he could, recognizing that the law left Maart's marriage unprotected and could not compel his master to sell him. He addressed a letter to Theunissen in which he suggested that he "forgive" what had passed and "take Maart's wife again into his service and restore Maart to his favor." There is no record of Theunissen's response.[65]

One feature of Maart's marriage was common to most other marriages between slave men and free women: it was a hostage to the relationship between the master and mistress and the slave's wife because the master and mistress ordinarily employed the free wife as a servant. For example, Jack, a slave belonging to Willem Basson (not the Willem Johannes Basson named above), claimed that his master had punished him because he had protested his master's demand that his Khoisan wife leave her sickbed and go to work. Hugo Loedolff, a witness for Basson, agreed that Basson had ordered Jack's wife out of bed. Jack, he said, then became "excessively impudent" and was told several times "to be still." Jack, however, "persisted in talking very bad and being very impertinent." He showed no "contrition" when his master confronted him the following morning and, so, received twenty-four lashes with a cat-o'-nine-tails. Jack had deserted after the beating, but eventually returned to his wife and his master.[66]

A slave owner's irritation with the conduct of a slave's free wife sometimes ended, or threatened to end, the marriage. The assistant protector of slaves in Somerset reported a case that illustrates the point. About two years before the protector heard the story, the Khoisan wife of Adam, a slave, came to live on his master's farm. When Adam's master, Andries Piek[?], asked her to "enter his service," she refused. Piek then ordered her off the farm. Since that time she had lived in a straw hut on a piece of ground not far from Piek's property. Her relationship with Piek had continued to be strained, and Adam added to the tension by "going to his wife several times a night," as his master put it. Piek had finally forbidden Adam from seeing her at all, and Adam asked the protector to intervene on his behalf. The protector convinced Piek to allow Adam to visit his wife at "all reasonable times."[67]

Slave owners manipulated slave/free families as a means of controlling their slaves. Everyone involved understood the system, and the slaves deeply resented it. Apollos, a slave in Graaff-Reinet, went to the assistant protector of slaves when his master drove his wife, "a Hottentot woman" with whom he had "cohabited for a number of years," off the farm. The protector told Apollos that the law could not compel his master to let her return and that his best course would be to "ask it of his master as an indulgence."[68] Since Apollos had no right to demand that his master recognize the marriage, his only option was to conduct himself in such as way as to merit the privilege. The same assistant protector gave a slave named Esauw similar advice after his master had turned away his Khoisan wife of two years. The protector did, however, write a letter on Esauw's behalf.[69]

Slave women as well as slave men took free partners. These marriages were equally hostage to the masters' whim and equally likely to be broken. Jouviel, a slave belonging to Philip du Plessis, took a "Hottentot" husband, Cobus Cupido, and it was Cupido who traveled to the assistant protector's office in Graaff-Reinet to register a complaint on his wife's behalf. It was an effort to save his marriage. He told the protector that he and Jouviel lived together on du Plessis's farm and that they had been married for nine years. Jouviel had borne nine children, two of whom were still alive. Du Plessis had now driven Cupido off his farm, because, Cupido said, Du Plessis believed that he was a bad influence on his wife. Jouviel had earlier brought a complaint against her master that the protector had deemed "frivolous," and du Plessis was sure that Cupido had "incited" his wife's complaint. Du Plessis had decided that if there was to be peace within his household, Cupido would have to leave.

Cupido had indeed left and had found work paying £3 15s. a year. But he and Jouviel were so unhappy with the turn of events that he was willing to return to the farm at his former rate of £1 10s. a year, if only du Plessis would allow it. The protector could not force du Plessis to permit Cupido to return to his wife, but, after calling him into his office, he asked him to grant the couple this indulgence. Du Plessis refused. He said that Cupido "put thoughts of freedom and mischief into [Jouviel's] head." He "admitted the hardship of the Case," the protector reported, but believed "that this Course was necessary to secure the services of his Slaves and that while the law allowed him the right of Judging of what servants he would employ, he would persist in keeping Cupido from coming on his premises." The protector told Cupido that there was nothing more he could do.[70]

Du Plessis imagined that he had been forced to choose between the good of his slave's family and the good of his household. He chose the latter. He acknowledged the damage he had done by destroying his slave's family, but this family was merely a component of a larger whole. Its interests were subordinate to the interests of his household, his slave's interests to his own. Du Plessis also used the opportunity to voice his resentment against the laws and the officials that had intruded on the relations between master and slave. He, and Cape Colony slave owners generally, viewed the private sphere of the household as the personal domain of the patriarch.[71]

On occasion, slave women took free black men as their husbands. The concentration of the free black population in Cape Town meant that these marriages were predominantly an urban phenomenon. Free black men, unlike most slave men, worked for wages and commonly earned incomes that allowed them to rent and sometimes buy houses or apartments. With the masters' permission, they might set up housekeeping with their slave wives. Mariana, for instance, a Cape Town slave housemaid, "cohabited" with Dollie, a free black. This marriage ended badly. When the couple split up, Dollie refused to return the "bed and bedding and a trunk etc." that Mariana had left behind.[72]

In rare instances, slave women married Prize Negro men.[73] Clare, who was a Prize Negro, appealed for the protector's help when his wife, Rachel, was confined to her sickbed. Even though Rachel was "dangerously ill," her master and mistress would not call for "medical aid," Clare said. The protector summoned the master to his office and seems to have shamed him into action. Rachel's master claimed to have earlier called in a physician "who had given up all hopes of Rachel's recovery, that nevertheless his Wife [Rachel's mistress] would immediately send a Doctor again to see her."[74]

While slave men very seldom married free black women, and never whites, slave women often married free blacks, and they took white working-class husbands as a matter of course. The latter type of marriage was not without problems, but the difficulties seem to have stemmed less from the woman's putative race than from her status as a slave.

Slave Wives, White Husbands

Marriages between slave women and white men encountered problems much like the ones that other slave marriages faced. Husbands and masters often clashed over visiting rights, residence, and the care and treatment of the slave woman. The color of the man and woman seems seldom to have been an issue. Without suggesting it was a scandal, J. W. D. Moodie, who lived at the Cape during the 1820s and 1830s, mentioned the "many . . . English labourers at Cape Town [who] live in habits of intimacy with Malay [slave] girls."[75] Presumably the working-class white men who married slave women had little status to lose.

A case involving Annet, a twenty-year-old slave woman, and Richard

Knowles, a mason who had immigrated to the Cape from England, illustrates some of the points at which marriages between slave women and white men were constrained.[76] Annet arrived at the office of the assistant protector of slaves in Somerset with many things on her mind. She complained that her master, Petrus Cornelis Clase, threatened to beat her until "she might wash herself in her blood," that he did not supply her with sufficient clothing, and that he had stolen a goat and two kids that belonged to her. Most importantly, Clase had "driven away" Knowles, her "husband," "with whom she [had] cohabited for some time" and by whom she had a child. She asked for a license to marry Knowles, who had accompanied her to Somerset, and for permission to baptize her child. The protector summoned Clase to his office and asked him whether he would allow the couple to marry. Clase, the protector recorded, "positively refused his Consent to the marriage." He denied having threatened Annet and said that he had "no objection" to the baptism, but was unalterably opposed to the marriage. He had purchased Annet from his father-in-law, and ever since that time she and Knowles had behaved very improperly.

Clase claimed that Annet had run off to visit Knowles when he was engaged at his trade "at some distance" from the farm and that she was "in general" highly disobedient and negligent in her duties. When Knowles was on the farm, his presence added to the tension. Once, when Clase was "rebuking" Annet for some misconduct, Knowles had attempted to stop him, challenging Clase to strike him instead of his wife. Annet and Knowles, the protector wrote, "admitted" that Clase's account was "correct in great measure."

After hearing Knowles's testimony, the protector thought that he "seemed to entertain an opinion that upon being married to Annet he would acquire more authority over her than is Consistent with the Masters [sic] Title to her Services." This would not do, and the protector reported that Knowles "was put right on that point." The protector did not believe that a formal marriage was in order, but he did effect "an amicable arrangement between the parties." Clase agreed to allow Knowles to return to his farm and to grant the couple permission to marry "if he should find that they Change their Conduct for the better towards him." The protector advised Knowles to find the means to purchase his wife's freedom, something the protector thought he could accomplish, provided he was "industrious and frugal."

There is little here that does not replicate the strains that existed between slave, Khoisan, and free black husbands and wives and their masters. Although the couple had lived together for some time, considered themselves husband and wife, and had produced a child, the law did not recognize their union. Because a master's rights over his slaves largely superseded the slaves' familial rights, Annet's master had it within his power to allow the marriage to prosper or cause it to fail. Annet had been punished, or at least rebuked, after having run away to reunite her temporarily 'broad marriage. When Clase punished his wife, Knowles had attempted to intervene; Clase had consequently thrown him off his farm. The only unusual aspect in this chain of events was Knowles's open challenge to Clase. Few slave, Khoisan, Bastaard Hottentot, or free black men would have dared to step between their master and their wife and implicitly threaten him, daring him to strike. Knowles, however, was not only a white man in a racially stratified slaveholding society but an Englishman confronting a Boer in a colony that the British had taken from the Dutch. He had a standing in the settler community that no slave or other nonwhite could match, a much more secure base from which to challenge his wife's master.

Marriages between slave women and white men were most common in Cape Town, if only because there the population of both slaves and single white men was the most concentrated. The men involved were not invariably English. For instance, Salia, a Cape Town slave, at one time had an English lover, but the man had disappeared and left her pregnant. A few years later, Carel Becker, whose name suggests that he was an Afrikaner, approached the protector of slaves and said that he was "desirous of purchasing Salia and one of her Children, of which [he] was the Father." Becker was not a rich man. He added that he could only buy his family's freedom "if the price was reasonable." Salia's master, the socially prominent Michiel van Breda, asked a very high price for the family. The protector reported that Becker promised to "try to collect the Sum demanded," though he appeared "to have no reasonable prospects of doing so."[77]

Money was often the obstacle over which slave women and their white husbands stumbled in their attempts to legitimate their marriages and free their families. This was the case for Candace, a Cape Town slave, who lived with her white husband, William Spratt. She told the protector that Spratt was willing to buy her freedom, "have her Christened, and marry her." The couple's plans fell apart because of her husband's failure to match her master's price and the protector's inability to bargain it down.[78]

Sometimes if a white husband wished to live with his wife, he was forced to hire her from her master or mistress. For example, Rachel, a Cape Town slave belonging to the widow le Seur, told the guardian of slaves that "she had for six years been allowed to hire herself out to the man with whom she cohabited, at 18 rix-dollars per month." The arrangement had recently come to an end. Her husband "was no longer able to pay that sum," and her mistress was not sympathetic. She "refused to receive less from him, and let out [Rachel] to another person for 12 rix-dollars per month," despite the husband's offer to meet the lower price. After an investigation, the guardian decided that there was nothing he could do for the couple.[79]

The families the Cape slaves created assumed a variety of forms, and many produced children. But whether the fathers were slave or free, black or white, the children followed the condition of their mothers, who were most often slaves or apprentices. As a consequence, the protectors' and special justices' reports shed considerable light on slave childhoods.

Bitter Harvest

Far too much that can be known about slave and apprentice children involves violence. This is not just a function of the sources. Violence lay at the heart of slavery, and nothing was more likely to cause conflict between slave parents and slave owners than the violence that slave owners directed at their children. Slave owners believed that their authority over slave children was supreme, and that if slave parents claimed any authority of their own, they did so not by right, but as an indulgence. Slaves and apprentices resented slaveholding society's denial of what they saw as their natural parental rights. Mothers and fathers fought continually with their masters and mistresses over the degree to which their children were to be disciplined, by whom, and for which offenses. Some slave owners recognized the depth of parental passion and turned it to their own ends. The family became one of the means by which masters controlled their slaves, not merely because members of slave families had something to lose, but because some slave owners used the family as an instrument of violent coercion.

Slave owners sometimes tried to delegate the patriarchal (or matriarchal) authority over slave children to the biological parents. Abraham, a fifteen-year-old slave, was whipped by his father at his mistress's insistence, even though, Abraham said, he had done nothing wrong. The assistant protector of slaves in Stellenbosch looked into the matter and determined that Abraham's mistress had demanded the beating because of "some disrespectful language, which [Abraham] held with one of the other Slaves respecting [her]."[80] Ceasar, an apprentice in the Graaff-Reinet district, was another parent who found himself involved in disciplining his own child. When his master took Ceasar's son, Adam, to the special justice for punishment, Ceasar admitted that Adam had recently been drunk and that he "is very disobedient and will not attend to his Master's orders or mine." The justice sentenced Adam to receive twenty lashes.[81] There is no telling whether Ceasar adopted his master's view of proper servile behavior as a mask, thought that his son's actions were foolish, serving only to make a hard life rougher, or believed that Adam was truly in the wrong.

Masters and mistresses could not always co-opt slave and apprentice parents. John Rens, a Malmesbury farmer, once spoke of his apprentice Jacob's relationship with his son. The son often neglected his duties while tending the farm's horses, and as a result the animals had done "considerable damage" to Rens's crops. Rens claimed that he did not punish Jacob's son himself; instead he "frequently" sent him to his father for "correction." Jacob, however, did not always fulfil his fatherly duties as far as Rens was concerned. Instead of punishing his son, Rens said, he "rather encourages him or makes some careless reply about it."[82]

Like Jacob, another Malmesbury apprentice, Anthony, seems to have been able to maintain a considerable degree of psychological independence. Anthony charged his master with having assaulted him after a clash over the punishment of his child. He told the special justice that he entered his master's house one evening and heard his master beating one of his children in the hall. He complained to his master's son, who told him that "it would do the Child good." Anthony replied "that now & then it might but that every day was too much." The master's son repeated Anthony's words to his father, who then struck Anthony in the face several times for his insolence.[83] Anthony's crime was to assert his natal rights and implicitly deny his master's superior claims. When Alie, a slave, saw his master's father whip his son, he asked, "Old Master why do You beat my Child" and attempted to stop him. Alie's master, like Anthony's, beat him for having dared to presume that his parental rights were as valid as his master's patriarchal authority.[84]

As Anthony's and Alie's cases demonstrate, violence directed at their children sometimes drove slaves and apprentices to the protectors or special justices in search of support. Regina, for instance, "assisted" her young son, Klaas, when he traveled to the protector to charge his master and another white man with beating him with a doubled whip.[85] Steyn, an apprentice housemaid, pressed charges against her master's son for assaulting her daughter. She said that John Oberholster had been in "a great passion" when he whipped her daughter, Magalder, and that he had continued to strike her even after she fell to the ground. A witness, another apprentice, confirmed that Oberholster had been "angry." He said that he had "distinctly" counted thirty-one blows and that they had fallen with "great force." A second witness, this one a white man, agreed that Oberholster had been in a "passion" and had badly beaten Magalder. He added that Steyn had become "very impertinent" when Oberholster beat her daughter and had "followed him a hundred Yards or thereabout."[86]

Violence was pervasive. It was the foundation on which slavery rested. It was a language people had learned to use to communicate with each other. U. B. Phillips, the first major historian of American slavery, once described the southern plantation as "a school . . . of civilization."[87] This was hardly an adequate characterization, as succeeding generations of historians have demonstrated, but it was not entirely wrong. Slavery was indeed a school of sorts. At the Cape, slavery might inadequately, though not incorrectly, be termed a "school of violence."[88] Slaves sometimes responded to the violence and degradation in their lives by lashing out at their children, their spouses, and their comrades. Children were especially at risk.

A slave mother, for instance, saw the protector of slaves throw out her complaint against her mistress when he learned of the violence she had directed at her own son. Jasmina, a Cape Town housemaid, claimed that her mistress had slapped her for no apparent reason. Her mistress, the widow Schickerling, told the story differently. She said that on the day in question she "had reason to speak" to Jasmina about the carelessness of her work. The slave answered "excessively impudently." After Schickerling scolded her for her insolence, Jasmina chased her own son out of the house, into the yard, and began to beat him in a "shameful manner." Schickerling followed and attempted to rescue the boy from his mother. In the ensuing "scuffle," she said, she might have pushed her slave, but she had not slapped her. She added that, from the "expressions" that Jasmina had used while beating her son, she had believed "she had an intent to take away his life." Schickerling's daughter-in-law supported the elder woman's testimony. She said that she had witnessed the beating and had heard Jasmina say that she would not stop until she killed the boy. Theunis, a slave, had seen Jasmina leaving her mistress's house "in a most violent passion," dragging her son by the collar. All the witnesses agreed that the spark that ignited Jasmina's rage had been the tongue-lashing her mistress had given her.[89] Rather than strike back at her mistress, Jasmina chose the safest, most readily available target.

Slave owners commonly intervened when slave and apprentice parents assaulted their children. Their motives, no doubt, were mixed. On the one hand, the sight of a child, toward whom they may well have developed an honest affection, being abused would have prompted humane concern. On the other hand, slave parents who disciplined their children unavoidably asserted parental rights that were incompatible with the patriarchal ideology of slavery. Elements of this conflict emerge from the record of Jasmina's complaint, as they do in a case that Cupido, a slave, pressed against his master, Andries Petrus Lubbe, a wheat farmer in the Clan William district.

Cupido told the assistant protector of slaves that his master had given him thirteen stokes with a cat-o'-nine-tails, over his "bare buttocks" because he had "Chastized his Child Davis"—the product of his marriage to a free woman.[90] Later the same day, in the field, Lubbe had beaten him again. Cupido said that the trouble had begun early one morning when his master asked him why he had punished his son the preceding evening, and Cupido told Lubbe that Davis had disobeyed him. According to Cupido, Lubbe was not satisfied with his answer: he ordered two slaves, April and Pero, and a "free person of Color," Danzer, to hold Cupido down while he whipped him. After the beating, Cupido had fallen behind the other workers while reaping hay; Lubbe, Cupido said, had noticed and again ordered Cupido to be laid out on the ground and beaten.

April, Pero, and Danzer told the tale differently. They testified that Lubbe had initially whipped Cupido for having "ill treated" Davis. His master had beaten him a second time not only because he had fallen behind in his work, "for which he stated to be unwell and could not keep up," but because he had provoked Lubbe "by his improper language." The three said that Cupido had declared "that their Master could do with him what he pleased that day, even if he should like to hang him," but "he Should [continue to] do with his Wife and Child, what he pleases, as they were free persons." Speaking in his own defense, Lubbe admitted that he had beaten his slave on the two separate occasions. The first time, he said, "was to prevent him from Committing a Murder on his Child Davis, as he frequently Committs Crueltyes on that Child." The second whipping was due to Cupido's "improper Conduct in presence of my other slaves April, Pero and the Hottentot Danzer."

The violence that Jasmina and Cupido directed at their children was not uncommon among slaves and apprentices. The prevalence of family violence raises the question of how it came to be the case. Writing about slavery in the American South, Nell Irvin Painter argues that slave parents routinely beat their children in order "to make them regard obedience as an automatic component of their personal makeup that was necessary for survival in a cruel world." Such parents knew that their children's' lives would be easier if they learned to obey without asking questions and to take a beating without complaining.[91] Painter's arguments are compelling, but they seem insufficient in the face of the sort of extreme violence that we have just examined.

Recent studies of violence in families and institutions suggest other answers. Writing of violence in late-twentieth-century South Africa, Wilma Hoffman and Brian McKendrick observe that "violence produces a bitter harvest of more violence." "This fact," they continue, "is one of the most consistently supported findings in the entire scientific research literature on human behavior. People repeat behaviors to which they have been exposed—if violence has been used to try to control and shape their own behaviour, they will in all probability try to use violence to influence the behaviour of others."[92] Slave owners exposed their slaves and apprentices to a lifetime of physical abuse. From early childhood onward, violence was the principal means by which slave owners controlled and subordinated their slaves. Slave parents learned from the example of their masters and mistresses that authority was expressed and obedience was commanded by the whip, the sjambok, the fist, and the open hand. When they disciplined their children, they used the techniques that they had been taught. While this argument explains the "legitimate" violence of a parent or patriarch, it may not be enough to account for the abusive violence of parents such as Jasmina and Cupido.

Linda Gordon's study of family violence in nineteenth- and twentieth-century Boston suggests ways in which the argument can be extended. Gordon insists that definitions of "violence" and "abuse" are not fixed, but have shifted over time and space. Since they have been "historically and politically constructed," there is no single standard against which they might be judged. Standards vary across class, culture, and individual psychology. Child abuse is particularly difficult to define sharply "because it is so often connected to or confused with [legitimate] punishment." Nevertheless, Gordon is able to define "violence" and "abuse," relying to a large extent on the (still diffuse) conventions of the period she studies.[93]

Gordon accepts the argument that adults who were abused as children will be more likely than others to abuse children of their own. But she believes merely to cite an "intergenerational repetition of violence" is not to go far enough. She identifies several "stress factors" that contribute greatly to child abuse; among them are poverty, unemployment, alcoholism, and interracial and interethnic hostility. Perhaps most important is a "subjective version" of the "cycle of violence" thesis. Child abusers, she finds, may not have been victims of child abuse, but they "feel themselves to have been victims" of personal and impersonal forces. They "experience themselves as powerless, their wishes disrespected by their children." These feelings, she adds, "may accurately reflect their actual social and economic status."[94]

Cupido, Jasmina, and slaves like them "abused" their children. To make this assertion is to accept the standards that their contemporaries set. The intensity of the violence they directed against their children shocked the witnesses who appeared before the protectors and special justices. Even in a society inured to harsh physical discipline, slaves and slave owners might agree that some violence was excessive or unwarranted. Slaves who abused their children probably, and quite reasonably, "experienced" themselves as victims. They were poor, powerless, and the objects of racial oppression and class exploitation. These factors, shared by all slaves and exacerbated by some weakness within the emotional makeup of a few, predisposed them to turn against their children when a catalyst ignited their fury.

It is probable that few slaves and apprentices routinely abused their children. The violence of masters and mistresses was always a more serious threat to the physical and emotional well-being of slave children and adults than violence within the slave community. Extreme parental violence underscores the severity of the damage slavery inflicted on those who were enslaved. The only way in which slaves could be sure of escaping such damage was to escape slavery itself. Slaves did this in a variety of ways. As we have seen, some slaves lived relatively autonomous lives as hired-out laborers or as virtual labor tenants.[95] Some slaves, especially young men, ran away.[96] Most slave parents did not have the opportunity to hire themselves out or to work as labor tenants; for them, running away was unattractive, because it almost always required them to leave their children behind. There existed another possible means of escape. Although it was a difficult task, slave families sometimes pooled their resources to buy their way out of slavery.

Families and Freedom

Some slaves were able to buy their freedom or the freedom of family members. It was never easy. Throughout the eighteenth century and into the nineteenth, the employers and slave owners of the Cape faced a labor shortage.[97] White workers were scarce; Khoisan resisted incorporation into the colonial labor market; and the importation of slaves was erratic. As a result, the price of slaves was persistently high and rose even higher after the abolition of the slave trade in 1808. Few slave owners were willing to part with their slaves, even if a slave had managed somehow to raise the necessary money, and until the 1820s no law or custom compelled them to do so.

The slaves' chances of buying their way out of slavery improved following the promulgation of ordinance 19 in 1826. The ordinance made manumissions compulsory if the slave were able to offer a fair price for himself or herself or for a family member.[98] When the government published the ordinance, the slave owners howled in protest. They held that this was an intolerable attenuation of their property rights.[99] But the evidence regarding the slave owners' long-term response to the compulsory manumissions is ambiguous. Eight years after the promulgation of the ordinance, the principal protector of slaves observed that the "Generality of Slave Holders . . . except in a very few Instances . . . [had not] been indisposed to meet reasonable proposals for Emancipating their Slaves." He cautioned, however, that "the prices of good Slaves have been, and even still are, extravagantly high."[100] Despite the protector's optimism, slave owners often resisted compulsory manumissions. And despite their best efforts, most slaves found it impossible to raise enough money to buy their freedom. Slaves whose liberty was purchased for them under compulsion tended to have been freed with money supplied by family members who were free blacks. But on rare occasions, slaves and apprentices did manage to buy a family member's freedom.

Floris, a Cape Town slave, was one of the few. A baker, he raised the R.100 he needed to purchase the liberty of his three-year-old son, April.[101] The transaction had not gone smoothly. April's master, J. F. Beck, who had consented to free the child and had taken the money, died before signing April's deed of manumission. The trustees of his estate had stalled when Floris asked that they release his son. He turned to the protector of slaves for help, taking with him the agreement to free April that Beck had signed. Confronted with the document, the trustees complied with Beck's wishes and manumitted the child.[102]

At the same time that he was struggling to purchase his child's freedom, Floris was also working to free his wife. He could not, however, free his wife; her price was too high and her master was uncooperative. He told the protector that he had asked a Mr. Botha to buy his wife, Mariana, from the estate of her late master—the J. F. Beck mentioned above. Both Floris and Mariana were to serve Botha until Floris had paid back Mariana's purchase price of R.980. Botha, he said, now refused to abide by his promise and claimed to have bought Mariana unconditionally. At the protector's hearing, Botha denied that he had refused to free Mariana. He said that he had told Floris that he would free her when Floris repaid her purchase price and was willing to stand by this agreement if Floris could come up with the money within two months. Floris said that he would try to find the money, though apparently without much hope. Even a skilled slave craftsman who worked full-time on his own account would have had difficulty raising nearly R.1,000, and Floris, a baker, was in no such position. The protector recorded that the case had been "adjusted by Floris going back to Mr. Botha's service."[103]

Fritz, another Cape Town slave, was also able to buy his children's freedom, and again the price was R.100. Fritz applied to the protector in the name of his children, Damon and Maria. He told the protector that he had R.100 that he hoped to pay toward their manumission; he asked the protector to approach his master, Philip Leeb, on his behalf. The negotiations moved quickly. Leeb agreed that R.100 was a fair price for the children. After accepting the money and signing the deeds of manumission, he gave the money back to Fritz and undertook "to have the two Children Baptized and to support them during their minority."[104] This was an unusually happy outcome, an indulgence of the sort that masters and mistresses sometimes granted to especially favored slaves.

Far more often, it was not a slave but a free-black husband, father, or grandfather who raised the funds needed to buy the freedom of a wife, child, or grandchild. Free blacks, especially men and particularly in Cape Town, often possessed skills that allowed them to command a substantial wage. Unlike slaves who hired out their own time, they did not pay any of their earnings to a master or mistress as hire money. Free blacks were, however, often forced to rely on a slave owner's goodwill.

The case of Camonie, a slave, and January, her free black grandfather, illustrates many of these points.

Camonie appeared at the protector's office in Cape Town hoping that he could help her win freedom for herself and her child. She told the protector that, prior to her death, her late mistress "had benevolently directed that a period of six weeks should be allowed to her to look out for any person who was willing to make any favorable arrangement in the purchase of herself and two Children Regina 3 Years and Leonora 18 Months." But no guardian angel had appeared. The protector, however, learned that Camonie had a free-black grandfather, January, who was the "principle [sic] Servant" of a wealthy cattle dealer and that he earned "very liberal wages." He "was immediately sent for." When January heard about the agreement between his granddaughter and her late mistress, he promised "to enter into any arrangements within his means." The protector called January's employer into his office and persuaded him to advance his servant R.800 for the purchase of Camonie and her children. January was to repay the loan either in cash or in services rendered. The family was manumitted only three days after the case had been opened, "to the infinite joy of January and Camonie, and the sincere gratification of the Protector."[105]

Several persons played important roles in the drama that freed Camonie and her daughters. Her late mistress made freedom possible by granting her the opportunity to search for someone willing and able to free her. The structure of Camonie's slave/free extended family allowed her to tap the necessary financial resources. Because her grandfather was a skilled worker, he had the wherewithal to borrow the money, even if he did not have enough cash at hand. January's employer stepped on stage at the critical moment, lending money to a favorite and perhaps indispensable employee. The protector, of course, brought the players together.

A mistress's kindliness similarly allowed a free-black father to purchase the freedom of his two-month-old son. Manuel, a Cape Town free black, asked the protector to help him buy the liberty of his boy, Onverwacht. The child's mother, a slave belonging to the widow Eckard, had recently died, probably in childbirth. Manuel said that he could pay R.100 for Onverwacht and asked the protector to approach his mistress with the offer. Eckard happily accepted Manuel's terms. "After having executed Onverwacht's Deed of Manumission," in a sincere gesture of affection, "[she] presented Manuel with the 100 Rix Dollars in token of her remembrance of the faithful Services of Onverwacht's late Mother."[106]

Although free blacks earned higher wages than all but the most fortunate slaves, they were, nonetheless, members of the Cape's working class. The great majority were poor; a few were tolerably well off. Many could not produce the cash needed to purchase a family member's freedom. Some of them, with the protector's help, managed to buy freedom on the installment plan. Apdul [*sic*], of Java, another free-black Capetonian, came to the protector with a proposal that he hoped would result in freedom for his wife and children. He was willing to offer R.3,000 for his wife, Saartje, and their four children; he offered to put R.1,700 down in cash, a very large sum, and to pay the balance in installments. Saartje's mistress, the widow Heydenrych, was "very old and infirm," and her son represented her at the protector's office. He said that his mother would accept only payment in full, unless Apdul could find someone to guarantee the balance. The protector reported that "Apdul after some further negotiation brought 700 Rix Dollars more, and found Security for the remaining 600." The family was soon freed, and the protector did not hesitate to congratulate himself for the part he played. If it had not been for his "Solicitation," he wrote, Saartje and her children were likely to have remained slaves: "The mother was still a young woman . . . and her eldest daughter had nearly attained Womanhood, and would soon have borne Children and which would have of course raise these Persons Value."[107] Indulgence had its place within the institution of slavery, but as the actions of the widow Heydenrych's son make clear, calculations of profit and loss were never far from the surface.

Dina, a slave housemaid, also enlisted her extended family, a free/slave combination, to secure her own freedom and that of her children. Her father, Jan of Batavia, a Cape Town free black, applied for the protector's help on her behalf. He told the protector that "some time earlier" he had purchased the freedom of one of his grandchildren from Dina's former mistress and that of two others from her present master, I. J. Blanckenberg. The manumission of the youngest of his grandchildren had been Blanckenberg's "free gift." Jan now wanted to buy and free Dina, but Blanckenberg asked for £100 (R.1,333), £25 more than he could raise. After making a series of inquiries, the protector determined that Dina "was a most valuable Slave and well worth £150 Sterling." Blanckenberg said that he "had already made considerable sacrifices for Jan" and refused to lower her price. Jan eventually found the additional £25, bought his daughter, and freed her.[108] Jan, like many free blacks, was willing to shoulder heavy financial burdens to free his family. Blanckenberg, like many masters, felt some affection for his slaves, but was not prepared to allow sentiment to cloud his judgment about what was in his own best interest.

Money was consistently a problem for free blacks who wished to buy freedom for family members. Philip Ryklief, a free black in Cape Town, tried to secure a loan from the colonial government in his attempt to buy his family's freedom. He wrote to the guardian of slaves and asked his help in securing a R.2,000 loan from the Government Bank. He offered "to give security for the amount and to discharge the Sum of 150 Rix Dollars per Quarter." The guardian wrote a letter of inquiry to the bank's directors, who replied that "the Regulations prevented any Loan being made to Philip Ryklief upon the terms offered." The guardian went over the directors' heads and asked the lieutenant governor to "authorize the advance." Again he and Ryklief met defeat. The "answer expressed His Honor's regret that present Circumstances of the Bank prevented him from acceding to the Guardian's recommendation."[109]

Female free blacks were even less likely than males to have at hand the funds necessary to free a family member. For instance, Annilie, a free woman, who had been born a slave, approached the guardian seeking help in purchasing her mother, Philidia. She said that she could offer her mother's master, J. Jurgens, R.300, but he demanded R.1,000. The guardian interviewed Jurgens, who called Philidia a "very valuable" slave; he said R.300 was far less than she would fetch on the open market; he would not accept a lower price. The guardian explained to Annilie that, because of "the smallness of the Sum offered by her he did not think it adviseable" to press the matter, "which would only lead to expense without any possibility of a satisfactory decision."[110] There is no evidence that the guardian attempted to arrange for an individual or the government bank to lend Annilie the necessary money, probably because of her sex. Since free women were shut out of most trades, their earning power was even more constrained than that of free-black men.[111] Unable to raise the necessary funds to buy the freedom of their children and themselves, women, both slaves and free blacks, as well as a handful of men, turned to an organization called the Cape of Good Hope Philanthropic Society for Aiding Deserving Slaves to Purchase Their Freedom.

Deserving Freedom

A group of liberal English-speakers, including several civil servants, merchants, and nonconformist clergymen, founded the philanthropic society in Cape Town in 1828. Their society, they said, was "the most benevolent, most interesting association ever formed in this colony." Its purpose was to abolish slavery at the Cape "gradually . . . without violence, without violation of the property of others." The society's plan was a simple one. They would solicit monetary contributions from sympathetic persons and, with those funds, lend young, female slaves enough money to buy themselves.[112] In practice, the society seems instead to have helped family members purchase the girls' freedom. While the Society's title spoke of aiding "Deserving" slaves, R. L. Watson, who has written extensively on the matter, believes that "Deserving" meant little more than belonging to a master or mistress who was willing to sell for "the right price."[113]

Girls and very young women were essential to the philanthropic society's plan to end slavery gradually. As more and more of them were emancipated, more and more children would be born free. In time, all young women who had once been slaves would have been purchased and freed, and no new slaves would be born. Concurrently, the older generation born into slavery would die away. Slavery would end peacefully (in about 1910, if the society had had its way), and with no violence done to slave owners' property rights. The society explicitly disavowed any possibility that the passing of slavery would upset the social hierarchy of the Cape. It pledged not to "break asunder those bonds of attachment, which so often exist between the female slave and her mistress." Instead, the society would train the freed girls to be proper servants.

The society chose to free girls, rather than boys. The fact that the status of a child derived from the mother, not the father, certainly argued in favor of freeing female slaves as a means of ending slavery by degrees. But the fact that girls were triply subordinated—as females, as slaves, and as nonwhites—also meant that to free a girl was not to remove the assumption that her social role was to serve her betters. And girls could not grow up to be men. Free-black men not only presented a potential physical threat, their work as craftsmen made many of them more likely to break out of the bonds of dependence than were free-black women.

The sentimentalization of women and the family by evangelical British Christians of the early nineteenth century, of whom the expatriate founders of the philanthropic Society were representative, also played a

role in the decision to free girls, not boys. As Pamela S   pointed
out, the period of amelioration and emancipation coinc   as pointed
ish middle-class preoccupation with gender relations.[114]   h a Brit-
social disruption of industrialization seemed to have provo   the
of the family" that was destined to rip apart the fabric of soc   the
and mothers had left their homes and entered the factories o   isis
tile industry, depriving their children of care and moral instruct
their husbands of the comforts of home. If not checked, the coll
the family would inevitably "sweep the nation into turbulent, unch
and perilous times of chaos and anarchy"; it was both a cause and i
of the erosion "of traditional moral and social bonds and restraint
the unbridled and irresponsible indulgence of individual lusts a
selfish appetites."[115] The answer was to valorize and reinforce the ser
that a woman's proper role was to be the "natural comforter and dome
tic muse" to her family.[116]

The end of slavery, though sincerely hoped for by members of the co
lonial philanthropic society, would present them with the problem of re-
constructing the social hierarchy of the Cape. A servile population freed
from the bonds of slavery would have been as potentially threatening as
an industrial working class. The Cape of Good Hope Philanthropic Society planned to use women and the family to control the process. Although slave girls could not conform to the norms of middle-class propriety, they were seen to be gentler, more delicate, more easily damaged,
and more easily trained than boys and, hence, more deserving of freedom. The freed family could be the foundation on which a properly
subordinated, sober, and industrious, nonwhite working class could be
built, if the mothers of that class played their proper role. The society,
which very much hoped for this result, planned to do its part.

Evidence drawn from the protectors' records bears out the sugges-
tion that the society was very much concerned to preserve the existing
social hierarchy. For instance, it provided Clara, a Cape Town slave, with
the funds needed to free her two daughters, whose late mistress had
expressed her hope that they would be "sold for their freedom . . . in
consideration of [her] faithful services." After the girls were freed,
the society apprenticed them as servants, moving the protector to remark that they had been "put in a way to become good Members of the
Community."[117]

The society achieved the same end in a more complicated case. Constantia's late mistress, the widow Morel, had consented to manumit her
daughter, Sara, for R.150. Constantia had applied to the society for help

release the necessary funds. Meanwhile, R.150 had

and it had vo~~~ecutors of the Morel estate "through another Chan-

been paid t~~l been freed. Constantia discovered that her new mas-

nel," and ~ manumit her for the same R.150. When she asked the

ter was ~d the money it had allotted for Sara's freedom on her

socie~~~ned that the society's rules would not allow the money to

ow~~~at way. She asked the protector to intervene. The protector

h~~~e secretary of the society and brought the matter to "a very

~ermination." The funds were given to Constantia, and she

. The protector noted that "in consideration" of the society's

~d as a means of having her Child well brought up," Constantia

~er at the disposal of the Philanthropic Society to apprentice

as a servant.[118] Although the society had not supplied the

free Sara, it had managed to insist that for her good and for

of the community she would be apprenticed. As a servant, she

rn to play her proper role in Cape society.

~s, the protector and the society joined forces with a slave

free all of the family's members. Candasa, a slave who lived in

n but belonged to the wife of the resident magistrate of Graaff-

~ad the chance to free her family if she could raise sufficient

She told the protector that her mistress had given her permission

~rchase the freedom of herself and her children for R.1,800; she

~ded help finding the money. Since Candasa bore "a most excellent

~haracter," the protector applied to the philanthropic society on her

behalf. Her two daughters were quickly bought out of slavery. The soci-

ety, however, would not supply funds to buy Candasa, an adult, and her

son, a male. Candasa's slave husband somehow "procured a portion of

the money" needed to free them, and with the protector's assistance, "a

subscription [was] set on foot, the remainder was obtained and Candasa

and her other Child were emancipated."[119] The public fund-raising ef-

fort that helped Candasa and her family buy their way out of slavery was

a remarkable phenomenon.

The protector helped Carolus, a Cape Town free black, in much the

same way. He was one of the few fathers who freed his children with

the society's help. By the time he visited the protector, three of his chil-

dren had been manumitted, but his wife and two other children re-

mained enslaved. Carolus could not afford to buy them, but the protec-

tor came to his aid. Because Carolus was "a very industrious Person and

having a very good Character," the protector assisted "him in getting up a Subscription which at length amounted to as much as . . . the purchase money."[120]

Candasa and Carolus were probably impressive and likeable, fully deserving of the support that they received. Yet the colonists' response to them was in fact more than just a gesture of admiration. In this period, when both the local administration and the imperial state were engaged in the process of making the slaves fit for freedom and were looking for ways to discipline other members of the working classes, "industrious" men and women, "having a very good Character," were those who would receive official approval, encouragement, and support.

Slave and apprentice families varied tremendously. Most were composed exclusively of slaves or apprentices, but reaching out to other members of the working class was one of the ways in which the slaves coped with the chronically unbalanced sex ratio. Slaves thus created families with Khoisan, free blacks, Bastaard Hottentots, and poor whites. These families served to define the boundaries of the working-class communities of the early nineteenth century, the embryos of the post-emancipation "coloured" communities.

Slaves and apprentices created their own families, but not precisely as they would have wished. The demography of the slave population was one of the reasons that double-headed families—families with both a mother and father present, the form that slaves preferred—were not universal. Masters and mistresses were equally influential in determining the shape of slave families, sometimes interfering, but typically allowing their slaves to marry and create families. Slave owners may have done so simply out of humanity, but they would also have calculated the probable profit from the birth of slave children and recognized that married slaves and slave parents tended to be less rebellious than unmarried and childless slaves. If slave owners acquiesced in the formation of slave families, the reform laws of the 1820s and 1830s promoted it. The men in London and at the Cape who sponsored, drafted, and implemented the laws believed that the slaves had to be made fit and qualified for freedom. The family was to be one of the principal instruments in transforming the slaves into sober, industrious, and properly subordinated free wage laborers.

The families that the slaves and apprentices created did indeed fit them for freedom, but in ways that the abolitionists, parliamentarians, colonial officials, and philanthropists did not anticipate and that masters and mistresses feared. The slaves looked forward to the day in which they would become free, but not to becoming, while free, disciplined and subordinated wage laborers. Within their families, they had been able to resist in tangible ways the patriarchal ideology that sought to reduce them to infantilized, subject members of their master's household. As they assumed the roles of mother and father, roles that slave-holding ideology assigned only to their masters and mistresses, slave parents subverted natal alienation and realized much more of their human potential than they otherwise would have. Children grew up looking to their parents, not just to their masters and mistresses, as sources of authority and as protection from the forces of soul murder and social death.

Slaves and apprentices could not escape the household, as the petty humiliations and awful heartbreaks of slavery constantly reminded them. But in their families, they learned that one of the most important meanings of true freedom would have to be emancipation from their master's household. On 1 December 1838, thousands of former apprentices left those households, taking their families with them.

EPILOGUE

Resurrection

I had crossed de line of which I had so long been dreaming. I was free; but there was no one to welcome me to de land of freedom, I was a stranger in a strange land.

—HARRIET TUBMAN, AMERICAN SLAVE

The heavens wept on Emancipation Day. At dawn on 1 December 1838, the skies opened and a cold, gray rain swept across the land. For three days, the deluge and the chill continued: rivers flooded, and snow draped the shoulders of the mountains of the western Cape. Not for a generation had there been such curious weather, so late in the season. The former apprentices, the freedpeople, understood: the rains were God's tears, shed for those who had died in chains.[1]

Seventy-two years later, a frail former slave named Katie Jacobs remembered the day and its storms.[2] When she first saw her husband on the morning of their liberation, Jacob was "in a violent passion," his clothing soaked through to the skin. The couple shared a 'broad marriage, having belonged to different masters and having lived on neighboring farms not far north of Cape Town. Jacob Jacobs's boss, a cruel and violent man, had been "mad with rage" on Emancipation Day. "Early in the morning," Katie said, "he armed himself with a gun, mounted a horse, and drove every former apprentice off his farm. At the boundary, he warned that the first that was found trespassing on his land would be shot down." Katie found it "no wonder" that Jacob had been so angry "on the day of joy and humiliation and prayer."

Katie's master responded differently to emancipation, as did she. Her *"baas* and missus" were "somewhat irritated at the news of our . . . liberation." Still, they wanted her to stay. Jacob, however, "at first appeared determined to leave the district where he had suffered so much" and refused Katie's master's offer of employment for cash wages, housing, and board. Her master and mistress had been "on the whole kind," Katie said, and she "was not overjoyed at the prospect of leaving them." On hearing Jacob's decision, Katie reported, her mistress "wept at the idea of my leaving her." "'No; you must stay!' the mistress cried. 'Think of my son, whom you have suckled and nursed, and who has now grown so fond of you. What will become of him? No; you must stay; you cannot go.'" "Finally," Katie said, her husband "gave way." The offer of a steady job relieved some of the frightening uncertainty of freedom. The pressure of a stubborn wife's desire to stay probably sealed the issue. Jacob decided that the couple would settle on Katie's master's farm. They stayed on for another three or four more years.

Thinking back, Katie mentioned one other memory of her liberation. Shortly after Emancipation Day, she and Jacob regularized their marriage before God and the state. They and, as she recollected, "hundreds of ex-slaves" who lived in the district, visited Durban (now Bellville, a suburb of Cape Town)[3] and kept the Rev. Mr. Beck, of the Cape Auxiliary Missionary Society, busy with baptisms and marriages "from morning to night."

For Katie and Jacob and all of the former apprentices, Emancipation Day was a time of social rebirth. Jacob left his violent master, never to return. He and Katie united themselves as a couple, never to be separated, except by death. Their marriage soon received the sanction of church and state. The couple made their own decisions about where to work and where to live. They answered to no master, only to themselves. Social death was no more.

In telling the story of Emancipation Day, Katie Jacobs touched on questions that must shape any understanding of the transition from slavery to freedom: family, work, mobility, and the evolving relationships between white masters and mistresses and their newly freed servants and laborers. Underlying each of these themes, as Pamela Scully notes, were the larger questions about the ways in which emancipation would affect the structures of class, gender, and racial domination at the Cape.[4]

The social relationships that had existed under slavery and apprenticeship had disappeared. In combination with the colonial government's commitment to laws that were formally color blind, emancipation had given the freedpeople substantially more bargaining power relative to their masters. This revolution demanded that white supremacy adapt if it were to survive.[5] Nor could family and gender relations, within the community of former apprentices and beyond it, remain the same. Emancipation had given the freedpeople the chance to liberate themselves from the slave owner's household. Most took the opportunity. As they reunited broken families, freedmen began to assume to role of household patriarch. Behind the inextricably knotted questions of class, color, and gender was the central issue, the deceptively simple question everyone in the Cape Colony in some way had to confront: What did freedom mean?

For Jacob Jacobs, as for so many other freedpeople, the first test of freedom was mobility. Would he be free to travel unmolested through the colony? Would he be able to choose his employer and place of residence? His former master had, of course, forced him off the farm at gunpoint, but it seems certain that he would have left in any case. His master had treated him badly, and, as we shall see, severe masters found it difficult to retain their freed laborers. It was his decision, not his master's, to go directly to his wife on emancipation morning. He determined where he and Katie would spend their first night. Neither Jacob nor Katie had any intention of remaining a 'broad husband and wife. Like other freedpeople, they used their newly acquired mobility to unite their marriage. Jacob was also inclined to use his new mobility to seek out work under the best possible conditions. He may have hesitated to hire himself to Katie's master because he wanted to see what other offers he might draw. Another test of freedom was to establish in practice the right he now possessed to determine for himself to whom he would sell his labor and under what conditions.

Katie seems to have reacted to freedom more cautiously than Jacob. To be sure, her strongest memory of Emancipation Day was of her husband coming to her, and her first significant act after her liberation was to legitimate her marriage. But for Katie, freedom was ambiguous. It threatened to destroy human relationships that she deeply valued. She was "not overjoyed" about the possibility of leaving her master and mistress. She seems to have felt a genuine affection for her former owners and, one supposes, for their child, whom she had nursed. Her identity as a member of her master's household was not something that she could easily dismiss. On the other hand, her sense of herself as Jacob's wife pulled her toward him. She was caught between habits of dependency and a longing for autonomy. In the end, Katie seems to have managed a compromise, gathering in her family while retaining a place in the her former master's household.

Emancipation was also a moment of crisis for Katie's and Jacobs's masters and mistresses. The anguish that Katie's mistress felt when it appeared likely that Jacob would take Katie away was certainly authentic. Katie was a favorite servant and an intimate one, having wet-nursed her mistress's son. Her mistress may have believed that she was about to loose a companion as well as a servant. It would also have occurred to her that there would be more work for her to do if Katie moved on. She was as dependent on her servant as her servant was on her. Race and class informed her sense of herself, as they did most masters and mistresses at the Cape. She must have wondered who she would be if she were not the mistress of nonwhite servants. The passion with which she pleaded with Katie to stay indicates that her dependence on her servant was as psychological as it was material. The questions confronting everyone at the Cape were of both the body and the spirit. Neither can be ranked above the other.

The Abolition Act had plunged the colony into an unknown that held both promise and dread. The issues that the people of the Cape faced were similar to those that freedpeople, government officials, and former slave owners addressed in every society in which slaves were freed during the nineteenth century. As Eric Foner has argued, the "conflict between the freedmen's desire for autonomy and the planters' demand for a disciplined labor force unites the history of . . . societies in the aftermath of emancipation." While the result of this struggle over the meaning of freedom was by no means preordained, the state commonly entered the fray on the side of the former slave owners, thus seeing to it that the outcome would not favor the ex-slaves. Rigid social and political dichotomies between former master and former slave, racist ideologies, the former slaves' economic dependence and insecurity "seem always to survive the end of slavery."[6]

At the Cape, the colonial state deferred to the goals of the British cabinet and the Colonial Office. The secretary of state rather neatly declared his views on emancipation in an 1837 circular dispatch to the governors of the various slave colonies. On the one hand, "the great cardinal principle of the law for the abolition of Slavery is that the apprenticeship of the emancipated Slaves, is to be immediately succeeded by personal freedom, in that full and unlimited sense of the term, in which it is used in reference to the other subjects of the British Crown." On the other hand, freedom had its limits. The freedom that the former apprentices enjoyed "must of course . . . be that of men living in civil society. . . . Their privileges cannot be unconnected with restrictions."[7] Just what those restrictions might be was indicated by the coercive nature of an order in council regulating the relations between masters and freed servants that the secretary transmitted to the governors of British Guiana, Trinidad, Saint Lucia, and Mauritius. Under such legislation, Frederick Cooper writes, "slaves would be freed of the tyranny and violence of the individual slave owner, but not from the subordination, poverty, and powerlessness of the plantation economy."[8] Indeed, the order sanctioned the imprisonment at hard labor for up to two weeks of any servant who "neglected to perform his stipulated work, or . . . performed it negligently or improperly." Masters who mistreated their servants were subject only to fines, except for the crime of ignoring judicial orders.[9] The clear purpose of this piece of legislation was to reinforce the subordination of workers to their employers. But its role in buttressing the racial hierarchy in the former slave colonies must not be overlooked, despite its color-blind language.

William Cohen contends that in former slaveholding societies, the interpretation of "laws that omitted mention of race . . . reflected a mutual understanding and community of interest among all whites to see that they were applied *particularly* to black laborers."[10] While this was certainly the case at the Cape, the colonial state could not impose constraints on the freedpeople as liberally as governments in the West Indies. It had to contend with ordinance 50 of 1828, which protected "Hottentots and other free Persons of colour" from "certain obnoxious usages and customs" designed to restrict their mobility and tie them to settler farms by force of law.[11] At emancipation, the former slaves became "free Persons of colour," protected from the most obvious and attractive forms of labor coercion. The local administration and the settlers did not get around the problem until the passage of the Masters and Servants Ordinance of 1842. By then, as George Fredrickson notes, "the relationship between white and nonwhite corresponded so closely to a European-type class division, [that] the settlers found they could exercise effective control without recourse to legalized social discrimination. Technically color-blind master-servant laws giving the upper hand to employers could thus operate in a de facto racist fashion."[12]

As important as were the actions of the colonial state and the former slave owners, a search for the meaning of freedom must begin with the freedpeople. Because the freedpeople wanted more for themselves than the exploitation and oppression that the colonial government and the masters hoped to inflict upon them, freedom became a terrain of struggle. Its meaning emerged from the daily skirmishing between the former apprentices, the masters, and the colonial government over mobility, family, labor, and a host of other issues. Few of the skirmishes played out in anything like a straight-forward manner. As Barbara Fields has noted, freedom was a "constantly moving target."[13] It is the opening moments of this struggle, the moments that set the scene for the long fight ahead, that are the concern of this chapter.

Each of the thirty-six thousand apprentices freed in the Cape Colony would have had a story to tell about emancipation day. Every tale would have revolved around the great themes of race, gender, class, and the meaning of freedom and yet would have varied in its particulars. While few narratives as complete as Katie Jacobs's can be found, others can be reconstructed from the archival material that is available. The details matter. The meaning of freedom will appear only if the particulars of the former apprentices' stories are told.

The First Test of Freedom

Emancipation Day was not an occasion for frivolity and wild abandon. Katie Jacobs had captured the mood well when she described it as a "day of joy and humiliation and prayer."[14] Uniformly, observers described the behavior of the former apprentices in terms such as "quiet, proper, and peaceful."[15] For one of *De Zuid-Afrikaan*'s correspondents in Tulbagh, the most striking event of the day was the weather. Four days of driving rain, beginning on 1 December, damaged buildings, destroyed crops, and injured livestock. For whites, the wet and bitter cold prompted what might be called an alternative folk-explanation of the phenomenon: "We look upon this weather as *providentially* happening . . . [it] occasioned the avoidance of idle assemblages, and its consequences; and also prevented . . . improper rejoicings and drunkenness, from which nothing but evil must have arisen."[16] The governor, Major General Sir George Napier, was similarly pleased that "every thing passed off in perfect quietness" throughout his colony. He was equally happy to note that "the Churches of the various denominations were filled with the freed Apprentices returning thanks to the Almighty and the British Government for this great and just boon."[17] There was more to emancipation than churchgoing, but the sight of the freedpeople at worship was the day's most comforting sight as far as the officials and colonists were concerned. As it turned out, the former apprentices were not just in church; they were everywhere. On emancipation day, the Cape was a colony in motion.

Freedom came at midnight and, in Graham's Town at least, most of the apprentices, perhaps two hundred of them, were already at prayer in the Wesleyan chapel. The local newspaper reported that they had gathered from town and countryside to spend "the last remaining hours of their state of thraldrom [*sic*] in religious exercises. The midnight hour, the moment of emancipation, found them on their knees in the solemn exercise of prayer; a few seconds after 12 o'clock they arose and joined in singing with no ordinary fervour, the beautiful doxology, 'Praise God from whom all blessings flow.'"[18] In the towns and villages of the colony, from Cape Town to Graaff-Reinet, the reports were much the same: the vast majority former apprentices were orderly and sober. Even though few had been baptized, many of them went to church.[19] In Stellenbosch, "notwithstanding the inclemency of the weather the missionary chapel . . . was crowded to excess at three different services . . . and many who could not gain admittance, remained outside, near the door, and windows endeavouring to catch some portion of the service."[20] In Cape Town, ministers at both the so-called Scotch Church and the missionary chapel on Long Street preached to large congregations of freedpeople—more than five hundred at one of the services.[21] Edward Williams, who led the London Missionary Society station of Hankey in the eastern Cape, addressed another gathering of freedpeople, taking his text from 1 Peter 2:15–16: "For so is the will of God, that with well doing ye may put to silence the ignorance of foolish men: As free, and not using your liberty for a cloke of maliciousness, but as the servants of God."[22]

Not every former apprentice went to church on emancipation day— two thousand at most—but even those who did not attend services generally behaved with restraint. Very few towns reported instances of drunkenness, and the few that there were amounted to very minor breaches of the peace. In Swellendam, the special justice locked a handful of inebriated former apprentice revelers in jail, allowed them to sleep it off, and released them in the morning with instructions "to quit the Village immediately."[23] In Cape Town, which had the largest and most concentrated apprentice population in the colony and a reputation for wantonness as "the Tavern of the Seas,"[24] the police reported no criminal activity at all on 1 December—a marked change from the eight preceding Saturdays.[25] The single instance of public frolic that has entered the record from that well-documented day was the work of a troupe of whites. *De Zuid-Afrikaan* reported that the day "passed over without any extraordinary occurrence. . . . With the exception of some few individuals, who had masqueraded themselves as blacks, riding through the streets in a chaise, followed by a concourse, the greatest part children, and a small band of young boys, proceeding through the streets with a flag."[26] No other source seems to have reported this curious episode. Was it a mockery of emancipation, a reference to the premature celebrations of four years earlier, when the abolition of slavery had not meant the end of bondage?[27] A veiled assertion of the continuity of racial privilege? Perhaps. It seems to have been the single frivolous display, and it was carried out by members of the ruling race, not by freedpeople.

Most members of the emancipated class neither drank nor prayed nor frolicked; they took a holiday and took to the road. Thousands of freedpeople left the farms and households in which they had been enslaved and apprenticed, leaving for a day or forever. The justice of the peace in Paarl reported that on 1 December "an extra-ordinary number" of former apprentices visited the village "or passed through on their way to other places."[28] In Graaff-Reinet, "a great number" of freedpeople "repaired to this village respectably dressed, orderly, sober and peaceable in their conduct."[29] Former apprentices from the surrounding countryside traveled to Worcester for church services, and the "late Apprentices" of Koeberg "flocked into the Village" of Malmesbury.[30] Not only did freedpeople crowd into Stellenbosch for the three worship services, filling the chapel to overflowing each time, but a "good number of them" left the village for Cape Town.[31] A variety of motives had sent the former apprentices on their way.

The most powerful reason was, perhaps, simply to "demonstrate to themselves that their old masters and mistresses no longer owned or controlled them."[32] As a black preacher was to tell his congregation of newly freed American slaves a generation later, "You ain't, none o' you, gwinter feel free till you shakes de dus' ob de Ole Plantation offen yore feet an' goes ter a new place whey you kin live out o' sight o' de [master's] house."[33] The yearning to unite families was another of the incentives that prompted movement. Although the freedpeople would never have heard the phrase *natal alienation*, virtually all had experienced its heartbreak. Most slave and apprentice parents and children, husbands and wives, brothers, cousins, sisters, and aunts had never been able to share a home.[34]

Emancipation provided the opportunity to strengthen the ties of kinship and, sometimes, to unite families for good. Jacob Jacobs would have gone directly to his wife, Katie, whether or not his master had run him off the farm. Cathryn, another former apprentice, took her two young children with her when she left the farm of Piet de Vos two days after emancipation, going first to visit her husband at the farm on which he lived and then to see her mother in the village of Worcester. She told a colonial official, who questioned her in the course of an investigation into the activities of her former master, that she intended shortly to return to her husband for good. Another of de Vos's former apprentices, Amilie, left the farm to prevent the breakup of her marriage. She said that she "had an inclination" to stay with her mistress, but, when de Vos had ordered her husband to leave, she had gone with him.[35]

The need to move in order to unify or preserve families often intersected with a desire to establish independent households and to educate the children. Less than two months after emancipation, the Wesleyan missionary in the Somerset district reported that families of freedpeople had settled on mission land near the village with the "urgent wish" to have their children instructed in "moral and common useful Learning."[36] Similarly, several former apprentice husbands and fathers called on the resident magistrate of Worcester to request that he set aside "a small allotment" of public land near the village on which they might settle their families. They told him that they hoped to send their children to the missionary society's school and attend services in the chapel. They were also well aware that they would be able to earn more money as day laborers in the village than by hiring themselves to any single employer.[37] A combination of motives was at work here: the desire to cement family ties, the hope of upward mobility through education and higher wages, the assertion of independence from a master, and the need to worship God.

Ties not only of kinship but of friendship, too, took freedpeople off the farms and out of their masters' households. When September's master asked him if he intended to remain on the farm after emancipation, he said that he did, but that he "wished first to go and visit [his] friends."[38] On 4 December, a group of former apprentices in Uitenhage threw "a public tea party" for "their brothers and sisters in freedom." The former apprentices bore the cost of the party themselves and, according to a newspaper account, it was "respectably attended."[39] The mutuality that bound together the slave/apprentice community continued to bring them together in freedom.

Once the initial excitement of emancipation faded, the freedpeople settled down to the task of earning their daily bread. Their new mobility allowed them to search for better working conditions and greater rewards than they had known as slaves and apprentices. Some freedpeople wanted simply to find less violent masters and less grueling work. Jacob Jacobs, for instance, wished to quit the district "where he had suffered so much" at the hands of his former master.[40] The words of the former apprentice Present, another refugee from Piet de Vos's farm, reflect a similar stance. In answering questions about his reasons for leaving his master's farm two days after he was freed, Present said that he "had no inclination to remain there any longer . . . because I had to labor too hard."[41] It was a widespread phenomenon. Colonial officials in Worcester and Graaff-Reinet both reported that many freedpeople had sought new employers, particularly those whose masters had been "in any way remarkable for harshness or rigour." The report from Graaff-Reinet added that all were "now quietly turning their mind to earn a livelihood."[42] This last observation points toward an important aspect of emancipation. Settler spokesmen and conservative historiography notwithstanding, the former apprentices did not withdraw from the Cape labor market.[43]

The freedpeople wanted better conditions. The former apprentices did cease their labors in the momentary excitement of emancipation, but the interlude was short, and they soon returned to work. Many, it is true, did not return as properly subordinated laborers. They knew that they had to work to eat, but they were also determined to use their freedom to extract wages sufficiently high to ensure that they would eat better as freedpeople than they had as slaves. The settlers' contradictory denunciations of worker behavior reflect this tension (see below). As in the United States, "the abolition of slavery meant not an escape from all labor, but an end to unrequited toil. . . . Freedmen wished to . . . free themselves from subordination, and carve out the greatest measure of economic autonomy."[44]

More than a few of the former slave owners realized immediately that worker mobility had fundamentally altered the relations between masters and servants. Some tried to deny their workers the right to move. On Emancipation Day, one master in the eastern Cape told his former apprentices that "they were now free, and could do what they pleased in regard to remaining in his service." He said that he hoped that they would continue to work for him, and the former apprentices agreed to stay on. But when a group of them asked permission to attend a thanksgiving service at a mission station, the master refused and told them that "if they went, they should not set foot again on his premises." The freedpeople chose to leave.[45] Piet de Vos, mentioned above, also asked several people on his farm to continue to work for him. One of those who accepted his offer said that he first wanted to visit Worcester. De Vos told him "that he wanted no people on his place running about"; the price of continued employment was immobility. It was a price this former apprentice refused to pay, and he left.[46] Former apprentices knew that they were bound to earn a living, but they also knew that they were no longer bound to their masters.

New Relations of Production

Despite evidence that the former apprentices were ready to work, able to work, and indeed already working on farms and in households throughout the colony, the anguished howls of former slave owners unable to secure a sufficient workforce were heard across the land. One set of complaints claimed that the freedpeople were idle. They squatted on public lands and at the mission stations, it was claimed, and refused to work. Another set of complaints argued that the freedpeople demanded wages that were impossibly high. If they received wages approximating their outrageous demands, they then worked only until they had satisfied their limited wants and returned to idleness. These final charges begin to address the crucial issue. In the wake of emancipation at the Cape, there was a labor shortage of a kind. But it existed only to the degree that the former slave owners could not find enough former apprentices willing to work for the wages, and under the conditions, offered.

In the days and weeks after emancipation, there were frequent reports of ample supplies of labor. In Paarl, according to an official, there was no reason to worry about the harvest of 1838. The "extraordinary number" of freedpeople who had visited or passed through the village "flocked to the Corn farmers in unusual numbers, and many others . . . entered into engagements of service in the Village and neighborhood" as soon as the rains cleared.[47] In Stellenbosch, "great numbers" similarly went to the grain farms to harvest the crop.[48] As these comments suggest, many masters adapted quickly, if unhappily, to the new relationship between them and the freedpeople. This was so much the case that some observers believed that very little had changed following emancipation day. After a brief inspection tour of the countryside during the first week of freedom, the special justice in Worcester reported that it could not "be even perceived that so great a change, or indeed, that any change at all had taken place."[49] Some weeks later, a private citizen writing from Uitenhage used remarkably similar language. "Everybody remained in the *status quo*" after 1 December, "and not the most scrutinizing observer would have discovered that so great a change [as emancipation] had taken place."[50] These writers were reacting to the return of workers to the farms and the households. They saw labor power at work, and from a distance the scene seemed familiar. They were wrong, and the masters and former apprentices knew it.

The freedpeople's ability to come and go at will gave them considerably more bargaining power than they had previously possessed. It was not something the ruling race allowed to pass unchallenged. In the wake of emancipation, the relations of production were very much in flux as masters and servants experimented with a variety of labor arrangements, some of which would survive and some of which would not. This fluidity is mirrored in the comments of contemporaries. No single pattern of labor relations or behavior by the former apprentices emerged. Pieter Barend Botha of Tulbagh remembered that "most" of the freedpeople in his neighborhood stayed with their masters, "and the few who chose to go did not stay away long but soon returned to their former homes."[51] The resident magistrate of Caledon (who was the former special justice of Swellendam) reported that "many" of the "emancipated negroes" in his district remained at work "with their old Masters during the Harvest, but intending, when that is over to leave them."[52] In Malmesbury, the special justice found that, "with a few exceptions," the freedpeople continued to work for their former owners. But this by no means meant that they continued to live under the masters' supervision. The freedpeople, he wrote, were "inclined to live on, or near the farms on which they have resided," if they had been "well treated."[53] None of these observers spoke of a labor crisis.

On the other hand, A. J. Louw of Koeberg, a frequent correspondent to *De Zuid-Afrikaan,* the voice of the Dutch-speaking farmers, spoke for many masters when he claimed that emancipation had created a critical labor shortage. He wrote that "the final termination of Slave Apprenticeship . . . created an indescribable confusion, and gave the Agriculturalists a severe shock." He wrote that his former apprentices had "all left [his] service, and they roam about."[54] Yet Louw had adjusted to the new exigencies and had not lost his crop. His grain had been harvested, for wages, by itinerant laborers (former apprentices) from the wine country.[55] If Louw experienced a labor crisis, it was of his own making. He seems not to have made any of the more significant changes that many other colonial farmers made in an effort to secure a reliable supply of workers.

One of the most striking improvisations of the day was an evolving system of labor tenancy. This system might be interpreted as an extension of informal rights to garden plots and pasturage for livestock that the freedpeople had enjoyed as slaves and apprentices.[56] One former slave owner from Wynberg in the Cape district claimed that masters in his neighborhood had begun to offer labor tenancy to prospective employees even before Emancipation Day. In doing so, they had stolen the labor of other men. They "induced servants to quit their masters by holding out to them an independent means of subsistence. They gave them small patches of land to construct habitations on, rent free; but with this condition, that they are to serve the landowner, whenever he shall think proper . . . which is generally twice a week." This system drew adult, male former apprentices away from masters who did not offer these arrangements at the same time that it removed their wives and children from the labor pool altogether. The proceeds from the garden plots were enough to support the men's families. Labor tenancy, the man from Wynberg believed, was unfair to other masters and "detrimental to the community."[57] A farmer from Wagonmaker's Valley in the Stellenbosch district also denounced the system of "granting patches of ground to the late apprentices, with permission to erect huts thereon for large families." It was, he wrote, the "main cause" of the labor crunch.[58] Events in Wynberg and Stellenbosch were not isolated. A missionary in the Swellendam district, writing in 1839, mentioned labor tenancy as "a common practice in these parts."[59]

At least one former slave owner, J. R. Louw of the Stellenbosch district, was prepared to defend his use of labor tenancy. Because he granted his workers "lodgings on [his] ground gratis," he had secured "eight stout boys" to work for him. Louw paid the men a small wage. Their wives and children did not work for him, instead growing the families' food on plots that he had given them "for sowing and gardening." Louw was not pleased with this state of affairs; it was a circumstance the freed workers had forced on him. He wanted the state to weigh in on his side and called for a "better law" to bind the workers to their masters. He apologized for having adopted labor tenancy, but explained that his "worn out brain" could think of no other way to obtain the labor he needed.[60]

White farmers who did not enter into labor tenancy arrangements with their workers had to hire them for wages. Here again, the master-servant relationship had radically changed. The relationship between an employer and a wage laborer was terminable by either party, often on short notice. In fact, for the masters, the most irritating aspect of the new dispensation was the reluctance and at times refusal of the former apprentices to enter into long-term labor contracts binding them to service. A. J. Louw, of Koeberg, who had managed to bring in his grain harvest using migrant wage laborers, was nevertheless angry that the former apprentices would "not hire themselves except by the day." The autonomy that day laborers possessed made them unreliable, according to Louw. They were cheeky as well. Louw complained bitterly about his inability to discipline these impudent servants. "They come to the field after the sun has risen, and if we look sour about it, they go away and abandon work."[61] A writer from Worcester echoed Louw's remarks. It was, he argued, only "with difficulty" that the freedpeople could be made to work for the former slave owners, "and if you get them, it is only per day; you can hardly prevail upon them to enter service by the month; and even in the latter case they leave before half the period is out."[62] The idea of signing contracts to bind themselves to former slave owners for lengthy stretches of time would not have appealed to the freedpeople. All realized that it was their mobility that made freedom meaningful. It allowed them to reunite their families, seek better conditions of labor, carve out a measure of independence, and establish some physical and psychological distance from their masters. They had escaped social death and saw no reason to turn back the clock.

The memory of the violence of slavery and apprenticeship was another factor that moved the freedpeople to shun long-term labor contracts. Some colonists understood this. A correspondent to *De Zuid-Afrikaan* who called himself "Meditator" and claimed to have long been involved in agriculture at the Cape, addressed the question of day labor in early 1839. He believed that the labor troubles of many farmers could be traced back to slavery. He agreed that "many of the emancipated blacks wish to hire themselves by the day, and few will take service for more than a month." He thought that farmers who complained about a shortage of labor had chosen to close their eyes to the truth. The former apprentices' "motives for acting in this cautious manner [were] very obvious." They "have been, in many cases, so accustomed to harsh treatment, and have seen their race suffer so much from bad masters, that they are unwilling to extend their services, until they ascertain the character of their employers." This writer felt confident "that good masters will experience . . . little difficulty in procuring servants. . . . The labouring population will soon discover where the best masters are to be found." He regretted, however, that "good masters" did not form the majority:

The bad, who I fear form the most numerous class, will never be able to obtain a good description of servants. . . . Is harsh treatment, then . . . a prominent feature of the African farmer's character? His natural disposition is, no doubt, similar to the rest of mankind;—the circumstances in which he has been placed, have tended to harden it, and to render him callous and indifferent to the feelings of others. His hand has been too familiar with the whip, the cat, and the samboc [sjambok].[63]

Freedpeople knew that freedom would have little meaning if the violence that had been such a large part of social death continued to dominate their lives.

"Meditator" may have been too pessimistic about the chances of "the most numerous class" of masters to secure the labor they needed. They, like A. J. Louw, who was not necessarily one of them, temporarily accepted expedients such as day labor and labor tenancy while they carefully plotted revenge.

New Gender and Family Relations

The freedpeople's' ability to unite their families and to redefine the relations within them presented their erstwhile masters and mistresses with another set of labor problems. Married couples attempted, with varying degrees of success, to reduce their dependence on their former masters as much as possible, seeking especially to withdraw children and married women from the labor market.[64] They looked for land on which to settle, whether in the towns and villages, on mission stations, or on public lands, in order to free themselves from dependence on an employer by producing for themselves. Those freedpeople who remained on their employers' property preferred labor tenancy because of the opportunity it presented for families to engage in relatively autonomous productive labor. The freedpeople did not always attain their goals. The circumstances that prevailed at the Cape after emancipation made it difficult to withdraw women's and children's labor fully or to secure access to productive land.

There was nothing, however, to stop freed couples from formalizing their marriages. At the opening of this chapter, we saw how Katie Jacobs, remembered that the freedpeople in her district kept the local missionary busy "from morning to night," performing marriage ceremonies.[65] Elsewhere, missionaries themselves reported that great numbers of freedmen and freedwomen exchanged vows.[66] The former apprentices sought two things for their marriages that most had been denied during slavery: spiritual sanction and legal protection. Religious and legal ties strengthened the bonds of affection that had held couples together when they were slaves. Formal marriage ceremonies also brought their unions recognition within colonial society and gave them a civil existence. Children were legitimated; property could be passed on to surviving spouses and heirs. Natal alienation was no more, and church, state, and society formally recognized its passing. Such regularization of marriage was not limited to the Cape. In the United States, as in other Western slave societies, "emancipation allowed blacks to reaffirm and solidify their family connections, and most freedmen seized the opportunity with alacrity."[67]

Couples moved quickly to restructure their marital and familial relations by withdrawing wives and children from the labor force. Many married freedwomen managed to avoid direct labor for a master at least temporarily. Commenting on the supposed colonial labor shortage, the editor of the *Commercial Advertiser* argued that it was only female domestic servants who were in short supply. He attributed this to two causes in particular: "A dislike among the laboring classes in this colony, to domestic occupations, particularly cooking. . . . [And the] retirement of a great number of female servants to their own homes, where their husbands being now free, are able to maintain them."[68] *De Zuid-Afrikaan* also noted the dearth of domestics and pointed with horror to the fact that "respectable families . . . are obliged to perform domestic services themselves."[69] Such lamentations over the scarcity of domestic servants could be heard in both urban and rural households.

As hard as married freedwomen tried to avoid the labor market, circumstances soon forced most to work with some regularity in the households and on the farms of the former slave owners. Their labor seems often to have been tied to the arrangements their husbands made with their employers. The resident magistrate of Worcester noted that freedmen who hired themselves to farmers in his district sometimes found that the farmers required their wives and children to work on the farm as well.[70] Two farmers, a wheat grower and a wine maker who entered the newspaper debate that raged over the labor issue in early 1839, noted that they paid cash wages to their female domestic servants.[71] It was never clear during the immediate postemancipation period, however, whether or not the women's and children's efforts to stay out of the labor market would succeed.

Unremarked upon by contemporaries was the new structure many of the freed families assumed. Scully has observed that the former slave owners and the colonial state promoted the patriarchal structure of the freed family, hoping to rely on freedmen to discipline family members.[72] Farmers, for instance, paid freedmen significantly higher wages than freedwomen, and they entered into labor-tenancy agreements only with male family heads.[73] But it also seems clear that the freedpeople themselves preferred, whenever possible, to form patriarchal families—that is, families headed by males, with wives, children, and other kin in subordinate positions. This was reflected in Katie Jacobs's personal narrative: she was prepared to leave the master and mistress, of whom she was fond, in order to follow her husband. Though, at first, she convinced him to stay on her master's farm, she later followed him from farm to farm and eventually to Cape Town's District Six, a working-class neighborhood that became the stuff of legend.[74] Amilie and Coloni, two freedwomen who left Piet de Vos's farm on 3 December, moved away contrary to their own preference because their husbands had decided to seek opportunities elsewhere. As one of them put it, "I had an inclination to remain with my Mistress, but when my husband went away I did so also."[75] Men took the lead in other ways. When, for instance, a party of freed families asked permission to settle on public land near Worcester, it was the men who approached the resident magistrate.[76]

The former apprentices' apparent readiness to construct patriarchal families is remarkable. Scholarship produced over the last generation has exploded earlier views of patriarchal families as a natural phenomenon. This scholarship has also destroyed the naive view of the family as a domestic unit in which each member naturally contributes in his or her gender-specific way to the welfare of the whole. This view supposed that, unless outside factors such as slavery intervened, men performed economically productive work, eschewed domestic labor, and controlled family resources; women (and children) worked within the household at unpaid labor; and all shared equitably in the rewards. Instead, the patriarchal family and the gender division of labor have been seen as human inventions. Because the gender division of labor results in the woman's economic dependence on the dominant male, the patriarchal family as been identified as one of the primary sites of women's oppression.[77]

Is it possible that, for freedwomen, freedom from slavery meant subordination to a husband and father? If so, emancipation was a backward step. During slavery and apprenticeship, the typical family had been matrifocal.[78] Slaves and apprentices could not have formed fully real-ized patriarchal families had they wanted to. Much of a patriarch's power over his kinfolk stems from his economic dominance, and most slaves had no income and no property. Nor could a male slave exercise the full range of patriarchal prerogatives. The male slave could not, for instance, protect his family from breakup by sale, loan, or will; he could not deny his master access to his wife's body, either by way of the lash or by rape.[79] There was room for only one patriarch in the master's household.

With emancipation, this changed. A master's patriarchal authority was no longer enshrined in law. There were few absolute restrictions on the formation of families among the former apprentices. Legal restric-tions on the freedpeople's' ability to earn an income and accumulate property fell away. At the same time, some married freedwomen with-drew themselves from the labor market and chose to forgo the chance to establish relative economic independence. They became, instead, de-pendent on their husbands, giving rise to another patriarchal family. If the patriarchal family is seen merely as a site of women's oppression, then one conclusion seems inescapable: Katie, Amilie, Coloni, and the other freedwomen had, in freedom, exchanged one master for another. But the freedwomen were not so foolish.

Though there were certain costs that the freedwomen had to pay when participating in the creation of male-headed families, the benefits were greater still. The older, "naive" view of the family was not entirely incorrect. It can be a domestic unit in which all members work toward some common good, and in which authority, if concentrated in one pair of hands, is at least shared. The sexual division of labor, to the degree the former apprentices were able to achieve it, in some ways helped to make freedom more, rather than less, meaningful. Freedwomen who devoted most of their labor to household production contributed to the structural integrity of families that, so recently, had been so fragile. During slavery and apprenticeship, slave family members were subject to dispersal at the whim of the master, his heirs, or his creditors. Part-ners often did not belong to the same master and did not live on the same farm or even in the same neighborhood. For all family members, the physical proximity and structural integrity that came with free-dom were precious things. In limiting themselves to work within their own households, the freedwomen were able to maximize the time they spent with their families. Scully argues that the women's reluctance to work within a master's home emerged out of the history of sexual abuse during slavery and apprenticeship.[80] This was surely an important consideration, but it was one among many.

A significant proportion of Cape freedwomen, but not all, as we have seen, would have wanted to establish the greatest possible physical and psychological distance between their families and the master and mistress. The time they spent outside of the enforced intimacy of the master's household was time they did not spend cooking for him, cleaning for him, suckling his child, or trying to fend off his advances. Since it was common for a domestic servant's younger children to stay near her while she worked, refusing employment within the master's household ensured that both she and the children were beyond the master's reach.[81] Freedwomen who avoided the labor market were also able to spend the greatest possible amount of time working for and with their families— minding their own children, cooking, sewing, cleaning, tending a garden plot, caring for livestock. Freedwomen thereby decreased the families' dependence on the wages earned by the freedmen, and hence, lessened the families' dependence on a master. Her labor belonged to the family in a way that her wage-earning husband's did not. The centrality of the freedwoman's position in the economic life of the family meant that the freed family was less patriarchal than it might at first appear.

A similar process followed emancipation in the American South. Married freedwomen tried to withdraw from the former slave owners' households and fields, though they did not always succeed. At the same time, freedmen asserted themselves at the head of the former slaves' households.[82] This does not mean, however, that the freedwomen had been forced into a subordinate role within their families or that they had created one for themselves. As Jacqueline Jones has argued, for married freedwomen "freedom had meaning primarily in a family context." "Freedwomen derived emotional fulfillment and a newfound sense of pride from their roles as wives and mothers. Only at home could they exercise considerable control over their own lives and those of their husbands and children and impose a semblance of order on the physical world."[83] Like the married freedwomen of the Cape, they found strength, not weakness, within their families. The families that they helped to re-create were the most important support in the freedpeople's struggles with their former masters and the state over the meaning of freedom.

Searching for a Home

Nearly half a century after Emancipation Day at the Cape, during the last days of Brazilian slavery, the abolitionist Joaquim Nabuco wrote that "freeing the Negro without freeing the land is but half an abolition."[84] Even in the Cape Colony, where antislavery sentiment was a weak and exotic growth, a few white voices had recommended that "respectable" freedmen be given plots of land on which they could raise crops, graze livestock, and build a home for their families. In 1834, as the end of slavery approached, the protector of slaves in Graaff-Reinet suggested "that the first step towards improving the colored classes, and even towards securing the Community against the disorder of the indolent, should be, to fix as many as possible of the industrious, *upon their own land.*" By *land* he meant garden lots, either in the existing towns or in newly created villages. By *colored classes* he meant the soon-to-be-freed slaves and the "Hottentots."[85] He saw several advantages to his plan. Prosperity would be hard work's reward, reinforcing the missionaries' messages of uplift and salvation. Having become productive members of society, industrious freedpeople and Khoisan would have an "interest in the preservation of order" and a great reluctance to call for reform or revolution. Their economic success would make them "an object for emulation" by the less hard-working members of their community.[86]

In 1837, Dr. John Philip, director of the London Missionary Society in the colony, and his son-in-law, John Fairbairn, editor of the *South African Commercial Advertiser*, also proposed that the government grant land to families of "Hottentots" and later to emancipated apprentices. The secretary of state was hostile to the idea. He thought that any plan to settle freedpeople on government land "appears . . . to be open to many serious, if not conclusive objections." "I should fear that the probable effect would be to perpetuate their poverty. . . . The most desirable result would be that they should be induced to work for wages as free labourers."[87] The secretary of state was not prepared to countenance the creation of an independent coloured peasantry—neither in the Cape nor in any of Britain's other slave colonies—because the colonial economies could not survive without some form of forced labor.[88]

The idea that the freedpeople needed land to make their freedom complete reappeared throughout the emancipation era. Sometimes the former apprentices themselves raised the question. Two months after emancipation, the resident magistrate in Worcester advised his superiors that several former apprentice tradesmen and laborers had asked for "a small allotment of Government ground adjoining this Town, to locate [their families] on." The magistrate believed that the men were deserving and that a grant of land would keep them and their labor power in the community, rather than their being lost to a mission station. But he could not bring himself to endorse the plan wholeheartedly: "I observe such a strong prejudice with the inhabitants against the locating of them [on government land], that I am almost reluctant to suggest any plan for that purpose."[89] Whites knew that access to land would decrease the freedpeople's dependence on them for subsistence, consequently diminishing the supply of labor and raising its price. Because of the opposition of both the local government and the local whites, there could never be land for the freedpeople without the vigorous support of the Colonial Office. That support never came. The former apprentices were thrown back on their own resources in their search for a measure of autonomy. For some, the search was successful.

Besides labor tenancy there were three important ways in which the freedpeople gained access to land in the immediate postemancipation period: they squatted on public land in the rural areas; they moved onto public land adjacent to the towns and villages; and they moved to the mission stations. The least significant of these options, at least in terms of the numbers of former apprentices involved, was squatting on vacant public land.

Prior to emancipation in 1838, the Cape's Legislative Council passed an ordinance prohibiting unauthorized squatting on government land.[90] Like most local ordinances of the day, it was a finely crafted statement of intent, but ineffective in practice. Because the government lacked a regular police force and had to rely on the highly inconsistent performance of the veld cornets, it lacked the capacity to enforce the ordinance.[91] But when law enforcement failed, the social geography of the Cape stepped in. Especially in the western districts, where two-thirds of the freedpeople lived, there was very little good vacant land to be found. Only a small number of former apprentices found land on which to raise a crop of vegetables, even a meager one, and to run a small flock of goats or sheep, thereby limiting their involvement with the labor market.[92]

It is impossible to say precisely how many freedpeople squatted on government land in the countryside. The number cannot have been large. Marincowitz estimates that a decade after emancipation there were one thousand squatters on public lands in the western Cape.[93] In 1851, testimony before the Legislative Council regarding a proposed new antisquatting ordinance indicated that there were sixteen squatter locations in the western Cape. The combined population could not have totaled more than twelve hundred.[94] There would have been even fewer squatters in the arid and sparsely populated eastern Cape. The number of former apprentice squatters in the first years after emancipation was probably well under a thousand.

Despite these low numbers, whites hotly denounced the squatters and demanded government action against them. In part, this was because whites blamed squatters for the theft of livestock and for other "depredations." More important was the distance that the squatters were able to establish between themselves and the labor market. *De Zuid-Afrikaan*, for instance, called for laws "whereby idle persons, thieves and vagabonds, are prevented from living upon the earnings of the laborious, and are then consequently indirectly compelled to seek for service, and for work, in accordance with the principle of the present *Poor Laws* in England." The newspaper denounced the existing labor law and demanded a more coercive statute. "We hope our Rulers will see the inefficiency of the system as at present . . . and the improper influence it must have on the minds of servants, and the Blacks in particular. . . . Protect the Blacks, but protect equally the Whites!"[95]

A larger number of freedpeople moved onto government land on the outskirts of the towns and villages in the Cape. According to Jane Sales, they did so because of the scarcity of land, elsewhere, for cultivation and herding and to be close to chapels and schools.[96] An equally powerful pull was the chance to escape the direct gaze of a master, yet be close to sources of casual employment for both craftsmen and agricultural laborers. Some of the former apprentices who visited the towns of the Cape on Emancipation Day stayed on, and more trickled in over the next few years. Again the numbers are approximate; perhaps three thousand former apprentices had entered the towns of the western Cape by 1848; another one thousand lived in the towns in the east.[97] Many of the former apprentices in the western districts quickly established a pattern of engaging in seasonal labor for the wheat growers and wine farmers and in occasional day labor. Income from these sources allowed them to live independently of any single master. In the eastern part of the colony, the emerging wool industry provided seasonal work.[98]

Life in the towns and villages was not easy. In Worcester, for instance, most freedpeople lived in shacks on a patch of ground that in winter was surrounded by pools of standing water. Their beds were "sheep skins spread on the bare ground."[99] Often they had so little food that they were extremely vulnerable to the periodic epidemic diseases that swept the Cape.[100] Many freedpeople nevertheless preferred the autonomy of a hut on government land to continued dependence on a master.

It is possible to be more precise about the number of freedpeople who moved onto the lands of the colonial missionary societies in the first months after emancipation. In March 1839, the colonial administration ordered the ministers in charge of each of the mission stations to answer a number of questions regarding their relationship with the former apprentices. What the officials most wanted to know was whether or not the missionaries were encouraging the freedpeople to leave their masters and join the stations and how many freedpeople had settled on mission land. The government was responding to widespread rumors that up to six thousand freedpeople had crowded into the stations. In circulating these reports, the former slave owners placed much of the blame for their inability to find a sufficient supply of compliant labor at the doorstep of the missionaries.[101]

The government's investigation showed that the rumors lacked substance. No more than nine hundred freedpeople had settled on the mission stations in the colony by April 1839. Only in the area around the Moravian mission of Genadendal, where the eastern border of the district of Swellendam met the western edge of the Stellenbosch district, had a sizeable percentage of the local freedpeople moved onto the mission lands. The 474 freedpeople living at the station represented about 12 percent of the freed population of the immediate neighborhood.[102] Although most of the freedmen who lived on the mission stations performed day labor for the local farmers, the access to at least a minimal amount of land allowed many of the freedwomen to confine their labor to the household.[103] The missionary at Bethelsdorp, for example, noted that the only former-apprentice family on his station sent the father and eldest son out to work, while the younger children and the mother stayed at home.[104]

There is no doubt that emancipation upset the Cape labor market. Some freedpeople managed to withdraw themselves from the labor market; some farmers could not obtain as much labor as they wanted at the wages and under the conditions that they were willing to offer. The principle causes of the immediate disruption were the movement of perhaps two thousand to twenty-five hundred freedpeople off the farms onto public lands and the mission stations, combined with the withdrawal of many married freedwomen from nonhousehold labor. Masters who could not adjust to the new circumstances cried foul. Agricultural production did fall modestly in 1838 and 1839. This decline, however, was not caused by a labor shortage alone. Heavy rains and cold destroyed crops in the southwestern Cape; drought plagued the districts east of Worcester; and an outbreak of measles severely affected many workers. It is thus uncertain how much of the decline in agricultural production can be blamed on the withdrawal of freedpeople from field labor. And recovery came quickly. By 1839, production figures were within the range of those achieved prior to emancipation.[105] So rapidly did the colonial farmers adjust to free labor that, as Robert Ross has shown, "the two decades after the emancipation of the slaves were a long boom for the agricultural economy of the colony."[106]

There was great fluidity in the social and economic arrangements at the Cape during the first months of freedom, but there was no significant, absolute shortage of labor. The former slave owners' problem was rather that there was a shortage of cheap, malleable, and, to them, properly subordinated labor. The problem of workers who were entirely too free was one that the colonists and the colonial government were determined to solve.

From Freedom to Coercion, From Slave to Coloured

In late 1833 and early 1834, soon after he received word of the passage of the Abolition Act, Lieutenant Colonel T. F. Wade, the acting governor of the Cape, sent a series of dispatches to the secretary of state reminding him of the colonists' chronic complaints about a labor shortage. Taking up the settlers' cause, he suggested that emancipation would only worsen the situation. Wade believed that "long before the period of the expiration of the Apprenticeship arrives," some law ought to be enacted for "the prevention and punishment of Vagrancy."[107] While it is true that many settlers and colonial officials were convinced that the livestock thefts committed by jobless and propertyless "Hottentot" vagrants had become a serious burden in the years after the promulgation of ordinance 50, the suppression of vagrancy was by no means Wade's sole object.[108] The acting governor was equally concerned about the ability of the farmers to coerce free people to work for them. The vagrancy law that he proposed would secure "a sufficiency of labourers to the colony by *compelling* not only the liberated apprentices to earn an honest livelihood, but all others who, being capable of doing so, may be inclined to lead an idle and vagabonding life."[109] Wade was not alone in his thinking. A demand for laws to restrict the mobility of the Khoisan and of the soon-to-be-freed slaves had been building ever since the promulgation of ordinance 50. Two historians have in fact referred to an "anti-vagrancy hysteria" among the settlers.[110]

Whites dreaded the consequences of emancipation. When that day dawned, according to the protector of slaves in Cape Town, "near Forty Thousand free People will be given to the existing coloured Population, of which there are at present at the least an equal number."[111] A protector of slaves in the eastern Cape explained that the settlers feared that the freedpeople would behave as the "Hottentots" had after ordinance 50 liberated them, preferring "a life of independence, to engaging in regular labor for hire." Independence meant sloth, as far as the settlers were concerned. The freed slaves would "lapse into wandering habits which [would] inevitably lead, as in the Case of Vagrant . . . Hottentots to incorrigible idleness and ultimately to crime."[112]

One of the first acts of the new governor, Major General Sir Benjamin D'Urban, who arrived in 1834 was to order his attorney general to draft a vagrancy ordinance. This was a delicate matter. The royal approval of ordinance 50 had included a clause forbidding the local administration to amend or repeal it without the sanction of the home government.[113] The ordinance had provided that "no Hottentot or other free Person of colour . . . shall be subject to any compulsory service to which other of His Majesty's Subjects . . . are not liable, nor to any hindrance, molestation, fine, imprisonment or punishment of any kind whatsoever, under pretense that such Person has been guilty of vagrancy or any other offence, unless after trial."[114]

Ignoring the dangers that ordinance 50 posed, the law that the attorney general proposed granted local magistrates the power to apprehend any "Hottentots" and persons of color that they "may reasonably suspect of having no honest means of subsistence." If those arrested could not prove otherwise, the magistrates might order them to the public works or hire them to settler farmers. The ordinance passed through the legislative council, but D'Urban withheld it, pending the approval of the Colonial Office.[115] The draft, said the historian W. M. Macmillan, "was well calculated to satisfy even the crudest demands of the white colonists." It was "a commonplace attempt . . . to get State sanction for a policy that would secure a plentiful supply of cheap, subservient, and exploitable labour."[116]

Macmillan had echoed the sentiments of those against whom the law had been written. Soon after the draft was published, missionaries connected to the London Missionary Society sponsored petitions condemning the law. Each was signed by scores of "Hottentots" and were addressed to the governor. Though the language is clearly that of the missionaries, the sentiments are those of the Khoisan.[117] Calling themselves the "coloured Inhabitants" of the Caledon mission station, one group acknowledged that "many of their brethren" had "a strong aversion . . . to labour for the agriculturalists." This was but a "consequence of the cruel treatment and the fraudulent dealings they have formerly met with." The proposed law would not remedy the situation. They were "convinced from bitter experience that if passed [the law] . . . would become an instrument of oppression."[118] The "colored Inhabitants of Graham's Town and it Vicinity" also condemned the draft.[119] They reminded the governor that they represented the "colored population [who were] the Natives and original proprietors of the soil." Since the promulgation of ordinance 50, they had "emerged from a condition of abject bondage to which they had been reduced partly by the Laws and partly by the lawless aggressions of the local authorities." The powers that the proposed law gave to local magistrates, they thought, amounted "to absolute despotism, and lays the whole free colored population prostrate before them and at their mercy." The government could not trust the administration of the law to "uneducated men, owners of Slaves . . . [with] no just notions of the feelings and privileges of mankind in a state of Civil Liberty."[120] The Colonial Office in London signaled its disapproval of the ordinance in 1835. Its most important objections, the secretary of state told D'Urban, were that it contravened ordinance 50 and that "the proposed enactments were at variance with the most established principles of personal freedom."[121] Hence, when emancipation came, the law regulating the relationship between master and servant was ordinance 50. It was not a law with which the masters were pleased.

Though ordinance 50 may have provided the Khoikhoi and other free persons of color less protection than colonists claimed, it nevertheless made it more difficult for farmers to bind them to labor.[122] Soon after his arrival, Governor Napier, who had replaced D'Urban in January 1838, ordered local officials to begin work on an ordinance designed to supersede ordinance 50 and regulate the "rights and duties" of masters and servants. Their model was the proposed "masters and servants" law that the Colonial Office had created for the West Indian slave colonies.[123] A draft of the Cape's Masters and Servants Ordinance was ready in mid-1839, seven months after emancipation. The preamble declared that it was "expedient to amend . . . the Laws regulating the relative rights and duties of Master, Servants, and Apprentices, and providing for the improvement of the labouring classes, and more particularly for

that class composed of persons of colour." It went on to define persons
of color as "Hottentots," all others covered under ordinance 50, and the
former apprentices. It specifically excluded Bantu-speaking Africans
and "any woman of colour . . . lawfully married to any European."[124] Napier was soon persuaded that the racially explicit language would not get
past the Colonial Office and he submitted a revised, race-neutral draft
for approval in January 1840.[125]

Though the law was now formally color blind, no one at the Cape
doubted what was understood: in practice, masters were to be white and
servants coloured. It more rigidly defined the duties of servants than
had ordinance 50 and "went far to allay the masters' alarm at abolition."[126] The law made a servant's neglect of work, refusal to work, desertion, insolence, and insubordination punishable by local magistrates.
Servants convicted of breaking contracts could either be fined or sentenced to hard labor; masters were subject only to fines.[127] The legal
scales had been weighted decisively on the side of the masters.[128] An order of the queen in council confirmed the ordinance in August 1842,
giving it the force of law.[129]

The draft vagrancy law and the Masters and Servants Ordinance were
labor legislation designed to do more than simply force free persons
into the service of settler farmers. Their purpose was to create and to
subordinate a coloured labor force. Ordinance 50, which had relieved
the "Hottentots and other free Persons of colour" of the most onerous
compulsions placed on them, and the Abolition Act, which had freed
the slaves, were symbols of "an old order in disintegration."[130] The old
order presupposed white domination of all other persons within the colony, especially the Khoisan and the slaves, the Cape's principal workforce. Since the economic well-being of the settlers and of the colony as
a whole depended on their combined labor, the new order that followed
slavery would have to invent new forms of class and race domination
that encompassed both freedpeople and Khoisan. After the emancipation of the slaves, it became convenient for the government and the settlers to view these two groups as one. The first draft of a masters and servants ordinance made this explicit, defining "Hottentots" and former
slaves as "persons of colour."[131] The draft ordinance, in so defining
Khoikhoi and former slaves, had not innovated. By 1839, this definition
was common. The words *coloured* and *persons of colour* seem to have entered the Cape from the usage in the British West Indies, by way of the
Colonial Office. In the West Indies, the terms distinguished free people
of mixed ancestry from those of purely European or African descent.

This usage found its way into ordinance 50; *free Persons of Colour* had referred to free blacks and Bastaard Hottentots, groups that colonial society distinguished from both whites and Africans. By 1834, the protector of slaves in the Eastern Division was referring to slaves and "Hottentots" as members of the "Colored Classes" or simply as "coloreds."[132] Beginning in 1837, the colonial blue books followed what was becoming a common practice by enumerating apprentices and Khoisan as the "Colored Population" in the population table.[133] No later than 1838, *coloured*, meaning the combined population of former slaves and Khoisan, had entered Cape Dutch as *gekleurde*, as if *coloured* were the past tense of the verb *to colour*.[134] In practice, speech, and, indirectly, in law, the colonists were inventing a racially defined, subordinate working class.

It is not certain when freedpeople and Khoisan began to think of themselves as "coloured." The "colored Inhabitants of Graham's Town" used the word to identify themselves and as a synonym for *Khoisan* ("the Natives, and original proprietors of the soil") in their antivagrancy-law petition of 1834.[135] In practice, as we have seen, the slaves and Khoisan often worked together under the same conditions, resisted the masters collectively, and intermarried and created families.[136] In much of their behavior, then, they had been acting for many years as if they were one people.

The invention of *coloured* was only beginning in the period of emancipation. Former apprentices, Khoisan, settlers, and officials all continued at times to draw distinctions between "Hottentots" and freedpeople. But the process of creating legally defined *and* self-identified coloured communities had begun its fitful run.

Notes

Preface

1. W. L. Burn, *Emancipation and Apprenticeship in the British West Indies* (London, 1937), 80.

2. Orlando Patterson, *Slavery and Social Death: A Comparative Study* (Cambridge, Mass., 1982); Ran Greenstein, "The Study of South African Society: Towards a New Agenda for Comparative Historical Inquiry," *Journal of Southern African Studies* 20, no. 4 (1994).

Introduction

1. The following narrative draws on the day book of the protector of slaves, Cape Town, Cape Archives Depot [CAD], Cape Town, South Africa, SO 5/9, vols. 3, 4, 5, 6, 8, and 9; the register of slaves, Cape Town and Cape district, CA, SO 6/15; and report, protector of slaves, Western Division, 26 July 1833, Public Record Office, London [PRO], CO 53/56.

2. Official documents customarily identified slaves by a given name and the name of their owner, as in "Jeptha, male slave belonging to Johannes van der Merwe." Slaves bearing two names appear in the record often enough, however, to suggest that slaves at the Cape commonly possessed a surname, whether or not their owners and the colonial state chose to recognize it.

3. See Timothy Keegan, *Colonial South Africa and the Origins of the Racial Order* (Cape Town, 1996); Robert Ross, *Beyond the Pale: Essays on the History of Colonial South Africa* (Hanover, 1993); Nigel Worden, "Adjusting to Emancipation: Freed Slaves and Farmers in Mid-Nineteenth-Century South-Western Cape," Wilmot James and Mary Simons, eds., *The Angry Divide: Social and Economic History of the Western Cape* (Cape Town, 1989); Mary Raynor, "Wine and Slaves: The Failure of an Export Economy and the Ending of Slavery in the Cape Colony, South Africa, 1806–1834," Ph.D. diss., Duke University, 1986; Robert C.-H. Shell, *Children of Bondage: A Social History of the Slave Society at the Cape of Good Hope, 1652–1838* (Hanover, 1994); and Pamela Scully, *Liberating the Family? Gender and British Slave Emancipation in the Rural Western Cape, South Africa, 1823–1853* (Portsmouth, N.H., 1997).

4. This marriage had almost certainly not been sanctioned by either church or state. Yet even the Colonial Office knew that slaves in the Cape as throughout the British Empire had long formed "connections which they regarded as matrimonial, although not solemnized according to the established Rules of Law. The effect is that such ties are sometimes disregarded, and too lightly dissolved": Glenelg to Napier[?], 15 September 1838, CAD, GH 1/125.

5. On the gentry, see Robert Ross, "The Cape Economy and the Cape Gentry," in *Beyond the Pale*, 13–49.

6. Cloete's thirty slaves placed him among the larger slaveholders in the Cape Colony.

7. Natalie Zemon Davis, *Fiction in the Archives: Pardon Tales and Their Tellers in Sixteenth-century France* (Stanford, Calif., 1988).

8. This line of thought is cribbed, of course, from Karl Marx, *The Eighteenth Brumaire of Louis Bonaparte* (reprint, New York, 1963), 15.

9. Apprenticeship, a four-year period of virtual slavery, preceded the slaves' effective emancipation in 1838. During apprenticeship, slaves were referred to in official language as apprentices. For a detailed discussion of both the protectors of slaves and the special justices, see chapter 2.

10. Patterson, *Slavery and Social Death: A Comparative Study* (Cambridge, Mass., 1982), 1–14, 207.

11. See also other works by Patterson: *Freedom*, vol. 1: *Freedom in the Making of Western Culture* (New York, 1991); *Rituals of Blood: Consequences of Slavery in Two American Centuries* (Washington, D.C., 1998).

12. Patterson, *Slavery and Social Death*, 207.

13. Patterson's work extends and complements M. I. Findley's efforts to define slavery; see, for instance, M. I. Findley, *Ancient Slavery and Modern Ideology* (Harmondsworth, Eng., 1983).

14. When he asserts that Patterson "offers only an elegant reconstruction of the ideologies of the dominators," Jonathan Glassman misreads *Slavery and Social Death;* see Glassman, "The Bondsman's New Clothes: The Contradictory Consciousness of Slave Resistance on the Swahili Coast," *Journal of African History* 32 (1991): 280.

15. Patterson, *Slavery and Social Death*, 13.

16. Patterson, *Freedom*, 21.

17. Patterson, *Slavery and Social Death*, 337.

18. Patterson, *Freedom*, 22.

19. Nell Irvin Painter, "Soul Murder and Slavery: Toward a Fully Loaded Cost Accounting," in Linda Kerber et al., eds., *US History as Women's History* (Chapel Hill, N.C., 1995), 127–28, 133–34.

20. Ibid., 130.

21. Ibid., 139.

22. Goderich to Lowry Cole, 29 February 1832, CAD GH 1/89.

23. Glenelg to Napier, 6 November 1837, CAD, GH 1/117.

24. Timothy Keegan, *Colonial South Africa and the Origins of the Racial Order* (Cape Town, 1996), 13.

1. The State of the Cape

1. See Leonard Thompson, *A History of South Africa* (New Haven, Conn., 1990), 54; and Eric A. Walker, *A History of South Africa* (London, 1928), 144–45.

2. Lowry Cole to Viscount Goderich, 4 April 1831, in Maud Lowry Cole and Stephen Gwynn, *Memoirs of Sir Lowry Cole* (London, 1934), 244.

3. The phrases *Cape of Good Hope* and *the Cape* can refer either to the geographical point at the tip of the Cape peninsula, to the peninsula and its continental hinterland, or, more commonly, and in the sense I use it throughout, to the colony as a whole.

4. The hunter-gatherers of southern Africa, once called Bushmen, are now commonly referred to as San. Pastoralists, known to the settlers as Hottentots, called

themselves Khoikhoi, a term that has become standard. *Khoisan* is often used to refer to the hunter-gatherers and Khoikhoi collectively and is the term I adopt here. On reduction to servitude, see Susan Newton-King, *Masters and Servants on the Cape Eastern Frontier, 1760–1803* (Cambridge, Eng., 1999).

5. Governor, Cape Colony, to sec. of state, 12 October 1809, CAD, GH 23/2.

6. A. J. Christopher, *Southern Africa* (Folkestone, Eng., 1976), 20.

7. See Robert Ross,"The Cape Economy and the Cape Gentry," in *Beyond the Pale: Essays on the History of Colonial South Africa* (Hanover, 1993), 13–49.

8. Christopher, *Southern Africa* 20; William M. Freund, "The Cape under the Transitional Governments, 1795–1814," in Richard Elphick and Hermann Giliomee, eds., *The Shaping of South African Society, 1652–1840* (Cape Town, 1989), 344.

9. Thompson, *South Africa,* 55–56.

10. There were many names by which the Dutch-speaking settlers were called at the time—(Dutch-)colonists, (Dutch-)settlers, inhabitants, Christians, whites, Boers, Afrikanders. Today their descendants are *Afrikaners,* a term that first appeared in 1703 and has since been in constant, if not always predominant, use. I use *Afrikaners* to refer to Dutch-speaking settlers in general and *Boers* to refer to Dutch-speaking farmers: see Richard Elphick, *Khoikhoi and the Founding of White South Africa* (Johannesburg, 1985), 227. On master-servant relations and settler resentments, see chapter 2.

11. Henry Lichtenstein, *Travels in Southern Africa, in the Years 1803, 1804, 1805, and 1806,* 2 vols. (reprint, Cape Town, 1928), 1:10.

12. Monica M. Cole, *South Africa,* 2nd ed. (London, 1966), 22–24, 34; Christopher, *Southern Africa,* 17–18.

13. Cole, *South Africa,* 60.

14. Cole, *South Africa,* 32–60 and Christopher, *Southern Africa,* 18–20.

15. Statement of population . . . Cape of Good Hope, 1808, enclosure to dispatch, governor, Cape Colony, to sec. of state, 16 October 1809, CAD, GH 28/2.

16. Derived ibid.; and Christopher, *Southern Africa,* 52.

17. In 1750, half the free adult male settler population owned slaves. The figure would have been approximately the same in the 1820s and 1830s. In 1824, there were 12,748 "Christian" men above the age of sixteen in the colony. In 1831, the nearest year for which numbers exist, 6,380 people owned slaves. It seems likely that, in the late 1820s as in 1750, half of the free adult male settler population owned slaves since the great majority of the slave owners were adult males: James C. Armstrong and Nigel Worden, "The Slaves, 1652–1834," in Elphick and Giliomee, *Shaping,* 129–34; return showing population . . . at the Cape of Good Hope . . . 1824, George McC. Theal, comp., *Records of the Cape Colony [RCC],* in 36 vols. (London, 1897–1905), 35:386–87; report, protector of slaves, 24 June 1831, PRO, CO 53/52.

18. Returns of "the total number of slaves in the various districts according to the several classes and values," CAD, SO 20/61.

19. Ross, *Cape of Torments: Slavery and Resistance in South Africa* (London, 1983), 24.

20. John Barrow, *An Account of Travels into the Interior of Southern Africa, in the Years 1797 and 1798* (London, 1801), 2:386.

21. Robert C.-H. Shell, *Children of Bondage: A Social History of the Slave Society at the Cape of Good Hope, 1652–1838* (Hanover, 1994), 40–65.

22. [Sam?] Sinclair, "Descriptive Account of the Voyages," Sinclair Papers, Archives and Papers, University of the Witwatersrand Library, Johannesburg, South Africa, A98, 24–25.

23. Statement of population, enclosure to dispatch, 1809, CAD, GH 28/2.

24. Verenigde Oost-Indische Compagnie. See chapter 2.

25. On the use of the term *Christian*, see, for instance, the critical remarks of the Christian missionaries George Champion and William Elliot: George Champion, *Journal of an American Missionary in the Cape Colony, 1835*, ed. A. R. Booth (Cape Town, 1968), 14, 20; Elliot quoted in R. L. Watson, *Slave Question: Liberty and property in South Africa* (Hanover, 1990), 173.

26. Richard Elphick and Hermann Giliomee, "The Origins and Entrenchment of European Dominance at the Cape, 1652–1840," in Elphick and Giliomee, *Shaping*, 523–24.

27. For more on free blacks, see especially chapter 7.

28. Statement of population, enclosure to dispatch, 1809.

29. Richard Elphick, *Khoikhoi*, 4–14.

30. Elphick, *Khoikhoi*, 12, 67–90 and passim; see also Henry C. Bredekamp and Susan Newton-King, "The Subjugation of the Khoisan, during the Seventeenth and Eighteenth Centuries," paper, Conference on Economic Development and Racial Domination, University of the Western Cape, Bellville, South Africa, 8–10 October 1984.

31. Statement of population, enclosure to dispatch, 1809, CAD, GH 28/2.

32. Ibid.

33. D. J. van Zyl, "Die Slaaf in die Ekonomiese Lewe van die Kaapkolonie, 1795–1834," *South African Historical Journal* 9 (November 1977): 8.

34. Armstrong and Worden, "Slaves," 129–34; Ross, *Cape of Torments*, 16.

35. Armstrong and Worden, "Slaves," 133.

36. Ibid., 110–12.

37. Ross, *Cape of Torments*, 13.

38. Robert C. H. Shell has done by far the most extensive work on the slave trade to the Cape; see, for instance, *Children of Bondage*, 40–65. See also Nigel Worden, *Slavery in Dutch South Africa* (Cambridge, Eng., 1985), 41–48, and Armstrong and Worden, "Slaves," 110–22.

39. *Gleanings in Africa . . . the Cape of Good Hope and Surrounding Country* (London, 1806), 60–61.

40. S. E. Hudson, "Slaves," *Kronos* 9 (1984): 48–49.

41. A burgher was a citizen of the Cape. All, with the rarest of exceptions, were white.

42. Worden, *Slavery*, 46–48.

43. Ross, *Cape of Torments*, 17.

44. Ross, *Cape of Torments*, 17–18; Worden, *Slavery*, 36–37; Andrew Bank, "Slavery in Cape Town, 1806 to 1834," M.A. thesis, University of Cape Town, 1991, 19–60.

45. Worden, *Slavery*, 39.

46. Derived from returns of "the total number of slaves," CAD, SO 20/61.

47. Colonial slave registry, Cape Town and district and the residency of Simon's Town, 1816–19, vols. 1–3, PRO, T 71/652–54.

48. J. W. D. Moodie, *Ten Years in South Africa: Including a Particular Description of the Wild Sports of that Country*, vols., 1 and 2 (London, 1835), 1:113–14.

49. Lichtenstein, *Travels*, 1:73.

50. Leonard Guelke, "Freehold Farmers and Frontier Settlers, 1657–1780," in Elphick and Giliomee, *Shaping*, 69–73; Worden, *Slavery*, 6–9.

51. Guelke, "Freehold Farmers," 73–77; Worden, *Slavery*, 19–26.

52. Robert Ross, "The First Two Centuries of Colonial Agriculture in the Cape Colony: A Historical Review," *Social Dynamics* 9, no. 1 (1983): 37.

53. Guelke, "Freehold Farmers," 77–84; Ross, "Two Centuries," 40–43.

54. Statement of population, enclosure to dispatch, 1809, CAD, GH 28/2.

55. Pieter van Duin and Robert Ross, "The Economy of the Cape Colony in the Eighteenth Century," *Intercontinenta* 7 (1987): 33–40; Cole, *South Africa*, 203–4.

56. Barrow, *Account of Travels*, 2:394–95. On the first and second British occupation of the Cape, see chapter 2.

57. Van Duin and Ross, "Economy," 45–50; Christopher, *Southern Africa*, 53. The most thorough overview of the wine economy in the eighteenth and nineteenth centuries is D. J. van Zyl's *Kaapse Wyn en Brandwyn, 1795–1860: Die Geskiedenis van Wynbou en Wynhandel in die Kaapkolonie* (Cape wines and brandies, 1795–1860: The history of wine farming and the wine trade in the Cape Colony) (Kaapstad [Cape Town], 1974).

58. Cole, *South Africa*, 176.

59. Van Duin and Ross, "Economy," 41–42.

60. Worden, *Slavery*, 23, 70.

61. Ross, *Cape of Torments*, 25.

62. Ross, *Cape of Torments*, 25–26; Worden, *Slavery*, 26–27, 88–89.

63. See chapters 3, 4, and 5.

64. Worden, *Slavery*, 88. See also chapter 5.

65. Elphick, *Khoikhoi and the Founding*, 12; Thompson, *South Africa*, 12.

66. Elphick, *Khoikhoi and the Founding*, 151–74; Cole, *South Africa*, 227.

67. Cole, *South Africa*, 227–28; van Duin and Ross, "Economy," 58 ff.

68. Christopher, *Southern Africa*, 44–46; Cole, *South Africa*, 102–3; van Duin and Ross, "Economy," 58; Elphick, *Khoikhoi and the Founding*, 224.

69. Cole, *South Africa*, 103.

70. Ross, "Two Centuries," 36.

71. Elphick, *Khoikhoi and the Founding*, 67–68, 112–14, 221–22; Bredekamp and Newton-King, "Subjugation," 5–6, 25–27.

72. See Susan Newton-King, "The Rebellion of the Khoi in Graaff-Reinet: 1799 to 1803," in Susan Newton-King and V. C. Malherbe, *The Khoikhoi Rebellion in the Eastern Cape, 1799–1803* (Cape Town, 1981).

73. Statement of population, enclosure to dispatch, 1809, CAD, GH 28/2.

74. Richard Elphick and V. C. Malherbe, "The Khoisan to 1828," in Elphick and Giliomee, *Shaping*, 30–31; Susan Newton-King, "The Enemy Within," paper presented to the conference on Slavery and After, University of Cape Town, Cape Town, South Africa, 10–11 August 1989, passim.

75. Bredekamp and Newton-King, "Subjugation," 26–30.

76. Worden, *Slavery*, 36.

77. Elphick and Malherbe, "The Khoisan," 28–29.

78. Worden, *Slavery*, 27. See also chapter 5.

79. See chapters 4 and 5.

80. Van Duin and Ross, *Cape Economy*, 88.

81. On gender, see chapter 3.

82. Those who write about slavery often distinguish between "societies with slaves" and "slave societies." In the first, slavery was an important component of the cultural, political, and economic life of the society, but, while it influenced those aspects of society, it did not define them: slavery was not "determinative." In a slave

society, on the other hand, slaves not only played a critical role in production and constituted a large proportion of the population, slavery itself determined the nature of social institutions: see Orlando Patterson, *Slavery and Social Death: A Comparative Study* (Cambridge, Mass., 1982), ix–xii; Worden, *Slavery,* 6–18.

83. On Afrikaans as a creole language, owing much to the linguistic input of the slaves, see Achmat Davids, "The Afrikaans of the Cape Muslims, from 1815 to 1915: A Socio-linguistic Study," M.A. thesis, University of Natal, Durban, 1991; and Ross, *Cape of Torments,* 14–15.

84. Freund, "Transitional Governments," 334–35.

85. M. I. Findley, *Economy and Society in Ancient Greece* (Harmondsworth, Eng., 1983), 99.

86. Andre du Toit and Hermann Giliomee, eds., *Afrikaner Political Thought: Analysis and Documents,* vol. 1: *1780–1850* (Berkeley, Calif., 1983), 71; see also, Worden, *Slavery,* 139.

87. Fiscal (legal officer) to governor, Cape Colony, 29 November 1797, quoted in du Toit and Giliomee, eds., *Afrikaner Political Thought,* 48.

88. Walker, *History,* 144–45.

89. Governor, Cape Colony, to sec. of state, 1 July 1808, CAD, GH 23/2.

90. William J. Burchell, *Travels in the Interior of Southern Africa,* 2 vols. (reprint, Cape Town, 1967), 1:27–28. See also Cowper Rose, *Four Years in Southern Africa* (London, 1829), 8.

91. Report, protector of slaves, Western Div., 20 January 1834, PRO, CO 53/57.

92. Hendrik Tobias Theron v. fiscal, appeal, CAD, GH 47/2/12.

93. Enclosure, governor, Cape Colony, to sec. of state, 29 February 1826, CAD, GH 28/11.

94. F. M. L. Thompson, *The Rise of Respectable Society: A Social History of Victorian Britain, 1830–1900* (Cambridge, Mass., 1988), 91–113; quote on 93.

95. On Islam, see chapter 7.

96. Armstrong and Worden, "Slaves," 192–93; Richard Elphick and Robert Shell, "Intergroup Relations: Khoikhoi, Settlers, Slaves, and Free Blacks, 1652–1795," in Elphick and Giliomee, *Shaping,* 214–24. Freund argues otherwise in, "Race in the Social Structure," *Race and Class* 18, no. 1 (1976): 53–67.

97. Stephen Jay Gould, *The Mismeasure of Man* (New York, 1981), 19–29, 30–42 and Winthrop D. Jordan, *White over Black: American Attitudes Toward the Negro, 1550–1812* (Baltimore, Md., 1969), 216–65, 482–541.

98. Keegan, *Colonial South Africa,* 13.

99. R. L. Watson, *The Slave Question: Liberty and Property in South Africa* (Hanover, 1990), 184–85.

100. W[illiam Wilberforce] Bird, *State of the Cape of Good Hope in 1822* (reprint, Cape Town, 1966), 349, 176.

101. Statement of the laws of the Colony of the Cape of Good Hope regarding slavery, *RCC,* 9:153.

102. Report, commissioners of inquiry to William Huskisson, on the police at the Cape of Good Hope, *RCC,* 35:137.

103. Ross, *Beyond the Pale,* 5, 69–110.

104. Elphick and Giliomee, "European Dominance," 536–37.

105. Ibid., 544, 549 (emphasis in original).

106. On soul murder, see Nell Irvin Painter, "Soul Murder and Slavery: Toward

a Fully Loaded Cost Accounting," in Linda Kerber et al., eds., *US History as Women's History* (Chapel Hill, N.C., 1995).

107. Orlando Patterson, *Slavery and Social Death: A Comparative Study* (Cambridge, Mass., 1982), 5–13.

2. "Breaking the Spell of Subjection"

1. This was the second British occupation of the Cape; see below.

2. Mary Isabel Raynor, "Wine and Slaves: The Failure of an Export Economy and the Ending of Slavery in the Cape Colony, South Africa, 1806–1834," Ph.D. diss., Duke University, 1986, 7.

3. G. E. Cory, "A Short History of Slavery at the Cape," MS, South African Historical Society Papers, Archives and Papers, A 241, Witwatersrand University Library, Johannesburg, South Africa, 4.

4. Seymour Drescher, *Econocide: British Slavery in the Era of Abolition* (Pittsburgh, 1977).

5. William Law Mathieson, *British Slavery and Its Abolition, 1823–1838* (London, 1926), 27.

6. John Barrow, *An Account of Travels into the Interior of Southern Africa, in the Years 1797 and 1798,* 2 vols. (London, 1801), 1:10.

7. Verenigde Oost-Indische Compagnie.

8. Richard Elphick, *Khoikhoi and the Founding of White South Africa* (Johannesburg, 1985), 71–102; Leonard Thompson, *A History of South Africa* (New Haven, Conn., 1990), 31–33.

9. William Freund, "The Cape under the Transitional Governments," in Richard Elphick and Hermann Giliomee, eds., *The Shaping of South African Society* (Cape Town, 1989), 324–34; Thompson, *South Africa,* 52–53.

10. Eric A. Walker, *A History of South Africa* (London, 1928), 125–28.

11. Freund, "Transitional Governments," 325, 328–39; see also, Susan Newton-King and V. C. Malherbe, *The Khoikhoi Rebellion in the Eastern Cape* (Cape Town, 1981).

12. Thompson, *South Africa,* 52–53; Walker, *South Africa,* 130–39.

13. Freund, "Transitional Governments," 337–38, 350–51, and passim.

14. George McC. Theal, *History of South Africa* (London, 1891), 115 ff.; Walker, *South Africa,* 144–45.

15. 47 Geo. 3, sess. 1, cap. 36.

16. David Eltis, *Economic Growth and the Ending of the Transatlantic Slave Trade* (New York, 1987), 4.

17. Other moments in his larger argument have been called into question; see below. For a vigorous defense of Williams, see Cedric J. Robinson's "Capitalism, Slavery and Bourgeois Historiography (or taking on ol' massa)," *History Workshop* 23 (spring 1987): 122–40.

18. Eric Williams, *Capitalism and Slavery* (reprint, New York, 1966), 52.

19. Eltis, *Economic Growth,* 4.

20. Drescher, *Econocide,* 3.

21. Ibid.; Robin Blackburn, *The Overthrow of Colonial Slavery, 1776–1848* (London, 1988), 35–36. For a scholarly example of the providential view, see Reginald Coupland's *The British Anti-Slavery Movement* (London, 1933).

22. Williams, *Capitalism and Slavery,* 134–35, 169.

23. Drescher, *Econocide,* 183.

24. Eltis, *Economic Growth,* 7.

25. David Brion Davis, "Reflections on Abolitionism and Ideological Hegemony," *American Historical Review* 92, no. 4 (1987): 797–98.

26. Blackburn, *Overthrow,* 295.

27. Eltis, *Economic Growth,* 11–12.

28. Freund, "Transitional Governments," 329; Raynor, "Wine and Slaves," 58. And below.

29. C. W. de Kiewiet, *A History of South Africa: Social and Economic* (Oxford, 1941), 35.

30. Freund, "Transitional Governments," 328.

31. Isobel Eirlys Edwards, *Towards Emancipation: A Study of South African Slavery* (Cardiff, Wales, 1942), 159.

32. Raynor, "Wine and Slaves," 8; de Kiewiet, *Social and Economic,* 36–37.

33. Dispatch and enclosure, governor, Cape Colony, to sec. of state, 25 July 1807, CAD, GH 23/1.

34. Governor, Cape Colony, to sec. of state, 15 December 1807, CAD, GH 23/1.

35. See Susan Newton-King, "The Labor Market of the Cape Colony, 1807–28," eds. Shula Marks and Anthony Atmore, *Economy and Society in Pre-Industrial South Africa* (London, 1980).

36. Raynor, "Wine and slaves," 36–37.

37. Governor, Cape Colony, to sec. of state, 21 March 1810, CAD, GH 23/2.

38. Quoted in Raynor, "Wine and Slaves," 12.

39. Ibid., 12–14.

40. Ibid., 15.

41. Newton-King, "Labor Market," 172–73.

42. James C. Armstrong and Nigel Worden, "The Slaves, 1652–1834," in Elphick and Giliomee, *Shaping,* 132.

43. Ibid., 180.

44. Christopher Saunders, "Liberated Africans in Cape Colony, in the First Half of the Nineteenth Century," *International Journal of African Historical Studies* 18, no. 2 (1985): 224, 227–30; R. L. Watson, "'Prize Negroes' and the Development of Racial Attitudes in the Cape Colony, South Africa," conference paper, University of Western Carolina, 15 April 2000, 2; see also Newton-King, "Labor Market," 179–80.

45. Dispatch, governor, Cape Colony, to sec. of state, 16 October 1809, CAD, GH 1809.

46. Proclamation of 1 November 1809, #1.

47. Ibid., #1 and #2. See also, Newton-King, "Labor Market," 176–77; W. M. Macmillan, *The Cape Colour Question: A Historical Survey* (London, 1927), 160–61.

48. Richard Elphick and V. C. Malherbe, "The Khoisan to 1828," in Elphick and Giliomee, *Shaping,* 41; Newton-King, "Labor Market," 177.

49. Macmillan, *Cape Colour Question,* 160.

50. Freund, "Transitional Governments," 336.

51. Raynor, "Wine and Slaves," 73–129; de Kiewiet, *Social and Economic,* 35–46.

52. *Parliamentary Debates, New Series, v. VII, 1823* (Hansard), cols. 1783–1801. On Islam at the Cape, see chapter 7.

53. Blackburn, *Overthrow,* 421.

54. David Brion Davis, *Slavery and Human Progress* (New York, 1984), 166.

55. Davis, *Slavery and Human Progress,* 169. See also Blackburn, *Overthrow,* 421–22;

William A. Green, *British Slave Emancipation: The Sugar Colonies and the Great Experiment* (Oxford, 1976), 100.

56. W. L. Burn, *Emancipation and Apprenticeship in the British West Indies* (London, 1937), 80.

57. Davis, *Slavery and Human Progress*, 192–94; Green, *British Emancipation*, 100–120; Burn, *Emancipation and Apprenticeship*, 80–82.

58. Edwards, *Towards Emancipation*, 91.

59. Cape proclamation, 18 March 1823, #5, #6, #7, #12, #13, and #24.

60. Davis, *Slavery and Human Progress*, 192.

61. Anthony Kendal Millar, *Plantagenet in South Africa: Lord Charles Somerset* (Cape Town, 1965), 158.

62. Davis, "Reflections on Abolitionism," 800.

63. Isobel Eirlys Edwards, *Towards Emancipation*, 93.

64. Ibid., 94.

65. Ibid., 97–99, 101; sec. to the Cape government to undersec. of state, 26 Sept. 1826, in George McC. Theal, comp., *Records of the Cape Colony* [*RCC*] (London, 1897–1905), 23:161.

66. Cape ordinance 19, 1826.

67. Ibid., #2–7, #12, #13, #17, #23, #33–39.

68. See below.

69. Memo, Burgher Senate, 30 June 1826, *RCC*, 26:90–94; memo to the Burgher Senate, 3 July 1826, ibid., 26:98–100; memo to the landdrost and heemraden of the Stellenbosch district, 10 July 1826, ibid., 27:110 ff.

70. Ordinance 19, #7 and #17.

71. Ibid., #33–38.

72. Order of the king in council, 2 February 1830, #22 and #26.

73. Hereafter I use *protector* to refer to the officeholders during the entire period of amelioration.

74. The slaveholders petitions may be found in the enclosures to a dispatch of the governor, Cape Colony, to sec. of state, 1 April 1831, PRO, CO 48/142. On the riot, see the dispatches of the governor to the sec. of state, 3 July and 4 December 1831, PRO, CO 48/143; *South African Commercial Advertiser*, 23 April and 17 September 1831.

75. On the protests, see governor, Cape Colony, to sec. of state, 19 June 1832, CAD, GH 26/69 and R. L. Watson, *The Slave Question: Liberty and Property in South Africa* (Hanover, 1990), 30–48, 116–34.

76. Cape ordinance 50, 1828; see also Elphick and Malherbe, "The Khoisan," 47–49; Keegan, *Colonial South Africa*, 104–6, 118–22.

77. De Kiewiet, *Social and Economic*, 38.

78. Raynor, "Wine and Slaves," 190–93.

79. For evidence of literate slaves, see their signed letters to the protectors in miscellaneous letters, CAD, SO 1/52.

80. See below.

81. Calculated from the reports of the guardians and protectors of slaves, PRO, CO 53/48–58.

82. Observations of the protector, December 1833, CAD, SO 3/20a.

83. Report, protector of slaves, assistant protector, Somerset, 28 May 1833, PRO, CO 53/55.

84. Report, protector of slaves, 24 June 1831, PRO, CO 53/52.

85. Calculated from the return of estimated traveling distances in hours on horseback, in enclosure, governor, Cape Colony, to sec. of state, 21 April 1831, PRO, CO 48/142.

86. Report, registrar and guardian of slaves, assistant guardian, Stellenbosch, 31 December 1827, PRO, CO 53/48.

87. Wayne Dooling in "Slaves, Slaveowners, and Amelioration in Graaff-Reinet, 1823–1830," B.A. thesis, University of Cape Town, 1989, 64.

88. Initially, district clerks acted as assistant guardians at a small additional salary. By 1831, the job had been given to the clerks of the peace, whose pay was not increased; see *Cape of Good Hope Blue Books*, 1827 and 1833. The principal protector frequently complained that his men had too little time to devote to their duties. See general observations, reports of the protector of slaves, Western Div., 25 December 1830, PRO, CO 53/51 and 26 July 1833, PRO, CO 53/56.

89. Report, registrar and guardian of slaves, 25 December 1826, PRO, CO 53/48.

90. Nigel Worden, *Slavery in Dutch South Africa* (Cambridge, Eng., 1985), 94–95.

91. Peter Philip, *British Residents at the Cape, 1795–1819* (Cape Town, 1981), 354.

92. General observations, report, protector of slaves, 25 December 1830, PRO, CO 53/51. I discuss the ideology and reality of Cape paternalism in chapter 3.

93. Quoted in Raynor, "Wine and Slaves," 275.

94. General observations, report, protector of slaves, Eastern Div., 24 December 1833, PRO, CO 53/57.

95. General observations, report, protector of slaves, Western Div., 26 July 1833, PRO, CO 53/56.

96. Report, protector of slaves, Western Div., 26 July 1833, PRO, CO 53/56.

97. Ibid., 7 January 1833, PRO, CO 53/55.

98. Edwards, *Towards Emancipation*, 122.

99. Raynor, "Wine and Slaves," 276–77.

100. See, for instance, assistant guardian of slaves, Stellenbosch, to the governor, Cape Colony, enclosure, governor, Cape Colony, to sec. of state, 9 April 1830, CAD, GH 26/60; and observations, protector of slaves, December 1830, CAD, SO 3/20a.

101. Raynor, "Wine and Slaves," 274.

102. Slave register, Cape district, CAD, SO 6/28. He sold both in 1831.

103. General observations, report, protector of slaves, 25 December 1830, PRO, CO 53/51.

104. Dispatch, sec. of state to governor, Cape Colony, 29 February 1832, CAD, GH 1/89.

105. Green, *British Emancipation*, 107.

106. Quoted in ibid., 107–8. See also sec. of state to the governor, Cape Colony, 22 April 1828, in report, guardian and registrar of slaves, 24 June 1827, PRO, CO 53/48.

107. Report, protector of slaves, assistant protector, Stellenbosch, 25 July 1833, PRO, CO 53/55.

108. Edwards, *Towards Emancipation*, 129.

109. Robert Ross, "The Rise of the Cape Gentry," *Journal of Southern African Studies* 9 (1983): 196–97.

110. See Edwards, *Towards Emancipation*, 128.

111. General observations, report, protector of slaves, Eastern Div., 14 August 1833, PRO, CO 53/56.

112. Confidential dispatch, governor, Cape Colony, to undersec. of state, 18 April 1831, CAD, GH 26/64.

113. E. Hengherr, "Emancipation and After: A Study of Cape Slavery and the Issues Arising from It," M.A. thesis, University of Cape Town, 1953, 11.

114. See one protector's reasoning in general observations, report, protector of slaves, Eastern Div., 14 August 1833, PRO, CO 53/56.

115. The phrase is Eric Hobsbawm's: "Peasants and Politics," *Journal of Peasant Studies* 1, no. 1 (1973): 13.

116. 3 & 4 Wm. 4. cap. 73.

117. Davis, *Slavery and Human Progress*, 200–201; Blackburn, *Overthrow*, 450–51.

118. 3 & 4 Wm. 4, cap. 73, #1; Cape ordinance 1, 1835.

119. 3 & 4 Wm. 4, cap. 73, #24.

120. Jacqueline Lalou Meltzer, "The Growth of Cape Town Commerce and the Role of John Fairbairn's *Advertiser*," M.A. thesis, University of Cape Town, 1989, 55. It has been common in South African historiography to contend that compensation money did not adequately cover the financial losses incurred as a result of emancipation, severely damaging the colonial economy. Meltzer convincingly refutes this argument. She finds that, on the contrary, compensation payments were an economic boon. For further confirmation of Meltzer's position, see Keegan, *Colonial South Africa*, 115–16.

121. The terms *praedial* and *nonpraedial* were not well defined in the Abolition Act; see Burn, *Emancipation and Apprenticeship*, 118, n. 4.

122. 3 & 4 Wm., cap. 73, #2–17.

123. Cape ordinance 1, 1835.

124. Ibid., chap. 3, #1; chap. 5, #1, #4–10, #11, #14, #15, #16.

125. Ibid., chap. 4, #1; chap. 6, #13.

126. Ibid., chap. 5, #3–8, #10, #11, #16; chap. 6, #13.

127. Edwards, *Towards Emancipation*, 177–78.

128. Mathieson, *British Slavery*, 243.

129. Burn, *Emancipation and Apprenticeship*, 105.

130. Blackburn, *Overthrow*, 441.

131. Letters, special justices of Cape Town, Stellenbosch, Paarl, and Tygerberg, n.d., in *Kronos* 9 (1984): 76–77.

132. Report, protector of slaves, Eastern Div., 24 December 1833, PRO, CO 53/57.

133. See the recollections of the former slave Katie Jacobs in *APO* (newspaper of the African Political Organization), Christmas number 1910, 9.

134. Special justice, Swellendam, to sec. to government, 23 February 1835, CAD, CO 441.

135. Journal of cases, special justice, Worcester, 18 February 1835, CAD, WOC, 19/29.

136. Edwards, *Towards Emancipation*, 180–81.

137. Enclosures, governor, Cape Colony, to sec. of state, 15 April 1836, CAD, GH 26/73; returns exhibiting the number and effect of punishments inflicted by the special magistrates of the . . . Cape, enclosure, governor, Cape Colony, to sec. of state, 19 December 1836, CAD, GH 26/77.

138. Criminal and civil notebooks, special magistrate, Malmesbury, 1835–38, CAD, CBY 3/1/1.

288 Notes to Pages 62-69

139. Both cases in the criminal record book, special magistrate, Worcester, 1835–36, CAD, WOC 19/26.

140. Burn, *Emancipation and Apprenticeship*, 334–59; Davis, *Slavery and Human Progress*, 298; Blackburn, *Overthrow*, 460–61.

141. Governor, Cape Colony, to sec. of state, 24 August 1838, CAD, GH 23/12.

142. Report, registrar and guardian of slaves, 24 June 1827, PRO, CO 53/48.

143. Dispatch, acting governor, Cape Colony, to sec. of state, 6 December 1833, CAD, GH 23/10.

144. Ibid. (emphasis in original).

145. Ibid.

146. Slave rebellions indeed followed attempts at amelioration, and sometimes mere discussions of amelioration, in the West Indies: Blackburn, *Overthrow*, 419–72. On the Cape Colony, see below.

147. Sec. of state to governor, Cape Colony, 29 February 1832, CAD, GH 1/89.

148. Raynor, "Wine and Slaves," 246–306; Dooling, "Slaves, Slaveholders, and Amelioration," 88.

149. Observations of the protector, December 1833, in confidential reports, protector of slaves, 1829–34, CAD, SO 3/20a.

150. For Truter's slaves, see Raynor, "Wine and Slaves," 96.

151. Truter to governor, Cape Colony, 25 May 1825, in appendix, minutes of the advisory council, 1825–26, PRO, CO 52/2.

152. This revolt has received much attention. The most thorough account is P. J. Warnich's "Die Toepassing en Invloed van Slawewetgewing in die Landdrosdistrik Tulbagh/Worcester, 1816–1830: The Application and Influence of Slave Laws in the Tulbagh/Worcester Landdrost district, 1816–30," M.A. thesis, University of Stellenbosch, 1988. Robert Ross's brief, trenchant analysis can be found in his *Cape of Torments: Slavery and Resistance in South Africa* (London, 1983), 105–16. Andre Brink's novel *A Chain of Voices* (Harmondsworth, Eng., 1983), is a brilliant treatment. See also, Watson, *The Slave Question*, 51–59, and Raynor, "Wine and Slaves," 174–89.

153. Ross, *Cape of Torments*, 105–16.

154. Ibid., 105.

155. *RCC*, 20:191–92.

156. *RCC*, 20:208–10.

157. Eugene D. Genovese has argued that one of the preconditions for a slave revolt is a divided ruling class "split either in warfare between slaveholding countries or in bitter struggles within a particular slaveholding country": Eugene D. Genovese, *From Rebellion to Revolution: Afro-American Slave Revolts in the Making of the Modern World* (New York, 1981), 11–12.

158. Ross, *Cape of Torments*, 107–8.

3. "A State in Miniature"

1. This brief narrative draws on the report of the protector of slaves, Eastern Div., Graaff-Reinet, 11 January 1833, PRO, CO 53/55.

2. Order of the king in council, 2 November 1831, #64–69.

3. I return to the subject of slave families in chapter 8.

4. I use the word *patriarchal* not as a synonym for male supremacy but to refer to a family structure in which fathers control the lives and labor of family members— wife, children, servants, and, in this case, slaves. See Linda Gordon, *Heroes of Their*

Own lives: The Politics and History of Family Violence, Boston, 1880–1960 (New York, 1989), 55–56.

5. David Herlihy, "Family," *American Historical Review* 96, no. 1 (1991): 2–3.

6. On how this played in the American South, see, for instance, Eugene D. Genovese, *The World the Slaveholders Made: Two Essays in Interpretation* (New York, 1971); idem., *Roll, Jordan, Roll: The World the Slaves Made* (New York, 1976); and, in contrast, James Oakes, *Slavery and Freedom: An Interpretation of the Old South* (New York, 1990).

7. Court of Justice to governor, Cape Colony, 14 January 1796, in Andre du Toit and Hermann Giliomee, eds., *Afrikaner Political Thought: Analysis and Documents, Vol. 1, 1780–1850* (Berkeley, Calif., 1983), 91–93.

8. For the details of the reform process, see chapter 2.

9. Memo, Burgher Senate to governor, Cape Colony, 30 June 1826, in George McC. Theal, comp., *Records of the Cape Colony* [*RCC*] (London, 1897–1905), 27:92.

10. Petition from agriculturalists of the Cape district, enclosure, governor, Cape Colony, to sec. of state, 1 April 1831, CAD, ZP 1/1/74 (microfilm); in Dutch and English.

11. *De Zuid-Afrikaan*, 25 May 1832—in Dutch and English.

12. Quoted in report, protector of slaves, Eastern Div., 14 August 1833, PRO, CO 53/56 (my emphasis).

13. J. S. Marais, *The Cape Coloured People, 1652–1937* (London, 1939), 5; S. E. Hudson, "Slaves," *Kronos* 9 (1984): 47.

14. Memo to landdrost and heemraden, Stellenbosch, 10 July 1826, *RCC*, 27:109.

15. See chapters 2 and 6.

16. Linda Gordon, *Heroes*, 251.

17. Robert C.-H. Shell, "Slavery at the Cape of Good Hope, 1680–1731," Ph.D. diss., Yale University, 1986, 1:233, 228.

18. Robert C.-H. Shell, *Children of Bondage: A Social History of the Slave Society at the Cape of Good Hope, 1652–1838* (Hanover, 1994), 206–27.

19. Herbert G. Gutman, *The Black Family in Slavery and Freedom, 1750–1925* (New York, 1976), 319.

20. Genovese, *Roll, Jordan, Roll*, 26.

21. A heavy whip, often made of hippopotamus hide, four to six feet long, and tapering to the thickness of a man's finger. It and its descendants have been in constant use in South Africa since at least the early eighteenth century. The modern police sjambok—called a quirt—is made of plastic. Like its predecessor, it is capable of cutting through clothes and skin.

22. Robert Ross, *Cape of Torments: Slavery and Resistance in South Africa* (London, 1983), 96–116.

23. Statement, laws regarding slavery, *RCC*, 9:147–48.

24. Anders Sparrman, *A Voyage to the Cape of Good Hope Towards the Antarctic Polar Circle Round the World and to the Country of the Hottentots and the Caffres from the Year 1772–1776*, 2 vols. (reprint, Cape Town, 1975), 2:259.

25. Shell, "Slavery at the Cape," 1:229.

26. Statement, laws regarding slavery, *RCC*, 9:147–48.

27. Until 1828, the Cape's chief legal officer was known as the fiscal.

28. Letter, fiscal to governor, Cape Colony, 16 March 1813, *RCC*, 9:144.

29. Opgaaf Roll, Cape district, 1825, CAD, J 56; Will and Testament, CAD, MOOC 7/1/120; slave register, Cape Town and district, CAD, SO 6/26.

30. This point is amply demonstrated in the case involving van Niekerk and his

slave Mey, in day book, assistant protector of slaves, Cape Town, vol. 4 and 5, CAD, SO 5/9; see also John Edwin Mason, "Hendrik Albertus and His Ex-Slave Mey: A Drama in Three Acts," *Journal of African History* 31 (1990): 423–45.

31. Report, protector of slaves, assistant protector, Uitenhage, 28 May 1833, PRO, CO 53/55; slave register, Uitenhage, CAD, SO 6/148.

32. Number of slave proprietors in each district . . . possessing . . . 8 slaves and under, enclosure, governor, Cape Colony, to sec. of state, 21 April 1831, PRO, CO 48/142.

33. Ross, *Cape of Torments,* 25.

34. Returns of "the total number of slaves," CAD, SO 20/61.

35. Ross, *Cape of Torments,* 25.

36. Ibid.

37. Calculated from *Cape of Good Hope Blue Book,* 1834, PRO, CO 53/71.

38. Figures in the report, protector of slaves, Western Div., 20 January 1834, PRO, CO 53/57.

39. Henry Lichtenstein, *Travels in Southern Africa in the Years 1803, 1804, 1805, and 1806,* 2 vols. (reprint, Cape Town, 1928), 1:57–58.

40. A. J. Christopher, *Southern Africa* (Folkestone, Eng. 1976), 44; James Walton, *Old Cape Farmsteads* (Cape Town, 1989), 18–19, 94; C. Graham Botha, *General History and Social Life of the Cape of Good Hope* (Cape Town, 1962), 208–9; personal observation, nineteenth-century farms, Western Cape Province, South Africa.

41. Walton, *Old Cape Farmsteads,* 94.

42. Nigel Worden, *Slavery in Dutch South Africa* (Cambridge, Eng., 1985), 92.

43. Report, protector of slaves, Western Div., 20 January 1834, PRO, CO 53/57.

44. Enclosure, governor, Cape Colony, to sec. of state, 29 July 1830, CAD, GH 26/61, 26/62.

45. Report, protector of slaves, assistant protector, Stellenbosch, 24 June 1831, PRO, CO 53/52.

46. Botha, *Cape History and Social Life,* 167, 221; Worden, *Slavery,* 92.

47. Lichtenstein, *Travels,* 1:130–32, 204.

48. Ibid., 1:138–39.

49. George Thompson, *Travels and Adventures in Southern Africa* (reprint, Cape Town, 1967), 1:46.

50. Report, protector of slaves, Eastern Div., Albany, 11 January 1833, PRO, CO 53/55.

51. Report, protector of slaves, Eastern Div., Somerset, 28 May 1833, PRO, CO 53/55.

52. John Barrow, *An Account of Travels into the Interior of Southern Africa, in the Years 1797 and 1798,* 2 vols. (London, 1801), 1:76–78, 2:401–2; Lichtenstein, *Travels,* 1:26.

53. William Burchell, *Travels in the Interior of Southern Africa,* 2 vols. (reprint, Cape Town, 1967), 2:177–78 (emphasis in original).

54. See chapter 4.

55. Botha, *Cape History and Social Life,* 1:167.

56. Robert Percival, *An Account of the Cape of Good Hope; Containing an Historical View* (London, 1804), 117.

57. Barrow, *Account of Travels,* 1:83–84.

58. [Samuel?] Sinclair, "Descriptive Account of the Voyages," unpub. ms., Archives and Papers, University of the Witwatersrand, A 98, 125.

59. *Gleanings in Africa . . . the Cape of Good Hope and Surrounding Country* (London, 1806), 267.

60. Burchell, *Travels*, 1:190.

61. Cowper Rose, *Four Years in Southern Africa* (London, 1829), 23–25.

62. Anne Barnard, *The Letters of Lady Anne Barnard to Henry Dundas, from the Cape and Elsewhere, 1793–1803*, ed. A. M. Lewin Robinson (Cape Town, 1973), 85–86.

63. [Edward Blount], *Notes on the Cape of Good Hope . . . in the Year 1820* (London, 1821), 28.

64. Barrow, *Account of Travels*, 1:47.

65. Burchell, *Travels*, 1:34.

66. Cowper Rose, *Four Years*, 32–33.

67. Percival, *Account*, 280.

68. Gilberto Freyre, *The Masters and the Slaves: A Study in the Development of Brazilian Civilization*, trans. Samuel Putnam, (New York, 1956), 349–50.

69. Ibid., 351.

70. *Gleanings*, 257–58.

71. Report, protector of slaves, Eastern Div., 23 January 1834, PRO, CO 53/57.

72. Report, protector of slaves, Cape Town, PRO, CO 53/52.

73. The following narrative is drawn from Dagvarings en Verklarings, 1832–1834, assistant protector of slaves, Stellenbosch, CAD, STB 22/165.

74. Barrow, *Account of Travels*, 1:80–81.

75. Botha, *Cape History and Social Life*, 221.

76. *Transactions of the Missionary Society, 1812*, vol. 3, (London, 1812), 296.

77. Slave register, Cape Town and Cape district, CAD SO 6/21, 6/22.

78. Marais, *Cape Coloured People*, 5.

79. Shell, "Slavery at the Cape," 1:269–73.

80. Orlando Patterson, *Slavery and Social Death: A Comparative Study* (Cambridge, Mass., 1982), 54–56.

81. Herbert Gutman, *The Black Family in Slavery and Freedom, 1750–1925* (New York, 1976), 230–56.

82. Report, registrar and guardian of slaves, 24 June 1827, PRO, CO 53/48; report, protector of slaves, Eastern Div., Graaff-Reinet, 14 August 1833, PRO, CO 53/56; report, protector of slaves, Eastern Div., Uitenhage, 11 January 1833; PRO, CO 53/ 55; report, protector of slaves, Western Div., Worcester, 18 February 1834, PRO, CO 53/57.

83. Report, registrar and guardian of slaves, 27 December 1826, PRO, CO 53/48.

84. Slave register, Stellenbosch, CAD, SO 6/85.

85. Dagvarings en Verklarings, 1832–1834, assistant protector of slaves, Stellenbosch, CAD, STB 22/165.

86. Report, protector of slaves, Western Div., assistant protector, Stellenbosch, 24 December 1834, PRO, CO 53/57.

87. By *wolves*, Cape colonists meant hyenas. Reports of slaves and apprentices carrying firearms are rare, but they appear often enough to indicate that in the eastern Cape the practice, confined as it was to trusted servants, was routine.

88. Minutes, special justice, Graaff-Reinet, 1835–38, CAD, GR 17/45.

89. Report, protector of slaves, assistant protector, Stellenbosch, 24 June 1831, PRO, CO 53/52.

90. Criminal record book, special magistrate, Worcester, 1835–36, CAD, WOC 19/26.

91. For a discussion of the possibilities of sisterhood between mistresses and female slaves in the American South, see Elizabeth Fox-Genovese, *Within the Plantation Household: Black and White Women of the Old South* (Chapel Hill, N.C., 1988), 34–35 and chapters 2 and 3, passim.

92. Lichtenstein, *Travels,* 2:140

93. S. E. Hudson, "Slaves," *Kronos* 9 (1984): 52.

94. W[illiam Wilberforce] Bird, *The State of the Cape of Good Hope in 1822* (reprint, Cape Town, 1966), 74.

95. Report, protector of slaves, Eastern Div., assistant protector, Uitenhage, 14 August 1833, PRO, CO 53/56.29.

96. This brief narrative draws on the day book, assistant guardian of slaves, Graham's Town, c.1826, CAD, GR 17/17. At the time of her court appearance, van Rooyen had recently given birth.

97. Day book, assistant protector of slaves, Graham's Town, c. 1832, CAD, GR 17/17.

98. Register of slaves, Albany, CAD, SO 6/2.

99. Letter and enclosures, special justice, George Town, to sec. to government, 13 October 1837, CAD, CO 465.

100. Report, protector of slaves, assistant protector, Stellenbosch, 24 June 1831, PRO, CO 53/52.

101. Sparrman, *A Voyage,* 1:101.

102. *Gleanings,* 63.

103. Percival, *Account,* 286.

104. Bird, *State of the Cape,* 73–74.

105. Hudson, "Slaves," 51.

106. General observations, report, protector of protector of slaves, 24 June 1831, PRO, CO 53/52; Hudson, "Slaves," 51; *Gleanings,* 64.

107. Blount, *Notes on the Cape,* 117.

108. Hudson, "Slaves," 51.

109. J. W. D. Moodie, *Ten Years in South Africa: Including a Particular Description of the Wild Sports of that Country,* vols. 1 and 2, (London, 1835), 1:199.

110. Hudson, "Slaves," 51–52.

111. *Gleanings,* 64.

112. Percival, *Account,* 291. Against these claims, there is the testimony of William Wilberforce Bird, once a customs official at the Cape, who argued that "no mistress in any decent rank of life ever dressed her female slave for prostitution, as has lately been stated, or would knowingly suffer a promiscuous intercourse to take place": Bird, *State of the Cape,* 75.

113. Hudson, "Slaves," 52.

114. Bird, *State of the Cape,* 74–75.

115. Barbara Bush, *Slave Women in Caribbean Society, 1650–1838* (Kingston, Jamaica, 1989), 14–17; Deborah Gray White, *Ar'n't I a Woman? Female Slaves in the Plantation South* (New York: 1985), chapter 1, passim.

116. For affectionate marriages between slave women and white men, see chapter 7.

117. O. F. Mentzel, *A Complete and Authentic Geographical and Topographical Description of the Famous and (All Things Considered) Remarkable African Cape of Good Hope* (reprint, Cape Town, 1944), 3:119.

118. Ibid. (reprint, Cape Town, 1919), 2:109.

119. Barnard, *Letters,* 93.

120. Hudson, "Slaves," 54.

121. Statement, laws regarding slavery, *RCC,* 9:152.

122. *South African Commercial Advertiser,* 24 September 1831.

123. Report, protector of slaves, Western Div., 20 January 1834, PRO, CO 53/57.

124. Day book, principal assistant protector of slaves, Graham's Town, c.1831, CAD, GR 17/17. *Cohabitated* is one of the euphemisms for sexual intercourse that is found in the records. It implies a sustained pattern of behavior.

125. Report, registrar and guardian of slaves, assistant guardian, Graaff-Reinet, 24 June 1827, PRO, CO 53/48.

126. Report, registrar and guardian of slaves, 25 December 1826, PRO, CO 53/48.

127. Report, protector of slaves, Cape Town, 24 June 1831, PRO, CO 53/52.

128. Report, protector of slaves, Eastern Div., assistant protector, Albany, 14 August 1833, PRO, CO 53/56 and Day book, assistant protector of slaves, Albany, n.d., CAD, GR 17/17.

129. Report, protector of slaves, Cape Town, 24 June 1831, PRO, CO 53/52.

130. Barnard, *Letters,* 93.

131. Hudson, "Slaves," 54.

132. Report, protector of slaves, Cape Town, 24 June 1831, PRO, CO 53/52.

133. Report, protector of slaves, Western Div., 28 May 1833, PRO, CO 53/55.

134. Report, registrar and guardian of slaves, 31 December 1827, PRO, CO 53/48.

135. See, for instance, White, *Ar'n't I a Woman?* 15–17, 23–25; Jones, *Labor of Love, Labor of Sorrow,* 11–12.

136. Gerda Lerner, *The Creation of Patriarchy* (New York, 1986), 88–89 (emphasis in original).

137. Nell Irvin Painter, "Soul Murder and Slavery: Toward a Fully Loaded Cost Accounting," in *US History as Women's History,* Linda Kerber et al., eds. (Chapel Hill, N.C., 1995), passim.

138. Willie Lee Rose, "The Domestication of Domestic Slavery," in Willie Lee Rose, *Slavery and Freedom,* expanded edition, ed. William W. Freehling, New York, 1982), 29.

4. "A Paradise, Even When Oppressive"

1. The following brief narrative draws on the report, protector of slaves, Eastern Div., Graaff-Reinet, 23 January 1834, PRO, CO 53/57.

2. Slaves who fetched the highest prices at auction—healthy slave men between the ages of roughly eighteen and twenty-eight—sold for between £150 and £190 in 1831–33: return of slaves sold at public auction, CAD, SO 10/19.

3. The protector's report and the slave register differ slightly as to the number of slaves: register of slaves, Graaff-Reinet, CAD, SO 6/62.

4. Rural slave owners routinely gave their adult slaves one or several "tots" of wine each day. While the wine was thought to ensure good health and stimulate vigorous work, it was also a debilitating form of social control; see Mary Isabel Raynor, "Wine and Slaves: The Failure of an Export Economy and the Ending of Slavery in the Cape Colony, South Africa, 1806–1834," Ph.D. diss., Duke University, 1986, 17–19; J. S. Marais, *The Cape Coloured People, 1652–1937* (London, 1939), 165, 196–98.

5. A springbok is a swift African gazelle. They are commonly brown.

6. Richard Elphick and Robert Shell, "Intergroup Relations: Khoikhoi, Settlers, Slaves, and Free Blacks, 1652–1795," in Richard Elphick and Hermann Giliomee, eds., *The Shaping of South African Society, 1652–1840* (Cape Town, 1989), 221–24.

7. Christopher Saunders, "Prize Slaves in the Pre-Emancipation Cape," unpublished MS, 8, 15–16.

8. For Prize Negroes on grain farms, see W. Procter, minutes of evidence, commissioners of eastern inquiry, 13 December 1826, CAD, ZP 1/4/1 (microfilm).

9. For an early mention of the incorporation of Bantu-speaking Africans into the colonial economy, see enclosures, governor, Cape Colony, to sec. of state, 30 July 1825, CAD, GH 28/11.

10. Minutes of evidence, 5 December 1826, Peter Lawrence Cloete, James Christiaan Faure, and William Duckett, commissioners of eastern inquiry, PRO, CO 414/2.

11. These generalizations are based on the examination of registers of slaves, Cape Town and Cape district, CAD, SO 6/15, 6/22, 6/28, Graaff-Reinet, CAD, SO 6/62, 6/73, and Stellenbosch, CAD, SO 6/84, 6/101.

12. Nell Irvin Painter, "Soul Murder and Slavery: Toward a Fully Loaded Coast Accounting," eds. Linda Kerber, et al., *US History as Women's History* (Chapel Hill, N.C., 1995), 129, 133.

13. Report, protector of slaves, Western Div., 28 May 1833, PRO, CO 53/55.

14. Report, protector of slaves, Western Div., assistant protector, Clan William, 20 January 1833, PRO, CO 53/55.

15. Report, protector of slaves, Western Div., Stellenbosch, 25 July 1833, PRO, CO 53/55.

16. Register of slaves, Cape Town and Cape district, CAD, SO 6/15 and SO 6/22; register of slaves, Stellenbosch, CAD, SO 6/101.

17. Minutes of evidence, Peter Lawrence Cloete, James Christian Faure, and William Duckett, 5 December 1826, commissioners of eastern inquiry, PRO, CO 414/2.

18. Henry Lichtenstein, *Travels in Southern Africa, in the Years 1803, 1804, 1805, and 1806*, 2 vols. (reprint, Cape Town, 1928), 1:67.

19. Report, protector of slaves, Western Div., Stellenbosch, 24 December 1834, PRO, CO 53/57.

20. Ibid., 24 June 1831, PRO, CO 53/52. On elderly slaves, see also Nigel Worden, *Slavery in Dutch South Africa* (Cambridge, Eng., 1985), 23.

21. Report, protector of slaves, Eastern Div., Albany, 14 August 1833, PRO, CO 53/56.

22. Ibid.

23. A. Bank, "Slavery in Cape Town, 1806 to 1834," M.A. thesis, University of Cape Town, 1991, 37–38; Population of the Cape Colony in 1827, in George McC. Theal, comp., *Records of the Cape Colony [RCC]* (London, 1897–1905), 35:81.

24. Lichtenstein, *Travels*, 2:102–4.

25. Ibid., 1:33–34. Cape slaves were noted for their music making. For other, sometimes less complimentary accounts of slave musicians, see [Edward Blount], *Notes on the Cape of Good Hope . . . in the Year 1820* (London, 1821), 106–7, and [Sam?] Sinclair, "Descriptive Account of the Voyages," unpublished MS, Sinclair Papers, Archives and Papers, A 98, University of the Witwatersrand Library, Johannesburg, 39.

26. William J. Burchell, *Travels in the Interior of Southern Africa* (reprint, Cape Town: Struik, 1967), 1:197–98.

27. Lists taken from the registers of slaves, Cape Town and district, CAD, SO 6/8 to 6/35; Graaff-Reinet, CAD, SO 6/58 to 6/77; Stellenbosch, CAD, SO 6/80 to 6/110.

28. *Cape Town Gazette and African Advertiser,* 10 February 1826.

29. Report, protector of slaves, Western Div., 20 January 1834, PRO, CO 53/57.

30. Jacqueline Jones, *Labor of Love, Labor of Sorrow: Black Women, Work, and the Family from Slavery to the Present* (New York, 1985), 11–12.

31. W[illiam Wilberforce] Bird, *The State of the Cape of Good Hope in 1822* (reprint, Cape Town, 1966), 73–74; see also my chapter 3.

32. Report, protector of slaves, Eastern Div., Albany, 14 August 1833, PRO, CO 53/56.

33. Report, registrar and guardian of slaves, 24 June 1827, PRO, CO 53/48.

34. I find no evidence to support Nigel Worden's claim that slaves drew a clear distinction between field workers and domestic slaves: Worden, *Slavery,* 90.

35. John Barrow, *An Account of Travels into the Interior of Southern Africa, in the Years 1797 and 1798,* 2 vols. (London, 1801), 1:43–44.

36. Report on slaves and the state of slavery, Cape of Good Hope, *RCC,* 35:374.

37. Report on the criminal law, *RCC,* 33:11–12; report on slaves, *RCC,* 35:374.

38. Report, protector of slaves, Cape Town, 24 June 1831, PRO, CO 53/52.

39. George Champion, *The Journal of an American Missionary in the Cape Colony, 1835* (Cape Town, 1968), 24.

40. Bank, "Slavery in Cape Town," 40, and population of the colony, 1827, *RCC,* 35:81.

41. Robert D. Thomson, "Journal," Archives and Papers, A 148, Witwatersrand University Library, 402–4. See also Robert Ross, *Cape of Torments: Slavery and Resistance in South Africa* (London, 1983), 74–75.

42. On payment problems, see letter, Thomas _____[?], to guardian [protector] of slaves, 8 March 1831, CAD, SO 1/51.

43. Champion, *Journal,* 3.

44. Bird, *State of the Cape,* 159.

45. Laws relating to free blacks in the . . . Cape, colonial memo, c.1826, CAD, M 142; *South African Almanack and Directory for 1827* (Cape Town, 1827), 122. The pay for a day's work would be approximately 2s. 3d; for an errand, 2 1/4d.

46. Bird, *State of the Cape,* 159.

47. Minutes of evidence, P. M. Brink, 8 December 1826 and Gerhardus Henry Meyer, 13 December 1826, commissioners of eastern inquiry, CAD, ZP 1/4/1 (microfilm).

48. Minutes of evidence, Gerhardus Henry Meyer, ibid.

49. Report on slaves, *RCC,* 35:362–63.

50. Minutes of evidence, P. M. Brink and Christopher Henry Olivier, 8 December 1826, commissioners of eastern inquiry, CAD, ZP 1/4/1 (microfilm).

51. Minutes of evidence, P. M. Brink, 8 December 1826, ibid.

52. Richard C. Wade, *Slavery in the Cities, 1820–1860* (New York, 1964), 38.

53. Bank, "Slavery in Cape Town," 34–35, 50.

54. Robert Percival, *An Account of the Cape of Good Hope; Containing an Historical View* (London, 1804), 110; Burchell, *Travels,* 1:11n.

55. Bird, *State of the Cape*, 157; Bank, "Slavery in Cape Town," 41.

56. Bird, *State of the Cape*, 148–49. See also Ross, *Cape of Torments*, 18 and Worden, *Slavery*, 38–39.

57. Report, protector of slaves, Western Div., 20 January 1834, PRO, CO 53/57.

58. Report, protector of slaves, Western Div., 26 July 1833, PRO, CO 53/56.

59. Burchell, *Travels*, 1:39; Percival, *Account*, 147–48; Lady Anne Barnard, *The Letters of Lady Anne Barnard to Henry Dundas from the Cape and Elsewhere, 1793–1803* (Cape Town, 1973), 38; Hudson, "Slaves," 63.

60. Report, protector of slaves, 24 June 1831, PRO, CO 53/52.

61. Bank, "Slavery in Cape Town," 35.

62. *Cape of Good Hope Government Gazette*, 3 March 1826.

63. Ibid., 3 February 1826.

64. Rabe and Read, register of slaves, Cape Town and district, CAD, SO 6/28 and *The African Court Calender and Directory for MDCCCXVII* (Cape Town, 1817), 95; Roux, register of slaves, Stellenbosch, CAD, SO 6/101.

65. *Zuid-Afrikaan*, 2 July 1830. See also Bank, "Slavery in Cape Town," 32.

66. Report, protector of slaves, assistant protector, Stellenbosch, 24 June 1831, PRO, CO 53/52.

67. Report, protector of slaves, 24 June 1831, PRO, CO 53/52.

68. Report, registrar and guardian of slaves, 31 December 1827, PRO, CO 53/48.

69. Eugene D. Genovese, *Roll, Jordan, Roll: The World the Slaves Made* (New York, 1974), 393.

70. Minutes of evidence, Hermanus Schutte and John Cannon, 6 December 1826, commission of eastern inquiry, PRO, CO 414/2.

71. Minutes of evidence, P. M. Brink and Christopher Henry Olivier, 8 December 1826, commissioners of eastern inquiry, CAD, ZP 1/4/1 (microfilm).

72. Report, protector of slaves, Western Div., 26 July 1833, PRO, CO 53/56.

73. Report on slaves, *RCC*, 35:373.

74. Minutes of evidence, John Cannon, 6 December 1826, commission of eastern inquiry, PRO, CO 414/2.

75. Report, protector of slaves, Western Div., 20 January 1834, PRO, CO 53/57.

76. See chapter 2.

77. Report, protector of slaves, Western Div., 26 July 1833, PRO, CO 53/56.

78. Register of slaves, Cape Town and district, CAD, SO 6/22.

79. Reports of the protector of slaves, Western Div., 28 May 1833 and 20 January 1834, PRO, CO 53/55 and 53/57.

80. Report, protector of slaves, Eastern Div., Graaff-Reinet, 23 January 1834, PRO, CO 53/57.

81. Report, protector of slaves, Western Div., 26 July 1833, PRO, CO 53/56.

82. Report, protector of slaves, 24 June 1831, PRO, CO 53/52.

83. Day book, assistant protector of slaves, Graham's Town, in report, protector of slaves, Eastern Div., 11 December 1832, CAD, GR 17/17.

84. Criminal record book, 1835–36, special magistrate, Worcester, CAD WOC 19/26.

85. Quoted in Genovese, *Roll, Jordan, Roll*, 393.

86. In chapters 5, 6, and 7, we encounter other circumstances in which pride and self-confidence developed.

87. Quoted in Wade, *Slavery in the Cities*, 246.

5. "An Unprofitable Waste, Unfit for Culture"

1. The recent immigrants were the "1820 Settlers," whom the Cape government placed in the eastern Cape to secure the colonial hold on conquered Xhosa land; see Leonard Thompson, *A History of South Africa* (New Haven, Conn., 1990], 55–56.

2. W[illiam Wilberforce] Bird, *State of the Cape of Good Hope in 1822* (reprint, Cape Town, 1966), 92–93.

3. John Barrow, *An Account of Travels into the Interior of Southern Africa, in the Years 1797 and 1798,* 2 vols. (London, 1801), 1:10, 2:29.

4. [Edward Blount], *Notes on the Cape of Good Hope . . . 1820* (London, 1821), 57.

5. George Thompson, *Travels and Adventures in Southern Africa* (reprint, Cape Town, 1968), 3:86–87.

6. J. W. D. Moodie, *Ten Years in South Africa: Including a Particular Description of the Wild Sports of that Country,* 2 vols. (London, 1835), 1:113–14.

7. Robert Ross, "The First Two Centuries of Colonial Agriculture in the Cape Colony: A Historical Review," *Social Dynamics* 9, no. 1 (1983): 40; Pieter van Duin and Robert Ross, "The Economy of the Cape Colony in the Eighteenth Century," *Intercontinenta* 7 (1987): 8, 58.

8. See chapter 4.

9. Robert Percival, *An Account of the Cape of Good Hope; Containing an Historical View* (London, 1804), 176–77.

10. Blount, *Notes on the Cape,* 71.

11. Thompson, *Travels,* 3:150, 150n.

12. Percival, *Account,* 176–81. On wine, see also *Gleanings in Africa . . . the Cape of Good Hope and Surrounding Country* (London, 1806), 205–8; Blount, *Notes on the Cape,* 71–73; Bird, *State of the Cape,* 110–12.

13. Mary Isabel Raynor, "Wine and Slaves: the Failure of an Export Economy and the Ending of Slavery in the Cape Colony, South Africa, 1806–1834," Ph.D. diss., Duke University, 1986, 58, 60–61.

14. This is the same man as the Pieter Laurens Cloete encountered in chapter 4.

15. Minutes of evidence, Peter Lawrence Cloete, 5 December 1826, commission of inquiry, PRO, CO 414/2.

16. Evidence, Hendrik Oostwald Eksteen, ibid.

17. Evidence, James Christiaan Faure, ibid.

18. Faure evidence, ibid. These Khoisan "apprentices" would have been indentured as children under the terms of Governor Cradock's proclamation of 23 April 1812, and are not to be confused with the ex-slave apprentices of the period 1834–38.

19. Evidence, Hendrik Oostwald Eksteen, ibid.

20. Civil commissioner, Stellenbosch, to sec. to government, 6 February 1830, enclosure, governor, Cape Colony, to sec. of state, 18 July 1830, CAD, GH 26/61.

21. Evidence, Peter Lawrence Cloete, 5 December 1826, commission of inquiry, PRO, CO 414/2.

22. Bird, *State of the Cape,* 111–12; *Gleanings,* 207; Blount, *Notes on the Cape,* 71.

23. Robert Ross, *Cape of Torments: Slavery and Resistance in South Africa* (London, 1983), 26; see also Worden, *Slavery,* 25–26.

24. Bird, *State of the Cape,* 112; *Gleanings,* 208.

25. Reports of the protector of slaves, Western Div., Stellenbosch, 25 July 1833,

PRO, CO 53/55 (case of Isaak of Pieter Cilliers), 24 December 1834, PRO, CO 53/57 (case of Louis of Willem Marais). On labor, see also Raynor, "Wine and Slaves," 67–70.

26. Register of slaves, Cape Town and Cape district, CAD, SO 6/15.

27. Ibid.

28. Report, protector of slaves, Western Div., Stellenbosch, PRO, CO 53/55.

29. Raynor, "Wine and Slaves," 59. On the wine boom see chapter 1.

30. Dagvarings en Verklarings, assistant protector of slaves, Stellenbosch, 1832–34, CAD, STB 22/165.

31. Moodie, *Ten Years,* 1:114–17.

32. Blount, *Notes on the Cape,* 58–60; Moodie, *Ten Years,* 1:117. See Deuteronomy 25:4.

33. Moodie, *Ten Years,* 1:117–21; Blount, *Notes on the Cape,* 58–62; *Gleanings,* 270–71.

34. See chapter 7.

35. Report, protector of slaves, Western Div., Stellenbosch, 24 December 1834, PRO, CO 53/57.

36. Minutes of evidence, Christopher Henry Olivier, 8 December 1826, commission of inquiry, PRO, CO 414/2; report, protector of slaves, Eastern Div., Beaufort, 14 August 1833, PRO, CO 53/56 (case of Louis of Christiaan Le Roux).

37. Civil commissioner, Worcester, to sec. to government, 6 January 1830, and civil commissioner, Uitenhage, to sec. to government, 2 January 1830, enclosures, governor, Cape Colony, to sec. of state, 18 July 1830, CAD, GH 21/61.

38. Evidence, W. Proctor, 13 December 1826, PRO, CO 414/2.

39. Report, protector of slaves, assistant protector, Somerset, 28 May 1833, PRO, CO 53/55.

40. Dagvarings and Verklarings, assistant protector of slaves, Stellenbosch, 1832–34, CAD, STB 22/165; report, protector of slaves, Eastern Div., George, 14 August 1833, PRO, CO 53/56; minutes of evidence, W. Procter, 13 December 1826, commission of inquiry, PRO, CO 414/2.

41. Evidence, Peter Lawrence Cloete, 5 December 1826, commission of inquiry, PRO, CO 414/2; see also minutes of evidence, W. Procter, 13 December 1826, ibid.

42. Thompson, *Travels and Adventures,* 3:91–92.

43. Ibid., 3:92–93; see also chapter 1.

44. Richard Elphick, *Khoikhoi and the Founding of White South Africa* (Johannesburg, 1985), 154–70.

45. Richard Elphick and V. C. Malherbe, "The Khoisan to 1828," in Richard Elphick and Hermann Giliomee, *The Shaping of South African Society, 1652–1840* (Cape Town, 1989), 28.

46. Leonard Guelke, "Freehold Farmers and Frontier Settlers, 1657–1780," in Elphick and Giliomee, *Shaping,* 87.

47. Report, protector of slaves, Eastern Div., Graaff-Reinet, 23 January 1834, PRO, CO 53/57.

48. Minutes, special justice, Graaff-Reinet, 1835, CAD, GR 17/145.

49. Oorlams were San who had either been born into Boer households or captured in raids as children and raised in them, speaking the creole Dutch of their masters and working on settler farms as subordinate agricultural laborers: Martin Legassick, "The Northern Frontier," in Elphick and Giliomee, *Shaping,* 368–69.

50. Africa's deposition, general observations, report, protector of slaves, Eastern Div., 30 June 1834, PRO, CO 53/58.

51. It might be asked why Africa did not simply run away from his master. The difficulty of obtaining food, clearly evident in his depositions, and his responsibilities toward his family would have been reasons enough to detain him.

52. While historians have documented these arrangements, they have not studied them in detail. See J. S. Marais, *The Cape Coloured People, 1652–1937* (London, 1939), 167–68; Clifton Crais, "Slavery and Freedom along a Frontier[:] The Eastern Cape, South Africa: 1770–1838," *Slavery and Abolition* 11, no. 2 (1990): 201–3.

53. Statement, laws regarding slavery, in George McC. Theal, comp., *Records of the Cape Colony [RCC]* (London, 1897–1905), 9:152–53.

54. Cape ordinance 19 1826, #28.

55. Introduction, Ira Berlin and Philip D. Morgan, *Slavery and Abolition* 12, no. 1 (May 1991): 1.

56. Peter J. Parish, *Slavery: History and Historians* (New York, 1989), 34–35.

57. I have borrowed this turn of phrase from Parish, ibid.

58. Report, protector of slaves, Eastern Div., 24 June 1834, PRO, CO 53/58.

59. General observations, report, protector of slaves, Western Div., 28 May 1833, PRO, CO 53/55.

60. The sums of £5 to £15 a year are almost certainly optimistic; see below.

61. General observations, report, protector of slaves, 25 December 1830, PRO, CO 53/51.

62. General observations, report, protector of slaves, Western Div., 28 May 1833, PRO, CO 53/55.

63. Criminal record book, special magistrate, Worcester, 1835–36, CAD, WOC 19/26; register of slaves, Worcester, CAD, SO 6/132.

64. Ibid.

65. Report, protector of slaves, Eastern Div., Graaff-Reinet, 14 August 1833, PRO, CO 53/56.

66. Report, protector of slaves, Western Div., Stellenbosch, 25 July 1833, PRO, CO 53/55.

67. Report, protector of slaves, Eastern Div., Graaff-Reinet, 11 January 1833, PRO, CO 53/55.

68. Significant though they were, these holdings never approached the size of white farmers' herds and flocks. A white stock farmer with a mid-sized holding might possess four thousand to six thousand sheep and several hundred head of cattle; wealthier stockmen sometimes owned more than ten thousand sheep and as many as two thousand head of cattle: see Burchell, *Travels*, 2:113; Thompson, *Travels and Adventures*, 1:55.

69. Report, protector of slaves, Eastern Div., Graaff-Reinet, 28 May 1833, PRO, CO 53/55.

70. The following brief narrative relies on a report, ibid., PRO, CO 53/57.

71. Ordinance 19, 1826 and the order of the king in council, 2 February 1830, had cleared up any ambiguity surrounding the control of the slaves' property by investing them with full rights over their property; see chapter 2.

72. Mantatees were Sotho-speaking African refugees from north and east of the Cape Colony who found work on settler farms.

73. Elphick and Malherbe, "The Khoisan," 17, 30–31, 45; civil commissioner, Swellendam, to sec. to government, 6 January 1830, enclosure, governor, Cape Colony, to sec. of state, 18 July 1830, CAD, GH 26/61.

74. Report on the Hottentots, *RCC,* 35:315.

75. J. B. Peires, *House of Phalo: A History of the Xhosa People in the Days of Their Independence* (Berkeley, Calif., 1981), 104–5, and Susan Newton-King, "The Labor Market of the Cape Colony, 1807–1828," in Shula Marks and Anthony Atmore, eds., *Economy and Society in Pre-Industrial South Africa* (London, 1980), 193–95.

76. Report, protector of slaves, Eastern Div., Somerset, 28 May 1833, PRO, CO 53/55.

77. Ibid., Graaff-Reinet, PRO, CO 53/57.

78. Peires, *House of Phalo,* 91–92, 119.

79. Day book, assistant protector of slaves, Graham's Town, in report, protector of slaves, Eastern Div., 11 December 1832, CAD, GR 17/17.

80. Civil cases, resident magistrate, Uitenhage, 22 October 1838, enclosure, governor, Cape Colony, to sec. of state, 8 September 1841, CAD, GH 28/17.

81. Report, protector of slaves, Eastern Div., Somerset, 14 August 1833, PRO, CO 53/56.

82. Report, protector of slaves, assistant protector, Somerset, 25 June 1831, CAD, SO 3/7.

83. Report, protector of slaves, Eastern Div., Graaff-Reinet, 14 August 1833, PRO, CO 53/56.

84. Day book, assistant guardian of slaves, Graham's Town, in CAD, GR 17/17. The identification of Retief as the trek leader may be found in Marais, *Cape Coloured People,* 167.

85. Elphick, *Khoikhoi,* 62.

86. William Beinart, "Production and the Material Base of Chieftainship: Pondoland, c.1830–80," in Marks and Atmore, eds., *Economy and Society,* 134.

87. Peires, *House of Phalo,* 32.

88. S. Daniel Neumark, *Economic Influences on the south African Frontier, 1652–1836* (Stanford, Calif., 1957), 37.

89. Report, protector of slaves, Eastern Div., Graaff-Reinet, 14 August 1833, PRO, CO 53/56.

90. Day book, assistant protector of slaves, Graham's Town, in CAD, GR 17/17.

91. Report, protector of slaves, assistant protector, Somerset, 28 May 1833, PRO, CO 53/55.

6. *"Words Will Not Suffice"*

1. Marx quotes J. Steuart with approval in Karl Marx, *Capital: A Critique of Political Economy,* vol. 1 (reprint, New York, 1977), 1027–28n.

2. Cited in Orlando Patterson, *Slavery and Social Death: A Comparative Study* (Cambridge, Mass., 1982), 2.

3. Patterson, *Slavery and Social Death,* passim.

4. The very title of Robert Ross's pioneering study of slavery in the Cape Colony reflects the centrality of violence: see Ross, *Cape of Torments: Slavery and Resistance in South Africa* (London, 1983).

5. Anders Sparrman, *A Voyage to the Cape of Good Hope . . . 1772–1776,* 2 vols. (reprint, Cape Town, 1975), 2:256–57.

6. Statement, laws regarding slavery, in George McC. Theal, comp., *Records of the Cape Colony* [*RCC*] (London, 1897–1905), 9:144, 9:147–48.

7. Cape ordinance 19, 1826, #12–13.

8. See chapter 2.

9. Report, registrar and guardian of slaves, 31 December 1827, PRO, CO 53/48.

10. Order of the king in council, 2 February 1830, #22 and #26. The order became law in the Cape in 1831.

11. Memo, agriculturalists of Graaff-Reinet to governor, Cape Colony, 11 December 1830, enclosure, governor, Cape Colony, to sec. of state, 1 April 1831, PRO, CO 48/142; see also other memos, ibid.

12. General observations, report, protector of slaves, Eastern Div., 14 August 1833, PRO, CO 53/56.

13. Patterson, *Slavery and Social Death*, 2–3, 13.

14. Nell Irvin Painter, "Soul Murder and Slavery: Toward a Fully Loaded Cost Accounting," in Linda Kerber et al., eds., *US History as Women's History* (Chapel Hill, N.C., 1995).

15. I base this claim on an examination of the slaves' and apprentices' complaints against their masters in reports of the protectors of slaves, 1826 to 1834, PRO, CO 53/48–58; journals of the special justices in Simon's Town, 1835–38, CAD, SMT 5/1/4; journal of the special magistrate, Malmesbury, 1835–38, CAD, MBY 3/1/1; minutes, special justice, Graaff-Reinet, 1835–38, CAD, GR 17/45.

16. Nigel Worden, *Slavery in Dutch South Africa* (Cambridge, Eng., 1985), 106–7.

17. Minutes, special justice, Graaff-Reinet, 1835–38, CAD, GR 17/145.

18. Letter, special justice, Clan William, to sec. to government, 18 April 1837, CAD, CO 465.

19. Report, protector of slaves, Eastern Div., Graaff-Reinet, 23 January 1834, PRO, CO 53/57.

20. Worden, *Slavery*, 88–91.

21. Report, protector of slaves, Western Div., 28 May 1833, PRO, CO 53/55.

22. Report, protector of slaves, assistant protector, Swellendam, 28 January 1834, PRO, CO 53/57.

23. Robert Percival, *An Account of the Cape of Good Hope; Containing an Historical View* (London, 1804), 280. See also John Barrow, *An Account of Travels into the Interior of Southern Africa*, 2 vols. (London, 1801), 1:47; Cowper Rose, *Four Years in Southern Africa* (London, 1829), 32–33.

24. Report, protector of slaves, Eastern Div., Somerset, 14 August 1833, PRO, CO 53/56.

25. Report, protector of slaves, Western Div., 24 June 1831, PRO, CO 53/52.

26. Both cases in report, protector of slaves, 25 December 1830, PRO, CO 53/51.

27. Worden, *Slavery*, 89.

28. Henry Lichtenstein, *Travels in Southern Africa, in the Years 1803, 1804, 1805, and 1806*, 2 vols. (reprint, Cape Town, 1930), 2:95–96.

29. Ross, *Cape of Torments*, 30–31; Worden, *Slavery*, 89, 109.

30. Ross, *Cape of Torments*, 30.

31. Worden, *Slavery*, 89.

32. Report, protector of slaves, Western Div., Stellenbosch, 7 January 1833, PRO, CO 53/55.

33. Eugene D. Genovese, *Roll, Jordan, Roll: The World the Slaves Made* (New York, 1974), 15.

34. See chapter 7 for more about Christianity and the slaves.

35. Dagvarings en Verklarings, assistant protector of slaves, Stellenbosch, 1832–34, CAD, STB 22/165.

36. Sparrman, *Voyage*, 1:274.

37. Register of slaves, Cape Town and district, CAD, SO 6/15.

38. Ibid., CAD, SO 6/21 and 6/22.

39. Report, protector of slaves, 24 June 1831, PRO, CO 53/52.

40. Report, protector of slaves, Western Div., Stellenbosch, 25 July 1833, PRO, CO 53/55.

41. Ross, *Cape of Torments*, 34.

42. Minutes, special justice, 1835–38, Graaff-Reinet, CAD, GR 17/45.

43. For a discussion of some of this literature, see Peter J. Parish, *Slavery: History and Historians* (New York, 1989), 73–74.

44. On a "hierarchy of prejudices," see Robert C.-H. Shell, *Children of Bondage: A Social History of Slave Society at the Cape of Good Hope, 1652–1838* (Hanover, 1994), 228 ff.

45. W[illiam Wilberforce] Bird, *State of the Cape of Good Hope in 1822* (reprint, Cape Town, 1966), 73–74; J. W. D. Moodie, *Ten Years in South Africa: Including a Particular Description of the Wild Sports of that Country*, 2 vols. (London, 1835), 1:197–201.

46. D. Denyssen to Lt. Col. T. Reynall, 27 February 1813, in Andre du Toit and Hermann Giliomee, eds., *Afrikaner Political Thought, Analysis and Documents, Volume One: 1780–1850* (Berkeley, Calif., 1983), 57.

47. Fiscal to governor, Cape Colony, 16 March 1813, *RCC*, 9:144–45.

48. Court of Justice to governor, Cape Colony, 14 January 1796, quoted in du Toit and Giliomee, *Afrikaner Thought*, 92.

49. James C. Scott, *Domination and the Arts of Resistance: Hidden Transcripts* (New Haven, Conn. 1990), 193.

50. James C. Scott, *Weapons of the Weak: Everyday Forms of Peasant Resistance* (New Haven, Conn. 1985), 29.

51. Mary Isabel Raynor, "Wine and Slaves: The Failure of an Export Economy and the Ending of Slavery in the Cape Colony, South Africa, 1806–1834," Ph.D. diss., Duke University, 1986, 130 ff., quote on 132; Worden, *Slavery*, 119 ff.; Ross, *Cape of Torments*, 29–37 and passim.

52. George M. Fredrickson and Christopher Lasch, "Resistance to Slavery," in Ann J. Lane, ed., *The Debate over Slavery: Stanley Elkins and His Critics* (Urbana, Ill., 1971), 226–28.

53. James Scott, *Weapons of the Weak*, xv–xvi, 291–92, 295 (my emphasis).

54. Ross, *Cape of Torments*, 117; Worden, *Slavery*, 120–21.

55. Scott, *Weapons of the Weak*, 38.

56. Report, protector of slaves, 24 June 1831, PRO, CO 53/52.

57. Report, protector of slaves, Western Div., 20 January 1834, PRO, CO 53/57.

58. Report, registrar and guardian of slaves, 24 June 1827, PRO, CO 53/48.

59. Report, protector of slaves, Eastern Div., Somerset, 28 May 1833, PRO, CO 53/55.

60. A classic discussion of moral economy may be found in James C. Scott's *The Moral Economy of the Peasant: Rebellion and Subsistence in Southeast Asia* (New Haven, Conn., 1976).

61. This brief narrative draws on the day book, assistant protector of slaves, Cape Town, vols. 4 and 5, CAD, SO 5/9.

62. Report, protector of slaves, assistant protector, Stellenbosch, 24 June 1831, PRO, CO 53/52.

63. Report, protector of slaves, Eastern Div., 23 January 1834, PRO, CO 53/57.

64. Report, protector of slaves, Western Div., 20 January 1834, PRO, CO 53/57.

65. Confidential reports, protector of slaves, 1829–34, observations of the protector, December 1830, CAD, SO 3/20a.

66. Peter Kolchin, *Unfree Labor: American Slavery and Russian Serfdom* (Cambridge, Mass., 1987), 315.

67. Report, protector of slaves, Eastern Div., Graaff-Reinet, 23 January 1834, PRO, CO 53/57.

68. Report, protector of slaves, Eastern Div., Uitenhage, 11 January 1833, PRO, CO 53/55.

69. On the slaves and religion, see chapter 7.

70. Criminal and civil notebooks, special magistrate, Malmesbury, 1835–38, CAD, MBY 3/1/1.

71. Report, protector of slaves, Western Div., Stellenbosch, 25 July 1833, PRO, CO 53/55.

72. Criminal and civil notebooks, 1835–38, special magistrate, Malmesbury, CAD, MBY 3/1/1.

73. Ibid.

74. Report, protector of slaves, Western Div., 20 January 1834, PRO, CO 53/57.

75. Sparrman, *A Voyage*, 1:318.

76. Criminal and civil notebooks, 1835–38, special magistrate, Malmesbury, CAD, MBY 3/1/1.

77. Memo appended to special justice, Worcester, to sec. to government, 22 February 1838, CAD, CO 476.

78. Minutes, special justice, 1835–38, Graaff-Reinet, CAD, GR 17/145.

79. Criminal and civil notebooks, 1835–38, special justice, Malmesbury, CAD, MBY 3/1/1.

80. This is apparently a reference to service during the Frontier War of 1834–35.

81. Minutes, special justice, 1835–38, Graaff-Reinet, CAD, GR 17/45.

82. Report, protector of slaves, Western Div., 20 January 1834, PRO, CO 53/57.

83. Minutes, special justice, Graaff-Reinet, 1835–38, CAD, GR 17/45.

84. Ibid.

85. Report, protector of slaves, Western Div., Stellenbosch, 7 January 1833, PRO, CO 53/55.

86. Criminal record book, 1835–36, special justice, Worcester, CAD, WOC 19/26.

87. Criminal and civil notebook, 1835–38, special justice, Malmesbury, CAD, MBY 3/1/1.

88. Nigel Worden argues that in the eighteenth century most slaves "condoned" theft from their masters and mistresses, but strongly disapproved of stealing each other's property: Worden, *Slavery*, 99–100. Evidence drawn from the protectors' of slaves and special justices' reports suggests that nineteenth-century slaves and apprentices shared the first part of this ethic, but were not universally committed to honoring the second.

89. Barrington Moore, quoted in Scott, *Weapons of the Weak*, 245 (emphasis removed).

90. Worden, *Slavery*, 127. See also Ross, *Cape of Torments*, 11–12.

91. Report on slaves, *RCC*, 35:352.

92. Report, protector of slaves, Western Div., 28 August 1834, PRO, CO 53/58.

93. For example Ross, *Cape of Torments*, 38–53, 81–95.

94. On compensation, see chapter 2.

95. Circular letter, assistant commissioners of slave compensation to civil commissioners, 28 November 1834, CAD, SO 20/4a.

96. The figures in this paragraph are derived from "the returns of the total number of slaves," CAD, SO 20/61.

97. See above.

98. See chapter 4.

99. Report, registrar and guardian of slaves, 24 June 1827, PRO, CO 53/48.

100. Confidential reports, protector of slaves, 1829–34, observations of the protector, December 1833, CAD, SO 3/20a.

101. Raynor, "Wine and Slaves," 59.

102. Ross, *Cape of Torments*, 84.

103. *Cape Town Gazette and African Advertiser,* 13 January to 29 December 1826; *Cape Government Gazette,* 6 June to 28 December 1832.

104. Deborah Gray White, *Ar'n't I a Woman? Female Slaves in the Plantation South* (New York, 1985), 70.

105. *Government Gazette,* 20 June 1834.

106. Ross, *Cape of Torments*, 34.

107. Report, protector of slaves, Eastern Div., Graaff-Reinet, 23 January 1834, PRO, CO 53/57.

108. Report, protector of slaves, Western Div., 20 January 1834, PRO, CO 53/57.

109. *Government Gazette,* 16 December 1831.

110. Ibid., 7 February 1834.

111. *Graham's Town Journal,* 20 February 1834.

112. Special justice, Graaff-Reinet, to justice of the peace, Fort Beaufort, 23 July 1835, CAD, GR 17/44.

113. Minutes, special justice, Graaff-Reinet, 1835–1838, CAD, GR 17/45.

114. Ibid.

115. Criminal and civil notebooks, special magistrate, Malmesbury, 1835–1838, CAD, MBY 3/1/1.

116. *Government Gazette,* 7 February 1834.

117. Minutes, special justice, Graaff-Reinet, 24 April and 12 May 1835, CAD, GR 17/45.

118. Report, protector of slaves, Western Div., 20 January 1834, PRO, CO 53/57.

119. Report, protector of slaves, 24 June 1831, PRO, CO 53/52.

120. Robert Percival, *An Account of the Cape of Good Hope; Containing an Historical View* (London, 1804), 127.

121. See Joshua Penny, *The Life and Adventures of Joshua Penny, a Native of Southhold, Long-Island, Suffolk County, New York* (reprint, Cape Town, 1982).

122. S. E. Hudson, "Slaves," *Kronos* 9 (1984), 63; Ross, *Cape of Torments*, 57.

123. Nigel Penn, "*Droster* Gangs of the Bokkeveld and the Roggeveld, 1770–1800," unpublished MS, 1; Ross, *Cape of Torments*, 38–53.

124. Report, registrar and guardian of slaves, assistant guardian, Stellenbosch, 31 December 1827, PRO, CO 53/48.

125. Report, registrar and guardian of slaves, 24 June 1827, ibid.

126. Ross, *Cape of Torments*, 54–72; Hudson, "Slaves," 62–63.

127. Ross, *Cape of Torments,* 56.

128. Ibid., 62–63.

129. Ibid., 41–48, 81, 88–89; James C. Armstrong and Nigel Worden, "Slaves," in Richard Elphick and Hermann Giliomee, eds., *The Shaping of South African Society, 1652–1840* (Cape Town, 1989), 160.

130. Sparrman, *A Voyage,* 2:126; Worden, *Slavery,* 125.

131. Report, protector of slaves, Eastern Div., Graaff-Reinet, 23 January 1834, PRO, CO 53/57.

132. A.K., "Frederick Opperman: Cape Slave," *Christian Express,* July/August 1891, eds., in Francis Wilson and Dominique Perrot, *Outlook on a Century: South Africa, 1870–1970* (Lovedale, E. Cape Province, 1973), 45–57.

7. "A Faith for Ourselves"

1. PRO, CO53/55, report, protector of slaves, Eastern Div., Uitenhage, 11 January 1833.

2. The reference, is of course, is to W. E. B. Du Bois's classic examination of African-American double consciousness; see Du Bois, *The Souls of Black Folk: Essays and Sketches.*

3. Elizabeth Elbourne and Robert Ross, "Combating Spiritual and Social Bondage: Early Missions in the Cape Colony," in Richard Elphick and Rodney Davenport, eds., *Christianity in South Africa: A Political, Social, and Cultural History* (Oxford, Eng., 1997), 34.

4. Both Christianity and Islam were also deployed in defense of slavery.

5. Barnabus Shaw, *Memorials of South Africa* (reprint, Cape Town, 1970), 184; Shaw's trans.

6. See R. L. Watson, *The Slave Question: Liberty and Property in South Africa* (Hanover, 1990), 172.

7. J. S. Marais, *The Cape Coloured People, 1652–1937* (London, 1939), 168.

8. Report on slaves, in George McC. Theal, comp., *Records of the Cape Colony [RCC]* (London, 1897–1905), 35:366.

9. Ibid.

10. Quoted in Watson, *Slave Question,* 174.

11. Karen Armstrong, *History of God: The 4,000 Year Quest of Judaism, Christianity, and Islam* (New York, 1993), xix.

12. Paul Radin, "Forward," in Clifton H. Johnson, ed., *God Struck Me Dead: Voices of Ex-Slaves* (reprint, Cleveland, 1993), viii.

13. Joao Jose Reis, *Slave Rebellion in Brazil: The Muslim Uprising of 1835 in Bahia* (Baltimore, Md., 1993), 114.

14. Robert W. Hefner, "World Building and the Rationality of Conversion," in Robert W. Hefner, ed., *Conversion to Christianity: Historical and Anthropological Perspectives on a Great Transformation* (Berkeley, Calif., 1993), 3.

15. Jonathan N. Gertsner, "A Christian Monopoly: The Reformed Church and Colonial Society under Dutch Rule," in Richard Elphick and Rodney Davenport, eds., *Christianity in South Africa,* 22.

16. Richard Elphick and Robert C.-H. Shell, "Intergroup Relations: Khoikhoi, Settlers, Slaves, and Free Blacks, 1652–1795," in Richard Elphick and Hermann Giliomee, eds., *The Shaping of South African Society, 1652–1840* (Cape Town, 1989), 186–87.

17. Muriel Horrell, *The Education of the Coloured Community in South Africa, 1652 to 1970* (Johannesburg, 1970), 3.

18. Elphick and Shell, "Intergroup Relations," 188–90.

19. Timothy Keegan, *Colonial South Africa and the Origins of the Racial Order* (Cape Town, 1996), 27.

20. Gertsner, "Christian Monopoly," 24, 27.

21. Leonard Guelke, "Freehold Farmers and Frontier Settlers, 1657–1780," in Elphick and Giliomee, *Shaping*, 96; Gertsner, "Christian Monopoly," 23.

22. Henry Lichtenstein, *Travels in Southern Africa in the Years 1803, 1804, 1805 and 1806* (reprint, Cape Town, 1930), 2:447.

23. Gertsner, "Christian Monopoly," 26.

24. Keegan, *Colonial South Africa*, 84.

25. Elphick and Shell, "Intergroup Relations," 188–89.

26. Marais, *Cape Coloured People*, 169.

27. Report on slaves, *RCC*, 35:366.

28. Quoted in Elphick and Shell, "Intergroup Relations," 188.

29. Truter to Cradock, 17 September 1812, *RCC*, 8:489; see also Elphick and Shell, "Intergroup Relations," 188–190; Gertsner, "Christian Monopoly," 17–18.

30. Caledon to Castlereagh, 4 February 1808, CAD, GH 23/1.

31. Achmat Davids, *The Mosques of Bo-Kaap: A Social History of Islam at the Cape* (Athlone, Western Cape Province, 1980), 100–101; "The Afrikaans of the Cape Muslims, from 1815 to 1915: A Socio-linguistic Study," (M.A. thesis, University of Natal, Durban, 1991), 37. The exact year of the mosque's opening is the subject of much debate; see Abdulkader Tayob, *Islam in South Africa: Mosques, Imams, and Sermons* (Gainesville, Fla., 1999), 45.

32. S. Dangor, "In the Footsteps of the Companions: *Shaykh* Yusuf of Macassar (1626–1699)," in Yusuf da Costa and Achmat Davids, eds., *Pages From Cape Muslim History* (Pietermaritzburg, 1994), 23–46.

33. Tayob, *Islam in South Africa*, 23; Suleman Essop Dangor, *A Critical Biography of Shaykh Yusuf* (Westville, KwaZulu-Natal, 1982), passim; *Boorhaanol Islam* 29, no. 2 (1994): 2. To this day Yusuf is venerated as a saint, and his *kramat* (tomb) overlooking False Bay has been a place of pilgrimage since at least the end of the eighteenth century.

34. The name, derived from *mardycka* or *maredhika*, is sometimes read as implying that they were free people: Ebrahim Mahomed Mahida, *History of Muslims in South Africa: A Chronology* (Durban, 1993), 1–2.

35. Achmat Davids, "Politics and the Muslims of Cape Town: A Historical Survey," *Studies in the History of Cape Town* 4 (1981): 177–78.

36. Achmat Davids, "Muslim-Christian Relations in Nineteenth-Century Cape Town, 1825–1925," *Kronos* 19 (November 1992): 84. M. A. Bradlow disagrees vehemently with this assertion, claiming that in the late eighteenth and early to mid-nineteenth centuries there was a "ferocious" level of state repression; however, he fails to disentangle the discrimination slaves and free blacks suffered and the harassment they endured from the toleration of the religion many of them practiced—a difficult task, admittedly, but one that must be performed: M. A. Bradlow, "Imperialism, State Formation, and the Establishment of a Muslim Community at the Cape of Good Hope, 1770–1840: A Study in Urban Resistance": M.A. thesis, University of Cape Town, 1988, 133.

37. Bradlow, "Imperialism," 2–3. Others have divided this history into similar

periods; see Davids, "Afrikaans," and Abdulkader Tayob, *Islamic Resurgence in South Africa: The Muslim Youth Movement* (Cape Town, 1995).

38. Bradlow, "Imperialism," 2–3, 120 ff.

39. *Tariqa* translates literally as path, or way, but conventionally (as above), order or brotherhood.

40. Bradlow, "Imperialism," 120 ff. Among the tariqa at the Cape, Bradlow mentions the Khalwatiyyah and the Qadariyyah.

41. Andrew Bank, *The Decline of Urban Slavery at the Cape, 1806 to 1843* (Cape Town, 1991), 111.

42. Bradlow, "Imperialism," 85.

43. Many of the texts Shaykh Yusuf produced while living in the Indonesian archipelago have survived and are housed in archives in Malaysia and the Netherlands.

44. The veneration of saints and the visitation of their tombs is consistent with Sufi practice elsewhere in the world; see Mervyn Hiskett, *The Development of Islam in West Africa* (London, 1984), 9.

45. Suleman Essop Dangor, *Shaykh Yusuf*, passim.

46. Achmat Davids, "Men of Power and Influence: The *Kramats* of Constantia," unpub. MSS, 1, 7–8, 13–14.

47. Achmat Davids, "Afrikaans" 29–30.

48. Yusuf da Costa, "The Influence of *Tasawwuf* on Islamic Practices at the Cape," in da Costa and Davids, *Pages,* 129–35.

49. Cited in Tayob, *Islam in South Africa,* 22–23.

50. Bradlow, "Imperialism," 126.

51. See, for instance, Davids, *Mosques,* and Shell, "From Rites and Rebellion: Islamic Conversion at the Cape, 1808–1915," *Studies in the History of Cape Town,* 5 (1984): 1–46.

52. Carl Peter Thunberg, *Travels at the Cape of Good Hope, 1772–1775* (reprint, Cape Town, 1986), 47–48.

53. Davids, *Mosques,* 100.

54. Ibid., 100–101, and "Afrikaans," 37. The exact year of the mosque's opening is the subject of some debate; see Tayob, *Islamic Resurgence,* 45.

55. Tuan Guru: loosely, Honored teacher.

56. Bradlow, "Imperialism," 4.

57. Achmat Davids, "Alternative Education: *Tuan Guru* and the Formation of the Cape Muslim Community," in Yusaf da Costa and Achmat Davids, *Pages from Cape Muslim History* (Pietermaritzburg, 1994), 53, 55.

58. On free black slave owners, see, for instance, Davids, "Afrikaans," 31–38

59. Ibid., 33.

60. Davids, "Alternative Education," 48–49. Tuan Guru was well within the mainstream of Islamic thought. As Ralph Willis notes, "It must be remembered that Muhammed, the Prophet of Islam, was . . . a slaveowner. . . . And since the tenets of Islam are tethered so tightly to the *sunna* (model) of its Prophet, it is no surprise to discover that slavery [commands] . . . such a wide presence in the social annals of Islam": Willis, *Slaves and Slavery in Muslim Africa,* vol. 1: *Islam and the Ideology of Enslavement* (London, 1985), viii. The Quran itself "urges, without actually commanding, kindness to the slave and recommends, without requiring, his liberation by purchase or manumission": Bernard Lewis, *Race and Slavery in the Middle East: An Historical Inquiry* (New York, 1990), 6.

61. The formal grant of religious freedom came in 1804.

62. Evidence of Imam Muding, 13 December 1824, imperial blue book, papers relating to the condition and treatment of native inhabitants of southern Africa, 18 March 1835, 207.

63. Davids, "Alternative Education," 51, and Imam Muding, imperial blue book, 210.

64. Robert Shell, "From Rites to Rebellion: Islamic Conversion, Urbanization, and Ethnic Identities at the Cape of Good Hope, 1797 to 1904," *Canadian Journal of History* (December 1993), 413–18.

65. Elizabeth Elbourne, "Early Khoisan Uses of Mission Christianity," conference paper, "People, Power, and Culture: The History of Christianity in South Africa, 1792–1992," University of the Western Cape, August 1992, 5.

66. Truter to Cradock, 17 September 1812, *RCC,* 8:489 (emphasis in original).

67. H. T. Colbrooke, "Note III," in W[illiam Wilberforce] Bird, *State of the Cape in 1822* (reprint, Cape Town, 1966), 349.

68. Cradock to van Ryneveld, 30 May 1812, *RCC,* 8:431.

69. Truter to Cradock, 17 September 1812, *RCC,* 8:489 (emphasis in original).

70. Denyssen to Foster, 30 September 1812, *RCC,* 8:498.

71. Proclamation, 9 October 1812, *RCC,* 8:500.

72. Abraham Leslie Behr, "Three Centuries of Coloured Education: Historical and Comparative Studies of the Education of the Coloured People in the Cape and the Transvaal, 1652–1952": Ed.D. thesis, Potchefstroom University for Christian Higher Education, 1952, 158; Horrell, comp., *Education of the Coloured Community,* 10.

73. Report, commission of the Court of Justice, n.d. [1813], CAD, GH 28/6.

74. Edgar Lionel Maurice, "The History and Administration of the Education of the Coloured Peoples of the Cape, 1652–1910, vols. 1 and 2," B.A. thesis, University of Cape Town, 1946, 1:93–94; see also Behr, "Coloured Education," 160–61.

75. See chapter 2.

76. Behr, "Coloured Education," 170.

77. Report on slaves, *RCC,* 35:364–65.

78. Gerstner, "Christian Monopoly," 28–29; Elbourne and Ross, "Combating Bondage," 32–33.

79. Freund, "Society and Government in Dutch South Africa: The Cape and the Batavians, 1803–1806," Ph.D. diss., Yale University, 1971, 333.

80. Watson, *Slave Question,* 164–65.

81. Marais, *Cape Coloured People,* 168; Freund, "Society and Government," 338–39.

82. Watson, *Slave Question,* 164; Freund, "Society and Government," 328.

83. Elbourne and Ross, "Combating Bondage," 39.

84. Keegan, *Colonial South Africa,* 102.

85. Freund, "Society and Government," 336.

86. Elbourne and Ross, "Combating Bondage," 42.

87. J. du Plessis, *A History of Christian Missions in South Africa* (London, 1911), 95.

88. *Report of the Committee of the Cape Town Auxiliary Missionary Society* (Cape Town, 1825), 4.

89. *The Third Report of the Cape Town Missionary Society, Auxiliary to the London Missionary Society* (Cape Town, 1827), 12.

90. *The Sixth Report of the Cape Town Missionary Society, Auxiliary to the London Missionary Society* (Cape Town, 1830), 8.

91. Du Plessis, *Christian Missions,* 203.

92. *The Fifth Report of the Cape Town Missionary Society, Auxiliary to the London Missionary Society* (Cape Town, 1829), 8.

93. Marais, *Cape Coloured People,* 171.

94. Elbourne and Ross, "Combating Bondage," 42.

95. Bird, *State of the Cape,* 76.

96. Shaw, *Memorials,* 152.

97. Ibid., 13, 179.

98. Report, registrar and guardian of slaves, 25 December 1826, PRO, CO 53/48.

99. Report, protector of slaves, assistant protector, Albany, 14 August 1833, PRO, CO 53/56.

100. Elbourne and Ross, "Combating Bondage," 41.

101. Report, Cape Town Auxiliary Missionary Society, 1825, 4.

102. Shaw, *Memorials,* 13 and 179.

103. Colebrooke, "Note III," 349.

104. Shaw, *Memorials,* 152.

105. Behr, "Three Centuries of Coloured Education," 135.

106. Keegan, *Colonial South Africa,* 281–85.

107. Marais, *Cape Coloured People,* 169–70.

108. James Backhouse, *A Narrative of a Visit to the Mauritius and South Africa* (London, 1844), 95.

109. Shaw, *Memorials,* 147; in the same vein, see also 13.

110. Report, Cape Town Auxiliary Missionary Society, 1825, 3–4.

111. Report on slaves, *RCC,* 35:364–65; Marais, *Cape Coloured People,* 169.

112. Evidence of Imam Muding, 13 December 1824, *Parliamentary Papers, Imperial Blue Book, 18 March 1835, Papers Relating to the Condition and Treatment of Native Inhabitants of Southern Africa,* 208.

113. Shaw, *Memorials,* 146.

114. *Report of the Stations of the London Missionary Society, South Africa, 1839* (Cape Town, 1840), 14; see also *Report of the Cape Town Auxiliary Missionary Society for 1840* (Cape Town, 1840), 6–7.

115. Du Plessis, *Christian Missions,* 98.

116. Elbourne and Ross, "Combating Bondage," 42.

117. Shaw, *Memorials,* 147. The passage is from Matthew 11:28.

118. Elbourne and Ross, "Combating Bondage," 42.

119. Shell, "From Rites to Rebellion," 413–18. On Prize Negroes, see chapter 1.

120. Ibid., 410–11, 419, 456–57.

121. Orlando Patterson, *Freedom: Volume I: Freedom in the Making of Western Culture* (New York, 1991), 21.

122. Davids, "Afrikaans," 38.

123. J. W. D. Moodie, *Ten Years in South Africa: Including a Particular Description of the Wild Sports of that Country, Vols. 1 and 2* (London, 1835), 1:200; John Schofield Mayson, *The Malays of Cape Town* (reprint, Cape Town, 1963), 12; Colebrooke, "Note III," 349–50.

124. Shell is, however, wrong to suggest that non-Muslim, non-Christian slaves did not honor the dead with burial rites or celebrate the birth of a child. See, for instance, Robert Semple, *Walks and Sketches at the Cape of Good Hope* (London, 1803), 30–33.

125. In this discussion of Elliot, I draw heavily on Watson, *The Slave Question,* 172–176.

310   Notes to Pages 199–205

126. Quoted in Watson, *The Slave Question,* 173.

127. Richard Elphick, "Writing about Christianity in History: Some Issues of Theory and Method," conference paper, University of the Western Cape, 12 August 1992, 2.

128. Cited in Hefner, "World Building," 26.

129. Ibid., 17.

130. Richard M. Eaton, *The Rise of Islam and the Bengal Frontier, 1204–1760* (Berkeley, Calif., 1993), 116.

131. Armstrong, *History of God,* xix.

132. Shell, "From Rites to Rebellion," 410 and passim.

133. Robin Horton, "On the Rationality of Conversion, Part I," *Africa* 45, no. 3 (1975): 220 and passim.

134. Hefner, "World Building," 21, 23, 28.

135. Elizabeth Elbourne, "Early Khoisan Uses of Mission Christianity," conference paper, University of the Western Cape, South Africa, August 1992, 1.

136. Shell, "Rites to Rebellion," 411.

137. Sura 2:163.

138. Imam Muding, imperial blue book, 18 March 1835, 207–8.

139. Davids, "Alternative Education," 48–56 and "Afrikaans," 29.

140. *Malay* was a local term for Muslim.

141. See Steven Feierman and John M. Janzen, eds., *The Social Basis of Health and Healing in Africa* (Berkeley, Calif., 1992).

142. Achmat Davids, "'The Revolt of the Malays': A Study of the Reactions of the Cape Muslims to the Smallpox Epidemics of Nineteenth-Century Cape Town," *Studies in the History of Cape Town* 5 (1983): 67. On white belief in Malay magic, see, for instance, J. W. D. Moodie, *Ten Years,* 1:197–200; Henry Lichtenstein, *Travels,* 1:107.

143. Davids, "Revolt of the Malays," 67–68.

144. Ismail Abdulla argues that *Islamic medicine* is a problematic term since the Quran has little to say about healing and since many of the physicians who worked within the Islamic world and contributed to medical learning were Jews, Christians, and Zoroastrians: Abdulla, "Diffusion of Islamic Medicine into Hausaland," in Feierman and Janzen, eds., *Health and Healing,* 177–78.

145. Ibid., 190.

146. Shell, "Rites to Rebellion," 426.

147. Achmat Davids, "The Survival of Islam," in da Costa and Davids, *Pages,* 62.

148. Davids, "Afrikaans," 30.

149. Davids, "My Religion is Superior," 63.

150. Davids, *Mosques,* 110–11 and "Afrikaans," 30.

151. See below.

152. That is *khalifah,* an archaic term for the ratiep.

153. Court of Justice, sentences, 1812–13, CAD, CJ 805, no. 37.

154. George Champion, *Journal of an American Missionary in the Cape Colony, 1835,* ed. A. R. Booth (Cape Town, 1968), 20.

155. Alfred W. Cole, *The Cape and the Kafirs; Or Notes of Five Year's Residence in South Africa* (London, 1852), 44–46.

156. *Cape Monthly Magazine* 10 (December 1861): 356–58.

157. Mirza Abu Taleb Khan, *The Travels of Mirza Abu Taleb Khan in Asia, Africa, and Europe, during the Years 1799, 1800, 1801, 1802, and 1803,* vols. 1 and 2, trans. Charles Stewart (London, 1810), 1:70–72.

158. Seyyed Hossein Nasr, introduction to Nasr, ed., *World Spirituality: An Encyclopedic History of the Religious Quest*, vol. 20: *Islamic Spirituality: Manifestations* (New York, 1991), xv.

159. Fazlur Rahman, *Islam*, 2nd ed. (Chicago, 1979), 134.

160. John Esposito, *Islam: The Straight Path* (New York, 1991), 101.

161. Armstrong, *History of God*, 226–27.

162. Nasr, introduction, xiii.

163. Armstrong, *History of God*, 213.

164. William Stoddart, *Sufism: The Mystical Doctrines and Methods of Islam* (New York, 1985), 56.

165. Rahman, *Islam*, 152.

166. Abdur-Rahman Ibrahim Doi, "Sufism in Africa," in Nasr, *Islamic Spirituality*, 293.

167. Osman Bin Bakar, "Sufism in the Malay-Indonesian World," in Nasr, *Islamic Spirituality*, 272.

168. Da Costa and Davids, *Pages*, 135.

169. Davids makes this point in "Afrikaans," 30.

170. The language is borrowed from Nathan Irvin Huggins, *Black Odyssey: The Afro-American Ordeal in Slavery* (reprint, New York, 1990), lxxxv.

171. Imam Muding, imperial blue book, 18 March 1835, 207.

172. Huggins, *Black Odyssey*, lxxxv.

8. *"Habits of Intimacy"*

1. The following narrative is drawn from special magistrate, Uitenhage, to sec. to government, 8 June 1835, CAD, CO 441.

2. Cape ordinance 1, 1835, cap. 4, #1.

3. The Abolition Act protected husbands and wives and parents and children from separation by sale and testament, but did not address problems such as September's: 3 & 4 Wm., cap. 73, #x.

4. Statement, laws regarding slavery, in George McCall Theal, comp., *Records of the Cape Colony* [*RCC*] (London, 1897–1905), 9:150.

5. Orlando Patterson, *Slavery and Social Death: A Comparative Study* (Cambridge, Mass., 1982), 5–10.

6. See chapter 2.

7. Cape ordinance 19, 1826, #18, #22, #23.

8. Order of the king in council, 2 February 1830, #46.

9. I have borrowed the concept of a "porous" family from Lawrence Stone; see Stone, *The Family, Sex, and Marriage in England, 1500–1800* (New York, 1977), 85.

10. Nigel Worden, *Slavery in Dutch South Africa* (Cambridge, Eng., 1985), 95; Robert Ross, *Cape of Torments: Slavery and Resistance in South Africa* (London, 1983), 16.

11. See below.

12. James Armstrong and Nigel Worden have found that by 1833, 53.2 percent of the slaves were under twenty-five years of age, indicating that they had been born after the abolition of the slave trade and must have been born in the Cape. Of course, many older slaves were also Cape-born: James C. Armstrong and Nigel Worden, "The Slaves, 1652–1834," in Richard Elphick and Hermann Giliomee, eds., *The Shaping of South African Society, 1652–1840* (Cape Town, 1989), 132.

13. My ideas about matrifocality and matriarchy have been shaped to a large

degree by the thinking of Hildred Geertz and Nancy Tanner; both in Tanner, "Matrifocality in Indonesia and Africa and among Black Americans," in Michelle Zimbalist Rosaldo and Louise Lamphere, eds., *Women, Culture, and Society* (Stanford, Calif., 1974), 131–35.

14. Herbert G. Gutman, *The Black Family in Slavery and Freedom, 1750–1925* (New York, 1976), 135, and chapter 3, passim; Deborah Gray White, *Ar'n't I a Woman? Female Slaves in the Plantation South* (New York, 1985), 75, 153–54.

15. Stone, *Family, Sex, and Marriage,* 21–22.

16. I have uncovered no evidence of homosexual relationships among the slaves during the nineteenth century. Such relationships almost certainly existed, but as far as I am aware, they were unrecorded. For evidence of homosexuality among slaves in the seventeenth and eighteenth centuries, see Robert Ross, "Oppression, Sexuality, and Slavery at the Cape of Good Hope," *Historical Reflection* 6, no. 2 (1979): 431–32, and Worden, *Slavery,* 96.

17. Willie Lee Rose, "The Domestication of Domestic Slavery," in Rose, *Slavery and Freedom,* expanded ed., ed. William W. Freehling (Oxford, Eng., 1982), 30, 32.

18. John W. Blassingame, *The Slave Community: Plantation Life in the Antebellum South* (2nd rev. ed., New York, 1979), 191, 149–91; Jacqueline Jones, *Labor of Love, Labor of Sorrow: Black Women, Work, and the Family from Slavery to the Present* (New York, 1985), 12–13.

19. The reference is to Christopher Lasch, *Haven in a Heartless World: The Family Besieged* (New York, 1977).

20. Returns of the total number of slaves, CAD SO 20/6; Armstrong and Worden, "Slaves," 133.

21. Ross, *Cape of Torments,* 25.

22. Calculated from figures in *Cape of Good Hope Blue Book,* 1834, PRO, CO 53/71.

23. Calculated from report, protector of slaves, Western Div., 20 January 1834, PRO, CO 53/57.

24. Population of the Cape, 1827 in *RCC,* 35:81. After this date, and until 1838, free blacks and Khoisan were incorporated as "white."

25. Ross, *Cape of Torments,* 16.

26. See below.

27. I borrow these terms from Lawrence Stone; see Stone, *Family, Sex, and Marriage,* 93 ff., 221 ff., 325 ff.

28. William J. Burchell, *Travels in the Interior of Southern Africa,* 2 vols. (reprint, Cape Town, 1967), 1:33–4.

29. On Islam at the Cape, see chapter 7. On Islamic marriage ceremonies, see William Wright, *Slavery at the Cape of Good Hope* (reprint, New York, 1969), 16; Ross, "Oppression and Sexuality," 426.

30. Wright, *Slavery at the Cape,* 15; W[illiam Wilberforce] Bird, *State of the Cape of Good Hope in 1822* (reprint, Cape Town, 1966), 74.

31. Special justice, Swellendam, to sec. to government, 3 January 1837, CAD, CO 465.

32. The following narrative relies on enclosure, special justice, Worcester, to sec. to government, 29 March 1836, CAD, CO 452.

33. Memo annexed to letter, special justice, Worcester, to sec. to government, 29 March 1836, CAD, CO 452.

34. Report, protector of slaves, Western Div., 26 July 1833, PRO, CO 53/56.

35. Mrs. Jooste is not otherwise identified.

36. Report, protector of slaves, Western Div., Worcester, 20 February 1833, PRO, CO 53/55.

37. Ibid., 13 August 1833, PRO, CO 53/55.

38. Ibid., Cape Town, 24 June 1831, PRO, CO 53/52.

39. Report, protector of slaves, assistant protector, Stellenbosch, 24 June 1831, PRO, CO 53/52.

40. Report, registrar and guardian of slaves, assistant guardian, Graaff-Reinet, 24 June 1827, PRO, CO 53/48.

41. Report, protector of slaves, Western Div., 28 May 1833, PRO, CO 53/55.

42. Criminal record book, special magistrate, Worcester, 1835–36, CAD, WOC 19/26.

43. Report, protector of slaves, Western Div., 26 July 1833, PRO, CO 53/56.

44. Ibid., Cape Town, 25 December 1830, PRO, CO 53/51.

45. See chapter 7.

46. Report, protector of slaves, assistant protector, Somerset, 28 May 1833, PRO, CO 53/55.

47. Report, protector of slaves, Eastern Div., Graaff-Reinet, 23 January 1834, PRO, CO 53/57.

48. The terms *bushman* and *bushwoman* were used to refer to the San.

49. Report, protector of slaves, Eastern Div., Graaff-Reinet, 11 January 1833, PRO, CO 53/55.

50. Criminal record book, special justice, Worcester, 1835–1836, CAD, WOC 19/26.

51. Statement, laws regarding slavery, *RCC,* 9:147, 150.

52. See chapter 2 and above.

53. Report, protector of slaves, assistant protector, Somerset, 28 May 1833, PRO, CO 53/55.

54. On hire money, see chapter 4.

55. Report, protector of slaves, Western Div., 26 July 1833, PRO, CO 53/56.

56. Minutes, special justice, Graaff-Reinet, 1835–38, CAD, GR 17/45.

57. The following narrative draws on enclosures to the memo, William Thomas Brown, CAD, CO 3968.

58. Mrs. Brown is not otherwise identified in the documents.

59. After whipping was banned in 1831, the law prescribed leg stocks as punishment for slave women.

60. Report, protector of slaves, Western Div., Worcester, 20 February 1833, PRO, CO 53/55.

61. Ibid., Cape Town, 25 December 1830, PRO, CO 53/51.

62. Ross, *Cape of Torments,* 46, 106; Worden, *Slavery* 95.

63. F. M. L. Thompson, *The Rise of Respectable Society: A Social History of Victorian Britain, 1830–1900* (Cambridge, Mass., 1988), 93.

64. Free blacks may have held a certain amount of prejudice against slaves, despite (or because of) most of them having had slave forebears. Lodewyk, a Cape Town slave, once charged David, a free black, with assault. David did not deny the charge "but pleaded in justification . . . having found Complainant with his Sister in a suspicious manner in the Streets on the Evening in question": report, protector of slaves, Western Div., 26 July 1833, PRO, CO 53/56.

65. Report, protector of slaves, Western Div., 28 May 1833, PRO, CO 53/55.

66. Ibid.

67. Ibid., Eastern Div., 14 August 1833, PRO, CO 53/56.

68. Ibid., Eastern Div., Graaff-Reinet, 14 August 1833, PRO, CO 53/56.

69. Ibid.

70. Report, protector of slaves, Eastern Div., Graaff-Reinet, 23 January 1834, PRO, CO 53/57.

71. See chapters 2 and 3.

72. Report, protector of slaves, Western Div., 26 July 1833, PRO, CO 53/56.

73. For Prize Negroes, see chapter 2.

74. Report, protector of slaves, Western Div., 26 July 1833, PRO, CO 53/56.

75. J. W. D. Moodie, *Ten Years in South Africa: Including a Particular Description of the Wild Sports of that Country,* 2 vols. (London, 1835), 1:199.

76. The following narrative draws on the report of the protector of slaves, Eastern Div., assistant protector, Somerset, 14 August 1833, and table D, ibid., PRO, CO 53/56.

77. Reports, protector of slaves, Western Div., 28 May 1833, PRO, CO 53/55 and 26 July 1833, PRO, CO 53/56.

78. Report, registrar and guardian of slaves, 25 December 1826, PRO, CO 53/48.

79. Ibid., 25 December 1826; also 24 June 1827; both PRO, CO 53/48.

80. Report, protector of slaves, assistant protector, Stellenbosch, 24 June 1831, PRO, CO 53/52.

81. Minutes, special justice, Graaff-Reinet, 1835–1838, CAD, GR 17/45.

82. Criminal and civil notebooks, special magistrate, Malmesbury, 1835–1838, CAD, MBY 3/1/1.

83. Ibid.

84. Report, protector of slaves, Eastern Div., Uitenhage, 28 May 1833, PRO, CO 53/55.

85. Ibid., Graaff-Reinet, 14 August 1833, PRO, CO 53/56.

86. Minutes, special justice, Graaff-Reinet, 1835–38, CAD, GR 17/45.

87. Ulrich Bonnell Phillips, *American Negro Slavery: A survey of the Supply, Employment and Control of Negro Labor as Determined by the Plantation Regime* (reprint, Baton Rouge, 1966), 342.

88. Ross makes a similar point in *Cape of Torments,* 1.

89. Report, protector of slaves, Western Div., 20 January 1834, PRO, CO 53/57.

90. The following narrative draws on the report of the protector of slaves, Western Div., Clan William, 20 January 1833, PRO, CO 53/55.

91. Nell Irvin Painter, "Soul Murder and Slavery: Toward a Fully Loaded Cost Accounting," in Linda Kerber et al., eds., *US History as Women's History* (Chapel Hill, N.C., 1995), 133.

92. Wilma Hoffman and Brian McKendrick, "Part 4: Violence in Institutions," in Brian McKendrick and Wilma Hoffman, eds., *People and Violence in South Africa* (Cape Town, 1990), 339.

93. Linda Gordon, *Heroes of Their Own Lives: The Politics and History of Family Violence, Boston 1880–1960* (New York, 1988), 3, 177.

94. Ibid., 172–73, 193.

95. See chapters 4 and 5.

96. See chapter 6.

97. See chapters 1 and 2.

98. Cape ordinance 19, 1826, #33–38.

99. See chapter 2.

100. Report, protector of slaves, Western Div., 20 January 1834, PRO, CO 53/57.

101. Skilled slave artisans in Cape Town earned between R.30 and R.40 a month if their masters allowed them to hire out their own time. They might return one-half to two-thirds of their earnings to their owners in hire money; see chapter 4.

102. Report, protector of slaves, Western Div., 26 July 1833, PRO, CO 53/56.

103. Ibid.

104. Ibid., 28 May 1833, PRO, CO 53/55.

105. Ibid.

106. Ibid., 20 January 1834, PRO, CO 53/57.

107. Report, protector of slaves, Cape Town, 24 June 1831, PRO, CO 53/52.

108. Report, protector of slaves, Western Div., 28 May 1833, PRO, CO 53/55.

109. Report, registrar and guardian of slaves, 31 December 1827, PRO, CO 53/48.

110. Ibid.

111. See chapter 4.

112. R. L. Watson, *The Slave Question: Liberty and Property in South Africa* (Hanover, 1990), 74, 78, 81.

113. Ibid.

114. Pamela Scully, *Liberating the Family? Gender and British Slave Emancipation in the Rural Western Cape, South Africa, 1823–1853* (Portsmouth, N.H., 1997), 6 ff.

115. F. M. L. Thompson, *The Rise of Respectable Society*, 85.

116. Susan Groag Bell and Karen M. Offen, *Women, the Family, and Freedom: The Debate in Documents* (Stanford, Calif., 1983), 18.

117. Report, protector of slaves, Western Div., 28 May 1833, PRO, CO 53/55.

118. Ibid.

119. Ibid.

120. Report of the protector of slaves, 24 June 1831, PRO, CO 53/52.

9. Epilogue

1. The weather was widely commented upon. See *De Zuid-Afrikaan* 7 December and 14 December 1838; civil commissioner, Worcester, to sec. to government, 4 December 1838, CAD, CO 476. The former apprentices' interpretation comes from a folk tale current in the "coloured" community in the Cape Province as recently as forty years ago, and perhaps still: Andre du Toit, personal communication, 8 February 1989. Drought continued in the eastern Cape.

2. The following brief narrative relies on Katie Jacobs, interview, *APO* (newspaper of the African Political Organization), Christmas number, 1910. Jacobs describes events that she remembers has having occurred on 1 December 1834, the official end of slavery and the beginning of apprenticeship. The details of her recollections, however, unambiguously confirm that the correct date is 1 December 1838. Robert Shell kindly brought this interview to my attention.

3. J. P. Duminy, *Twilight over the Tygerberg* (Kommetje, Western Cape Province, 1979), 3.

4. Pamela Scully, *Liberating the Family? Gender and British Slave Emancipation in the Rural Western Cape, South Africa, 1823–1853* (Portsmouth, N.H., 1997), 2–3.

5. For whites who chose not to adapt, there was the option of trekking beyond the Orange River. George M. Fredrickson writes: "The emancipation of slaves . . . impelled a portion of the white population to leave the colony and establish independent republics where racial inequality was constitutionally sanctioned and de facto

African enslavement, under the guise of 'apprenticeship,' was widely practiced": George M. Fredrickson, "After Emancipation: A Comparative Study of White Responses to the New Order of Race Relations in the American South, Jamaica, and the Cape Colony of South Africa," in David G. Sansing, ed., *What Was Freedom's Price?* (Jackson, Miss., 1978), 77.

6. Eric Foner, *Nothing but Freedom: Emancipation and Its Legacy* (Baton Rouge, 1983), 20, 37.

7. Circular dispatch, sec. of state to governors of the British Slave Colonies, 6 November 1837, CAD, GH 1/117.

8. Frederick Cooper, *From Slaves to Squatters: Plantation Labor and Agriculture in Zanzibar and Coastal Kenya, 1890–1925* (New Haven, Conn., 1980), 42.

9. Order of the queen in council, 7 September 1838, enclosure to dispatch, sec. of state to governor of Cape Colony, 15 September 1838, CAD, GH 1/125.

10. William Cohen, cited in Willie Lee Rose, "Jubilee and Beyond: What Was Freedom?" in Sansing, ed., *What Was Freedom's Price?*, 8 (emphasis in original).

11. Cape ordinance 50, 1828, #1; see chapter 2; see also below.

12. Fredrickson, "After Emancipation," ibid., 88–89.

13. Quoted in Rebecca J. Scott, "Exploring the Meaning of Freedom: Postemancipation Societies in Comparative Perspective," in Rebecca J. Scott et al., eds., *The Abolition of Slavery and the Aftermath of Emancipation in Brazil* (Durham, N.C., 1988), 20.

14. Katie Jacobs interview, 9.

15. *De Zuid-Afrikaan*, 14 December 1838—describing Tulbagh.

16. Ibid. (emphasis in original).

17. Napier to Glenelg, 6 December 1838, CAD, GH 23/12.

18. *Graham's Town Journal*, 6 December 1838.

19. Special justice, Cape Town, to sec. to government, 5 December 1838, CAD, CO 476; special justice, Graaff-Reinet, to sec. to government, 6 December 1838, CAD, CO 476; *Commercial Advertiser*, 5 December 1838.

20. Special justice, Stellenbosch, to sec. to government, 10 December 1838, CAD, CO 476.

21. The "Scotch Church" was St. Andrew's Presbyterian. G. C. Cuthbertson, "The Impact of the Emancipation of the Slaves on St. Andrew's Scottish Church, Cape Town, 1838–1878," in Christopher Saunders and Howard Phillips, eds., *Studies in the History of Cape Town*, vol. 3 (Cape Town, 1980), 49–50.

22. Edward Williams to directors, LMS, 20 December 1838, CAD, ZP 1/3/13 (microfilm). The meaning of these verses may be clearer in the Revised Standard Version: "For it is God's will that by doing right you should put to silence the ignorance of foolish men. Live as free men, yet without using your freedom as a pretext for evil; but live as servants of God." While this, as Chris Lowe has mentioned to me, is hardly liberation theology, it is also not as oppressive as might have been feared; see, for instance, 1 Peter 2:18.

23. Former special justice, Swellendam, to sec. to government, 4 December 1838, CAD, CO 476.

24. Cape Town's nearly six thousand apprentices comprised one-third of the town's population; see table 1.3.

25. *Commercial Advertiser*, 5 December 1838.

26. *De Zuid-Afrikaan*, 7 December 1838.

27. For the low-key celebrations on 1 December 1834, see Edna Bradlow, "Eman-

cipation and Race Perceptions at the Cape," *South African Historical Journal* 15 (1983): 18.

28. Justice of the peace, Paarl, to sec. to government, 6 December 1838, CAD, CO 2775.

29. Special justice, Graaff-Reinet, to sec. to government, 6 December 1838, CAD, CO 476.

30. Special justice, Worcester, to sec. to government, 7 December 1838, CAD, CO 476; special justice, Malmesbury, to sec. to government, 6 December 1838, CAD CO 476.

31. Special justice, Stellenbosch, to sec. to government, 10 December 1838, CAD, CO 476; *De Zuid-Afrikaan,* 7 December 1838.

32. Leon F. Litwack, *Been in the Storm So Long: The Aftermath of Slavery* (New York, 1980), 297.

33. Cited ibid.

34. See chapter 7.

35. Cathryn and Amilie's depositions in letter and enclosures, special justice, Worcester, to sec. to government, 16 December 1838, CAD, CO 476.

36. Thomas Hodgson to governor, Cape Colony, 25 January 1839, CAD, CO 485.

37. Resident magistrate, Worcester, to sec. to government, 12 February 1839, CAD, CO 2788.

38. September's deposition in letter and enclosures, former special justice, Worcester, to sec. to government, 16 December 1838, CAD, CO 476.

39. Letter to the editor, *Commercial Advertiser,* 3 January 1838.

40. Interview, Katie Jacobs, 9.

41. Present's deposition in letter and enclosures, special justice, Worcester, to sec. to government, 16 December 1838, CAD, CO 476.

42. Special justice, Graaff-Reinet, to sec. to government, 6 December 1838, CAD, CO 476; special justice, Worcester, to sec. to government, 7 December 1838, CAD, CO 476.

43. See, for instance, *De Zuid-Afrikaan,* 6 April 1839; letter to the editor, *De Zuid-Afrikaan,* 28 December 1838; C. R. Kotze, "A New Regime," in C. F. J. Muller, ed., *500 Years: A History of South Africa* (5th ed., Pretoria, 1988), 141. The exception to this rule—the withdrawal of married freedwomen—is discussed below.

44. Eric Foner, *Reconstruction: America's Unfinished Revolution* (New York, 1988), 103.

45. Jane Sales, *Mission Stations and the Coloured Communities of the Eastern Cape, 1800–1852* (Cape Town, 1975), 123.

46. September's deposition, letter and enclosures, special justice, Worcester, to sec. to government, 16 December 1838, CAD, CO 476.

47. Justice of the peace, Paarl, to sec. to government, 6 December 1838, CAD, CO 2775.

48. Special justice, Stellenbosch, to sec. to government, 10 December 1838, CAD, CO 476.

49. Special justice, Worcester, to sec. to government, 7 December 1838, CAD, CO 476.

50. Letter to the editor, *Commercial Advertiser,* 3 January 1839.

51. Memoir of Pieter Barend Botha, typescript, private collection, Jean Blankenberg, Cape Town.

52. Resident magistrate, Caledon, to sec. to government, 11 December 1838, CAD, CO 476.

53. Special justice, Malmesbury, to sec. to government, 6 December 1838, CAD, CO 476.

54. Letter to the editor, *De Zuid-Afrikaan,* 28 December 1838; see also letters to the editor, ibid., 8 and 22, February 1839, 8 March 1839.

55. Ibid.

56. See chapter 5.

57. Letter to the editor, *De Zuid-Afrikaan,* 8 March 1839.

58. Ibid., 8 February 1839.

59. Quoted in J. N. C. Marincowitz, "Rural Production and Labour in the Western Cape, 1838 to 1888, with Special Reference to the Wheat Producing Districts," Ph.D. diss., University of London, 1985, 35.

60. Letter to the editor, *De Zuid-Afrikaan,* 8 March 1839.

61. Ibid., 28 December 1838.

62. Ibid., 22 February 1839.

63. Ibid., 13 April 1839.

64. Pamela Scully's recent work confirms this argument, which appears in John Edwin Mason, "'Fit for Freedom': Slavery and Emancipation in the Cape Colony, South Africa, 1806 to 1842," Ph.D. diss., Yale University, 1992; see Scully, *Liberating the Family?,* 81 ff. Unmarried freedwomen, single mothers, and those who supported kinfolk had little choice but to work for a master. When I speak of married couples, I do not mean to refer only to those who have been married under the laws of the Cape or an organized religion; as in chapter 7, I refer to all who considered themselves to be husband and wife. I use *family* to indicate all those who live together in a "domestic unit" or who bore responsibilities of kinship toward one another.

65. Katie Jacobs interview, 9.

66. Marincowitz, "Rural Production and Labour," 53.

67. Foner, *Reconstruction,* 84.

68. *Commercial Advertiser,* 23 March 1839.

69. *De Zuid-Afrikaan,* 5 April 1839.

70. Resident magistrate, Worcester, to sec. to government, 12 February 1839, CAD, CO 2788.

71. *Commercial Advertiser,* 13 April 1839; *De Zuid-Afrikaan,* 19 April 1839.

72. Scully, *Liberating the Family?* 83.

73. See Katie Jacobs, *APO* Christmas number, 1910, 9; letter to the editor, *South African Commercial Advertiser,* 13 April 1839; letter to the editor, *De Zuid-Afrikaan,* 19 April 1839.

74. *APO* Christmas number, 1910, 9.

75. Depositions of Amilie and Caloni, enclosures, former special justice, Worcester, to sec. to government, 16 December 1838, CAD CO 476.

76. Resident magistrate, Worcester, to sec. to government, 12 February 1839, CAD CO 2788.

77. For a discussion of these assumptions in American women's history, see Nancy A. Hewitt, "Beyond the Search for Sisterhood: American Women's History in the 1980s," in Ellen Carol DuBois and Vicki L. Ruiz, eds., *Unequal Sisters: A Multicultural Reader in U.S. Women's History* (New York, 1990), 1–14.

78. This is more fully developed in chapter 8.

79. This is not to deny resistance, by both female and male slaves, to the master's sexual demands. But it is in the nature of slavery that such resistance ordinarily failed; see chapter 3.

80. Scully, *Liberating the Family?*, 81.

81. For some of the horrors of a slave childhood, see chapters 4 and 7.

82. Jacqueline Jones, *Labor of Love, Labor of Sorrow: Black Women, Work, and the Family from Slavery to the Present* (New York, 1985), 45–63; Litwack, *Been in the Storm So Long*, 244–46.

83. Jones, *Labor of Love, Labor of Sorrow*, 58.

84. Quoted in Foner, *Nothing but Freedom*, 34.

85. The protector's use of *colored* to incorporate both slaves and Khoisan is a point of interest to which I shall return.

86. General observations, report, protector of slaves, Eastern Div., 24 June 1834, PRO, CO 53/58 (emphasis in original).

87. Dispatch, sec. of state to governor, Cape Colony, 9 November 1837, CAD GH 1/117.

88. See Raynor, "Wine and Slaves," 319–20.

89. Resident magistrate, Worcester, to sec. to government, 12 February 1839, CAD, CO 2788. An "inhabitant" was invariably white; see chapter 1.

90. Raynor, "Wine and Slaves," 319–20.

91. See, for example, civil commissioner, Stellenbosch, to Field Cornet de Kock, 9 April 1839, CAD, STB 20/68; civil commissioner, Stellenbosch, to Field Cornet Vos, 26 April 1839, CAD, STB 20/68.

92. Marincowitz, "Rural Production and Labour," 41–45; Raynor, "Wine and Slaves," 319–20.

93. Marincowitz, "Rural Production and Labor," 29.

94. *Proceedings . . . Committee of the Legislative Council, Respecting the Proposed Ordinance "To Prevent the Practice of Settling or Squatting"* (Cape Town: Government of Cape Colony, 1852).

95. *De Zuid-Afrikaan*, 3 May 1839 (emphasis in original).

96. Sales, *Mission Stations*, 123–24.

97. Estimates from, Marincowitz, "Rural Production and Labor," 29, and *Proceedings . . . Committee of the Legislative Council.*

98. Sales, *Mission Stations*, 122.

99. *De Zuid-Afrikaan*, 14 June 1839.

100. Ibid., and civil commissioner, Stellenbosch, to Revs. Luckhoff and Edwards, 25 April 1839, CAD, STB 20/68.

101. See *De Zuid-Afrikaan*, 15 February 1839; *South African Commercial Advertiser*, 23 March 1839.

102. The mission station figures are from the replies to government circular, emancipated apprentices, various dates, 1839, CAD, CO 485. This figure is not completely accurate because two of the missionaries counted families, not individuals. The estimate of 12 percent is derived from the above figure and returns of the total number of slaves, CAD, SO 20/61.

103. Marincowitz, "Rural Production and Labour," 36–37.

104. Reply to government circular, re emancipated apprentices, Bethelsdorp, 22 March 1839, CAD CO 485.

105. Nigel Worden, "Adjusting to Emancipation: Freed Slaves and Farmers in

Mid-nineteenth-century South-Western Cape," in Wilmot G. James and Mary Simons, eds., *The Angry Divide: Social and Economic History of the Western Cape* (Cape Town, 1989), 34; Robert Ross, "Emancipations and the Economy of the Cape Colony," (typescript), 6–9.

106. Ross, "Emancipations and the Economy," 6.

107. Quoted in W. M. Macmillan, *The Cape Colour Question: A Historical Survey* (London, 1928), 234.

108. Marais, *Cape Coloured People*, 180–81.

109. Macmillan, *Cape Colour Question*, 234 (emphasis in original).

110. Richard Elphick and Hermann Giliomee, "The Origins and Entrenchment of European Dominance at the Cape, 1652-c.1840," in Richard Elphick and Hermann Giliomee, eds., *The Shaping of South African Society, 1652–1840* (Cape Town, 1989), 556.

111. General observations, report, protector of slaves, Western Div., 28 August 1834, PRO, CO 53/58.

112. General observations, report, protector of slaves, Eastern Div., 24 December 1833, PRO, CO 53/57.

113. Macmillan, *Cape Colour Question*, 219.

114. Cape ordinance 50 1828, #2.

115. Macmillan, *Cape Colour Question*, 234–35; Marais, *Cape Coloured People*, 182–83.

116. Macmillan, *The Cape Colour Question*, 235, 243.

117. Edna Bradlow, "The Khoi and the Proposed Vagrancy Legislation of 1834," *Quarterly Bulletin of the South African Library* 39, no. 3 (1985): 101–2.

118. Petition of the Caledon Mission Station to governor, Cape Colony, 11 August 1834, CAD, LCA 6, annex, LC.

119. Throughout the early nineteenth century, both spellings, *colored* and *coloured*, were used.

120. Petition of the colored inhabitants of Graham's Town, n.d., CAD, LCA 6, annex, LC.

121. Dispatch, sec. of state to governor, Cape Colony, 11 March 1835, CAD, GH 1/104.

122. Elphick and Giliomee, "European Dominance," 555–56.

123. Circular dispatch, sec. of state to governors of the British slave colonies, 6 November 1837, CAD, GH 1/117.

124. *Graham's Town Journal,* 1 August 1839.

125. Dispatch, governor, Cape Colony, to sec. of state, 30 January 1840, CAD, GH 23/12.

126. Elphick and Giliomee, "European Dominance," 556.

127. Cape ordinance 1, 1841, chap. 5, #3–8.

128. Macmillan, *The Cape Colour Question*, 256.

129. Dispatch, sec. of state to governor, Cape Colony, 28 September 1842, CAD, GH 1/150.

130. Elphick and Giliomee, "European Domination," 556.

131. *Graham's Town Journal,* 1 August 1839.

132. General observations, report, protector of slaves, Eastern Div., 24 June 1834, PRO, CO 53/58.

133. *Cape of Good Hope Blue Book,* 1837.

134. *De Zuid-Afrikaan,* 7 December 1838. In modern Afrikaans, "Coloured" is *Kleurling.*

135. Petition of the colored inhabitants of Graham's Town to governor, Cape Colony, n.d. [1834], CAD, LCA 6, annex LC.

136. See chapters 4, 5, 6, 7.

Index

Official documents customarily identified slaves and others only by a given name. Parenthetical information indicating location and sometimes owner has been added to such names to distinguish among individuals.

Port Elizabeth, 193
Portugal, 20, 22
Present (Graaff-Reinet), 138
Present (Somerset), 156–57
Present (Worcester), 258
Pretorious, Isaac, 140
Pretorius, Mathias Jacobus, 173
Pretter, Mrs., 226
"Prize Negroes," 44, 104, 113, 178, 198, 230
property rights: of slave owners, 10, 49–50, 56, 184, 190, 239, 244; of slaves/apprentices, 120, 126, 135–36, 142–43, 208
prostitution, 94
protectors of slaves (officials): as administrators of slavery reform laws, 2, 7, 49–50, 52–58, 112; slave owners and, 55, 57, 71
punishments, 147–52; for apprentices, 60, 62; beatings/whippings as, 9, 48, 53, 60, 74, 145–46, 159; confinement in stocks as, 3, 60; domestic correction and, 48, 62, 73–74, 145; moral economy and, 157–59, 169; sale into rural districts as, 112; for slave owners/former masters, 58, 60, 253; slavery reform laws and, 4, 48–51, 60, 145–46; for slaves/freed persons, 57, 60, 70, 91, 105–6, 253
purchase of freedom, 49–50, 119, 121, 127, 135, 140–41, 184, 232, 239–47
Putter, D. I. G., 152

Qadariyyah, 187
Quinn, John, 32

Rabe, Johannes, 118
Raby, Christiaan, 147
Rachel (Cape Town), 233
Rachel (Western Div.), 161–62, 230
Rachiel, 68–69
racial hierarchies, 10, 30, 32–34, 152–53, 182–83, 196, 252–53, 274–76
Radin, Paul, 180
Rafferty, Mrs. John, 195

Rafudeen, Muhamed Auwais, 188
rape, 93–101
ratiep, 187, 203–7
Raynor, Mary, 43, 55–56, 129, 154
Read, James, 118
Read, James, Sr., 192
Regina (Albany), 91–92
Regina (Graaff-Reinet), 234–35
Regina (Worcester), 221–22
Reis, Joao Jose, 180
religious life, 176–207; Christianity and, 46–47, 177–79, 181–84, 189–90, 192–98; Emancipation Day and, 254–55; Islam and, 32, 46, 177–80, 184–90, 197–207, 215
Rens, John, 234
Rens, Justinus, 74
resistance, 146, 177; escape, 155, 165–74; everyday subversions, 152–65, 174; families and, 212–13; social resurrection and, ix–x, 11. See also riots and rebellions
Retief, Piet, 141
Rifa'iyyah, 206
riots and rebellions, 174; by apprentices, 61; by colonists/settlers, 39; by Khoisan, 28, 39, 49; by slave owners, 51; by slaves, 49, 53, 59, 66–67, 288 n. 146. See also resistance
Roche, Pierre, 163
Rogers, George Jackman, 54–55, 63, 97–98
Roos, Francois Jacobus, 83–84
Roos, Philemon, 151
Rose, Cowper, 80–81
Rose, Willie Lee, 101, 212
Roset, 142
Rosetta, 223–24
Rosette, 215–17
Rosie, 1
Rosina, 3
Ross, Robert, 28, 34, 66, 152, 154–55, 167–68, 172, 193, 195, 197, 272
Rousseau, Jean-Jacques, 73
Roux, Adriaan, 118
Roux, Jacobus Petrus, 106
runaways, 155, 165–74, 238
Ryklief, Philip, 243

Reconsiderations in Southern African History

Milton Shain, *The Roots of Antisemitism in South Africa*

Timothy Keegan, *Colonial South Africa and the Origins of the Racial Order*

Ineke van Kessel, *"Beyond Our Wildest Dreams": The United Democratic Front and the Transformation of South Africa*

Benedict Carton, *Blood from Your Children: The Colonial Origins of Generational Conflict in South Africa*

Diana Wylie, *Starving on a Full Stomach: Hunger and the Triumph of Cultural Racism in Modern South Africa*

Jeff Guy, *The View across the River: Harriette Colenso and the Zulu Struggle against Imperialism*

John Edwin Mason, *Social Death and Resurrection: Slavery and Emancipation in South Africa*